VICTIMOLOGY

VICTIMOLOGY

A CANADIAN PERSPECTIVE

Jo-Anne M. Wemmers

UNIVERSITY OF TORONTO PRESS

Library and Archives Canada Cataloguing in Publication

Wemmers, Jo-Anne M., 1964–, author

    Victimology: a Canadian perspective/Jo-Anne M. Wemmers.

Includes bibliographical references and index.
Issued in print and electronic formats.

ISBN 978-1-4426-3483-1 (softcover).—ISBN 978-1-4426-3484-8 (hardcover).
ISBN 978-1-4426-3485-5 (HTML).—ISBN 978-1-4426-3486-2 (PDF)

    1. Victims of crimes—Canada. 2. Victims of crimes. 3. Victims of crimes—Services for—Canada. 4. Victims of crimes—Services for. I. Title.

HV6250.3.C3W46 2017   362.880971   C2017-900726-2
                                         C2017-900727-0

We welcome comments and suggestions regarding any aspect of our publications—please feel free to contact us at news@utphighereducation.com or visit our Internet site at www.utppublishing.com.

North America
5201 Dufferin Street
North York, Ontario, Canada, M3H 5T8

2250 Military Road
Tonawanda, New York, USA, 14150

ORDERS PHONE: 1–800–565–9523
ORDERS FAX: 1–800–221–9985
ORDERS E-MAIL: utpbooks@utpress.utoronto.ca

UK, Ireland, and continental Europe
NBN International
Estover Road, Plymouth, PL6 7PY, UK
ORDERS PHONE: 44 (0) 1752 202301
ORDERS FAX: 44 (0) 1752 202333
ORDERS E-MAIL: enquiries@nbninternational.com

Every effort has been made to contact copyright holders; in the event of an error or omission, please notify the publisher.

This book is printed on paper containing 100% post-consumer fibre.

The University of Toronto Press acknowledges the financial support for its publishing activities of the Government of Canada through the Canada Book Fund.

Printed in Canada

This book is dedicated to my parents.

CONTENTS

ILLUSTRATIONS

CHAPTER 1

EVOLUTION OF THE NOTION OF CRIME VICTIM

Victimology is an exciting new science, which has evolved in recent years into a well-defined domain of research. To develop a sound understanding of victimology, one must begin with key concepts regarding victims and criminal justice. Words such as "victim" and "crime" are notions that many of us take for granted and use without giving them much thought. But what does the word "victim" mean? When did it enter into our language and how? Who is a victim? What is a crime? What is the role of victims in the criminal justice system? What are the rights and obligations of crime victims? These are all fundamental questions. In this chapter we will examine the meaning of these basic concepts to understand the implications and limitations of these labels.

The Word "Victim"

If victimology is the study of victims, then what is a victim? According to the *Oxford Dictionary* (1989), this word originates from the Latin word *victima*. It first appeared in the English language in 1497. However, its original meaning was not at all related to criminality. In the fifteenth century, the word "victim" referred to "a living creature sacrificed to a deity or in performance of religious rite." The first time it was applied to a person was in reference to Jesus Christ, as an offering for mankind. According to Van Dijk (2009), the theologian Johannes Calvin used the word *victima* in 1536 as a special name for Jesus Christ in an elaboration of the sacrificial nature of the Crucifixion. It was not until the seventeenth century that it was used to refer to any person who is put to death, tortured, or severely hurt (1660). Finally, in 1781, it began to be used much like we use it today, namely to refer to "one who suffers some injury, hardship or loss, is badly treated or taken advantage of" (*Oxford Dictionary*, 1989).

The original meaning of the word "victim," which refers to religious sacrifice, can still be found in the word for victim used in Dutch and German. In Dutch, a victim is a *slachtoffer*. This word consists of two parts: the word *slacht*, which means to slaughter, and the word *offer*, which means a gift to God or the gods. In German, a victim is an *Opfer*, which means sacrifice. Following an exhaustive study of the word "victim" in Western languages as well as modern Hebrew and Arab, Van Dijk (2009) claims that, without exception, those affected by crime (i.e., the victims) are referred to with words denoting sacrifice or sacrificial objects.

The identity of "victim" is not one we value much because of the negative association of suffering and sacrifice associated with it (Dunn, 2012). Instead, some people prefer the word "survivor" to the word "victim" (Booth, 2016; Fattah, 2010). A "survivor" is someone "who continues to live or exist in spite of perils" (*Oxford Dictionary*, 1989). This certainly sounds more positive than someone who suffers. While these concerns are valid, it is important to understand that before one can be a "survivor," one must first suffer victimization. The recovery process following victimization (see Chapter 4) can only begin once the victim recognizes his or her suffering. As soon as the individual defines the event as a crime, she or he seeks recognition and validation from others, and it is important for the recovery process that this support is received (Hill, 2009; Ruback & Thompson, 2001; Strobl, 2010). Being a victim is not a permanent state (Fattah, 2010). However, recovery from crime starts with being a victim.

First appearing in the eighteenth century, the "victim of crime" is a relatively new concept. Yet crime is as old as humankind. In the Old Testament of the Bible, the story of Cain and Abel describes the murder of Abel (Gen. 4:1–16). Sons of Adam and Eve, Cain killed his brother, Abel, in a fit of jealousy after God accepted Abel's offering but not Cain's. While the Bible details the murder of Abel, there is no reference in the book of Genesis to Abel as a victim. Instead, the focus of the text is on God punishing Cain, thus highlighting the importance of retribution. How was it possible to understand crime without having a concept representing victims of crime? To understand how we can address crimes without the notion of a victim we must examine the evolution of criminal justice and the role of the victim within it.

Who Is a Victim?

As we have seen, in modern English the word "victim" refers to the person who is hurt or injured as a result of an event. More specifically, it refers to the person who *directly* suffered harm or injury as a result of an event. For example, the person who was murdered or the person who was raped, robbed, or whose home was burglarized.

However, besides the direct victim, other people, such as family and friends of the direct victim, may also suffer loss. The death of a loved one can have a tremendous impact on family members, both financially and emotionally. In some cases—for example, crimes that target members of a particular social, political, religious, or ethnic group—the entire community can be impacted (Wemmers, Lafontaine, & Viau, 2008). We will return to this topic in Chapter 4, where we identify different possible groups of victims and present a typology of victims.

Some authors argue that the concept of "victim" is a social construction that emerges interactionally (Dunn, 2012; Quinney, 1972; Strobl, 2010). In other words, victims are "produced" though practical and political activity. The meaning of objects, including victims, is not inherent in the object; rather, it is something that is conferred upon them as they are interpreted (Holstein & Miller, 1990). A victim cannot be taken for granted (Quinney, 1972). The postmodern criminologist Nils Christie's (1985) work on the "ideal victim" highlights the social meaning given to the victim label and how we are reluctant to recognize individuals as victims when they do not meet our expectations. According to Christie, the ideal victim is vulnerable, doing something respectable at the time of their victimization, and victimized by a stranger. "Bad victims," those who do not meet our expectations, do not elicit sympathetic reactions by others. For example, a women involved in prostitution who is raped by one of her clients is a "bad victim" according to Christie and, therefore, people will not tend to be sympathetic and will blame her for her victimization.

Deconstructing the meaning of the word "victim" in the literature, one finds that victimologists have often tended to focus on conventional crimes (Quinney, 1972). Victims who threaten the existing social order or who suffer because of that order do not fit into conventional criminology and, therefore, are often excluded from the criminological image of victimization. Victimologists, however, need not restrict their research to conventional society and its institutions (Strobl, 2004, 2010). This argues in favour of a broad image of the victim, which includes victims of nonconventional crimes, such as victims of the police, wars, and oppression.

In contrast, Fattah (2010) argues that victimologists have defined victims too widely and too loosely. He emphasizes the subjective character of being a "victim." By defining victims broadly, one risks including people as victims who neither define nor perceive themselves as victims. As previously noted, the subjective appraisal of victimization is vital in victimology. While one should be careful not to impose the "victim" label on others, this does not mean that victims are always necessarily aware of their victimization. There are countless examples of cases in which people are victims of crime but do not know it. Think of environmental crimes or corruption in government—whole communities may be victims of these crimes and may never know it. Nevertheless, how people frame their experiences affects their needs and their recovery process and, therefore, being a victim is highly subjective.

Legally, there is not one agreed-upon definition of who is a victim that is common across different bodies of law or jurisdictions. In international law, the United Nations *Declaration of Basic Principle of Justice for Victims of Crime and Abuse of Power* (hereinafter the UN Declaration) provides the following definition for victims:

> "Victims" means persons who, individually or collectively, have suffered harm, including physical or mental injury, emotional suffering, economic loss or substantial impairment of their fundamental rights, through acts or omissions that are in violation of criminal laws operative within Member States, including those laws proscribing criminal abuse of power. . . .
>
> The term "victim" also includes, where appropriate, the immediate family or dependents of the direct victim and persons who have suffered harm in intervening to assist victims in distress or to prevent victimization. (UN General Assembly, 1985, Art. 1–2)

This is a broad definition. It includes anyone who has suffered harm as a result of an offence, including indirect victims. It is also broad in the sense that it goes beyond crimes and includes abuses of power by the state.

The *Canadian Victims Bill of Rights* uses a narrower definition. According to article 2 of the Bill of Rights:

> *victim* means an individual who has suffered physical or emotional harm, property damage or economic loss as the result of the commission or alleged commission of an offence. (Department of Justice Canada, 2015a)

While one might argue that family and friends suffer emotional harm as a result of the victimization of their loved one, article 3 of the Bill makes it clear that these individuals are not considered victims under the Bill of Rights. According to article 3 "if the victim is dead or incapable of acting on their own behalf," the victim's spouse, partner, relative, dependent, legal guardian, or caregiver may exercise the victim's rights on his or her behalf. Hence, while family and friends are able to use these rights, they are not considered to be victims themselves but are instead representatives of victims. It is also important to note that, according to this definition, recognition as a victim is not dependent on whether an offender has been tried and convicted of the offence. Thus, victim status is independent of the criminal justice process.

While the word "victim" is often reserved for those who have directly experienced crime, it is important to bear in mind when we study victimology that the field is much broader and includes far more than just the direct victims of crimes for which an offender has been found guilty. This will be discussed further in Chapter 4.

The Word "Crime"

Strictly speaking, crimes are acts that are identified in a nation's criminal laws. Thus, a person commits a crime when they break one or more of the laws found in a criminal code. While some acts, such as murder or theft, are universally considered crimes and can be found in criminal codes around the world, not all criminal codes are the same. What may be a crime in one country may not be a crime in another. For example, in 1999 Belgium became one of the first Western countries to introduce legislation making forced marriage a criminal offence, and it was not until 2015 that it became a crime in Canada (Lamboley, 2016). While it is only recently that Western nations have begun to include forced mariage in their criminal codes, already in 1948 the Universal Declaration of Human Rights recognized protection against forced marriage as a universal human right. This shows that what is or is not considered a crime can change over time, and even when there is agreement that something is unacceptable, it may not be labelled a crime. Another example is the crime of human trafficking—or modern slavery, as it is sometimes called (Aronowitz, 2009). This is a horrendous crime that causes immense human suffering and, while it is not a new phenomenon, it was only introduced into the Canadian Criminal Code in 2005. Prior to that, human trafficking was not considered a crime in Canada (Jimenez, 2013). Hence, crime is a social construct.

The Role of Victims in Criminal Justice

To understand the place that victims occupy in our criminal justice system, we have to go back to the origins of criminal justice. As we have seen, crime is as old as humankind, and we find examples of crimes such as murder and theft in the Old Testament of the Bible. Already in ancient Egypt, in 4000 BCE, the Egyptians had developed their own legal system. The Egyptian king, the pharaoh, created laws by deciding what was legal and what was illegal, and judges applied these laws. The Hebrew judicial system dates back to 1200 BCE (Reichel, 1994). This system was already in place when Moses received the Ten Commandments from God. In these ancient systems, when two opposing parties were involved in a conflict they would present their dispute to a judge who would hear both parties and make a decision. A classical example of this kind of justice is the story of King Solomon, found in the Old Testament (1 Kings 3:16–22). Thus, judicial systems have existed in societies for thousands of years. However, in this early stage, criminal law and civil law were not yet separate.

In early tribal societies it was the family or the clan that controlled social relations. Even though the notion of criminality did not exist yet, these early societies did recognize certain behaviours as unacceptable, or *mala in se*. An offence was an act against the family of the victim on behalf of the family of the offender. When a person committed an unacceptable act, such as murder or theft, the victim or the family of the victim would have the right to retribution. The entire family of the offender would share responsibility for the wrong committed. This led to the "vendetta" or "blood feud" in which the family of the injured or murdered victim sought vengeance on the offender or his family. Thus this system of "private vengeance" gave a certain place to the victim, which the family or clan sought to avenge, through reparation by the offender and his family or clan (Schafer, 1968).

According to the victimologist Stephen Schafer (1968), when the early nomadic tribes began to settle in regions the stability of the community became more important and reactions to victimization began to change, becoming less severe. The vendetta presented a threat to the safety and stability of the community. In this respect, the Code of Hammurabi (1750 BCE) is significant. This Code includes over 200 laws, including the principle of *lex talionis*, or "an eye for an eye," which is often mistakenly considered a justification for revenge when in fact it introduced limits on retaliation, insisting that one respect rules of proportionality. Instead of retaliating, victims or their families could also negotiate with the offender to obtain reparation.

According to Schafer (1968), victim compensation is reflective of the level to which a society has evolved. For example, the Saxons and the Germans introduced the notion of *wergeld*, which meant that the offender would pay compensation to the victim or, in the case of death or if the victim was a woman, the victim's family. In exchange, the victim's family would renounce the vendetta after a murder or injuries (Allinne, 2001; Schafer, 1968). The agreement between the victim or the victim's family and the offender would effectively close the case (Viau, 1996). However, if the offender failed to respect the agreement, he would become an "outlaw"—stigmatized and outcast by the community and outside the protection of the law, meaning that anyone who killed him would enjoy impunity (Schafer, 1968; Jacob, 1974).

Schafer (1968) refers to this time as "the golden age of victims," because they and their families had an important role to play in the criminal justice

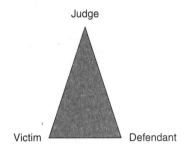

Judge

Victim   Defendant

FIGURE 1.1: Schafer's Golden Age of Victims

process, and reparation was a key objective of the justice process. In this sense, the victim and the offender were on equal footing: They both presented their case to a judge who would decide on their case. As such the duel changed from one of arms to one of words (Allinne, 2001; Reichel, 1994). However, if citizens were responsible for keeping the peace, they were also responsible for prosecuting their offender. Early justice systems pitted accusers against the accused. There were no police or public prosecutors, so it was up to the victim or his or her family to build a case, which meant finding witnesses and evidence and presenting them to the judge.

If this was the "golden age of victims," then why did the word "victim" not enter our vocabulary until much later? In these early societies, the notion of the individual did not yet exist, and it would not exist until the Middle Ages. That is not to say there were not any great individuals, but the *concept* of the individual as an important object of concern or study did not yet exist. The person's status as emperor, king, or serf was more important than an individual human being. While the notion of the individual first emerged in the Middle Ages, it was not until the Renaissance (*c.* 1500–1700 CE) that it became engrained in thought (Leahey, 1980). It was only once we began to think of people as individuals that the concept of the victim, which is essentially an individual who has suffered an injury, could enter into our vocabulary, and this occurred in the eighteenth century.

This system underwent a shift in England during the Middle Ages (476–1453 CE). There was a gradual change in perceptions of crime and social order, moving power away from the family or clan and toward the state. The king was at the head of the state, citizens were expected to keep "the king's peace," and interventions were made in the king's name. It was around the twelfth century that the state gradually began to intervene in criminal prosecutions in England and impose sanctions on offenders (Laurin & Viens, 1996). Under the reign of Henry II (1154–1189) a process of centralization was instigated, gradually giving greater powers to the king. In 1166, he introduced the *Assize of Clarendon*, an act that introduced several serious offences as *crimes* that fell under the king's jurisdiction (Doak, 2008). Prior to that, these offences had been viewed as *torts* or wrongs between citizens. Some argue that this change happened to keep the peace and prevent crime (Laurin & Viens, 1996). However, others argue that the Crown wanted to increase its power and riches, and therefore insisted on receiving all compensation paid by offenders to their victims and their families (Schafer, 1968; Ashworth, 1986). This is called a "fine" and it continues to exist today in many criminal justice systems. Thus, crime ceased to be a private affair between families, and the state increasingly became a stakeholder in criminal justice.

This change was not unique to England. In France, King Philip IV introduced the first Crown prosecutors in 1303. Gradually, these Crown prosecutors came to play an increasingly important role in the criminal justice process, at first beside the victim or complainant until they eventually took over the prosecution (Allinne, 2001). The division between criminal and civil law, which was triggered by the introduction of the king's justice, led to the decline of victims' rights (Baril, 1985). According to Schafer (1968), the "golden age of victims" came to an end once the state monopolized sanctions.

Little by little, the criminal justice system came to focus on the relationship between the state and the offender, while the victim became a mere **witness** to the crime. More specifically, the victim became a witness to a crime against the state. Moreover, if found guilty of a crime, the defendant would no longer have to make reparation to the victim or his or her family, but instead would have to repay the debt to society. As a result, reparation became increasingly rare in the criminal justice system, until it almost disappeared altogether (Baril, 1985). It was not until the end of the nineteenth century, instigated by thoughtful debate at many international conferences on penology, that reparation was reintroduced into criminal justice (Schafer, 1968).

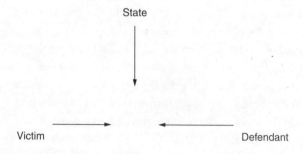

FIGURE 1.2: Intervention by the State

Today in Canada we continue to sometimes refer to the public prosecutor as a *Crown counsel* or *Crown attorney*, in reference to their function of intervening on behalf of the queen (or the state). When charges are laid against a defendant, this is done in the name of *Regina*, or the queen, not in the name of the victim; the victim has become a witness to a crime against the state. Civil law continues to deal with conflicts between individual citizens, but certain acts are considered particularly unacceptable, and these are called *crimes*. These acts, which are defined in the Criminal Code, are handled by the criminal justice system. Figure 1.3 shows the principal actors in the criminal justice system, which shows that the state has now completely replaced the victim. Today, the criminal justice process involves three main actors: the judge, the state, and the defendant.

Not much has changed since the late eighteenth century, by which time a clear division had evolved between criminal jurisdiction and tort (Kirchengast, 2006). One could even argue that the role of victims is somewhat more limited today following the creation of the police and a well-organized public prosecution, which is responsible for laying charges against the accused (Viau, 1996). While victims continue to exercise a certain power in their decision whether or not to report a crime to authorities, it is not up to victims to decide whether or not to prosecute a case. This power stays in the hands of the public prosecutor who, as we saw, represents the state.

In practice, the public prosecutor will often bear in mind the victim's wishes. For example, in the case of family violence, a victim who really does not want to see his or her family member criminally prosecuted may be an uncooperative witness and, therefore, the prosecutor may not believe it is worthwhile to pursue the case. However, this is definitely not the only factor that the prosecutor will take into consideration, and the prosecutor can prosecute an uncooperative witness for contempt of court. Viau (1996) cites the

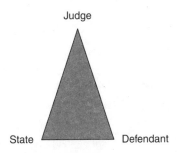

FIGURE 1.3: The Modern Criminal Justice System

example of *R. v. Moore* (1987), in which the Territorial Court of the Northwest Territories condemned a victim of conjugal violence for refusing to testify against her spouse. In the 1980s and 1990s, throughout Canada and the United States, many police forces introduced mandatory arrest policies for cases of conjugal violence in an effort to protect women from undue pressure by violent spouses. By taking away all choice from the victim, it was thought that women would be sheltered from pressure to retract their complaint (Johnson & Dawson, 2011). However, mandatory policies have also been strongly criticized for taking power away from women and, therefore, discouraging women from calling the police (Finn, 2013; Ford, 1991; Landau, 2000).

The victim's personal wishes are by far not the only element that the public prosecutor will want to consider. As a representative of the state, the prosecutor must above all consider the interests of society. Other relevant factors include the risk that the offender is believed to pose to the safety of others, whether this is his or her first offence or a repeat offence, and the nature of the crime committed.

Civil Litigation

Victims can pursue offenders in civil courts, which, like the early courts of antiquity, involve two parties who present their case to a judge. As we have seen, originally there was no distinction between civil and criminal law. This changed when certain acts came to be seen as crimes. In civil law, rather than using the terms "victim" and "accused," courts refer to the one who lodges the complaint as the "plaintiff" and the one against whom the complaint is lodged as the "defendant." These terms describe well the roles of both parties before the court: One makes a complaint and the other defends him or herself. Both parties have equal standing and can be represented by a lawyer.

Because civil laws place victims and offenders on equal footing, some would argue that it is a better system for victims (Christie, 1977; Van Swaaningen, 1999). For many of the acts described in the Criminal Code there exists similar offences in the civil code. A classic example is the case of O.J. Simpson, who was accused of killing his ex-wife, Nicole Brown Simpson, and her boyfriend, Ronald Goldman, in June 1994. After being found not guilty by a criminal court for the murders, the family members of the victims pursued a civil case against Simpson and won. Civil courts cannot impose prison sentences, but like the courts of antiquity they can demand that the offender pay compensation to the victim. In the O.J. Simpson case, the jury awarded US$33.5 million to the victims' families in compensatory and punitive damages. This example illustrates that victims can privately pursue their offender where they set their terms and make their demands, they call their own experts, and they have control.

However, victims of crime rarely sue their offenders. There are many reasons for this. To begin with, civil litigation is expensive. The parties involved in litigation have to pay all costs themselves: lawyers' fees, court fees, expert consultancy fees, and so on. If the plaintiff wins, then they may be able to get back some of their costs. However, they may not win, and even if they do there is no guarantee that the defendant will ever actually pay up. For example, in the O.J. Simpson case, although Simpson was worth millions at the time of the murders, 20 years after the judgment the Goldman family has only received 1 per cent of what Simpson was ordered to pay (Wells, 2014). Beside the costs involved, civil litigation fails to provide victims with the same level of public recognition and validation as the criminal courts. It also puts a tremendous burden on victims, not only financially but also psychologically. While victims want to be considered in the criminal justice process, they do not necessarily seek decision-making power, which many view as a burden (Shapland, Wilmore, & Duff, 1985; Wemmers & Cyr, 2004).

Rights of the Accused

The rise in power of the state and its absolute dominance in matters of criminal justice meant that authorities could commit atrocities of justice without any consequences. At the will of the king, a person could be thrown into prison and never come out. Once the state ousted victims from the criminal justice process, there was an imbalance of power between the omnipotent state and the individual accused of a crime (Doak, 2008; Kirchengast, 2006). The accused had very little protection other than the *lex talionis*, which limited the retaliation that could be inflicted on an offender and also any protection based on his social standing (Baril, 1985). Such abuses of power led to the development of human rights instruments to protect the rights of individuals and groups.

As early as the thirteenth century in England, the Magna Carta (or "great charter," which is the English translation) was drafted in response to the tyranny by King John. Written in 1215, this charter is the first-known example of an effort to bridle the power of the king and to introduce legal measures protecting individual freedom (Lagelée & Manceron, 1998). For example, article 39 outlines limitations on the ability of the king to imprison or exile "free men." Free men were, at the time, nobility, and the limitations outlined in the Magna Carta did not apply to women or men of lower social standing.

In the seventeenth century, under the influence of Protestant doctrine, the notion of individual rights emerged, in particular the necessity to protect individuals against tyranny by the state. In 1689, a first Bill of Rights was introduced in England. Suspicious of the arrival of a new king following the marriage of William of Orange with Mary, the daughter of King James II, the English noblemen wrote the Bill of Rights in an effort to prevent future abuses of power from occurring (Lagelée & Manceron, 1998). The notion of a bill of rights was later reintroduced by revolutionaries in the eighteenth century.

Many of the great philosophers of the eighteenth century were also instrumental in the move to limit the power of the state and introduce rights of the accused. In 1764, Cesare Beccaria (1738–94) wrote a critique of criminal justice in eighteenth-century Europe. Beccaria argued that punishment should be proportional with the crime committed and that the law should be applied equally to all regardless of whether you are the head of state or a simple citizen. According to Beccaria, people should be punished in the same way independent of the poverty or wealth of the offender. This is referred to as "rule of law." Hence, the focus shifted from the actor (the offender) to the act (the crime). Beccaria also demanded the introduction of laws protecting offenders from abuses of power by the state. His work was highly influential for the development of the rights of the accused and was a source of inspiration for both the American (1776) and the French (1789) revolutions.

The American and French revolutions were of monumental importance for the development of legal rights of the accused. Dissatisfaction with the British monarchy in the American colonies led to the introduction of the Virginia Declaration of Rights (1776), which later provided the basis for the American Constitution (1791). These documents aimed to limit the power of the state to avoid abuses of power in the newly founded country. The Virginia Declaration of Rights included legal rights for those accused in criminal matters, such as the right to be informed of any accusations and evidence, and the right to a speedy and fair trial by peers (article 8). Similarly, the French Déclaration des droits de l'homme et du citoyen (Declaration of the Rights of Man and of the Citizen) includes safeguards from arbitrary arrest and detention (article 7) and the presumption of innocence (article 9).

By the nineteenth century, the rights of the accused in matters of criminal law were already well established (Baril, 1985). Offenders' rights were reinforced with legal guarantees and recognized in bills of rights. These declarations, enshrined in constitutional law, gave persons accused, condemned, and imprisoned certain inalienable rights, including the following:

- the presumption of innocence
- the right to a fair and public trial
- the right to protection against arbitrary imprisonment
- protection against cruel punishment

In Canada, these rights are found in the Charter of Rights and Freedoms, which was adopted in 1982 when the Constitution was repatriated from Britain. Articles 7 to 14 of the Charter address legal guarantees, such as protection against arbitrary detention (article 9) and, in case of arrest or detention, to be informed promptly of the reasons (article 10). The Charter rights of the accused in Canada are enforceable rights, as indicated in article 24 of the Charter:

> Anyone whose rights or freedoms, as guaranteed by this Charter, have been infringed or denied may apply to a court of competent jurisdiction to obtain such remedy as the court considers appropriate and just in the circumstances.

Rights of Victims

While the Charter offers legal rights to the accused, it does not provide rights to victims of crime. It may seem odd that human rights instruments like the Charter would include extensive rights for those accused of having committed crimes but not mention victims of crime. After all, victims are human, too. To understand this apparent imbalance, it is important to recall the history of criminal law.

As we have seen, criminal law has evolved over time, and the state gradually replaced the victim in the legal process (Doak, 2008; Viau, 1996; Young, 2005). The result is that today in the countries belonging to the common law legal tradition, such as England, Canada, and the United States, the criminal justice process is founded on the state laying charges against the accused. While many different criminal justice systems exist, it is important to note that across legal traditions the focus of the trial is on proving the guilt of the accused. In common law countries that have an adversarial criminal justice system, there are only two parties: the state and the accused. It is the state's job to prove that the accused is guilty, and it is the defence's job to show reasonable doubt. The judge is like an umpire who makes sure that the rules are followed.

In this context, victims do not need rights because their freedom is not at stake. Victims are witnesses to crimes against the state. For example, in Canada, victims' involvement in the trial is completely up to the prosecution and the defence. If either thinks that it is important that the victim testify, the victim will be subpoenaed (i.e., ordered) to do so. However, if the case does not go to court (e.g., because it is plea bargained), or if the victim is simply not required to testify, then the victim will essentially be shut out of the criminal justice process until the sentencing hearing when they may make a victim impact statement (see Chapter 10). Victims, who once had a place in laying charges against the accused, have been completely pushed out and replaced by the state (Kirchengast, 2006; Schafer, 1968). They have been rendered powerless against an omnipotent state that has the power to force them to testify as well as the power to shut them out. Thus, while the rights of the accused became strengthened in an effort to limit the power of the state, victims and witnesses became increasingly marginalized in the criminal justice system (Laurin & Viens, 1996). Not surprisingly, this has led to calls for victims' rights.

What are the legal rights and obligations of victims? Like all citizens, victims have the right to report a crime to the police. They also have a right to protect themselves (s. 34 of the Criminal Code) in certain circumstances and to defend their property (s. 35). Victims of crime may also request reparation at sentencing. The principle of restitution of property and compensation for damages was introduced in the Criminal Code in 1892 (Laurin & Viens, 1996). Restitution orders have recently received new interest following the adoption of Bill C-32 in 2015, which introduced a new, standardized form for victims to submit a Statement on Restitution at sentencing (form 34.1; s. 737.1(4)). Certain victims in certain circumstances can also request a publication ban (s. 539.1) or that the public be excluded from the court (s. 486.1).

However, victims do not have the right to a fair trial. It is not the victim who is on trial—victims are witnesses to crimes against the state. Like any other witness, if the victim receives a subpoena he or she is obliged to appear in court. While the accused may simply be asked to promise to appear in court, witnesses are ordered to do so (s. 698). If the victim does not appear as a witness after being subpoenaed, then a warrant can be issued for his or her arrest (s. 704.1) and he or she can be detained for up to 30 days (s. 707.1). In contrast, the accused cannot be made to testify (art. 11c of the Charter).

The accused can, however, choose to represent him or herself, in which case he or she can question witnesses, including victim-witnesses, who are obliged to answer these questions (s. 545.1). The case of Gilles Dégarie illustrates the difference between the rights of the accused and those of the victim during the trial (see Box 1.1). In recent years, the Criminal Code has been modified to prevent the accused from personally cross-examining certain witnesses. Since 2005, the accused is prohibited from personally cross-examining any child victim-witnesses, unless the judge finds that this would hinder the proper administration of justice (s. 486.3(1)). In principle, adult victim-witnesses (18 years of age or older) may be personally cross-examined by the offender who chooses to represent him or herself. However, following the adoption of Bill C-32 in 2015, adult victims of sexual assault and criminal harassment may ask the judge to prohibit the offender from personally carrying out the cross-examination and, if such an order is made, the judge shall appoint counsel to conduct the cross-examination (s. 486.3 (2)).

BOX 1.1: THE CASE OF GILLES DÉGARIE

In 2000, Gilles Dégarie was found guilty of sexual assault and sentenced to 15 years in prison by the Court of Quebec. During the trial, Mr. Dégarie chose to represent himself, which was his right; however, as such he cross-examined the victim-witness himself. For two days the victim was interrogated by the man who sexually assaulted her. After sentencing, Dégarie appealed his case. At the appeal hearing, the victim-witness was once again called to testify. Fearing that she would again be subject to cross-examination by Dégarie, she refused. In doing so, she risked being held in contempt of court (s. 708). In the end the judge at the appellate court decided that she would not be asked to testify again and that the court would instead use the transcripts from the first trial (Cédilot, 2001).

Victims are also obliged to allow authorities to retain their stolen property as evidence in the trial. This can be inconvenient for victims, who could have to wait years before the trial is over, so section 491.2 of the Criminal Code allows authorities to return stolen property to the victim and use a photograph of it instead. However, whether or not authorities choose to use photographic evidence or retain the victim's property is at their discretion (Laurin & Viens, 1996).

The above rights and obligations are all legally enforceable; they are procedural rights found in the Criminal Code. In addition to these rights, many provinces have drafted their own bill of rights for victims, which include access to information, reparation, protection, and support. In 2015, the federal government adopted the Canadian Victims Bill of Rights (Bill C-32). However, nowhere in Canada do these bills of rights for victims include enforceable rights, and to become real the rights must be accompanied by victim standing and meaningful remedy (Beloof, 2005). Victims' rights are discussed in detail in Chapter 7.

Victims' Rights as Human Rights

This brings us to the core issue: Victims are witnesses to a crime against the state. If crimes truly were directed at the state and not committed against individuals, then this dual-party configuration would make sense. However, in reality crimes are committed against individuals. And these individuals—the victims of crime—seek recognition of the crimes committed against them. While victims are sensitive to the public interest in crime, in their view crime is an offence against society as well as an offence against the victim (Shapland et al., 1985; Wemmers & Cyr, 2004). They do not understand why the state does not recognize them in any role other than as witnesses. The fundamental difference between a tort and a crime is not that crimes do not affect individual victims, but rather that a tort is private and does not include the state while a crime affects society as well. As Doak (2008) points out, "What constitutes a 'crime' as opposed to a 'tort' is purely dependent upon how crime is defined within any given society" (p. 27). It is a subjective judgment by the victim who defines the act as a crime and reports it to the police. Hence, when the criminal justice system views the victim as a witness to a crime against the state, this is fundamentally opposed to the victim's perspective and, inevitably, he or she will be disappointed.

Victims' rights are viewed by some authors as human rights (Doak, 2008; Garkawe, 2005; Wemmers, 2012). Much like the seventeenth-century movement to enshrine the rights of the accused in law and limit the power of the state, we see a similar movement playing out today with respect to victims' rights. Rights are only meaningful if they confer entitlements as well as obligations on people. The monopoly of power of the state in the criminal justice process has silenced victims, rendering them mere witnesses to a crime against the state. It is our ability to exercise our rights, using our free will and rational choice, that gives meaning to the notion of human dignity. Without this ability, victims will remain voiceless objects of the criminal justice system who are forced to forfeit their individual human rights in the interest of society. We need to acknowledge the victim as a person before the law who has rights and privileges. In following a human rights approach, we recognize victims' interest in the criminal justice process. This is a victim-centred approach and one in which victims are at the heart of how we try to understand victimization.

Conclusion

In sum, victims have many obligations and few legal rights. Over the centuries, the victim's role as an active participant, responsible for the complaint and the prosecution, has been transformed to that of a witness. The state has taken over the burden of prosecution from victims, but in doing so it also changed the focus of criminal prosecution. The offence is no longer viewed as an act against the victim but as a crime committed against the state. By taking a victim-centred approach, we will examine victimization and its consequences from the victim's perspective and use this to understand the implications for justice for victims.

CHAPTER 2

HISTORY OF VICTIMOLOGY

If the notion of "crime victim" is relatively recent in our language, then the science of victimology is an even newer concept. Returning to origins of victimology, we identify dominant approaches in victimological research. Ironically, early victimologists focused almost exclusively on the victim–offender relationship and victims' participation in their victimization. They were criminologists, and they developed elaborate typologies of victims aimed at explaining crime. Under the influence of the victims' movement, victimological research shifted its focus from victims' contributions to crime to understanding the impact of crime, the needs of victims, and the experiences of victims in the criminal justice system. In this chapter we will trace the evolution of the science of victmology and examine the factors that played a role in the emergence of the victims' movement.

The Early Years

One of the first-known studies to systematically examine crime victims was Willem Nagel's doctoral dissertation, which he researched and wrote in 1937 in the Netherlands. Nagel conducted interviews with victims of crime to understand their perceptions and needs (Van Dijk, 2011). While he was still working on his dissertation, World War II broke out. From 1940 to 1945 the Netherlands was under German occupation, and Nagel, who was active in the Dutch resistance, had his work confiscated by the German police (Kirchhoff, 2010). When the war ended, he reconstructed his research using mainly data from court files. He defended his thesis in 1947, and it was published two years later (Nagel, 1949). While it includes data on victims, the data are less extensive than he originally intended (Van Dijk, 2011). Willem Nagel went on to become a professor of criminology at Leiden University in the Netherlands, and throughout his academic career he published extensively on the need to give more attention to victims of crime, both in criminological research and in criminal justice (Nagel, 1959, 1963). However, Nagel published his research in Dutch instead of English, so his early work is not well known outside of the Netherlands (Kirchhoff, 2010). Nevertheless, it constitutes one of the first-known empirical studies on victims.

The work of Hans von Hentig is often recognized as one of the first studies in victimology. Published in 1948, his book *The Criminal and His Victim* examines the relationship between the criminal and the victim. Born in Germany, Von Hentig (1887–1974) moved to the United States before the outbreak of World War II. When his book was published in 1948, Von Hentig worked as a professor at Yale University. Hans von Hentig was a criminologist, and his interest in the victim was solely criminological. He was not concerned about victims and how they were impacted by crime. Instead, he wanted to study victims to understand crime and criminals. According to Von Hentig,

> In most crimes the perpetrator is hidden, the victim—dead or alive—available. With a thorough knowledge of the interrelations between doer and sufferer new approaches to the detection of crime will be opened. (1948, p. 450)

He believed that with this knowledge we could also prevent crimes from happening in the first place. Using homicide data from the United States and Germany, Von Hentig paints a picture of the complex relationship between the criminal and victim in his book. However, Von Hentig never used the word "victimology."

The first person to use the word "victimology" in a publication was Fredric Wertham. An American psychiatrist, Wertham published a book in 1949 titled *The Show of Violence*, in which he introduced the word "victimology." He argues that "(t)he murder victim is the forgotten man … [and to] understand the psychology of the murderer we need to understand the sociology of his victim. What we need is a science of victimology" (1949, p. 259). This is the only reference to victimology in Wertham's book, and he does not elaborate any further or provide a definition of victimology. However, it is evident that, like Von Hentig, Wertham views victimology as a way to understand the criminal.

Other early works on victims include the work of Rhoda Milliken, a police officer in Washington, DC, who published a paper in 1950 on the suffering of victims of sexual violence. In 1952, R. Tahone, public prosecutor at the Court of Appeal in Liège (Belgium), published an article on the notion of consent in which he argued that victims' compliance did not diminish the criminal nature of their victimization nor did it hinder prosecution. In England, the British penal reformer and magistrate Margery Fry spoke publicly in the 1950s about the state's responsibility toward victims and their need for compensation (Fry, 1959).

Building on Von Hentig's work, in 1954 Henri Ellenberger (1905–93) published an article on the psychological relationship between victims and offenders. Originally from Switzerland, Ellenberger immigrated to the United States and then later to Montreal. Ellenberger quotes a 1920s' novel by Franz Werfel: "It's not the assassin but the victim who is guilty" (1954, p. 104). In this novel, a boy who suffered years of abuse at the hands of his father one day kills his father. According to Ellenberger, this example illustrates how a person can be a victim as well as an offender. Like Von Hentig, Ellenberger argued that studying the relationship between victims and their offenders would allow us to explain and, hence, prevent victimization.

Another key figure in the birth of victimology is Benjamin Mendelsohn (1900–98). Born in Romania, Mendelsohn studied law and worked as a defence lawyer. In 1956, he published his seminal work *A New Branch of the Bio-Psycho-Social Science: Victimology*.[1] In it, he provides a detailed definition of victimology and argues for the creation of a new science that is independent of criminology. He paints a portrait of victimology that could include all kinds of victims, not just crime victims. Victimology, according to Mendelsohn, is the opposite of criminology. Instead of focusing on criminals and crime, it focuses on victims and victimization. Like Von Hentig, Mendelsohn believed that the primary objective of victimology is *prevention* through education. Mendelsohn contended that through research we could better understand the role of the victim in crime and use this information to prevent others from becoming victims, as well as offer victims the support they need to avoid becoming victims again in the future.

Mendelsohn argued that both society and criminology had completely forgotten about the victim. He claims that historically "victims have not been sufficiently studied, sufficiently defended in justice, or sufficiently supported by public opinion"[2] (1956, p. 95). He asked why a society that showed compassion and humanity for law-breakers was totally disinterested in the victim, who in addition to suffering the consequences of the crime also bore the burden of evidence as a witness in the criminal justice system. Mendelsohn argued that our disinterest in the victim is because the victim is "inoffensive" (p. 95). The science of victimology would change this, making victims the key object of study.

....

1 Translated from French to English by the author. Original title: *Une nouvelle branche de la science bio-psycho-sociale: La victimologie.*
2 Translation from French to English by the author: « De tous temps, la victime n'a pas été suffisamment étudiée, suffisament défendue en justice, ni suffisamment soutenue par l'opinion publique dans la vie sociale. »

Hence, Mendelsohn was sensitive to the needs of victims and he recognized the consequences of crime for victims, the important role that victims play as witnesses in the criminal justice system, and the general lack of interest for the plight of crime victims.

Mendelsohn's vision for the future of victimology was remarkable. In setting the parameters of this new science, Mendelsohn asked if victimology should include mass victimization, political victims, as well as international victims. Mendelsohn conceded that it was "premature" to discuss the inclusion of these groups at this early stage in the development of victimology, and therefore he concentrated on victims of crime. However, in recent years the notion of mass victimization has gained importance in victimology. This is due in part to the establishment of the **International Criminal Court** in 2002, which was inconceivable in 1956.

Another prominent figure in the history of victimology is Marvin Wolfgang (1924–98), professor of criminology at Penn State University in the United States. In 1958, Wolfgang published his research on the role of the victim in homicide. Like Von Hentig, Ellenberger, and Mendelsohn, Wolfgang was interested in the victim to better understand and explain crime. Studying police files, Wolfgang found that in many cases of homicide it was the victim who had started the conflict. He referred to this phenomenon as *victim precipitation* (1958), which became an important concept in the early years of victimology as scholars sought to understand the victim–offender relationship (Silverman, 1975).

Real interest in victimology began on both sides of the Atlantic Ocean after World War II. The idea of victimology was planted before the war, but the germination of this idea was interrupted by the war and only picked up again after the war was over (Mendelsohn, 1963). One could argue that the birth of victimology, like human rights, was inspired by the atrocities committed during the war. While we can find the odd reference to the massacres committed during World War II in the early writings on victimology, these are the exception. For example, in his book *The Show of Violence*, Wertham (1949) mentions the mass murders committed by the Nazis in World War II, and Mendelsohn (1956) raises the question of mass victimization a few years later. However, there is no systematic study of mass victimization or genocide in these early writings. The first victimologists focused largely on victims of conventional crime. The early works in victimology were largely inspired by criminologists and criminal justice professionals who, in their effort to understand crime, introduced the notion of "victim" into academic discussions on crime. Subsequently, interest emerged not only in the role of victims of crime but also in the plight of victims as the forgotten party of the criminal justice system.

The Dissemination of Victimology

In 1956, Mendelsohn argued that this new science of victimology would need its own institutions and academic journals. Two years after the publication of Mendelsohn's seminal work, Professor Paul Cornil (Brussels) organized a conference on victimology in 1958. Technically, this was an international conference since it brought together Dutch and Belgian participants. They included professors Willem Nagel (Leiden University) and Willem Noach (Utrecht University) from the Netherlands, as well as the Belgian professor Willy Callewaert (University of Gent) (Mendelsohn, 1963; Screvens, 1959). The following year, in April 1959, the Belgian journal *Revue de droit penal et de criminologie* published a special issue on victimology.

As we saw, throughout the 1950s many academics, both in Europe and in North America, began to take an interest in crime victims. In 1960, Denis Szabo hired Henri Ellenberger as a professor at his newly founded School of Criminology at the Université de Montréal. Ellenberger would go on to have an important influence on the development of victimology at the school, where he directed students such as Ezzat Fattah, who became a prominent author in victimology and founded the School of Criminology at Simon Fraser University in British Columbia. Fattah published an article titled "Some Problems that Victimology Poses for Criminal Justice"[3] in 1966. Like Ellenberger, Fattah's early work focused on the victim–offender relationship. In 1971, Fattah's doctoral thesis was published under the title *Is the Victim Guilty?*[4] In it he examines the role of the victim in cases of armed robbery involving homicide. Fattah went on to publish several books in victimology, including *Understanding Criminal Victimization: An Introduction to Theoretical Victimology* (1991).

The first international symposium on victimology with participants from around the world was held in Israel in 1973 (Drapkin & Viano, 1974). Three years later, in 1976, a second international symposium was organized by Stephan Schafer in Boston. In 1979, the third international symposium on victimology took place in Münster, Germany, under the leadership of Hans Joachim Schneider, and it was at this symposium that the World Society of Victimology (WSV) was created. Since then, the WSV has organized international symposia on victimology every three years. More recently, we have also seen the integration of victimology into mainstream criminology with the creation of a

....

3 Translated from French to English by the author. Original title: *Quelques problèmes posés à la justice pénale par la victimologie.*
4 Translated from French to English by the author. Original title: *La victime est-elle coupable?*

division on victimology within the American Society of Criminology (2012) and the European Society of Criminology (2014).

The first academic textbook written on victimology was by Stephen Schafer (1968). The title, *The Victim and His Criminal*, was a reference to Von Hentig's seminal work, *The Criminal and His Victim*. The first academic journal dedicated to victimology was *Victimology: An International Journal*, which first appeared in 1976 and was edited by Emilio Viano in the United States. In 1988, the *International Review of Victimology* was founded in the United Kingdom by John Freeman in collaboration with Leslie Sebba and David Miers and continues to be a key resource for victimologists. Today, there are numerous journals that deal with victimology, including *Violence and Victims*, *Journal of Traumatic Stress*, and *Victims and Offenders*.

In addition to international symposia and academic journals, international research institutes for victimology have emerged: Tokiwa International Victimology Institute (TIVI) at Tokiwa University in Japan (2003–16) and the International Institute of Victimology (INTERVICT) at the University of Tilburg in the Netherlands, established in 2005. These centres bring together academics from around the world and promote research and training. Many universities now offer courses in victimology, and some offer whole programs in this area (Muscat, 2010; Waller, 2011). With these developments, Mendelsohn's vision for victimology has become a reality.

The Field of Victimology

Since its early beginnings, victimology has struggled with delineating its boundaries. Sparked by Mendelsohn's plea for a separate science of victimology, one of the first debates in the area was whether or not victimology is a branch of criminology or a separate science; there continues to be an absence of consensus among victimologists today about the boundaries of their field (Fisher & Jerin, 2014; Karmen, 2010).

An overview of the field reveals three main approaches in victimology (Bienkowska, 1992; Kirchhoff, 1994, 2010). The first is *penal victimology*, which considers victimology as a branch of criminology and is focused on victims of crimes. This approach is advocated by authors such as Andrew Karmen (2010) and Ezzat Fattah (2008). The second approach is *general victimology*. It includes victims of all types, including victims of accidents and natural disasters. This approach is advocated by authors such as John Dussich (Dussich, Underwood, & Petersen, 2003) and Sam Garkawe (2004). The third approach is a *human rights approach*. Advanced by authors such as Robert Elias (1985), this approach focuses on human-made victimizations of all kinds, including genocide, torture, and slavery.

Advocates of penal victimology argue that, while criminology long neglected the victim, it should include the study of victims and victimizations. According to Fattah (1991, 2008, 2010), by limiting itself to criminal acts victimology restricts itself to that which is measurable and well defined. By focusing on crime, victimology remains objective and neutral and avoids becoming political. Authors such as Hans von Hentig took the approach of penal victimology, which focused on understanding the crime. Willem Nagel (1963) argued that while criminology had in the past neglected the victim, this was a mistake and victimology should be part of criminology. More recently, Ezzat Fattah (2008) has argued that "attempts to divorce victimology from criminology" were "misguided" (p. 1). According to Karmen (2010), most victimologists adhere to this approach and view victimology as a subfield of criminology that studies crime victims. Undoubtedly, most research in victimology has focused on victims of conventional crimes.

However, if victimology is limited to the study of crimes, then the criminal code of any particular jurisdiction essentially sets its research agenda. Clearly it is possible that some things are immoral but not criminal. For example, abuses of power by the state may not constitute crimes in the legal sense but would clearly be considered immoral. Hence, rather than being neutral and objective, penal victimology may in fact promote a conservative "law and order" agenda because it fails to question the state (Elias, 1985).

General victimology is inclusive and does not exclude any victims. This approach recognizes that the word "victim" is used in many different contexts besides criminal victimization. As a result, victimology covers much more than criminology and is justified as a separate science. Because of its broad scope, general victimology allows us to study crimes by the state and examine criminal victimization as a symptom of a more general social victimization. For example, the burning of brides in parts of India and Pakistan following the refusal of the bride's family to pay additional dowry can be viewed as an expression of the structural victimization of women in these societies (Schneider, 2001). This broad approach recognizes that victimization is a subjective appraisal rather than the result of some objective, external criteria. Also, general victimology emphasizes the similarities in people's reactions to different types of victimization, such as natural disasters, accidents, and criminal events. **Post-traumatic stress disorder**, for example, can be experienced following any sort of traumatic event and is not limited to crime victims.

However, in general victimology everyone is a victim, so the limits of the science are blurred. Moreover, people's reactions to intentional acts of victimization are structurally different than unintentional ones, such as natural disasters and accidents. When intentionally harmed by another human being, common reactions include anger and loss of faith in others (Baril, 2002; Shapland & Hall,

2007). These reactions are unique to human-made victimizations and do not occur when the victimization is the result of a natural disaster (Baril, 2002). Moreover, the causes of human-made victimization versus natural disasters are different. Understanding the causes of a tsunami requires very different knowledge (i.e., exact sciences) than understanding the causes of a robbery. Hence, if the objective of victimology is to explain and prevent victimization, then it does not make sense to include victimizations that are not human-made.

The third approach is a victimology of human rights. The American political scientist Robert Elias (1985, 1993) argued that if victimologists adhered too closely to legal definitions of crime, they would become pawns of law and order regimes. This problem is illustrated in the case of Maher Arar (see Box 2.1). In Elias's view, human rights violations should be included in the domain of victimology. Hence, victimology should study victims of acts committed by other human beings such as robbery, assault, rape, as well as genocide, torture, and slavery. Examining the reactions of victims of the Pinochet Regime in Chile (1973–90), Kirchhoff (1994) argues that the reactions of victims of abuses of power by the state are similar to those of crime victims. This human rights approach is also reflected in the United Nations (1985) *Declaration of Basic Principles of Justice for Victims of Crime and Abuse of Power*, which considers victims of crime as well as those who are victims of abuses of power by the state. According to Kirchhoff (2010), this approach to victimology is the most accepted one.

BOX 2.1: VICTIM OR OFFENDER? THE CASE OF MAHER ARAR

On 26 September 2002, Maher Arar, a Canadian engineer, was stopped at John F. Kennedy Airport in New York on a layover flight from Tunis to Canada. Arar was born in Syria in 1970 and had resided in Canada since 1987. The American officials suspected him of being a member of Al-Qaeda. He was detained, questioned, and held in solitary confinement for nearly two weeks. However, he was never accused. He was then sent by the CIA to Syria rather than allowed to return home to Canada. He was held and tortured in Syria for 11 months.

On 5 October 2003, Arar was finally allowed to return to Canada. Upon his return he began to seek recognition of innocence and publicly denounced his experience. In 2006, a commission of inquiry published its findings in relation to Arar. It established that there was *no evidence* that Mr. Arar had committed a crime or of there being a link between him and terrorist activity. Arar appeared to have fallen victim to overzealous law enforcement in what had become a witch hunt against terrorism.

Following publication of the commission's report on 28 September 2006, the commissioner of the RCMP issued an apology to Arar for the role of the RCMP in his arrest and detention. The RCMP commissioner resigned soon afterwards in light of his behaviour in this case. In addition, the Canadian government settled out of court with Arar and agreed to pay him $10.5 million in compensation plus an addition $1 million to cover legal fees. Prime Minister Stephen Harper issued a formal apology on behalf of the Canadian government.

Maher Arar's experience highlights the limitations of penal victimology in terms of who is a victim and what is the object of victimology. Following the approach of penal victimology, cases like this would be excluded from the domain of victimology. Arar was a suspect and not a victim of a conventional crime. However, following the human rights approach, cases like Arar's, in which an individual's human rights were violated by the state, fall within the realm of victimology.

Expanding on the human rights perspective, some authors argue that victimization itself is a violation of the human rights of the victim (Doak, 2008; Wemmers, 2012). In this approach, any violation of human rights falls within the domain of victimology. It excludes natural disasters such as earthquakes and tornados, which may be traumatic but do not constitute a violation of a person's human rights. This limits victimology to the study of human-made victimizations and allows the science to focus on understanding the causes of victimization. With this knowledge we can help prevent victimization as well as address the consequences of victimization when prevention fails. Hence the human rights approach is the most suitable of the three approaches found in the literature. Following this approach, victimology is the scientific study of victimizations attributable to the violations of human rights, including crimes, and reactions toward both victimization and victims (Kirchhoff, 1994, 2010).

But is victimology separate from criminology when it focuses only on human-made victimizations? The object of criminology is crimes, while the object of victimology is violations of human rights. In so far as crimes constitute a violation of victims' human rights, the two domains overlap. However, where violations of human rights are not considered crimes, the two fields are distinct. In recent years, there has been growing interest among criminologists in studying crimes against humanity and using the human rights approach in criminology (Hagan, Rymond-Richmond, & Parker, 2005; Parmentier & Weitekamp, 2007). Following the creation of the International Criminal Court (ICC), criminologists have become increasingly interested in questions related to gross violations of human rights (Wemmers, 2009a). Hence, while this human rights approach may have originated in victimology (Elias, 1993), it has since carried over into criminology. Here we see how victimology, which is the intellectual product of criminology, has matured to become a source of knowledge and inspiration *for* criminology, influencing the kinds of questions that criminologists focus on (Wemmers, 2009a).

Typologies of Victims

In their effort to understand the causes of crime, many of the early pioneers in victimology developed typologies of victims. Von Hentig's typology (1948), takes into consideration the psychological, social, and biological factors associated with victimization. Chapter 12 of his book is provocatively titled "Victim's Contribution to the Genesis of Crime," in which he describes certain characteristics that make individuals at risk of victimization. To begin with, he describes what he refers to as "general types" of victims (see Table 2.1). This group consists of people who are at risk of victimization because of their physical vulnerability, such as young people, the elderly, and women, as well as groups that are at risk based on their social vulnerability, such as immigrants and minorities. His second category consists of psychological types of victims, such as persons suffering from depression, the acquisitive or greedy personality, and socially isolated individuals.

Von Hentig's typology is in many ways offensive by today's standards. Not only does he squarely place at least some of the responsibility for the crime on the victims' shoulders, he highlights the victims' immorality. However, it is important to remember that his work was a product of its time. Although we may now consider some of Von Hentig's ideas socially reprehensible, they illustrate how reactions to victimization are, in part, socially determined.

TABLE 2.1: Von Hentig's Typology

I. GENERAL TYPES	II. PSYCHOLOGICAL TYPES
Young	The depressed
Female	The acquisitive
Old	The wanton
Mentally defective and deranged	The lonesome and the heartbroken
Immigrants, minorities, dull normals	The tormentor
	Blocked, exempted, and fighting victims

We must be careful not to simply disqualify his work because of how his ideas are presented. Essentially, his typology is based on victims' vulnerability, which is still considered a risk factor today and is found in many contemporary criminological theories, such as rational choice theory. We will return to some of Von Hentig's ideas when we discuss polyvictimization in Chapter 5.

Another popular typology is that of Benjamin Mendelsohn (1956). Mendelsohn's typology focused on the relationship between the victim and the offender and, in particular, the victim's behaviour with respect to the offender. Mendelsohn did not just consider victims' contribution to the crime; his typology was based on the victim's degree of culpability or guilt (see Table 2.2). At one extreme we find the innocent victim, such as a child. This was considered to be the *ideal victim* according to Mendelsohn. At the other extreme lies the guilty victim, who because of mental illness suffers from hallucinations and falsely accuses another person of a crime that never occurred. In between these two extremes lie victims with varying degrees of guilt.

TABLE 2.2: Mendelsohn's Typology

CATEGORY	SUBCATEGORIES
1. The entirely innocent victim	
2. The less guilty victim; victim by ignorance	
3. The victim equally guilty as the offender; the voluntary victim	a. Suicide b. Euthanasia
4. The victim more guilty than the offender	a. Provocative victim b. Imprudent victim
5. The guilty victim	a. Victim-offender: e.g., self-defence b. The imaginary victim

The American sociologist Marvin Wolfgang (1958) found empirical support for the hypothesis that victims were sometimes responsible for their victimization. Studying almost 600 cases of criminal homicide, Wolfgang discovered that in more than one out of every four cases it was the victim who had initiated the conflict. He referred to this phenomenon as *victim precipitation*. Wolfgang's work on victims led him to eventually develop a new typology, together with his colleague Thorsten Sellin, which was based on the type of victimization rather than the type of victim (Sellin & Wolfgang, 1964):

1. Primary victimization: Personalized or individual victims.
2. Secondary victimization: Commercial establishments such as department stores. The victim in this case is impersonal, commercial, and collective.

3. Tertiary victimization: A diffuse victimization that extends to the larger community and includes offences against the public order, social harmony, or the administration of government.

4. Mutual victimization: Cases in which the participants engage in mutually consenting acts (e.g., buying and selling sex).

5. No victimization: Offences that could not be committed by an adult and are commonly referred to as "juvenile status offences," such as running away from home.

Work on typologies continued well into the 1970s. While most typologies focused exclusively on conventional crimes, some authors, such as Quinney (1972), suggested that the field of victimology be expanded to include victims of war and abuses of power. This view of victimology gave rise to new typologies of victims. Stephen Schafer (1977), for example, created a typology that integrated notions already found in earlier typologies, such as vulnerability and victim–offender relations, and added a new category—political victims. The latter were not crime victims but victims of abuses of power. Their recognition as victims did not depend on domestic law but on international standards and norms. Schafer's typology contained five categories:

1. Unrelated victims
2. Provocative victims
3. Biologically weak victims
4. Socially weak victims
5. Political victims

However, despite the inclusion of victims of abuses of power, Schafer's typology, like those before it, focused exclusively on direct victims. All of these typologies fail to include individuals who may not have directly been the object of a crime but may have suffered harm nonetheless. For example, the family and friends of crime victims who were nowhere near the victim at the time of the crime may also be traumatized and suffer both material and intangible losses following the victimization of their loved one (Armour, 2002). We will return to the question of typologies of victims in Chapter 4.

The Victims' Movement

The victims' movement first emerged in the United States in the 1970s (Maguire, 1991). Influenced by several factors, the victims' movement strove to improve the plight of the crime victim. However, unlike other social movements, which are characterized by public protests and marches, the victims' movement did not involve public demonstrations by crime victims. By and large, the birth of the victims' movement was led by academics and civil servants (Rock, 1986). The absence of victim involvement in the early years of the victims' movement is curious and distinguishes it from other social movements (Elias, 1993). Factors that led to the birth of the victims' movement include the crime rate and the spirit of the times, which was marked by a general questioning of the status quo. This led to numerous social movements, in particular the women's movement, and political activism. In the following section each of these factors will be discussed in relation to how it affected the evolution of the victims' movement.

The Crime Rate

The **crime rate** refers to the number of offences registered by the police. Generally, crimes are registered when the victim reports the crime to the police. Except for certain crimes, which are only known when the police stop the offender, such as drunk driving, it is rare that police discover crimes without the help of the public and victims in particular. In the 1960s, the crime rate began to increase, and this trend did not stop until the early 1990s when the crime rate finally stabilized. Interestingly, we can find this trend in Canada, the United States, and Europe.

In Canada, the Uniform Crime Reporting Survey (UCR), which is the system used by police to register and count crimes, was introduced in 1962. Between 1962 and 1980, the number of crimes per 100,000 inhabitants in Canada grew by 300 per cent (Logan, 2001). The crime rate in Canada reached a peak in 1991, when over 10,000 incidents were registered for every 100,000 Canadians (see Figure 2.1). The next year it began a steady decline, and in 2015 5,195 incidents were registered for every 100,000 inhabitants (Allen, 2016).

The crime problem was even bigger in the United States, where the registered crime rate grew by 400 per cent between 1960 and 1980 (Bureau of Justice Statistics, 1991). At the same time that law enforcement authorities were registering unprecedented crime levels, the first victimization survey was conducted in the United States (see Chapter 3 for a discussion of the evolution of the victim survey). The victimization survey revealed that victim cooperation with authorities was problematic, and many crimes went unreported. The results were alarming for authorities because they revealed that the **dark number** of crime—that is, the crimes that go unreported to authorities—was as much as 10 times larger than what was often assumed (Baril, 1985). This amplified the crime problem and added to ongoing concerns that crime was out of control.

Not surprisingly, it is during this period that crime first became a political issue (Fiselier, 1978; Garland, 2001). In the United States as well as in

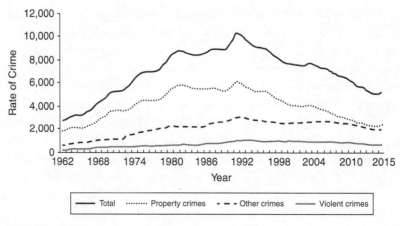

Source: Allen, 2016.

FIGURE 2.1: Police-Reported Crime Rates in Canada, 1962–2015

many other industrialized countries, governments actively searched for solutions to the crime problem, which seemed to be spiralling out of control. For example, governments began to fund research into effective policing in an effort to gain control over crime. One important study in this context was the Kansas City experiment (Kelling, Pate, Dieckman, & Brown, 1991). Carried out in the 1970s, this study sought to examine the impact of police surveillance methods on crime rates. It revealed that police surveillance was not only expensive, it was also *not* associated with less crimes being committed. Changing the police organization would not reduce the crime rate. The police needed the cooperation of the population if they hoped to reduce the crime rate. While police surveillance did not impact the crime rate, it was found to be associated with public satisfaction with the police. Hence, while the police could not control crime on their own, they could influence their relationship with the public. These results ultimately led to the creation of *community policing* to improve collaboration between the public and the police (Brodeur, 2003; Fijneault, Nuijten-Edelbroek, & Spickenheuer, 1985).

Policy and Research

The ever-increasing crime rate of the 1960s and 1970s explains, at least in part, the interest of policymakers in crime victims. Unable to directly control crime, authorities tried to control victims. Many of the first victim policies introduced aimed to improve the treatment of victims in the criminal justice process in the hope that this would encourage victim cooperation (Garland, 2001; Wemmers, 1996). In 1967, the President's Commission on Law Enforcement and Administration of Justice in the United States indicated that victim and witness cooperation in the criminal justice system posed a serious problem. In the early 1970s the Law Enforcement Assistance Administration (LEAA) gave grants to certain organizations to help victims and witnesses. In 1974, the LEAA funded eight pilot projects on victim-witness support. Located in the offices of the public prosecution, these projects aimed to produce better witnesses for the state. The idea was that by addressing the needs of victims, they would make better witnesses at trial. Victim-witness support expanded rapidly, and by 1979 there 220 of these programs throughout the United States (NOVA, 1988).

The mushrooming of victim support services across the United States led to the creation of a National Organization for Victim Assistance (NOVA) in 1975. This nonprofit organization was meant to act as an umbrella organization for local victim support services, providing training and research as well as advocating for victims' rights and services (Young, 2001). Similarly in England and Wales, the National Victims Assistance Support Scheme was established in 1979 as an umbrella body for local schemes (Van Dijk, 1988). In Canada, there have been several unsuccessful attempts to create a national victim support organization, the most recent being the Canadian Association for Victim Assistance, which organized national symposia in 2005 and 2006. However, due to a lack of funding these initiatives were unable to continue.

In Canada, the victims' movement was dominated by academics and civil servants (Roach, 1999; Rock, 1986). An important figure in the birth of the victims' movement in Canada was Irvin Waller, a professor of criminology at the University of Ottawa. In 1978, Waller published a study on the effects of burglary on victims (Waller & Okihiro, 1978). Soon after, Waller went on to become the director general of research at what was then called the Solicitor General of Canada (today this department is known as Public Safety Canada). Paul Rock (1986) describes Waller as a "moral entrepreneur" who was a major force behind the development of victim policies in Canada (p. 104). He introduced victimology and the American victims' movement to the federal government. An important event in this context is the 1981 annual meeting of NOVA, which was held in Toronto (Waller, 2011).

In 1982, the theme at the Quebec Society of Criminology's biannual conference was crime, victims, and community. As we saw, in Quebec victimology had been an important topic since the creation of the School of Criminology at the Université de Montréal in 1960. However, in the 1970s Ezzat Fattah left Montreal to create the School of Criminology at Simon Fraser University in British Columbia and his mentor, Henri Ellenberger, retired. A young criminologist, Micheline Baril, was a researcher at the Université de Montréal's

International Centre for Comparative Criminology and a professor at the School of Criminology. A talented researcher, her first publication on victims was a study on the effects of robbery on small business owners, which was published in 1977 (Cusson, 1993). In 1983, she published a pioneering study in which she examined the experiences of victims in the criminal justice system (Baril, Durand, Cousineau, & Gravel, 1983). In addition to being a scholar, Baril was also an activist. In the early 1980s she created the first victim support service in Montreal and, in 1984, she founded the advocacy group Association québécoise Plaidoyer-Victimes (Normandeau, 2000).

The first national seminar on victims' rights and the judicial process was organized in 1985 by the Canadian Criminal Justice Association (CCJA). The CCJA brings together researchers and practitioners in the field of criminal justice and corrections from across Canada to improve criminal justice. It publishes Canada's only bilingual criminological journal, the *Canadian Journal of Criminology and Criminal Justice*. At the end of the three-day conference in 1985 participants recommended that a national consultation between stakeholders take place to develop "nationally-accepted guidelines to ensure the victims' rights to dignity, participation and services at each stage of the process" (Zambrowsky & Davies, 1987, p. 130). We will return to this discussion of victims' rights in Chapter 7.

Zeitgeist

The late 1960s and early 1970s was a socially volatile era. The spirit of the times, or *zeitgeist*, was one of social change. Increasingly, the postwar baby boomers and members of minority groups questioned the status quo. In the United States, for example, there was the civil rights movement, which aimed to end segregation. In Canada, and in particular in the province of Quebec, there was the Quiet Revolution, characterized by the secularization of Quebec society and the creation of a welfare state.

Criminologists also questioned the established order. The Nazi occupation of Europe during World War II had left a lasting impression on many young criminologists who spent the war years in prison or in hiding. They rejected the positivist, biological approach to deviance that characterized Nazi policies (Van Swaaningen, 1999). Authors such as Nils Christie and Louk Hulsman (1977) advocated the abolition of the criminal justice system. Christie (1977) argued that the criminal justice system "stole" crime (or as he called it, "conflict") from victims and, consequently, victims of crime had lost their rights to participate. Victims' dissatisfaction with the criminal justice system was used by abolitionists like Christie as an argument in favour of its abolition. Christie advocated a "paradigm shift" that would see the criminal justice system replaced with a "victim-oriented court," which would be a lay-court that excluded lawyers and included victims. We will return to abolitionism in Chapter 11 when we discuss reparative justice.

The Women's Movement

While early victimologists agreed that the victim had been forgotten, their main focus was not on helping victims but on studying them to understand and prevent crime. Highlighting the work of authors such as Mendelsohn, whose typology focused on the victim's degree of guilt, and Wolfgang, whose work on victim precipitation identified victims as instigators, feminists strongly criticized victimology and victimologists for blaming victims.

Rejecting the status quo, feminists drew attention to violence against women and children, bringing issues such as rape, incest, and family violence into the public domain (Baril, 1985). Feminist scholars conducted research on violence in intimate relationships, revealing the double victimization experienced by many of these victims: first by their attacker and then by society. For example, in the 1970s sociologist Lynda Lytle Holmstrom and Ann Wolbert Burgess, a professor in nursing, studied rape victims admitted to the emergency ward of a large city hospital. They followed the victims over a long period. In all, 61 of the victims' cases went to criminal court. They found that victims were often treated as though they had committed a crime and were responsible for the rape. In an effort to defend their client and raise a "reasonable doubt," the defence would often put the victim on trial and expose her sexual history or suggest that she invented the complaint to save her reputation (Holmstrom & Burgess, 1978).

Besides fuelling research, the women's movement was also behind the creation of new laws aimed at protecting women from sexual violence. In Canada, feminist scholars successfully argued for drastic changes to the Criminal Code regarding violence against women, hence changing definitions of key concepts such as "rape" and "self-defence" to better correspond with the experiences of women (Johnson & Dawson, 2011; Laurin & Viens, 1996). Protective measures, such as the so-called "rape shield," were introduced to prevent victims from being questioned about their sexual history, and publication bans were introduced to protect their privacy. We will discuss these changes in detail in Chapter 7 together with other victims' rights. Notwithstanding these changes, the criminal prosecution of sexual assault remains difficult for victims who continue to feel as though they are the one on trial (see Box 2.2).

Feminists were critical of anything that highlighted the victim as an actor because of victim blaming. Early research on the effects of victimization revealed that victims often felt guilty and blamed themselves for what happened (Bard & Sangry, 1979). These findings were reinforced by research on public reactions to victimization. Work by Melvin Lerner on a *just-world theory* showed

BOX 2.2: VICTIM GOES ON TRIAL

On 23 November 2003, a 14-year-old girl rang the doorbell of a home in Sainte-Catherine, Quebec. The young girl was in a state of shock, trembling, cold, injured, naked, and wet. She had jumped into the St. Lawrence River to escape her rapist. Earlier that night, around 11 p.m., Frederic Dompierre (18 years old) had telephoned her and invited her to go out with him and his friend, Steve Lapointe (17 years old). She accepted the invitation. They picked her up in their car and drove down to the St. Lawrence River, where they sat and drank beer. Later she was attacked by Dompierre, who raped her and tried to drown her, hitting her on the head with a rock. The young girl managed to get away and swam to a small island in the river. Dompierre coaxed her to return to land, promising to drive her home. Instead, he forced her to undress and tried to drown her again. Again she got away and swam to the small island, where she remained until Dompierre and Lapointe finally left. She then swam ashore and rang the doorbell of a nearby house. Dompierre was found guilty of sexual assault and was sentenced to seven years in prison. Lapointe, who did not participate in the violence but was present throughout the ordeal, pled guilty to lesser charges and testified against Dompierre.

At the appeal hearing in 2005, Dompierre's defence lawyer argued that the young girl was in part responsible for what happened. After all, she had accepted the boys' invitation, even though it was already late at night and she didn't have her parents' permission. According to the defence, this meant that implicitly she had given her consent. Feminist groups and the Quebec Bar Association reacted with outrage. The defence lawyer, Linda Bureau, argued that it was her job to defend her client and this case was about a couple of adolescents who were out to have a good time.

that people tended to blame the victim, even when objectively the victim was not at fault. Lerner, a professor in social psychology at the University of Waterloo, argued that people like to believe that the world is just and that people get what they deserve. Using a series of well-organized experiments with students, he studied their reactions to observing the victimization of another human being. According to Lerner, people's belief in a just world is so important to them that when they are confronted with injustice, they would rather change their perception than alter their belief in a just world. Hence, when confronted with an innocent victim, observers devalue and blame the innocent victim to maintain their belief in a just world (Lerner & Simmons, 1971; Lerner, 1980). Just-world theory corroborated the feminist standpoint that we were blaming victims even when it was clearly not their fault. Victim blaming became taboo.

The women's movement also fuelled the creation of services for victims. The first services for female victims of crime emerged in the United States. In 1972, the first rape crisis centres emerged in California and Washington, DC (NOVA, 1988). Soon afterwards, similar services for women victims began to emerge in Canada. In 1973, the first women's shelters were established in Alberta, British Columbia, Ontario, and Saskatchewan (Johnson & Dawson, 2011). In Quebec, the first women's shelters and rape crisis centres were established in 1975, and within a few years there were six rape crisis centres and 20 women's shelters across the province (Lemieux & Riendeau, 1996). Today, there are an estimated 911 victim service providers operating across Canada, including 137 rape crisis centres (Munch, 2012). In addition, there are some 550 women's shelters in Canada (Sauvé & Burns, 2009).

Political Activism

In this era of social movement, political activism by family members of victims began to emerge in the later part of the 1970s, further fuelling the victims' movement in the United States (Maguire, 1991). In 1977, Betty Jane Spencer, who had herself survived a horrendous violent crime and whose sons had been murdered, created Protect the Innocent, a nonprofit organization that fought for the rights of victims (Young, 2001). In 1978, after the murder of their 19-year-old daughter, Robert and Charlotte Hullinger founded Parents of Murdered Children (www.pomc.com) to reach out and help family members of other homicide victims while advocating to reduce murder (Waller, 2011). Two years later, in 1980, Mothers Against Drunk Driving (MADD) (www.madd.org) was created in the United States. These were all groups that were created by those whose lives had been impacted by victimization to help victims and advocate for victims' rights. Compared to governmental victim services, these groups were much more dynamic and diverse; however, they played a marginal role in the early development of services for victims, which, as we saw, was led by government-run initiatives (Elias, 1983; Van Dijk, 1983).

Despite its geographic proximity to the United States, in Canada victims themselves did not engage in activism until much later. In 1989, nine years after the creation of MADD in the United States, family members of victims of drunk drivers founded MADD Canada (www.madd.ca). In 1992, following the brutal murder of her daughter, Nadine, Priscilla de Villiers established Canadians Against Violence Everywhere and Its Termination (CAVEAT).

CAVEAT worked to change legislation and protect victims until 2001, when Priscilla de Villiers joined the Office for Victims of Crime of the government of Ontario and CAVEAT was dissolved.

In Quebec, victim activism did not take flight until after 2000. In 2002, following a wave of serious violent crime committed by organized criminals, a group of victims and family members of victims founded a group called the Innocent Victims of Organized Crime (RIVCO).[5] The group's mission was to secure special services, such as compensation for the innocent victims of organized crime. While the group managed to attract considerable attention from the media, it slowly dissolved over time and is no longer active. Three years later, in 2005, four fathers whose daughters had been murdered or were missing (and thought to have been killed) formed the Association for the Families of Murdered and Missing Persons (AFPAD).[6] A key figure in the creation of AFPAD and one of the founders is Pierre-Hugues Boisvenu, whose daughter, Julie, was raped and murdered in 2002. In 2010, he left AFPAD when he was appointed senator by the Conservative government under Prime Minister Stephen Harper.

Ideological Transformation of Victimology

The victims' movement transformed victimology from a scholarly branch of criminology to a social movement. Paul Rock (1986) referred to victimology as both a science and a social movement. Early victimologists, such as Ezzat Fattah (1999, 2010), were not happy with this transformation of victimology. According to Fattah (2010), the transformation resulted in two groups with opposed ideals, different agendas, and divergent philosophies.

The early pioneers in victimology, such as Fattah, Ellenberger, Wolfgang, Nagel, and Von Hentig, formed one side of the ideological divide. They were scientists who studied the victim to understand and explain crime. These scholars and researchers saw victimology as a branch of criminology. As we have seen, early victimologists developed elaborate victim typologies depicting the relationship between the victim and the offender. While they recognized that victims had long been forgotten, they were not interested in the victims' suffering per se—they were interested in preventing crime.

On the other side were "the feminists, the therapists, the social workers, as well as the social and political activists" (Fattah, 2010, p. 53) who aimed to

....

5 The French name of the organization is Regroupement des innocentes victimes du crime organisé, which is where the acronym RIVCO comes from.

6 The French name of the organization is Association des Familles de Personnes Assassinées ou Disparues.

improve the plight of crime victims. Although there was some criticism of the treatment of crime victims in the 1950s (Fry, 1959; Milliken, 1950; Tahone, 1952), it was not until the 1970s that research began to address the consequences of victimization for the victim. Clinical studies with victims of mass atrocities, such as the Holocaust, highlighted the effects of victimization on the individual (Maguire, 1991). From the 1970s onward, research in the United States focused increasingly on the psychological impact of victimization and, in particular, on post-traumatic stress disorder (Shapland & Hall, 2007; see also Chapter 4). Research also emerged on victims' negative experiences with the criminal justice system and the **secondary victimization** of crime victims by criminal justice authorities (Baril, 1984; Holmstrom & Burgess, 1978; Shapland, 1985; Symonds, 1980; Williams, 1984; see also Chapter 6). While this side included excellent researchers doing top-notch research, for some old-school victimologists they were not objective but were part of an advocacy movement and a political lobby (Fattah, 2010).

This ideological shift had a tremendous impact on the kinds of research carried out in victimology. While speaking at the Third International Symposium on Victimology in Münster, Germany, Denis Szabo (1979) identified typologies as a research priority for victimologists, and yet throughout the 1980s the opposite occurred: Work on victim typologies disappeared. By the late 1980s it had become taboo to examine a victim's role in crime. Victim support organizations like NOVA in the United States instructed those working with victims that they should always tell victims right away that "it's not their fault" to prevent them from blaming themselves. Victimization was considered a random event, and victim blaming was to be avoided. It was not until the 1990s, when research emerged on multiple victimization, that victimologists began to show a renewed interest in the victim as an actor (Davis, Taylor, & Titus, 1997).

Co-opting Victims

Fattah's critique of victimology as a political lobby and advocacy movement is not without basis. As we saw, government-run victim services, such as victim-witness support, were devised primarily for official needs. Even services that began as part of a grassroots, feminist movement, such as rape crisis centres, gradually evolved into mainstream services for victims in the criminal justice system (Van Dijk, 1988). The absence of systematic evaluation studies on the effectiveness of victim assistance is, according to Fattah (1999, 2010), evidence that these programs are not intended to help victims. Similarly, Elias (1993) finds that most government-run victim compensation programs in the United States fail to address the needs of victims. Typically these programs focus exclusively on the **direct victim** of violence, excluding victims of nonviolent crime as well as the family members of victims (see Chapter 9 for a detailed discussion of government-run compensation programs). If these programs are intended to help victims, Elias asks, then why exclude certain groups? This raises the question of whether these programs are not simply symbolic politics instead of programs with real substance (Elias, 1983). The victims' movement, Elias warns, has been taken over and manipulated by government (Elias, 1993).

While Elias's research is based on groups in the United States, his argument about the co-option of the victims' movement is equally relevant outside of the United States. In Canada, the recruitment of victims' rights leaders, such as Priscilla de Villiers and Senator Pierre-Hugues Boisvenu, into government is an excellent example of this. The government usurps strong, vocal leaders for victims' rights. Once they are part of government, they lose their independence and their ability to critique government policy.

Politicians developed their own, punitive conception of how to act in victims' interests, independent of research on victims' needs. The dominant discourse is on victims versus offenders (Roach, 1999; Wemmers, 2012). In this political rhetoric, punitive policies are presented as pro-victim (Garland, 2001; Roach, 1999). Conservative crime bills limiting the rights of the accused are named after prominent victims to create a sense that this is for victims. Garland (2001) gives the example of Megan's Law in the United States. Named after Megan Kanka, the young victim of an adult sex offender, Megan's Law requires authorities to make information available to the public about registered sex offenders.

This is not a purely American phenomenon. It can be found in Canadian law as well. An excellent example is Bill C-479, which received royal assent on 23 April 2015 and hence became law (*Corrections and Conditional Release Act*, c. 11). The short title of this Bill is *An Act to Bring Fairness for the Victims of Violent Offenders*, which would seem to suggest that the Bill presents new procedural rights for victims. However, the full title of Bill C-479 is *An Act to Amend the Corrections and Conditional Release Act (fairness for victims)*. This is a more apt description of the Bill, which introduces new limitations on the right to parole hearings for sentenced offenders without providing any new rights or services for victims. Victims' rights are presented as the opposite of offender rights, and any limitation of the rights of offenders is considered advancement for victims' rights (Roach, 1999).

Focusing the public debate on victims versus offenders, there is little discussion about how the state hinders victims' rights in the criminal justice system. The state is generally not conceptualized as crime victims' main obstacle. Yet, despite the multitude of services that have been developed over the years, most criminal justice authorities still view crime as victimizing the state or society, not the victim. As we saw in Chapter 1, this continues to be the central premise of the criminal justice system, where a victim's role is that of a witness to a crime against the state. While numerous laws have been introduced to curb the rights of the accused, victims in Canada still do not have a legal right to participate in the criminal trial other than as a witness (see Chapter 10). The victims' movement, Elias (1993) argues, has not fundamentally challenged society in the fields of crime control strategies, social policy, or otherwise.

This critical approach to victimology, which is exemplified in the work of authors such as Fattah (1999, 2010) and Elias (1993), is important to bear in mind throughout this book. Elias (1985) warns that victimologists risk becoming pawns of abusive governments if they limit their object of study to victims of crime and argues in favour of a victimology of human rights. He encourages victimologists to independently and objectively examine crime's social sources. Through research, victimology can contribute to breaking down misperceptions about victims and changing society and how it responds to crime. When evaluating victim-centred policies and programs it is important to ask who benefits from them and to be suspicious of programs that pursue other goals in the name of victims.

Conclusion

A product of criminology, victimology was born in the ashes of World War II to help explain crime. Early victimologists studied the role of the victim in the criminal incident and created typologies to classify victims. Yet, despite the commitment of early victimologists to prevention, crime continued to grow. Faced with an ever-increasing crime rate and the realization that the police had little direct power over the amount of crime committed, authorities desperately searched for ways to regain control over it. Academics teamed up with government to understand the consequences of crime and improve the plight of the victim. Introducing measures such as community policing and pro-victim policies, policymakers aimed to enhance victims' attitudes toward the criminal justice system and increase their collaboration with criminal justice authorities. The women's movement drew attention to women and children as victims. Feminists developed grassroots services for victims, while scholars challenged popular conceptions of vicitmization and denounced victim blaming.

Politicians used the rhetoric of the victims' movement to enhance public perceptions of and cooperation with criminal justice authorities. While much has been done and victim services have become mainstream, the victims' movement has not fundamentally challenged society in the fields of crime control strategies, social policy, or otherwise. Victims remain the forgotten party in criminal justice. Research can always be used to further political agendas. However, research that is empirical and independent can make a substantial contribution to society. The human rights approach to victimology ensures that the field is not dependent on legal definitions and political rhetoric. In the following chapters we will expand on this science of victimology and discover what it teaches us about victims and victimizations.

CHAPTER 3

VICTIMIZATION SURVEYS

One of the most important contributions of victimology to criminology has been the **victimization survey**. First developed in the United States in the 1960s, the victimization survey was originally introduced as a way to measure crime. However, over the years it developed into much more and provides us with insight into victims' characteristics as well as their attitudes and behaviours. Beginning with the history and evolution of victimization surveys, this chapter will examine what information victimization surveys are able to provide and discuss their strengths and limitations.

History

How to measure crime is a question that has preoccupied authorities for a long time. Early measures of crime included the number of people convicted by a court or the number of people in prison. Following the introduction of police forces in the nineteenth century, police statistics on crime levels gradually gained importance. Soon afterwards national governments began collecting standardized police statistics, and in the twentieth century national police statistics became a popular means to measure the crime rate. However, the traditional measures for counting crimes were based on offenders (e.g., prisoners) or offences (e.g., police statistics). They did not provide systematic information about victims and victimizations. The only exception was homicide statistics, which are always based on the number of victims found. This is why many of the first empirical studies in victimology focused on homicide: These crimes offered the only systematic data on victims that was available at the time.

Authorities have always known that not all crimes are reported to the police. These crimes remain hidden from authorities. The *dark figure* refers to unreported or undiscovered crimes (Gibbons, 1979; Wemmers, 2003).

The ever-increasing crime rate of the 1960s worried politicians and policy-makers, making crime a political item. In 1965, US President Lyndon Johnson created the President's Commission on Law Enforcement and Administration of Justice, and he appointed his attorney general, Nicholas Katzenbach, to chair the commission. The commission was mandated to understand crime and to make recommendations to stop the growing crime problem (Fiselier, 1978).

One of the first questions that the commission tackled was, "How much crime is out there?" Critical of police statistics and the obvious gap between the number of crimes committed and those reported to police, the commission examined alternative ways to measure crime. One alternative proposed was the self-report study, in which people are asked to disclose their criminal activity. Self-report delinquency studies are particularly well-suited for young offenders and relatively minor offences, but they are less helpful when it comes to serious crimes committed by adult offenders (Junger-Tas & Haen-Marshall, 1999). Hence, the idea was proposed to ask people about their experiences as a victim of crime, based on the idea that people may be more forthcoming about their victimization than they would be about their delinquency. The commission gave Albert Biderman and his colleagues Philip Ennis and Al Reis the task of carrying out the first victimization survey. Their objective was to better understand the frequency of victimization and people's attitudes toward crime and criminal justice authorities (Biderman, 1967; Reiss, 1967).

The first victimization survey used face-to-face interviews with adults aged 18 years and older. One of the most startling findings from the original survey was that the number of unreported crimes—the dark figure—was many times larger than what was thought. On average, only one in three victimizations were reported to police (Reiss, 1967). According to Albert Reiss's calculations, the gross estimate of offences was more than five times as great as police statistics showed. Hence, the growing crime problem was quite possibly an even bigger problem.

The research also revealed, however, an inverse relationship between fear of crime and attitudes toward the police (Reiss, 1967): Victims' attitudes toward the police influenced their decision whether or not to report a crime. These findings would later form the basis for the introduction of new policies and practices, such as community policing, which aimed to improve public attitudes toward the police (Garland, 2001; Wemmers, 2003).

Five years later, in 1972, the Bureau of Justice Statistics (BJS) introduced the National Crime Victimization Survey (NCVS). Today, the BJS annually publishes findings from the NCVS. Other countries soon introduced their own victimization survey. Since 1989, there is even an International Crime Victims Survey. Victimization surveys are now carried out regularly to track changes over time.

General Social Survey

Compared to the United States and Europe, Canada was relatively late to introduce its survey. The first victimization survey in Canada was carried out in 1982 by the research office of what was then called the Solicitor General of Canada (now known as Public Safety Canada) in collaboration with Statistics Canada. This first survey was conducted in seven large urban areas: Vancouver, Edmonton, Winnipeg, Toronto, Montreal, Halifax-Dartmouth, and St. John's (Solicitor General of Canada, 1985). A few years later, Statistics Canada fully took over the survey, which is now part of the General Social Survey (GSS).

Since its introduction, the survey has been carried out approximately every five years (in 1988, 1993, 1999, 2004, 2009, and 2014). This is much less frequently than the United States and England and Wales, where victimization data are collected annually (Flatley, 2016; Truman & Langton, 2015). After the initial pilot study in 1982, the surveys were no longer limited to urban areas, but they were limited to the country's 10 provinces. The rural nature of the territories poses specific challenges for data collection; it was not until 2004 that victimization data were available for the territories (De Léséleuc & Brzozowski, 2006). However, data on the territories are reported separately because they involve another sampling design (Perreault & Brennan, 2010; Perreault, 2015). Thus, reports on criminal victimization in Canada still only include the provinces.

The GSS focuses on eight types of crimes that fall under two general categories: crimes against persons and crimes against households. The crimes against persons included in the survey are (1) sexual assault, (2) robbery, (3) physical assault, and (4) theft of personal property. The household victimizations include (5) break and enter or burglary, (6) motor vehicle theft or theft of parts, (7) theft of household property, and (8) vandalism (see Table 3.1). Respondents are asked whether they experienced any of these crimes in the 12 months preceding the interview. Those who indicate that they did experience one or more victimizations are then asked several questions about each incident. For example, they are asked where the incident took place, whether they knew the offender, what impact the incident had on them, and whether they reported the incident to the police.

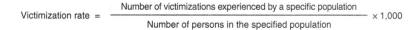

$$\text{Victimization rate} = \frac{\text{Number of victimizations experienced by a specific population}}{\text{Number of persons in the specified population}} \times 1{,}000$$

FIGURE 3.1: Victimization Rate

TABLE 3.1: Defining Criminal Victimization in Canada

TYPE OF VICTIMIZATION	DESCRIPTION
	Violent Victimization
Sexual assault	Forced sexual activity, an attempt at forced sexual activity, or unwanted sexual touching, grabbing, kissing, or fondling.
Robbery	Theft or attempted theft in which the perpetrator had a weapon or there was violence or the threat of violence against the victim.
Physical assault	An attack (the victim is hit, slapped, grabbed, knocked down, or beaten), a face-to-face threat of physical harm, or an incident with a weapon present.
	Nonviolent Victimization
Theft of personal property	Theft or attempted theft of personal property, such as money, credit cards, clothing, jewellery, a purse, or a wallet. (Unlike robbery, the perpetrator does not confront the victim.)
	Household Victimization
Break and enter	Illegal entry or attempted entry into a residence or other building on the victim's property.
Motor vehicle/parts theft	Theft or attempted theft of a car, truck, van, motorcycle, moped, or other vehicle or part of a motor vehicle.
Theft of household property	Theft or attempted theft of household property, such as liquor, bicycles, electronic equipment, tools, or appliances.
Vandalism	Wilful damage of personal or household property.

Source: Perreault, 2015.

The **victimization rate** refers to the number of incidents reported divided by the population in a particular region to obtain a standardized rate (see Figure 3.1). In 2014, the victimization rate for crimes against persons (i.e., violent crimes and personal theft) was 149 incidents per 1,000 Canadians aged 15 years and older. That same year the victimization rate for household crimes was 143 incidents per 1,000 households (Perreault, 2015).

$$\text{Prevalence rate} = \frac{\text{Number of victims in a specific population}}{\text{Number of persons in the specified population}} \times 1{,}000$$

FIGURE 3.2: Prevalence Rate

Another measure of the level of victimization is the **prevalence rate**. The prevalence rate is based on the number of individuals in the population who experienced at least one victimization during a specific time (Lauritsen & Rezey, 2013; see Figure 3.2). The key distinction between the victimization rate and the prevalence rate is whether the numerator consists of the number of victimizations or the number of victims. Any one person may experience one or more victimizations in a given period, so the victimization rate is generally higher than the prevalence rate. In 2014, approximately one in five Canadians aged 15 years and older reported that they or their household had been the victim of at least one victimization in the last 12 months (Perreault, 2015). This is a prevalence rate of 200.

For criminal justice policymakers, both the victimization rate and the prevalence rate provide useful information. Victimization rate data, which focuses on incidents, can be used to assess the needs of the criminal justice system. Criminal investigations, arrests, and prosecutions all begin with a criminal incident. In contrast, prevalence rate data can provide insight into the number of people requiring victim services (Lauritsen & Rezey, 2013).

Because these are standardized measures, both the victimization and prevalence rates allow us to compare rates across time while bearing in mind changes in population size. In 2014, victimization rates in Canada decreased for the first time since the survey was introduced (see Table 3.2). Similarly, the prevalence rate dropped: In 2014 it was 200/1,000, while in 1999 it was 260

TABLE 3.2: Victimization Rates in Canada, 1981–2014

YEAR	PERSONAL CRIMES (PER 1,000 INHABITANTS 15 YRS +)	HOUSEHOLD CRIMES (PER 1,000 HOUSEHOLDS)
1981	141[a]	369
1988	143[b]	216[b]
1993	144[c]	193[d]
1999	186[e]	218[d]
2004	199[e]	248[e]
2009	226[e]	237[e]
2014	149[f]	143[f]

a) In 1981 the rate was based on the population 16 years and older, Solicitor General of Canada (1983); b) Sacco & Johnson, 1990; c) Statistics Canada, 1994; d) Mihorean et al., 2001; e) Perreault & Brennan, 2010; f) Perreault, 2015.

(Mihorean et al., 2001), in 2004 it was 280, and in 2009 it was 260 (Perreault & Brennan, 2010).

However, when comparing rates it is important to bear in mind that the 2014 survey differed from previous surveys in that it included numerous reminders to respondents as to the reference period for all of the questions. This was done to discourage respondents from sharing information about victimization experiences that occurred outside of the survey's frame of reference and therefore exaggerated the level of victimizations (Perreault, 2015). This is referred to as *telescoping*, which effectively inflates victimization rates. Hence, it is unclear whether and to what extent the lower rates found in the 2014 survey reflect an actual reduction in victimization or if they are simply the result of this modified methodology.

Advantages of Victimization Surveys

Victimization surveys offer numerous benefits, which is why the United Nations Office on Drugs and Crime (2010) encourages member states to adopt the victimization survey as a standard tool to better understand their crime problem and how to address it. As mentioned earlier, before the introduction of the victimization survey there was no systematic data on victims and victimizations other than homicide statistics. Victimization surveys provide a wealth of previously unavailable information, which can be used in the development of crime prevention strategies and knowledge-based criminal justice policies (Aromaa, 2012).

One of the major benefits of victimization surveys is that they capture information on criminal incidents that are *not* reported to the police. Research has shown that for various reasons most victims do not report their victimization to the police. For example, according to the 2014 GSS, 67 per cent of victims did not bring the incident to the attention of the police. Reporting rates differ across type of offence: 67 per cent of violent victimizations, 63 per cent of household victimizations, and 79 per cent of personal property thefts were *not* reported to police (Perreault, 2015). Reporting rates vary across countries, too. Some countries, such as Austria, have reporting rates as high as 70 per cent of victimizations, while others, such as Mexico, have reporting rates of only 16 per cent of victimizations (Van Dijk, Van Kesteren, & Smit, 2007).

Besides measuring victimization and shedding light on the dark figure of crime, victimization surveys also provide a voice for victims (Aromaa, 2012; Van Dijk, 1999). They offer insight into the tangible and intangible consequences of criminal victimization, which is important to understanding the costs of crime for the individual victim as well as for society. Victims can express their needs for support, which is significant for the development of services for victims (see Chapter 4).

Victimization surveys also provide information about who becomes a victim of crime and identify risk factors as well as vulnerable groups. Besides individual victimization experiences, the survey provides insight into repeat and multiple victimization (Skogan, 1999). These concepts are discussed later in this chapter.

Surveys tap into people's attitudes and experiences. They measure attitudes toward authorities, such as satisfaction with police performance, as well as trust and confidence in the criminal justice system, which are vital for the legitimacy of the system and of those working in it (Hough, 2012; Tyler, 1990; Wemmers, 1996). Surveys also provide insight into public fear or concern about crime as well as what people have done about victimization to prevent further victimization. These are all key issues for policymakers interested in developing knowledge-based criminal justice policy (Aromaa, 2012).

When conducted regularly, victimization surveys provide insight into national as well as regional and even international trends. This information is particularly interesting when considered together with other sources of information about crime levels, such as police data (Aromaa, 2012; Skogan, 1999). After considering the disadvantages or limitations of victimization surveys, we will examine victimization findings together with police data.

Disadvantages of Victimization Surveys

Despite the benefits of self-reported victimization surveys, they do have limitations. To begin with, victimization surveys only include a few different types of victimization. All infractions without a direct victim, like white-collar crime, or where the victim is unable to speak, such as homicide, are necessarily excluded. Crimes against any organization, such as businesses and institutions, are also excluded. In addition, crimes that involve a degree of complacency on the part of the victim, such as drug offences or collusion, are excluded. The GSS only covers eight crimes.

Besides being limited to certain victimizations, surveys systematically exclude certain groups of people. Surveys will typically exclude children because the questionnaire is not adapted to their level of development. However, countries vary in terms of the age limit. For example, in Canada only people aged 15 years and older are interviewed (Perreault, 2015). In England and Wales the age limit is 16 years (Office for National Statistics, 2016), while in the United States children 12 years and older are included (Bureau of Justice Statistics, 2016). Surveys are often conducted by phone, which means that only people with a telephone can participate. As a result, those living in institutions, such as prisons, halfway houses, and hospitals, are systematically excluded. Also, individuals without a fixed address are excluded. Language barriers can also limit the participation of groups such as new immigrants who are unable to communicate in the local language. When considering victimization rates it is important to bear these groups in mind, which are not included in the data.

Victimization surveys are also limited in terms of how they define crimes. Respondents are not experts in law and are generally not familiar with the Criminal Code. Surveys measure victimization incidents rather than "crime" (Aromaa, 2012). In fact, they often avoid the word "crime" altogether. Instead they use accessible language to describe relevant incidents and situations that correspond with victimizations. Respondents are then asked if such things have happened to them over a given period, such as the last 12 months.

Subjectivity is also an issue. When does a disagreement become an assault? For example, if a hockey player hits an opponent on the head with his stick, is it an assault or is it just part of the game? The context in which an event takes place and the relationship between the victim and the offender are relevant for how the event is interpreted by the victim. Also, each of us judges an event differently depending on our age, gender, socioeconomic status, education, and so on. For example, when asked about violent victimization, victims tend not to label violence as a crime when it is caused by someone they know well (Brennan, 2016; Langton & Truman, 2014). The fact that victimization surveys are subjective and victimization is not independently validated by a third party is a problem if one's aim is to have an objective measure of crime. Aromaa (2012) argues that crime is an abstract and technical concept that is not well suited to be addressed in a population survey. He insists that victimization surveys do not measure "crime" but people's experiences. The criticism that surveys are subjective, however, is less problematic when we consider the survey as a means to provide insight into victims' experiences, attitudes, and behaviours rather than just as a tool to measure crime.

It is also important to bear in mind that people's memories are not perfect. Victimization surveys rely on respondents to recall and report events accurately. Two common errors people make are exaggeration and underestimation:

1. *Exaggeration:* The GSS asks about events that took place in the last 12 months. If someone experienced a victimization 13 months ago, then it should not be included in the survey. However, the victim may really want to talk about it and feels that it is important to report and therefore says that the event took place 11 months ago instead. This would inflate the observed rate of victimization artificially. Exaggeration is sometimes also referred to as telescoping (Perreault, 2015). Over the

years, survey techniques have improved to cope with this type of error. For example, if victims are first asked about lifetime victimization and then asked about victimization during the last 12 months, they will have an opportunity to talk about their experience and will be less inclined to modify the timeframe. This will generate qualitatively better data, and the researchers will be able to exclude the event when calculating the victimization rate during the last 12 months.

2. *Underestimation:* Contrary to exaggeration, victims may forget when exactly an event occurred. It may feel as though it was a very long time ago, so they don't mention it even though, in fact, it was 11 months ago. One way to help reduce the risk that victims will make this type of memory error is to help them to place important events on a timeline and then situate the victimization experience relative to these key events.

Clearly, victimization surveys, like any other method, are not perfect and have their limitations. Despite these limitations, they provide a wealth of information that simply is not available elsewhere.

Comparing Victimization Data with Police Data

Victimization surveys were meant to complement police data by shedding light on the dark figure. Despite their limitations, victimization surveys can be helpful when considered alongside other sources of information about crime, such as police statistics. Although both victimization surveys and police-reported data capture information on crime, they have many differences, including survey type, scope, coverage, and source of information (Perreault, 2015).

In Canada, the GSS is a sample survey, which in 2014 collected information on eight different types of victimization from approximately 33,000 noninstitutionalized individuals, aged 15 years and older, living in the 10 provinces. The survey is designed to ensure that these data represent only the noninstitutionalized Canadian population aged 15 years or over. In contrast, police-reported data (the Uniform Crime Reporting Survey, or UCR) is an annual census of all Criminal Code incidents and certain other federal laws that come to the attention of the police and are reported by them to Statistics Canada (Perreault, 2015).

Both the GSS and UCR shed some light on the crime rate. Since the early 1990s the UCR has registered a decreasing crime rate. In 2014, the crime rate in Canada was just over 5,000 per 100,000 population (people), which is the lowest rate on record since 1969 (Boyce, 2015). In contrast, victimization rates in Canada have not followed the same pattern (see Table 3.2). It was only in 2014 that victimization rates dropped sharply and, as mentioned earlier, it is unclear to what extent this is an artifact of the change in methodology or whether it is an actual decrease in victimization. While caution must be used when interpreting the results, it is nevertheless intriguing that findings from the GSS and the UCR do not show similar trends over time. It raises the question whether the UCR's declining crime rate reflects an actual decrease in crime or whether something else may be happening.

An important difference between police statistics and victimization surveys is the latter's ability to measure unreported victimization. As we saw, most victimizations are not reported to the police (Perreault & Brennan, 2010; Perreault, 2015). Since 1993, the rate of reporting has dropped steadily from 42 per cent to 37 per cent in 1999, 34 per cent in 2004, and 31 per cent in 2009 (Mihorean et al., 2001; Perreault & Brennan, 2010). The year 2014 marked the first time in 20 years that the reporting rate did not fall and remained stable at 31 per cent (Perreault, 2015).

There are many factors that can influence police-reported crime statistics, including the willingness of the public to report crimes to the police as well as changes in legislation, policies, and enforcement practices. In general, the more serious an incident, the greater the likelihood it will come to the attention of the police. Also, victims who want to make an insurance claim are obliged to report the crime to police to obtain compensation for any stolen or damaged property. Thus in 2014 incidents causing injury (45 per cent), those involving a weapon (53 per cent), or those that resulted in financial loss of $1,000 or more (70 per cent) were more likely to be reported to the police in Canada. In terms of type of victimization, robberies, break-ins, and theft of a motor vehicle or parts were reported to police at least 44 per cent of the time. However, only 5 per cent of sexual assaults were brought to the attention of the police in 2014 (Perreault, 2015). Once again, the seriousness of the victimization plays a role in a victim's decision to report as well as contextual factors: Victims are more likely to report sexual assault when the offender was a stranger, the victim suffered physical injuries, and the victim was not under the influence of drugs or alcohol (Wolitzky-Taylor et al., 2011).

Reasons for not reporting incidents vary depending on the crime and are linked to victims' expectations about the results. For example, 63 per cent of victims of violent crime said they did not report because it was a personal matter, while 27 per cent did not want to get the offender into trouble, and 18 per cent feared revenge (Perreault, 2015). Victims of sexual assault who chose not to report did so because they feared reprisal (68 per cent) or they did not want others (57 per cent) and in particular their family (59 per cent) to know (Wolitzky-Taylor et al., 2011). In Canada, some 12 per cent of sexual assault victims stated that they did not report the crime because they did not want to bring shame or dishonour to their family (Perreault, 2015). Other reasons for not reporting sexual assault include fear of the justice system (42 per cent) and that there was not enough proof (51 per cent) (Wolitzky-Taylor et al., 2011). As we saw in Chapter 2, nonreporting is a concern for governments, which effectively lose some control over crime when victimization is not reported to the police.

Risk of Victimization

Gender

Early victimization surveys found that men experienced more victimization than women (Fattah, 1991). However, this finding was in part an artifact of how victimization was measured and the inability of early surveys to adequately measure certain types of victimization that women are more at risk for than men, such as sexual assault and violence in intimate relationships. In the 1990s, much work was done to improve the measurement of violence against women in victimization surveys (Johnson & Dawson, 2011; Sinha, 2013). As a result, later surveys tended to find that men and women share similar overall victimization rates, but they fall victim to different types of crime (Gannon & Mihorean, 2005; Perreault & Brennan, 2010; Truman & Langton, 2015). Women have a greater risk of sexual violence, whereas men have a greater risk of physical assault. In 2014, the victimization rate for sexual assault in Canada was 37/1,000 for women and 5/1,000 for men, while the victimization rate for physical assault was 54/1,000 for men versus 43/1,000 for women (Perreault, 2015).

Age

In general, the risk of victimization decreases with age (Perreault, 2015; Truman & Langton, 2015). Regardless of the type of victimization, people have the highest risk of victimization between 15 and 24 years of age (Perreault & Brennan, 2010; Perreault, 2015). In particular, age is a key risk factor in violent victimization, and young adults between 20 and 24 years of age have the highest risk (Perreault, 2015; Truman & Langton, 2015).

However, it is important to bear in mind that the very young and the very old are not well represented in the victimization survey. Youth under 15 years of age are systematically excluded from the survey, and any seniors living in institutions like nursing homes are also excluded. Moreover, children and the elderly are typically victimized in the context of their family, and their dependent relationship with their aggressor makes it difficult and unlikely that they will report their victimization to police (Finkelhor, 1997).

David Finkelhor has extensively studied the victimization of children and youth in the United States and has developed a self-report survey, the Juvenile Victimization Survey, to measure the victimization of children and youth. He reports high rates of victimization among children: Nearly 60 per cent were exposed either directly or indirectly to violence in the past year, and almost half (46 per cent) were physically assaulted in the past year (Finkelhor, Turner, Ormrod, Hamby, & Kracke, 2009). Similar findings have been reported in Canada (Cyr, Clément, & Chamberland, 2014) and the United Kingdom (Radford, Corral, Bradley, & Fisher 2014). Using the Juvenile Victimization Survey, Cyr, Clément, and Chamberland (2014) found that 76 per cent of children and youth ages 2 to 17 in Quebec had experienced at least one victimization during their lifetime. While we need to be careful when comparing these findings with those from the general population, because each survey follows a different method, it does appear that children and youth report greater rates of victimization than adults (Lebeau, Wemmers, Cyr, & Chamberland, 2014). As Finkelhor (1997) points out, even if we were to assume that the rate of victimization for children under 15 years of age was zero (which it clearly is not), the high rate of victimization found in the general victimization survey among adolescents indicates that minors are more prone to victimization than adults. These findings and others like it have prompted Finkelhor and his colleagues to argue for the study of developmental victimology (Finkelhor, 1997), which is discussed in Chapter 5. As a result of the work done on the development of a victimization survey for children and youth, some countries, such as England and Wales, now routinely conduct a separate survey for children and youth ages 10 to 15 to better understand the victimization experiences of young people (Office for National Statistics, 2016).

Sexual Orientation

Targeting a person because of his or her sexual orientation is considered a hate crime in Canada (s. 718.2, Criminal Code). People who self-identify as homosexual and bisexual report significantly higher levels of violent victimization than those who self-identify as heterosexual (Perreault & Brennan, 2010; Perreault, 2015). In 2014, people self-identifying as bisexual recorded the highest violent victimization rate at 267 incidents per 1,000 Canadians, compared to 142/1000 for those self-identifying as homosexual and 69/1,000 for heterosexuals (Perreault, 2015).

Visible Minorities

Hate crimes can also target visible minorities. However, in Canada, immigrants and members of visible minority groups, religious minorities, or individuals whose language most often spoken at home differed from that of the majority in their province consistently have victimization rates similar to or lower than the average for Canadians (Perreault & Brennan, 2010; Perreault, 2015). For example, in 2014 rates of violent victimization were lower for those who self-identified as a visible minority (55/1,000) than for people who self-identified as a nonvisible minority (80/1,000) (Perreault, 2015). Also, rates were lower for immigrants (44/1,000) than for nonimmigrants (86/1,000) (Perreault, 2015). Among visible minorities, those who were born in Canada experience higher rates of violent victimization than visible minority immigrants. However, certain factors that are associated with a higher risk of victimization are also more common among Canadian-born visible minorities: They are often young (15–24 years), unmarried, and unemployed (Perreault, 2004).

Indigenous Peoples

Indigenous peoples consistently report higher rates of violent victimization than non-Indigenous people. Among respondents who self-identified as an Indigenous person, the rate of violent victimization was 160/1,000, while the rate for non-Indigenous peoples was 74/1,000. Among Indigenous peoples, First Nations have a higher rate of victimization (216/1,000) than respondents who self-identified as Métis (119/1,000) (Perreault, 2015). However, when other risk factors are taken into account the Indigenous identity is not associated with an increased risk of violent victimization, suggesting that other factors, such as poverty, lack of social cohesion, and gender, may be more important in explaining risk (Perreault & Simpson, 2016).

Indigenous women are particularly at risk of victimization in Canada. The rate of violent victimization reported by Indigenous women is almost three times higher than that of non-Indigenous women. More specifically, Indigenous women are more likely to be victims of conjugal violence than non-Indigenous women. They are also more likely to suffer injuries as a result of their victimization, to fear for their lives, and to experience psychological violence and financial exploitation than non-Indigenous women. Yet despite the high level of violence experienced by Indigenous women, they report experiencing less stress in their daily lives than non-Indigenous women (Brennan, 2011).

The Rural North

It was not until 2004 that a pilot survey was conducted in the territories. The survey was repeated in 2009 and 2014. Given the sparse population of northern Canada, irregular phone service, and language barriers, a different method for data collection was required. The results from these surveys reveal higher rates of victimization in the territories than in the provinces. In 2004, 37 per cent of residents aged 15 and older living in the territories reported being victimized at least once in the previous 12 months, whereas 28 per cent of provincial residents were victimized in this same period (De Léséleuc & Brzozowski, 2006). Five years later, in 2009, again over one in three (34 per cent) residents of the territories reported being victimized, and close to half (46 per cent) of all incidents were violent (Perreault & Hotton-Mahony, 2012). In 2014, 28 per cent of territorial residents reported being a victim of at least one crime. While this is down from the proportion in 2009, it remains higher than the figure reported in the provinces (18 per cent) (Perreault & Simpson, 2016). The rate of violent victimization for residents in the North is consistently higher than that of residents in the rest of Canada. It is also worth noting that Canada's North is predominantly populated by Indigenous people.

Income

People with an annual income of less than $20,000 have a greater risk of violent victimization than people with higher incomes, but they are less likely than people with a higher income to be a victim of theft of personal property (Perreault & Brennan, 2010).

Poverty is also associated with homelessness, and research suggests that the homeless are particularly vulnerable and at risk of victimization (Brassard & Cousineau, 2002). The GSS does not include homeless people, but respondents are asked if they have experienced homelessness in the past. People with a history of homelessness (e.g., those who had to live with someone else or in their vehicle because they had nowhere else to go) reported higher rates of violent victimization than people without such a history (Perreault, 2015).

Employment

Employment is associated with a low risk of victimization. In 2014, the violent victimization rate for Canadians with employment was 78/1,000, while it was 165/1,000 for respondents who were looking for paid work. Students also have a high rate of victimization: Their rate of victimization was 146/1,000 for violent crimes and 106/1,000 for theft of personal property (Perreault, 2015). However, this may also be related to age, since students tend to be in the 15–24 age group, which as we have seen is associated with a higher rate of victimization.

Drugs and Alcohol

People who report frequent use of drugs or drinking large quantities of alcohol in the preceding month are more likely to also report personal victimization, especially violent victimization. For example, in 2014 people who claimed to use cannabis everyday reported more violent victimizations (436/1,000) and personal theft (160/1,000) than those who did not use drugs in the preceding month (62/1,000 and 66/1,000, respectively). Distinguishing between cannabis use and other drugs, respondents who claimed to have used other drugs at least once during the preceding month had the highest rate of violent victimization (610/1,000) as well as theft (249/1,000) (Perreault, 2015).

The rate of violent victimization for people who reported drinking five or more alcoholic beverages in one sitting (i.e., binge drinking) in the preceding month was 127/1,000 compared to 58/1,000 for those who did not binge drink. Besides violent victimizations, binge drinking was also associated with a higher rate of theft of personal property (102/1,000 versus 64/1,000) (Perreault, 2015).

Marital Status

Victimization rates are also related to marital status (Perreault & Brennan, 2010; Truman & Langton, 2015). Single Canadians report more violent victimization (139/1,000) than those who are separated or divorced (108/1,000), in common law relationships (94/1,000), or married (40/1,000) (Perreault, 2015). However, this may also be associated with age and lifestyle, since single people tend to be younger and go out more than married people.

Lifestyle

The more often a person goes out in the evenings, the higher the risk of personal victimization. The violent victimization rate of people who go out almost every evening (21 or more times a month) is 141/1,000, and their rate of theft of personal property is 110/1,000, whereas for people who do not go out in the evening the rate of violent victimization is 34/1,000 and their rate of theft of personal property is 27/1,000 (Perreault, 2015). Age, marital status, employment, drug use, and binge drinking are all factors associated with lifestyle, which increases a person's risk of victimization.

Prior Victimization

The emergence of the victimization survey also sheds light on the phenomenon of **multiple victimization**. Early victimologists, such as Ezzat Fattah (1967), used the term "victim-recidivist" to describe someone with a general predisposition to become a victim of crime (p. 26). But the absence of a systematic database on victims and victimizations, other than homicide data, made it impossible to study this phenomenon. This changed with the introduction of the victimization survey.

For the first time researchers were provided with systematic information about who became a victim as well as about the victimizations they experienced. Not only did the survey allow researchers to examine victims and nonvictims in the population, it also provided information about the differential frequency of victimization among victims. To illustrate, according to the Canadian Urban Victimization Survey in 1981, there were 141 incidents of personal victimization per thousand persons, but there were only 115 victims of personal crime per thousand persons that year (Solicitor General of Canada, 1988). The lower value for prevalence rates as compared to victimization rates reflect multiple counting of survey respondents who were victims of a criminal incident on more than one occasion. Victimization surveys have confirmed that multiple victimization exists.

Multiple victimization is a general term that encompasses both repeat victimization, in which the individual reports being a victim of the same type of crime on multiple occasions, as well as cross-crime victimization or multiple crime-type victimization, in which the individual becomes a victim of different types of crimes (Hope, Bryan, Trickett, & Osborn 2001; Pease, 1998; Solicitor General of Canada, 1988). More recently, David Finkelhor and his colleagues have introduced the term **polyvictimization** to identify those individuals who experience multiple (i.e., three or more) types of victimization (Finkelhor, Ormrod, & Turner, 2007).

Multiple victimization means that a relatively small portion of the population experiences a lot of crime (Farrell & Pease, 1993). For example, in 2004 Canadians who reported having been the victim of more than one violent crime in the previous 12 months represented 2 per cent of the population but had experienced 60 per cent of all violent crimes. Among those individuals who reported victimization during the 12 months preceding the 2004 victimization survey, 38 per cent said that they had been victimized more than once. Of those, half were victimized twice while the other half were victimized three or more times (Perreault, Sauvé, & Burns, 2010).

Prior victimization experience seems to affect present victimization risk not only within crime types but also across crime types (Hope et al., 2001). In particular, people who suffered maltreatment as children seem to be more likely to be victims of violent crime as adults (Perreault, 2015). Child maltreatment is also associated with several other risk factors for violent victimization in adulthood, such as alcohol and drug use (Perreault, 2015). A high prevalence of physical or sexual violence in childhood is related to a higher level of physical violence against women in adulthood (European Union Agency for Fundamental Rights, 2014). While it is clear that past victimization increases the risks of future victimization, the mechanism or mechanisms behind this link are subject to debate. These findings underscore the necessity of developing theories of victimization that are capable of explaining risk. We will address this topic more in Chapter 5.

International Comparisons

Since 1989, Canada has participated in the International Crime Victims Survey (ICVS). The ICVS is a standardized survey developed to monitor the volume of victimization, perceptions of crime, and attitudes toward the criminal justice system in a comparative, international perspective. This survey was developed under the leadership of Jan van Dijk, a Dutch professor of criminology and expert in victimology. The survey was repeated in 1992, 1996, 2000, and 2005. It includes 10 different types of victimization: vehicle related crimes ((1) theft of a vehicle; (2) theft from a vehicle; (3) theft of a motorcycle or scooter; (4) theft of a bicycle); (5) burglary; (6) attempted burglary; (7) theft of personal property; and personal crimes ((8) robbery and attempted robbery; (9) sexual offences; (10) physical assaults or threats). Since its inception, the ICVS has been carried out in over 50 countries (Van Dijk, Van Kesteren, & Smit, 2007).

Compared to national surveys, however, the ICVS is based on smaller samples. For example, Canada's GSS in 2014 was based on a sample of 33,000 Canadians, whereas only 2,000 Canadians participated in the ICVS (Sauvé & Hung, 2008). Hence, nation-specific surveys produce higher-quality data on individual nations, but the ICVS provides better comparable data across countries.

One of the aims of the ICVS is to obtain figures of victimization to compare and describe differences in victimization rates and reporting between countries. Canada is often thought to have less crime and be a safer place to live than its neighbour to the south, the United States. Contrary to common perception, however, overall rates of victimization—burglary, robbery, and assault—are comparable between Canada and the United States. According to the 2004 survey, 17.2 per cent of Canadians aged 16 and older were victims of at least one crime being measured (Sauvé & Hung, 2008) compared to 18 per cent of Americans (Van Dijk et al., 2007). This is not a recent phenomenon, either: Both Canada and the United States have participated in the ICVS since its inception in 1989, and the two countries have consistently shown similar levels of victimization (Bouten, Goudriaan, & Nieuwbeerta, 2002).

In terms of reporting rates, compared to other countries participating in the ICVS Canadians have consistently reported less victimization to the police across all areas of the ICVS from 1989 to 2005 (Van Dijk et al., 2007). For example, in 2004–05, 53 per cent of victimizations on average were reported to police in the 30 countries that participated in the survey. However, only 47 per cent of victimizations were reported in Canada (Sauvé & Hung, 2008).

Besides victimization and reporting rates, the ICVS also includes several attitude measures. For example, findings from the first ICVS in 1989 showed that most Canadians favoured a nonprison sanction, but over time Canadians appear to have grown more punitive in their attitudes toward sentencing. This trend is not unique to Canada; attitudes in many industrialized countries, including England and Wales, Scotland, and the Netherlands, have become harsher, while attitudes in the United States and France have remained stable (Besserer, 2007).

Conclusion

The victimization survey is one of the most important contributions of victimology to criminology. Developed at a time of social unrest, when policymakers and politicians were concerned about the effects of crime on public authority, the survey was intended to shed light on the dark figure of crime as well as to inform policymakers about public attitudes toward crime and criminal justice authorities.

As a measure of the volume of victimization, the survey is incomplete. It is generally limited to direct victims of certain crimes. Many groups of victims are excluded systematically from the survey, which means that the survey necessarily provides an underestimate of the actual level of victimization.

Despite its limitations, the victimization survey does provide valuable information on victims and victimizations. It sheds light on who is at risk of becoming a victim, a multiple victim, and in particular it offers some insight into crimes that are not reported to the police. These surveys reveal that much victimization remains outside of the control of the state and law enforcement. Today victimization surveys have become a standard tool for policymakers, providing important information on the experiences and attitudes of crime victims.

CHAPTER 4

THE IMPACT OF VICTIMIZATION

Under the influence of the women's movement and, later, the victims' movement, victimological research gradually shifted in focus from a victim's role in
crime to the consequences of victimization. Research on the impact of victimization began to emerge in the 1960s and 1970s. Early studies on the impact
of victimization looked at serious violent crime such as terrorism and rape
(Crenlinsten, 1977; Holmstrom & Burgess, 1978). The introduction of victimization surveys provided insight for the first time into the consequences of a
wide variety of victimizations, including common crimes such as theft and
burglary. This was further complemented by research that documented the
strong impact of crimes generally considered less serious, such as burglary, on
the entire household (Maguire, 1980; Waller & Okihiro, 1978). By the 1990s,
the first longitudinal studies on the effects of crime began to emerge. In this
chapter we will present research on the impact of victimization. However,
before doing so, it is important to understand who is affected by crime.

The Victims

As we saw in Chapter 1, much of the work in victimology has focused on the
direct victims of crime. While this definition may work from a legal perspective, from a victimological perspective it is far too narrow. Earlier we described
victimology as the scientific study of victimizations attributable to violations of human rights, including crime, and reactions to both victimization
and victims. The effects of crime, especially serious crimes that include mass
victimization, can reach far beyond the direct victims and impact their family
and friends as well as their community. Hence the word "victim" can include
many different groups and, therefore, we need to identify the different categories or types of victims—we need a typology of victims. This will allow us
to better understand the breadth of the consequences of crime for victims.

As we saw in Chapter 2, typologies of victims were popular until the late 1970s, when focus shifted from explaining crime to helping victims. Earlier typologies were limited in that they focused exclusively on direct victims or on victimizations and failed to take into account the impact of victimization on others outside of the victim–offender dyad. Unlike the typologies viewed in Chapter 2, which focused on the causes of crime, a victim-centred framework focuses on the effects of crime on victims. Once we understand the consequences of victimization we can begin to identify and prioritize victims' needs. Using a victim-centred approach, four categories of victims can be identified based on one's emotional or psychological proximity to the victimization: (1) direct victims, (2) indirect victims, (3) secondary victims, and (4) tertiary victims.

1. The **direct victim** is the object of the victimization. This is the person who is unlawfully killed, disappeared, injured, assaulted, robbed, tortured, and so on. These individuals have directly suffered the effects of crime either by death, by undergoing physical or psychological harm, by otherwise being unlawfully arrested or detained, or by undergoing discriminatory actions or other violations of their human rights.

2. **Indirect victims** are those who are linked to direct victims in such a way that they too suffer as a result of that relationship. They are often the family members of a direct victim, who experience extreme hardship and pain because of the suffering of a family member or by being penalized because of their connection to that person—through serious socioeconomic deprivation, bereavement, the loss of a breadwinner, missed educational opportunities, family breakdown, police intimidation, or humiliation (Huyse, 2003). For example, a mother can suffer moral damages from the loss of a son, as well as material damage if she was economically dependent on him. Elsewhere in the literature they are referred to as *loved ones* or *co-victims* (Van Denderen, De Keijser, Kleen, & Boelen, 2015).

3. **Secondary victims** are individuals who have suffered harm in intervening to assist victims in distress or who witnessed the victimization. They are sometimes referred to as *third-level victims* (Brookes, Pooley, & Earnest, 2015). This group can be further subdivided into two groups: (1) those who are exposed to trauma directly, such as witnesses or bystanders who may have been traumatized because of what they witnessed, and (2) professionals who are repeatedly exposed to traumatic situations, including first responders such as police and paramedics as well as secondary care providers such as therapists, whose exposure is indirect but repeated because of their work assisting victims (Moulden & Firestone, 2007).

4. **Tertiary victims** refer to community members. A *community* is a social unit of any size that shares certain values or characteristics (McCold, 2004). This could be the geographic area where the crime took place—for example, the citizens of New York City following the attacks on the World Trade Center on 11 September 2001—or it could be a social group, such as an ethnic or religious group. The broader community can also be viewed as society, which, as we have seen, is represented by the public prosecutor in the criminal justice process. Exactly which community or communities are affected will vary depending on the nature of the victimization and the context in which it occurred. Less serious crimes will often have relatively little impact on society, while more serious crimes, and in particular crimes involving multiple victims (i.e., mass victimization), will have a greater impact on society. Hence, from a victmological standpoint, society is not always affected by crime, although it is from a legal standpoint.

Another group that can be identified are the family members of the offenders. They are sometimes referred to as *collateral victims* (Gagné, 2008). Depending on the circumstances, their lives can be profoundly affected by the crime, as they experience feelings of guilt, shame, and even financial loss as a result of the crime. It is important to keep in mind that victims of violence often know their offender (Langton & Truman, 2014; Perreault & Brennan, 2010). Hence, it is not unusual for an indirect victim to be the family or friend of the direct victim as well as the offender. However, for the time being, our focus is on the direct victims of crime and the people related to them and, therefore, collateral victims will not be discussed further here.

It is important to note that these categories are not mutually exclusive, and a person may fall under different categories simultaneously. For example, a person who experienced a violent attack in which he or she was injured and loved ones who were with the person at the time of the attack were murdered would be a direct victim (assaulted) and an indirect victim (loss of family) as well as a secondary victim (witness to violence). Similarly, secondary victims may well include neighbours, friends, and family of direct victims who witnessed the attack.

Furthermore, any one person may experience multiple victimizations and each time fall under different category. As we saw in Chapter 3, victimization surveys have consistently revealed that a relatively small portion of the population experiences a lot of crime (Farrell & Pease, 1993; Hope, Bryan, Trickett, & Osborn, 2001). Research on multiple victimization shows that the effects of each discrete victimization are cumulative (Alden, Regambal, & Laposa, 2008; Cougle, Resnick, & Kilpatrick, 2009; Shaw, 2001). Compared to one-time victims, individuals who experience multiple victimizations more often report experiencing health issues following victimization, such as sleeping problems and taking medication to help them sleep and calm down (Perreault, Sauvé, & Burns, 2010).

In the rest of this chapter we will use this typology to discuss the consequences of victimization for these four groups. This typology will show that the consequences of victimization are more pervasive than one might think, and when we focus exclusively on the direct victims of crime we miss a vast array of victims and victimizations.

Psychological Consequences

The psychological effects of crime often remain invisible—you do not see them. But unlike stolen property that can be replaced or broken bones that can heal, the psychological scars of victimization can last for years. In the following section we will consider the short- and long-term psychological effects of victimization for these different types of victims.

Direct Victims

Victimization surveys inform us about the short-term effects of criminal victimization on direct victims. Most victims, approximately four out of five, report being emotionally impacted by their victimization (AuCoin & Beauchamp, 2007; Perreault & Brennan, 2010; Shapland & Hall, 2007). One of the most common emotional responses to crime is anger (Gannon & Mihorean, 2005; Perreault & Brennan, 2010; Perreault, 2015; Shapland & Hall, 2007). Examining different waves of the Canadian victimization survey from 1999 to 2009, the percentage of victims experiencing anger has remained relatively stable at around one in three victims (Gannon & Mihorean, 2005; Mihorean et al., 2001; Perreault & Brennan, 2010). Other common emotions reported by victims include feeling upset or confused (Perreault, 2015).

Fear is another common reaction among victims. One in ten victims in Canada said that their victimization made them fearful and reported becoming more cautious or vigilant following the incident (Perreault & Brennan, 2010). In particular, victims of violence are more likely than victims of nonviolent crimes to report feeling fearful following their victimization (AuCoin & Beauchamp, 2007; Greenberg & Ruback, 1992). Victims of sexual assault and robbery are more likely to worry about their safety than victims of other types of crime (Leung, 2004). Compared to nonvictims, victims of crime also tend to be more fearful about future victimization, and their fear is not confined to the particular offence experienced but is a generalized high level of fear (AuCoin & Beauchamp, 2007; Shapland & Hall, 2007).

Emotional stress can also impact victims physically. While both victims of violent and nonviolent crimes sometimes experience sleeping problems, it is more common among victims of violent crime (AuCoin & Beauchamp, 2007). Difficulty sleeping may extend well beyond the first few days after the victimization. As many as 47 per cent of victims of violence report experiencing trouble sleeping for a month or more following their victimization (Langton & Truman, 2014).

Victims' reactions may vary depending on the characteristics of the offence. While victims of household crime are just as likely as victims of violent crimes to be affected emotionally, their reactions may differ (Perreault & Brennan, 2010; Perreault, 2015). Overall, victims of violence are slightly more prone to shock than anger compared with victims of household crime (AuCoin & Beauchamp, 2007; Perreault, 2015; Shapland & Hall, 2007).

The relationship between the victim and the offender can also affect how the individual reacts to the victimization. Survey data show that, for violent incidents, those victimized by a family member were more likely to report feeling upset and confused (42 per cent) compared to victims who had been assaulted by a stranger (19 per cent) or a friend (23 per cent) (AuCoin & Beauchamp, 2007). Similarly Langton and Truman (2014) found that nearly twice the proportion of victims of serious violence (defined as rape, sexual assault, robbery, or aggravated assault) committed by an intimate (60 per cent) or a relative (65 per cent) indicated that their victimization was severely distressing, compared to victims of serious violence by a stranger (31 per cent). Being victimized by someone you know and trust is more upsetting, distressing, and confusing than being victimized by someone you don't know.

Furthermore, victims' reactions may vary in relation to victims' characteristics. Females are more likely to report emotional effects as a result of violence than males (AuCoin & Beauchamp, 2007; Langton & Truman, 2014). In addition, a larger proportion of female victims (37 per cent) of violent victimization reported experiencing sleeping problems relative to their male counterparts (28 per cent) (AuCoin & Beauchamp, 2007). Females are more likely to experience socioemotional problems (i.e., distress, problems at work or school, problems in relationships) than males, regardless of the victim–offender relationship (Langton & Truman, 2014).

ASD and PTSD

Emotional reactions such as anger and fear are common short-term responses to victimization, and in most cases symptoms resolve rapidly. However, for some these emotions may turn into longer-term depressive effects that include sleeplessness and anxiety, and occasionally they will turn into a stress disorder, which can significantly limit the functioning of the individual, including his or her capacity to work and engage in social interactions.

Acute stress disorder (ASD) and post-traumatic stress disorder (PTSD) are psychological reactions that can develop after a traumatic event such as victimization. An event is considered traumatic if the person experienced, witnessed, or was confronted with one or a series of events that involved actual or threatened death, serious injury, or threat of physical integrity of self or others (American Psychiatric Association, 1994, 2013). The main difference between ASD and PTSD is the duration of symptoms. In the case of ASD, the symptoms last from two days to less than one month. If symptoms last one month or more, it is considered to be PTSD (American Psychiatric Association 1994, 2013).

The notion of PTSD was first introduced by the American Psychiatric Association in 1980 with the publication of the third edition of its *Diagnostics and Statistics Manual* (DSM-III). This was a milestone for victims because, for the first time, mental health professionals explicitly recognized the traumatic effects of criminal victimization. PTSD is based on the premise that the victims' mental health problems are the result of their traumatic experience. This validation was important for victims who, up until then, had been met with incomprehension and labelled as mentally ill. Earlier versions of the DSM included notions such as "gross stress reaction," which posited that the traumatic event had triggered a latent psychiatric illness (Wemmers, 2003). PTSD has undergone various modifications since its introduction in 1980, the most recent in 2013 with the publication of the DSM-V.

ASD/PTSD symptoms fall into four main categories: (1) intrusion, (2) avoidance, (3) negative alterations in cognitions and mood, and (4) alterations in arousal and reactivity. The intrusion symptoms consist of continually reliving the traumatic event day and night through intrusive memories, flashback episodes, and nightmares about the event.

The avoidance symptoms consist of avoiding any reminder of the traumatic event. Victims may go to great lengths and develop elaborate strategies to avoid thinking about the event (despite the intrusion symptoms cited above), speaking about the event, or being with people and objects that can awaken traumatic memories. This avoidance can be close to phobic avoidance.

Negative alterations in cognitions and mood represent a multitude of feelings. This includes a persistent and distorted sense of blame of self or others, feelings of alienation or isolation, a markedly diminished interest in typical activities, and an inability to remember key aspects of the event.

Finally, the arousal symptoms mean that victims experience physical (muscular) and emotional tension. This often manifests in a fight reaction. It is marked by aggressive, reckless, self-destructive behaviour. For example, victims may be constantly on guard even in the absence of any imminent risk. Victims can also suffer from sleep disorders, irritability, and concentration problems.

To be diagnosed with PTSD all four categories of symptoms must be experienced at the same time over at least one month, causing significant distress or impairment. For each category, the number of symptoms that must be identified depends on the cluster (see Box 4.1). In the case of ASD, the symptoms last from two days to less than one month.

BOX 4.1: POST-TRAUMATIC STRESS DISORDER

Criterion A: Stressor

The person was exposed to actual or threatened death, actual or threatened serious injury, or actual or threatened sexual violence, as follows (one required):

1. Direct exposure
2. Witnessing, in person
3. Indirectly, by learning that a close relative or close friend was exposed to trauma
4. Repeated or extreme indirect exposure to aversive details of the event(s) usually in the course of professional duties (e.g., first responders, collecting body parts)

Criterion B: Intrusion Symptoms

The traumatic event is persistently re-experienced in the following way(s) (one required):

1. Recurrent, involuntary, and intrusive memoires
2. Traumatic nightmares
3. Dissociative reactions (e.g., flashbacks), which may occur on a continuum from brief episodes to complete loss of consciousness
4. Intense or prolonged distress after exposure to traumatic reminders
5. Marked physiologic reactivity after exposure to trauma-related stimuli

Criterion C: Avoidance

Persistent effortful avoidance of distressing trauma-related stimuli after the event (one required):

1. Trauma-related thoughts or feelings
2. Trauma-related external reminders (people, places, sounds, smells, etc.)

Criterion D: Negative Alterations in Cognitions and Mood

Negative alterations in cognitions and mood that began or worsened after the traumatic event (two required):

1. Inability to recall key features of the traumatic event (usually dissociative amnesia that is not due to head injury, alcohol, or drugs)
2. Persistent (and often distorted) negative beliefs and expectations about oneself and the world (e.g., "I am bad")
3. Persistent distorted blame of self or others for causing the traumatic event or for the resulting consequences
4. Persistent negative trauma-related emotions (fear, horror, anger, guilt, shame)
5. Markedly diminished interest in (pretraumatic) significant activities
6. Feeling alienated from others
7. Constricted affect: persistent inability to experience positive emotions

Criterion E: Alterations in Arousal and Reactivity

Trauma-related alterations in arousal and reactivity that began or worsened after the traumatic event (two required):

1. Irritable or aggressive behaviour
2. Self-destructive or reckless behaviour
3. Hypervigilance
4. Exaggerated startle response
5. Problems in concentration
6. Sleep disturbance

Criterion F: Duration

Persistence of symptoms (A, B, C, D, and E) for more than one month.

Criterion G: Functional Significance

Significant symptom-related distress or functional impairment.

Source: American Psychiatric Association, 2013.

PTSD may be experienced together with dissociative symptoms. The new DSM-V introduced a new dissociative subtype of PTSD where the person both meets the criteria for PTSD and experiences high levels of depersonalization or derealization. *Depersonalization* refers to a state in which the person feels like an outside observer watching him or herself act (like in a dream). *Derealization* describes a state in which things feel unreal (APA, 2013). Dissociation can impede the victim from actively seeking help, which can make recovery all the more difficult.

The introduction of PTSD standardized the research on the impact of victimization, which up until then had used various measures to study the different effects of victimization. Since the 1980s, there has been tremendous growth in research on PTSD, and this standardization has allowed researchers to compare findings across studies and advance our understanding of the effects of victimization. Advances in research have led to PTSD undergoing several modifications over the years. However, the balance of work on the effects of victimization has swung so far toward work on PTSD that Shapland and Hall (2007) warn that researchers have neglected other emotional effects of victimization and types of victimization not associated with PTSD.

It is important to remember that while most victims are emotionally affected by victimization, most do not develop PTSD. Findings from the victimization survey indicate that one in seven victims experience symptoms consistent with PTSD (Perreault, 2015). Certain characteristics of the victimization, such as extreme violence and thinking you are going to die, increase the risk of developing mental health problems (Kilpatrick, Saunders, Veronen, Best, & Von, 1987). Exposure to criminal victimization and, in particular, interpersonal violence is more strongly related to the development of PTSD than exposure to an accident (Ozer, Best, Lipsey, & Weiss, 2003). Prevalence rates range from 35 per cent to 70 per cent for rape victims, from 2 per cent to 58 per cent for victims of physical assault, and from 18 per cent to 28 per cent for victims of robbery (Kessler, Sonnega, Bromet, Hughes, & Nelson, 1995; Kilpatrick et al., 1989). The victim's relationship to the perpetrator is also a factor, and victims who share a close relationship with the offender are more at risk of developing PTSD symptoms than victims who are not close to the offender (Martin, Cromer, De Prince, & Freyd, 2013). While PTSD is more likely when victimization is particularly serious, just because a victim does not develop PTSD does not mean that he or she was not negatively impacted by the experience.

Major Depression

Depression is frequently observed in crime victims and is well known to be a comorbid mental health disorder that can occur simultaneously with

ASD/PTSD (Breslau, Davis, Andreski, & Petersen, 1991; Kilpatrick et al., 1985). Depression symptoms include daily fatigue or loss of energy and feelings of worthlessness or guilt. People who suffer from depression also present impaired concentration and indecisiveness, and they suffer from insomnia or hypersomnia (excessive sleeping) almost every day. There is a marked reduction in interest or pleasure in almost all activities nearly every day. People feel restless or slowed down, and there is a significant weight loss or gain. Many times they also suffer from recurring thoughts of death or suicide (American Psychiatric Association, 1994, 2013).

Prevalence rates provide some insight into how often victims suffer depression. Kilpatrick, Edmunds, and Seymour (1992) found that in the United States women with life histories of physical assault were 3.31 times as likely to show life histories of depression, and recently assaulted women were 5.5 times as likely to present with depression as women who were not recently assaulted. Specifically, they found that 12.6 per cent of assaulted women versus 2.6 per cent of nonassaulted women met the criteria for active depression.

Substance Abuse

Research also reveals a high comorbidity between assault-related PTSD and substance abuse (Mills, Teesson, Ross, & Peters, 2006). In their study on traumatic events, Breslau and colleagues (1991) found that 45 per cent of those with PTSD also met the criteria for substance use or abuse, with 31 per cent meeting the criteria for alcohol abuse or dependence. Very few studies have looked at the origin of substance abuse, but using longitudinal survey data Kilpatrick, Acierno, Resnick, Saunders, and Best (1997) found evidence that rape and physical assault may lead to substance use and abuse in previously nonusing women. Specifically, they found that the likelihood of progression to substance use or abuse following assault in previously nonusing women was double that of nonassaulted women. This suggests that following a traumatic event victims will sometimes self-medicate in an effort to avoid trauma-related thoughts or feelings.

Stockholm Syndrome

First introduced in 1973 following a dramatic hostage taking at a bank in Stockholm, Sweden, the term "Stockholm syndrome" is accredited to the American psychiatrist Frank Ochberg (1978). In this particular case, one of the hostages developed a profound attachment to one of the hostage-takers, and she became outright hostile toward authorities. One year later, in February 1974, Patty Hearst, granddaughter of US multimillionaire William Randolph Hearst, was kidnapped by the Symbionese Liberation Army (SLA), an urban guerrilla group. A few months later, in April 1974, Patty was photographed wielding an assault rifle alongside other SLA members while robbing a San Francisco bank. The case captured the public's attention and made people ask how someone could side with a captor and adopt the same negative attitudes, blaming authority.

The term continues to be used to explain the sometimes surprising reactions of victims in cases of extreme violence and terror, such as battered woman syndrome and rape trauma syndrome (Adorjan, Christensen, Kelly, & Pawluch, 2012). According to Symonds (1980), Stockholm syndrome can appear in cases where victims have had prolonged contact with their offender. Concretely, the victim remains in a state of frozen fright and cooperates with the offender—seemingly of his or her own free will—because the victim is terrified. Strentz (1980) explains that the victim's need to survive is stronger than the drive to hate the person who put him or her in this situation. Hence, victims can do things that can be perceived as signs of complicity and appear odd and inexplicable to an outsider, but they are logical actions for the victim (Adorjan et al., 2012; Kirchhoff, 1999; Symonds, 1980).

Stockholm syndrome is not a recognized condition included in the DSM. Nevertheless, it is discussed here to remind us that victims can sometimes react unexpectedly to extreme stress and trauma. When working with victims, it is important to bear this in mind and not judge their behaviour.

Indirect Victims

Compared to direct victims, little research has been done on the effects of victimization on indirect victims. Yet indirect victims may undergo even greater stress than the direct victims themselves by virtue of the fact that the latter's coping mechanisms have been fully activated to deal with the situation while the former feel totally helpless and useless (Armour, 2002; Crenlinsten, 1977).

Fear can be contagious, and family and friends of the direct victim may experience increased fear and become mistrusting of others following the victimization (Ruback & Thompson, 2001). Friedman, Bischoff, Davis, and Person (1982) found that 80 per cent of people who comforted a victim after a victimization felt an increase in their own level of fear. Particular types of victimization that target social groups, such as hate crimes, can trigger fear among victims' family members as they worry about the safety of other family members (Barnes & Ephross, 1994; Bowling, 1994).

Much of the available research on indirect victims centres on family members of homicide victims (Armour, 2002; Van Denderen et al., 2015). For family members, the murder of a loved one is a different experience than deaths caused by illness, suicide, or accidents. As many as 9.3 per cent of adults in the United States have lost a loved one to homicide (Amick-McMullan, Kilpatrick, & Resnick, 1991). These victims are not included in the crime statistics and remain hidden. They are left to struggle with the fact that the death of their loved one was caused intentionally by a wilful act of violence by another person. In addition, media coverage of the crime and the criminal justice process can throw them into the public arena and strip them of their privacy at a time of great personal distress and sadness.

Complicated grief is a clinically significant grief reaction that occurs following the death of a loved one. While grief is a normal, healthy reaction to death, complicated grief obstructs the normal grieving process. The principal symptom of complicated grief is that the normal process is not occurring and the bereaved person is "stuck" in the grieving process. Loved ones often report difficulty moving on while the criminal justice process is ongoing (Armour, 2002). Complicated grief can be diagnosed when these symptoms persist for six months or more after a loss (Shear et al., 2011). These symptoms can cause substantial distress for the individual and have been associated with impaired quality of life, social isolation, maladaptive thoughts and behaviours, and increased suicide rates (Young et al., 2012). Unable to move on with their lives, these individuals may be unable to work or to function socially, which may add to their distress and isolation. This disorder affects 10 to 20 per cent of people suffering from the loss of a loved one in the United States (Jacobs, 1993; Middleton, Burnett, Raphael, & Martinek, 1996). The prevalence rate increases in the case of traumatic deaths (Field & Filanosky, 2009). People who are dealing with complicated grief can suffer from depression, PTSD, severe anxiety, disbelief, longing, anger, guilt, withdrawal, avoidance, and preoccupation with the deceased (Shear et al., 2011).

Moreover, violent crimes are more likely to be committed by someone known to the victim than by a stranger (Langton & Truman, 2014; Spungen, 1998). In Canada, police statistics on solved homicide cases indicate that 35 per cent of victims were suspected to have been killed by a family member. This percentage is much higher for female homicide victims than for male victims: 63 per cent of female homicide victims were thought to have been killed by a family member versus 21 per cent of male victims (Boyce & Cotter, 2013). This means that indirect victims will sometimes be a family member of both the victim and the offender. How these different and sometimes conflicting roles affect people in the case of intrafamilial homicide has not yet been sufficiently studied (Armour, 2002).

In the DSM-V, the definition of PTSD was modified to include indirect victims who do not actually witness the violence but learn about it after the fact. This is a significant development with respect to the recognition of indirect victims as victims. In fact, one in five family members and friends of homicide victims have been found to have developed PTSD (Amick-McMullan et al., 1991).

Family members of victims who have survived atrocities, such as the Holocaust and other gross violations of human rights, are also at risk of developing PTSD (Baranowsky, Young, Johnson-Douglas, Williams-Keeler, & McCarrey, 1998; Danieli, 1998). This is also referred to as *secondary traumatization* and the *intergenerational transmission of trauma* (Dekel & Goldblatt, 2008). In Canada, the residential school system had a devastating impact on generations of Indigenous families. Introduced in the 1880s, residential schools forcibly separated children from their families for extended periods and forbade them to acknowledge their Indigenous heritage and culture or to speak their own languages. Children lived in substandard conditions, and many experienced emotional, physical, and sexual abuse. While the last residential school in Canada finally closed its doors in 1996, the trauma created by the schools continues to impact Indigenous people through the intergenerational transmission of trauma (Bombay, Matheson, & Anisman, 2014; Menzies, 2006; Regan, 2011). We will return to this topic later when we discuss tertiary victims.

Secondary Victims

Witnessing crimes that victimize others may cause traumatic stress, anger, sadness, and grief (Bryant-Davis & Ocampo, 2005). According to the DSM-V, witnessing violence can be a source of stress and lead to ASD and PTSD. Among those who witnessed crime, 19 per cent reported problems sleeping (AuCoin & Beauchamp, 2007). Children and youth who witness violence have been found to suffer from PTSD symptoms as well as depression and anxiety (Ruback & Thompson, 2001).

In situations of mass victimization and gross violations of human rights, a large segment of the population will have directly experienced or witnessed violence, and this can result in high levels of stress, anxiety, and depression within the population. For example, research in Rwanda following the 1994 genocide found that five years after the event the prevalence rate of depression among a sample of 368 Rwandans was 15.5 per cent (Bolton, Neugebauer, & Ndogoni, 2002). In comparison, the prevalence rate of depression within the adult population in the United States is 6.7 per cent (Kessler, Chiu, Demler, & Walters, 2005). In another study, it was found that 25 per cent of adult Rwandans still suffered from PTSD eight years after the event (Pham, Weinstein, & Longman, 2004). In contrast, the prevalence rate of PTSD in the general population in Canada is 2 per cent, and the lifetime prevalence rate is 9 per cent (Van Ameringen, Mancini, Patterson, & Boyle, 2008).

According to the DSM-V, repeated exposure to the aversive details of the traumatic event can be a source of stress and can lead to ASD and PTSD. Trauma among first responders and other professionals who are in regular contact or a professional relationship with victims is often referred to as vicarious traumatization, secondary trauma, compassion fatigue, or burnout (Hill, 2009; McCann & Pearlman, 1990; Moulden & Firestone, 2007; Ruback & Thompson, 2001; Schauben & Frazier, 1995). For those who work in the criminal justice system (e.g., police) or in health services (e.g., therapists), exposure to trauma can be repetitive. Since the 1970s there has been extensive research on the effects of repeat exposure to secondary trauma among those working with victims. We will return to this topic in Chapter 8 when we discuss intervention with crime victims.

Tertiary Victims

Research shows that indirect exposure to crime can impact feelings of insecurity within entire communities and may create fear of crime (Brennan, 2011). Studying the relationship between neighbourhoods and crime levels, Fitzgerald (2008) reports that 12 per cent of the variance in people's fear is explained by neighbourhood factors. Cornaglia and Leigh (2011) examined the impact of regional crime rates on people who had not directly experienced victimization and found that the mental well-being of nonvictims of crime is significantly affected by violent crime in the area of residency. For communities, fear of crime is a determinant of the quality of life in the neighbourhood, which is related to economic activity, the amount of pedestrian and automobile traffic, and ultimately the health of the community (Ruback & Thompson, 2001).

While there has been relatively little research done on the impact of victimization on social groups, one exception is hate crime. By its nature, hate crime targets the individual and their ethnic, religious, or social group. Hate crimes convey a message of fear to all members of the community to which the specific individual belongs. Being a member of a target group may result in symptoms caused by awareness of potential victimization and the necessity of guarding against it (Craig-Henderson & Sloan, 2003). When victimization is hate motivated it enhances the impact of crime and increases trauma on community members (Bryant-Davis & Ocampo, 2005).

Much of the research on the impact of racial victimization on the group looks at fear of victimization. Visible minorities are more likely to be fearful of racial victimization than nonvisible minorities (Silver, Mihorean, & Taylor-Butts, 2004). This would seem logical, given that visible minorities have a greater risk of racial victimization. However, as with victimization in general, fear of victimization is not necessarily related to one's risk of victimization. For example, women tend to be more fearful of racial victimization than men, while men are at a higher risk of racial victimization (Bowling, 1994; Silver et al., 2004). However, survey data fail to capture the full range of possible ways in which racial victimization can affect the community. An underestimated aspect of racial victimization is how the ripple effects of racial victimization manifest themselves. Weiss (2005) gives an example of how community members socially isolated a victim in the hope that by not associating with the victim they would reduce their own risk of victimization.

Widespread and systematic violent victimization, such as genocide and war crimes, generates mass trauma (Herbert, Rioux, & Wemmers, 2014). In mass trauma, the effects are not only experienced at the individual level, but also by families and other community members, generating high levels of collective distress among members of the victimized community (Brookes, Pooley, & Earnest, 2015). Research with 286 refugees following their flight from their country of origin found that although most of them had not directly been victimized or experienced any direct threat in their home country, 72.4 per cent were suffering from severe trauma. According to the authors, fear of harm or threat was the basis of their trauma (Westermeyer & Williams, 1998). Hence, entire communities can be traumatized as a result of widespread victimization.

When mass trauma is part of a group's shared history, it is sometimes referred to as *historical trauma* (Bombay et al., 2014). Canada's residential schools are an example of historical trauma. Research suggests that historically traumatic events can continue to undermine the well-being of contemporary group members and that the effects of traumatic experiences are not only transferred across generations (intergenerational transmission), but these effects accumulate (Evans-Campbell, 2008). Studying the longitudinal effects of residential schools, Bombay and her colleagues (2014) found that the more generations that attended residential schools, the poorer the psychological well-being of the next generation.

Social Consequences

A common secondary and associated response to trauma includes difficulties in interpersonal relationships (Carlson & Dalenberg, 2000). Victimization survey data reveal that 21 per cent of direct victims of violence reported relationship problems with family or friends. Moreover, 80 per cent of the direct victims who experienced moderate to severe distress also experienced relationship problems (Langton & Truman, 2014). Experiencing difficulties in their relationships with others can compound the negative effects of victimization, contributing to victims' feelings of isolation.

Similarly, indirect victims, who experience many of the same affective and cognitive consequences of victimization, may also go through difficulties in their interpersonal relationships. Research with family members of homicide victims shows that they sometimes feel socially stigmatized by having a loved one murdered and may be shunned or blamed by others for the way the victim died or even for the way the victim lived (Armour, 2002).

Fear of crime has important implications at both the individual and community levels. Victimization can impact one's sense of safety and security, making people feel that they are no longer safe in their homes or their communities (Dugan, 1999). Using data from the National Crime Survey, a longitudinal panel survey of US dwelling units and their occupants, Xie and McDowall (2008) found that direct victims of violent and property crimes are more likely to move following their victimization, and the impact of violent crimes is larger than the impact of property crimes. They also examined the number of victimizations reported in one's neighbourhood, which they refer to as *indirect victimization*, and found that it too is associated with a higher likelihood of moving. According to the authors, victimization experienced by one household signals to others who live in close proximity that the neighbourhood is not safe. In other words, when people experience victimization either directly or indirectly, they will often decide to move away in an effort to restore their sense of security. Hence, at the community level, fear creates instability. This deteriorates social cohesion and breaks down informal social control mechanisms, which in turn fuels crime (Ruback & Thompson, 2001).

Physical Consequences

Unlike the emotional consequences of victimization, most victims of crime suffer either no physical injuries or very minor ones (Perreault, 2015; Shapland & Hall, 2007). In Canada, less than one in five victims of violent incidents suffer injuries (Perreault, 2015). Among those who do, most are relatively minor: One in four injured victims requires medical attention, and 20 per cent require bed rest (AuCoin & Beauchamp, 2007; Perreault, 2015). Similar findings are reported in England and Wales, where around 80 per cent of victims suffer little to no physical injuries (Shapland & Hall, 2007).

Physical injuries are limited to the direct victims of crime and first responders or witnesses who are injured when intervening or helping the victim. Indirect victims do not suffer physical injuries, but they may suffer the physical effects of emotional trauma, such as sleeplessness and loss of appetite.

Table 4.1 provides an overview of the different types of consequences that each group of victims may experience.

Financial Consequences

Victimization can also bring financial costs for the victim, his or her family, and society. When considering the financial costs of victimization we can

TABLE 4.1: Overview of Type of Victim by Type of Consequence

TYPE OF CONSEQUENCE	TYPE OF VICTIM			
	DIRECT VICTIMS	INDIRECT VICTIMS	SECONDARY VICTIMS	TERTIARY VICTIMS
Physical	x		x	
Psychological	x	x	x	x
Financial	x	x	x	x
Social	x	x	x	x

differentiate between *tangible* losses, such as lost or damaged property and medical expenses, and *intangible* costs, such as psychological pain and suffering.

Victims of property crime, particularly motor vehicle theft, often report tangible losses. However, the actual amount of losses resulting from property crime is relatively small: 60 per cent of household and property-related incidents in Canada resulted in a loss of under $500. One in three victims of property crime suffered losses valued at over $500, and 15 per cent suffered losses of more than $1,000 (AuCoin & Beauchamp, 2007; Besserer, Brzozowski, Hendrick, Ogg, & Trainor, 2001). For motor vehicle theft, the value of the stolen or damaged property is often much higher; in 91 per cent of such incidents, losses of more than $500 were reported (Perreault & Brennan, 2010). Often stolen and damaged property is not recovered, leaving the victim with net losses. Insurance will sometimes provide full or partial recovery, but not all Canadians have insurance and, in particular, victims with a low income are often uninsured (Solicitor General of Canada, 1985).

However, such figures are limited in that they only take account of direct losses arising from theft and damage to items. They ignore many consequential costs incurred by victims and their family, such as time spent cleaning up, time spent off work, and time spent assisting the criminal justice system or going to court (Shapland & Hall, 2007). They also fail to include funeral costs (in the case of homicide), medical expenses, and fees paid to a mental health professional such as a psychologist. These expenses may or may not be covered by private or public insurance, depending on the individual and where he or she lives.

In Canada, health care is public for permanent residents and citizens. However, not all medical fees are covered by public insurance. Health care programs are run by the provinces, so what they cover differs across the country. In Quebec, for example, besides the deductible required by many insurance programs, certain medications and services are not covered, such as psychological counselling. It is estimated that the average murder puts 1.5 to 2.5 people into counselling (Miller, Cohen, & Wiersema, 1996). However, as we have seen it is not only serious violent crime that can impact victims' psychological well-being. Many provinces have compensation programs for victims of violence, which will cover some of these expenses for some victims; these will be discussed in Chapter 9. However, when victims are not eligible for compensation and are left to carry the financial burden themselves, the costs can add up quite quickly.

Victimization can also entail a loss of income caused by the inability to work. One in four direct victims (28 per cent) of violent crime in Canada experienced difficulty carrying out their daily activities. On average, victims were able to return to their regular routine after 11 days (Perreault & Brennan, 2010). Based on their analysis of the National Crime Victimization Survey in the United States, Langton and Truman (2014) found that 18 per cent of victims of violence experienced problems at work or school following their victimization. As we have seen, indirect and secondary victims may also suffer trauma and, as a result, be unable to work for a period. If a person is unable to work or study because of the effects of the trauma, victimization can have significant consequences for their financial well-being.

Besides the loss of wages for the direct, indirect, or secondary victim who is unable to work because of trauma, Miller, Cohen, and Wiersema (1996) argue that the costs of crime also include productivity lost by co-workers and supervisors who need to recruit and train replacement workers. Based on a two-year multidisciplinary research effort to estimate the costs and consequences of personal crime for Americans, they calculate that personal crime costs Americans US$105 billion annually in medical costs, lost earnings, and public program costs related to victim assistance. Due to inflation, this value would be even higher today.

Besides the tangible costs of victimization, there is also the social cost of crime. But how do you put a dollar value on the cost of pain and suffering? It is not easy to quantify something as subjective and intangible as emotional pain. While it might seem cold and callus to try to put a dollar value on pain and suffering, such information is useful at the aggregate level. Without it, it is difficult to understand the value of victim support services. Monetary estimates of lost quality of life caused by fatalities can, for example, be based on the amount people routinely spend to reduce their risk of death (Leung, 2004; Miller, Cohen, & Wiersema, 1996). This concept is referred to as *contingent valuation* and it is derived from economics, where it is used in relation to labour market data on wages for risky jobs (Viscusi, 1993). Leung (2004) used contingent valuation together with victimization survey data on the number of victimizations and the proportion of victims feeling worried about their safety to calculate the cost of pain and suffering from crime in Canada. He estimates that the cost from all crimes was approximately $35 billion. When pain and suffering are taken into consideration, violent crimes are found to cost victims and society more than nonviolent crimes: $20 billion for violent crime versus $15 billion for property crime.

Attempts to quantify the intangible costs of crime have helped to reveal the burden of victimization on victims. Whereas early studies often focused exclusively on the tangible costs of crime, and thus concluded that property crimes were the most costly for victims, efforts to include intangible costs of crime show that violent crimes are in fact more costly (Klaus, 1994; Wemmers, 2003). To illustrate, the above study by Miller, Cohen, and Wiersema (1996) revealed that the aggregate tangible, out-of-pocket costs of rape were about US$7.5 billion, which is roughly equal to the tangible expenses for burglary victims and less than the approximately US$9 billion for larceny victims. However, burglary and larceny have less severe psychological effects on victims. When pain, suffering, and loss of quality of life are quantified, the cost of rape is approximately US$127 billion. This demonstrates the high cost of violent crime for victims and society.

Another possible measure used elsewhere in research on the cost of victimization is jury awards. However, in Canada jury awards are not publicly available and can be difficult to obtain (Leung, 2004). Moreover, civil claims tend to stem from traffic accidents, work accidents, or medical negligence cases rather than criminal victimization and, as a result, compensation claims have tended to reflect physical injury and downplay the emotional and social effects of crime (Shapland & Hall, 2007). Similarly, studies that calculate cost based on information from the labour market, like those by Leung (2004) as well as Miller, Cohen, and Wiersema (1996), fail to include the emotional and social effects that are unique to crime. While helpful, they should not be considered exhaustive or definitive.

Of course all these studies rely on data from national victimization surveys, which as we noted earlier exclude many groups of victims. Hence, much of the cost of victimization remains hidden from view and is not taken into consideration in these estimates.

Longitudinal Findings

There are very few longitudinal studies on the effects of victimization. Reactions to crime are influenced by social factors, which is a limitation of retrospective studies such as victimization surveys. Prospective longitudinal studies with control groups are, however, rare because of their organizational complexity and cost (Shapland & Hall, 2007). Determining whether crime victimization causally affects mental health is further complicated by the contribution of environment, family background, and behavioural factors. Failure to control for important risk factors, such as past victmization, stressful life events, age, employment status, and financial strain, when examining the relationship between crime victimization and mental health could lead us to draw erroneous conclusions about the impact of victimization (Freeman & Smith, 2014).

One of the few longitudinal studies on victims was conducted by Adriaan Denkers and Frans Willem Winkel in the Netherlands (Denkers, 1996; Denkers & Winkel, 1998). Based on a large sample from a general population telephone survey panel of 5,218 respondents, the objective of this study was to examine the impact of victimization on a person's well-being. The study is unique because it not only used longitudinal data and a control group, but it also included pre-victimization data on individuals' well-being. The sample included victims of all types of crime, regardless of whether or not they reported the crime to police, so the survey tends to include many less serious offences. Denkers and Winkel found that, as in other studies, victims report lower levels of well-being and higher levels of fear than nonvictims, and the effects of crime were more pronounced among victims of violent crimes than among victims of property crimes. However, when controlled for the premeasurement of satisfaction with life, victims hardly seemed to suffer a deterioration of well-being. Victims appeared to be "unhappier" than nonvictims, but to some extent they were already so before the crime took place. Differences in well-being between victims and nonvictims appeared to be a function of pre-crime factors.

The authors argue that "crime does not seem to shatter assumptions about the world and the self, but rather, those who are depicted by shattered assumptions seem to be liable to become victims of crime" (Denkers & Winkel, 1998, p. 157). These findings raise the question of whether, as some early victimologists argued, there is something about the victim that makes them prone to victimization. The only dependent measure that remained significant after controlling for the pre-crime measurement was perceived vulnerability. Those who experienced violent crime reported higher levels of perceived vulnerability than those who had experienced property crime or those who had not experienced any crime. After two months, victims of violent crimes appeared to have readjusted their perceived vulnerability. It is possible that those who felt especially vulnerable had previously experienced victimization. The study did not control for prior victimization, so it is impossible to exclude either possible explanation.

Norris and Kaniasty (1994; Norris, Kaniasty, & Thompson, 1997) undertook a longitudinal panel study of victims in Kentucky, examining levels of psychological distress following victimization. They drew a probability sample from a telephone crime survey of Kentucky residents in 1988. Respondents were classified as victims of violent crime in the past six months ($n = 171$), victims of property crime in the past six months ($n = 338$), and nonvictims in the past six months ($n = 298$). Each respondent was interviewed a second time six months later and again after another six months. In all, 522 people participated in all three waves. The researchers found that crime victims had greater psychological distress (i.e., fear, avoidance, depression, anxiety) than nonvictims at the time of the first interview, and victims of violent crime suffered more distress than victims of property crime. Moreover, they found a significant crime-by-time interaction effect: Victims got better over time while nonvictims remained stable. Most change occurred between interviews one and two. However, the authors did have to take into consideration possible re-victimization of the respondents over the 12-month period of their data collection. Using regression analysis, they found that when demographic variables as well as prior victimization were controlled for, experiencing a new, subsequent victimization was found to have significant effects on victims' distress symptoms. They also found that prior victimization was the best predictor of subsequent victimization. In addition, they examined various types of precautionary behaviour and found that victims were neither more nor less cautious than others. Hence, they concluded that victims are not to blame for their increased risk and that it is wrong to develop prevention policies based on the assumption that victims control their risk.

In Australia, Cornaglia and Leigh (2011) examined the mental health of crime victims and nonvictims in metropolitan areas using data from a large household-based panel survey, the Household, Income and Labour Dynamics in Australia (HILDA) survey, which follows households over time since it began in 2001. They examined data from the period 2001 to 2006. Mental health was measured in terms of nervousness, depression, and difficulties with daily activities because of emotional problems and tiredness. The authors found that when they controlled for time-stable individual risk factors (e.g., age, education) as well as dynamic variables (e.g., local unemployment rate) victimization did affect mental health, but this effect was only significant for violent victimization.

In another Australian study, Freeman and Smith (2014) also used data from the HILDA survey. The sample used records from 16,187 individuals with between two and ten years of annual survey data across the period 2002 to 2011. Mental heath was measured based on responses to questions relating to nervousness and emotional state in the preceding four weeks. Besides having longitudinal information about victimization and mental health, the authors were able to control for stable background variables (e.g., gender, past victimization) and numerous dynamic variables (e.g., partner status, employment status, financial prosperity, alcohol consumption, smoking status, physical activity, general health, social networks). They reported that victims of violence suffered significant alterations in their mental health following their experience of crime that could not be attributed to pre-existing time-stable factors (such as a history of child abuse) or the dynamic factors included in the model. However, for victims of property crime there was no statistically significant change in their mental health following their experience of the crime once other relevant time-stable and dynamic factors were controlled for. Examining gender differences, they found that becoming a victim of violent crime has a significant and negative impact on the mental health of both men and women, but the effect of violent victimization is more pronounced for females.

In another study, Hochstetler, DeLisi, Jones-Johnson, and Johnson (2014) used data from a national longitudinal study spanning 1986 to 1996 from the Americans' Changing Lives study. Face-to-face interviews were conducted in 1986, 1989, and 1996, and these three waves were used in the analysis. The authors aimed to understand the impact of victimization on depression while controlling for selection effects based on the rationale that victimization does not occur randomly and that the same variable that predicts victimization might well predict depression. To account for the selection problem, they adjusted for individuals' exposure propensity for victimization based on several predictor variables using inverse probability of treatment weighting. They found that criminal victimization predicts levels of depression and change in depression among a population of adults.

Using longitudinal data from the American National Crime Victimization Survey (NCVS), Bunch, Clay-Warner, and McMahon-Howard (2014) studied whether violent and property victimization changed victims' lifestyles. Propensity score matching was used to create matched groups of victims and nonvictims within the NCVS database. This study is unique methodologically because unlike most studies with victims, which simply examine victims' behaviour after the crime, this study includes pre- and post-test data as well as a matched control group of nonvictims, which allowed the researchers to isolate the effects of victimization on behaviour. Lifestyle was operationalized in terms of going out at night and shopping. The authors found that victimization does *not* influence lifestyles: Victims were no more or less likely to shop or to go out at night than matched nonvictims.

However, these large panel studies do have shortcomings. As we saw, victims are more likely to move than nonvictims (Xie & McDowall, 2008), which in this case could mean that only victims who did not move remained in the NCVS and HILDA samples. Hence, these samples may be biased, including only victims who reacted differently than most other victims by deciding not to move away.

These longitudinal studies illustrate the complexity of isolating the impact of crime from other factors that affect people's lives. Past victimization predicts future victimization. Studies that control for prior victimization find that violent victimization leads to a significant decline in mental health, and violent crime has a more severe and persistent impact on victims' mental health than property crime. While both men and women are emotionally affected by crime, women appear to be more strongly affected. Are people who have previously experienced victimization more vulnerable and, therefore, at greater risk of re-victimization? We will return to this question when we discuss polyvictimization in Chapter 5.

Recovery Process

Victimization does not take place in a vacuum, and as longitudinal studies presented above show, to understand the effects of victimization we need to take into consideration the victim's state before the victimization. Building on the work of Casarez-Levison (1992), Hill (2009) presents a model of victimization and recovery consisting of four stages: (1) pre-victimization, in which the victim's life has a certain order; (2) the actual victimization, which throws the victim into a state of disorganization; (3) transition, in which the victim tries to adjust to the long-term emotions and other effects and starts to give meaning to his or her victimization; and (4) reorganization, in which the individual finds a new balance. In the case of multiple or repeat victimizations, victims do not have a chance to reach stage 4 and integrate the experience into their lives before they are thrown back into the emotional turmoil of a new victimization experience (Finkelhor, Ormrod, & Turner, 2007; Shaw, 2001).

Stage 3 is vital for the successful recovery of the victim, and it is at this stage that the victim is likely to need the most help. Help can come from the victim's informal network of support (family and friends) as well as professionals (victim support services). Intervention with victims is discussed in detail in Chapter 8.

Victims who report their victimization to police are likely to come into contact with authorities in stages 2 and possibly 3. The police officer who arrives on a crime scene will likely be confronted with a victim who is confused and disoriented as he or she tries to figure out what just happened (Campbell & Raja, 1999; Campbell, Wasco, Ahrens, Sefl, & Barnes, 2001). Victims are very susceptible to reactions from others at these stages (Hill, 2009). We will return to this issue in Chapter 6 when we discuss secondary victimization.

Conclusion

Victimization surveys have helped us understand the short-term effects of victimization on direct victims. Surveys reveal that effects of crime vary considerably across victims and victimizations. While the majority of victims are emotionally impacted by the event, in most cases the effects dissipate within a few days, while others suffer serious, long-lasting effects. However, the limitations of victimization surveys apply equally when they are used to measure the effects of crime: They do not include all victims of all crimes, and they do not capture the long-term effects of crime or changes over time.

Longitudinal studies support the conclusion that victimization is not evenly distributed within the population and that prior victimization is a risk factor. They also show that when prior victimization is controlled for, violent victimization leads to a decline in mental health. Compared to property crime, violent crime has a more severe and persistent effect on mental health.

The concept of PTSD is important for victims and victimology. PTSD recognizes the traumatic impact that victimization can have on direct, indirect, and secondary victims. This validation and recognition of their experience is important. However, most victims do not develop PTSD, and by focusing on PTSD researchers risk neglecting other emotional effects of victimization and types of victimization not associated with PTSD.

There is a growing awareness that the effects of crime are felt beyond the direct victim. The indirect victims, secondary victims, and tertiary victims may all be impacted by victimization. With the exception of physical injury, which is experienced only by direct victims and possibly secondary victims who are injured during the crime, all types of victims may experience psychological, social, and financial consequences as a result of crime. All victims need be considered when we think about the impact of victimization.

CHAPTER 5

THEORETICAL VICTIMOLOGY

Over the past several decades, the field of victimology has grown tremendously, particularly through the introduction of victimization surveys and developments in the measurement of victimization and its impact on individuals. As we have seen, risk factors, in particular multiple victimizations, present important questions about why victimization happens and why it keeps happening to certain people. It is only once we can answer these questions that we can prevent victimization from happening in the first place. Thus, the main task of theoretical victimology is to explain the differential risks of victimization and the skewed distribution of victimization.

In this chapter we will examine theories explaining victimization and, in particular, re-victimization. Two main theoretical approaches in victimology are explored: (1) exposure theories, which include routine activities theory, opportunity theory, and rational choice theory; and (2) strain theory. We then discuss developmental victimology and research on polyvictimization and what each means for understanding victimization and its prevention.

Multiple Victimization

Explaining risk of victimization is not about blaming the victim. Although some early early researchers, such as Fattah (1971) and Hindelang, Gottfredson, and Garofalo (1978), explored the notion of victim proneness, this approach was strongly criticized by others who, as we saw in Chapter 2, argued against what they saw as blaming the victim (Bard & Sangry, 1979). At the same time, research on just-world theory showed how we tend to attribute blame to victims even when it was not their fault to maintain our belief in a just world (Lerner, 1980).

Subsequently, for years victimologists generally avoided questions pertaining to the etiology of victimization for fear that they would be seen to be putting blame on the victims. Systematic empirical research on the causes of victimization remained relatively rare, and instead research focused on the consequences of victimization, victims' needs, and the expansion of services. The end result was that victimology evolved into a predominantly applied science, but one that suffered a paucity of theoretical work (Wemmers, 2003; Zaykowski & Campagna, 2014).

This began to change in the 1990s, following work on multiple victimization (Farrell & Pease, 1993; Pease, 1998). As we saw in Chapter 3, research consistently shows that past victimization is associated with an increased risk for future victimization, which is true across crime types and data sources (Farrell, 1995; Farrell & Pease, 2001). Multiple victimization is a well-established finding that has been replicated across countries (Van Dijk, 1999) and across time (Farrell & Pease, 1993; Hindelang et al., 1978; Perreault, Sauvé, & Burns, 2010). A relatively small proportion of the population endures a large proportion of all criminal victimizations (Farrell & Pease, 1993; Finkelhor, Ormrod, Turner, & Hamby, 2005; Hope, Bryan, Trickett, & Osborn, 2001; Lauritsen & Davis-Quinet, 1995).

Moreover, as discussed in Chapter 4, the effects of multiple victimization are cumulative, and experiencing multiple types of crimes is particularly traumatic (Martin, Cromer, De Prince, & Freyd, 2013; Shaw, 2001). Victims who suffer re-victimization across crime types tend to show more trauma symptoms and are more anxious than victims who suffer repeat victimization of the same crime type (Finkelhor, Ormrod, & Turner, 2007). The age of onset, persistence, and the nature of the prior victimization are also important and have been found to increase one's risk of re-victimization. In particular, violent victimization that starts during the early developmental stages and is persistent is associated with subsequent victimization (Tillyer, 2013).

The phenomenon of multiple victimization is important for research with victims because it means that when we examine the effects of a victimization event without taking into consideration the person's history, as a researcher we can never be sure whether we are actually observing the effects of the particular victimization being studied or whether what we are seeing is in fact the cumulative impact of previous victimizations over the course of the person's lifetime. As a result, victimological research should examine victimization across the life course rather than studying individual victimization events (Tillyer, 2013).

The phenomenon of multiple victimization and the cumulative impact of re-victimization on the individual highlight the importance of theoretical work in victimology. If victimologists can explain victimization, then maybe we can help prevent victimization from happening in the future. However, any attempt to explain victimization must address both why victimization is sometimes an isolated event and why it is sometimes chronic. Victimological theories, therefore, must not only explain victimization but must also explain multiple victimization and, in particular, polyvictimization.

Explaining Re-victimization

Explanations of re-victimization generally fall into one of two broad categories: risk heterogeneity and state dependence. **Risk heterogeneity**, also referred to as *flag theory*, suggests that victims have some enduring characteristics or behaviours that repeatedly place them at risk for victimization (Farrell, Phillips, & Pease, 1995; Hope et al., 2001; Tseloni & Pease, 2003; Tillyer, 2013). For example, characteristics associated with risk of victimization, such as age, poverty, unemployment, drug and alcohol use, and lifestyle, increase the individual's risk of becoming a victim of crime (see Chapter 3). According to flag theory, these same characteristics place victims at risk for victimization and explain both the initial victimization as well as subsequent victimizations.

State dependence, also referred to as *event dependence* or *boost theory*, assumes that there is nothing that distinguishes victims from nonvictims before the initial victimization, but the initial victimization may boost or increase the probability of the victim continuing to be victimized (Farrell et al., 1995; Hope et al., 2001; Pease, 1998; Ruback, Clark, & Warner, 2014; Tseloni & Pease, 2003; Tillyer, 2013). In other words, previous victimization increases risk of future victimization by rendering the person more vulnerable (Bunch, Clay-Warner, & McMahon-Howard, 2014).

The idea that the victim is somehow prone to victimization raises a host of difficult empirical and moral issues that have plagued victimology since its beginning. Nevertheless, if victimology is going to contribute to the prevention

Heterogeneity (characteristics + behaviour) ➞ (Re-)victimization

FIGURE 5.1: Risk Heterogeneity

Victimization ➞ Boost ➞ Re-victimization

FIGURE 5.2: State Dependence

of victimization we need to address these difficult issues. Empirically it is difficult to detect the existence of either proneness or event dependency in their pure form. According to Hope and colleagues (2001), the processes are incompatible: Either victims were similar to nonvictims before their initial victimization, or they were not. To prove the existence of one process requires disproving the existence of the other.

Yet, while the two processes shaping victimization risk are in tension, they may nevertheless interact over the life course of people's everyday lives (Hope et al., 2001). Hence, rather than either/or *both* flag and boost may be at work (Lauritsen & Davis-Quinet, 1995; Pease, 1998). According to Pease (1998), prior victimization predicts future risk of victimization because it alters something about the individual (boost) *and* it signals some unmeasured tendency for victimization that persists over time (flag).

However, flag and boost theories do not specify which characteristics are important and why. For that we turn to theories on victimization. In particular, we will examine exposure theories and strain theory, which are both derived from criminology but which also serve to explain victimization.

Exposure Theories

First developed by criminologists to explain crime, **exposure theories** explain victimization by examining the environments victims are exposed to while also understanding what makes a target more vulnerable or attractive within such contexts (Zaykowski & Campagna, 2014). These theories approach victimization and crime as mundane, opportunistic, and rational behaviours rather than abnormal, pathological, purposeless, and mindless, and they start with the premise that criminals are not inherently different from noncriminals (Fattah, 1993). In victimology, exposure theories emphasize environmental, situational, and catalyzing factors, focusing on opportunity, motives, and the victim–offender interaction. In the following pages, three different theories that focus on the victim's environment will be discussed: rational choice theory, opportunity theory, and routine activity theory.

Rational choice theory (Cornish & Clarke, 1986) draws attention to the perspective of the offender with respect to the criminal event. It calls for a crime-specific analysis, examining rational and adaptive aspects of offending. Rational choice theory maintains that criminal victimization is rational behaviour and that the decision to engage in such behaviour is a lucid one. Rationality is relative and subjective. Neutralization techniques allow offenders to justify their behaviour. Offenders rationalize their behaviour by redefining it, or they may minimize the victim's suffering. Desensitization techniques include denial, depersonalization of the victim, blaming the victim, and devaluation of the victim (Fattah, 1993).

A key element in rational choice theory is target selection. The rational offender does not choose a victim at random. This is why certain groups are victimized more often than others. As rational operators, criminals, particularly those who commit property crime, select their victims or targets in a careful, rational manner. The rational choices criminals make, particularly with regard to target selection, are thought to be strongly influenced by victims' behaviours and characteristics, which make them vulnerable. For a motivated offender, a good target might be someone who is inattentive, perhaps because they are drunk or high. As we saw in Chapter 3, a high risk of victimization is associated with lifestyle, drug and alcohol use, and unemployment (Perreault & Brennan, 2010: Perreault, 2015).

Opportunity theory (Clarke, 2012; Mayhew, Clarke, Sturman, & Hough, 1976) emphasizes opportunities for crime, focusing on the characteristics of the situation or the environment in which crime takes place rather than the offender's characteristics. Victimization is thought to be a function of the people we associate with as well as where we live and where we spend our time. Lifestyles, travel routes, job situations, or other stable living patterns can repeatedly put individuals and their property at risk and create opportunities for victimization. As we saw in Chapter 3, situational factors, such as marital status, occupation, poverty, and unemployment, are strongly associated with risk of victimization. The availability of potential targets is also important in opportunity theory. For example, in developing countries with few automobiles, there will be less opportunity to commit car-related crimes. *Hot spots* refer to small geographic areas in which the occurrence of crime is frequent and, thus, there is a high concentration of crime (Farrell & Sousa, 2001; Sherman, 1995). An area may become a hot spot because it provides lots of opportunities for crime. For example, there may be a large number of motivated offenders or a concentration of attractive targets in the area.

Routine activities theory (RAT) (Cohen & Felson, 1979) posits that three factors are necessary for a crime to occur: (1) the presence of a motivated offender, (2) the presence of a suitable target, and (3) the absence of a capable guardian. Unless these three factors occur together, crime will not occur. One of the tenets of RAT and other lifestyle models (Hindelang et al., 1978) is that differential risks of victimization are, in part, a function of differential association with and exposure to motivated offenders and the absence of capable guardians. Criminal offending, especially juvenile delinquency, is often a group phenomenon, and individuals who associate with criminals have greater exposure to other active criminal offenders and may, therefore, be at risk of victimization themselves (Jensen & Brownfield, 1986). Furthermore, individuals often engage in crime while under the influence of drugs or alcohol, which may make them attractive targets for the co-offenders with whom they tend to associate (Mustaine & Tewksbury, 1998). Moreover, fellow offenders may make particularly attractive targets because they are unlikely to report the crime to police (Miller, 1998). Juveniles who experience one form of violence are likely to participate in routines or exhibit lifestyles that put them at risk for other types of violence (Nofziger & Kurtz, 2005). According to RAT, social activities that increase the level of association with or exposure to potential offenders (e.g., alcohol consumption, lifestyle) and increase target attractiveness increase the risks and the rates of victimization (Fattah, 1993).

The presence of a capable guardian will protect a person or object from victimization. A capable guardian could be another human being, a video camera, a dog, or anything else that reduces the offender's chance of successfully committing the crime without getting caught. Like other exposure theories, RAT assumes that offenders are rational. If a capable guardian is present, the motivated offender will move on and look for a suitable target without a capable guardian. Patterns of routine activities, including proximity to high-crime areas, exposure to criminal opportunities, target attractiveness, and guardianship, may help explain criminal victimization during one's life course (Wittebrood & Nieuwbeerta, 2000).

Findings from victimization surveys suggest that routine activity or lifestyle theory may explain re-victimization. Using data from the General Social Survey (GSS), Perreault, Sauvé, and Burns (2010) compared individuals who had been victims of a violent crime only once during the 12 months preceding the survey to those who experienced multiple victimizations during the same period. They found that the same characteristics that correlate with risk of victimization are also associated with risk of multiple victimization. Their analysis included nine background variables: age, gender, marital status, employment, income, urbanization, nighttime activities, drinking, and Indigenous status. However, survey data, which are based on a single interview, may not accurately capture victimization experiences across time.

Longitudinal research that follows victims over a period of time allows researchers to examine victimization experiences as they occur. Using data from the US National Crime Victimization Survey (NCVS), in which victims are interviewed every six months across three and a half years, Tseloni and Pease (2003) examined personal victimizations, which included rape, sexual assault, robbery, assault, threats, pickpocketing, and larceny. They found that victim characteristics and behaviours explained both prior and subsequent personal victimization. Similarly, Bunch, Clay-Warner, and McMahon-Howard (2014) also used the longitudinal data from the NCVS to examine risk of re-victimization. They reported that both the initial victimization and subsequent victimization seem to be attributable to pre-existing factors that distinguish victims from nonvictims and are not caused by the victimization event itself. These studies support risk heterogeneity as an explanation of victimization and re-victimization—in other words, victimization itself does not increase risk of re-victimization. However, these studies were based on a limited number of risk factors that were available in the victimization surveys. It is possible that individuals who experience re-victimization are different but in a way not measured in these studies.

It is also important to consider the time between victimizations. Research suggests that the risk of re-victimization is not constant and that it changes over time. In an extensive study of residential burglary in Saskatoon, Polvi, Looman, Humphries, and Pease (1990) found that after the initial burglary, households were almost four times more likely to be re-victimized. However, risk of re-victimization was the highest immediately after the first victimization and gradually reduced over time until eventually, by the eighth month, previously burglarized households had the same risk of victimization as nonvictimized households. Similar findings are reported by Guidi, Homel, and Townsley (1997) in Australia and Kleemans (1996) in the Netherlands, who also studied home burglaries. Hence, the risk of re-victimization seems to diminish over time.

Research with offenders convicted of burglary confirms that it is not unusual for them to return to a site that they previously robbed. They go back for things that they saw the first time and were unable to take or to look for new items that were bought to replace the items that were previously stolen (Bennett, 1995; Clarke, Perkins, & Smith, 2001). Revisiting a site that the offender is already familiar with is less risky for the offender than targeting a new site (Pease, 1998). These findings paint a picture of a rational offender who chooses his or her target carefully, including possibly returning to a target (Farrell et al., 1995). In other words, previous victimization makes victims a more attractive target for offenders, thus increasing their risk of re-victimization.

This temporal dimension is not unique to burglary and has been found in a variety of different types of victimizations, including domestic violence (Lloyd, Farrell, & Pease, 1994) and racial attacks (Sampson & Phillips, 1992). These findings suggest that re-victimization may be state dependent, at least in part, and that victimization experiences impact one's risk of re-victimization (Farrell et al., 1995). A flag alone is unable to explain why risk of re-victimization changes over time, and offenders' motives show how previous victimization boosts the risk of re-victimization.

The conclusion that both flag and boost processes may be at work is also supported by longitudinal research. Using a retrospective life-course victimization survey, Wittebrood and Nieuwbeerta (2000) find that re-victimization is partly explained by state dependence as well as by the effects of patterns of routine activities or lifestyle. Over time, as the effect of state dependence dissipates, victims' characteristics and behaviours continue to influence their risk of

Heterogeneity (characteristics + behaviour) ⟶ Victimization

⟶ Boost (target attractiveness) ⟶ Re-victimization

FIGURE 5.3: Exposure Theories, Risk Heterogeneity, and State Dependence

victimization. Hence, risk heterogeneity may explain the initial victimization and state dependence may explain the further increase in risk of re-victimization (see Figure 5.3).

These exposure theories attempt to explain the differential risks of victimization and the skewed distribution of victimization in time and space (Fattah, 1993). They offer a dynamic, three-dimensional model (victim–offender–situation) to explain criminal victimization. While victim characteristics and behaviours are only one dimension, they are an important one. Viewing victims as agents in crime prevention assumes that victims can actively reduce their risk of re-victimization by changing their behaviour (Davis, Taylor, & Titus, 1997; Wemmers, 2011a). For example, victims can reduce their vulnerability when they install an alarm system, go out less often at night, and do not walk alone. However, some characteristics, such as age, gender, and ethnicity, are impossible to change and others, such as employment and family income, may be difficult to change. Moreover, sociodemographic characteristics and behaviours may simply be symptomatic of other, deeper concerns that are not measured in victimization surveys, such as the individual's psychological well-being.

Social Learning

Before leaving environmental factors, it is important to consider social learning as a possible explanation of victimization and re-victimization. Social learning theories posit that victimization is a process by which norms, values, and expected behaviours are transmitted through interaction between victim and offender, family, friends, or more broadly society, media, and other cultural influences (Zaykowski & Campagna, 2014). Research has consistently revealed an overlap between victimization and offending (Berg, Stewart, Schreck, Simons, 2012; Radford, Corral, Bradley, & Fisher, 2014; Wemmers & Cyr, 2015). Lifestyle and routine activities theories explain this overlap through association: By associating with others who engage in criminal behaviour, one runs the risk of becoming a victim. Retrospective self-report studies on victimization and offending suggest that one of the best predictors for violent offending is prior violent victimization (Singer, 1986). Berg and colleagues (2012) found a strong association between violent victimization and offending, even when victim characteristics and behaviours (risk heterogeneity) are controlled for. They interpret this as evidence of social learning. Social learning is often used to explain the intergenerational transmission of violence, or the cycle of violence, as it is also called (Widom & Wilson, 2015). While no single factor explains delinquency, the finding that childhood victimization is associated with later delinquency is robust (Widom, Schuck, & White, 2006; Widom & Wilson, 2015). In other words, violence and favourable attitudes toward it are learned, which in turn boost one's risk of future victimization and offending.

Victimization not only teaches the victim about offending, it can also teach them about pain and suffering. As we saw in Chapter 3, victims sometimes feel guilty and blame themselves for their victimization. The attributions made by the victim are important. *Learned helplessness* posits that when people are repeatedly exposed to unavoidable, painful experiences, they come to expect that outcomes are unavoidable and that they are helpless (Abramson, Seligman, & Teasdale, 1978). Learned helplessness is a form of reactive depression, and individuals who attribute negative outcomes to internal, stable, and global causes are more likely to be depressed than those who attribute the same outcomes to external, unstable, and specific causes (Seligman, Abramson, Semmel, & Von Baeyer, 1979). When victims attribute an inability to avoid negative experiences to internal factors (e.g., "It is my fault") rather than external factors (e.g., "It is their fault") it leads to lowered self-esteem and poorer psychological adjustment (Abramson, Seligman, & Teasdale, 1978; Hassija & Gray, 2012). Research shows that the more negative life events individuals experienced during the last year, the more likely they are to blame themselves, suggesting that multiple and, in particular, polyvictims may be particularly prone to learned helplessness (Peterson, Schwartz, & Seligman, 1981).

In terms of risk heterogeneity and state dependence, social learning theories concur with state dependence. Regardless of whether it's due to learning to offend or learning that one is unable to avoid aversive events, both explanations consider victimization to boost the probability of future victimization.

Strain Theory

Like exposure theories, **strain theory** was originally developed as a theory explaining criminal behaviour. Robert Agnew's *general strain theory* (1992) posits that the accumulation of strains or stressors increases the likelihood of negative emotions like anger and frustration. Strain can be objective or subjective. *Objective strains* are events or conditions that are disliked by most members of a given group. *Subjective strains* are events or conditions that are disliked by the people who have experienced them. Examples of possible strains include the death of a loved one, loss of employment, sickness, witnessing violence, and criminal victimization. In other words, direct, indirect, secondary, and tertiary victimizations all constitute possible strains for those who experience them. A concentration of crime victimization and other misfortunes is associated with a concentration of social disadvantage (e.g., poverty, unemployment), both in people's lives and in the communities in which they live (Agnew, 1992, 2001; Hope et al., 2001).

When strains build up they create pressure for corrective action and, according to Agnew, crime is one possible response for reducing strain. As we saw earlier when we discussed exposure theories, individuals who engage in criminal activity and lead risky lifestyles are at increased risk of victimization. Several studies find a strong correlation between victimization and offending among adolescents (Fattah, 1991; Radford et al., 2014; Van Dijk & Steinmetz, 1983; Wemmers & Cyr, 2015). Longitudinal research by Ruback, Clark, and Warner (2014) examined substance use, depression, and offending as mediators of the link between victimization and re-victimization and found that, especially for males, violent offending was a significant mediator between victimization and re-victimization. Their offending behaviour and criminal lifestyle may expose them to other potential offenders, which according to routine activities theory puts them at risk of additional victimization in the future.

However, from a victimological perspective strain theory is particularly interesting because it considers the impact of victimization on the individual. As we saw in Chapter 4, the consequences of victimization can have a strong impact on the individual's well-being. Poorer, disadvantaged areas have higher rates of both theft of personal property and violent victimization (Hope et al., 2001; Perreault & Brennan, 2010). Victimization experiences may accumulate over time alongside other misfortunes in some people's lives, particularly among those who may also suffer from additional socioeconomic disadvantages. The accumulation of strain or stress from personal misfortune, poverty, unemployment, racism, social marginalization, criminal victimization, and poor health both in people's lives and in the communities in which they live may be a source of psychological distress, impacting their mental health and well-being (Hope et al., 2001).

The effects of victimization on the psychological well-being of victims may increase an individual's vulnerability and contribute to re-victimization. As we saw in Chapter 4, following victimization an individual may develop several symptoms such as post-traumatic stress, depression, anxiety, or dissociation. Post-traumatic symptomology includes avoidance. Efforts to avoid emotions that are related to the trauma might put the individual at risk of making unwise decisions because they avoid or block out important danger cues. Research on the impact of sexual violence on information processing suggests that individuals suffering dissociation may be less able to recognize dangerous situations and, as a result, are more likely to expose themselves to risk (Chu, 1992; Sandberg, Lynn, & Matorin, 2001). Victims suffering from mental health problems may be more vulnerable and less capable to defend themselves and, consequently, are at risk of re-victimization (Logan, Walker, Cole, & Leukefeld, 2002).

In addition, negative coping strategies following victimization, such as alcohol and drug use, may also make the individual vulnerable to re-victimization (Hill, 2009). As we saw, certain mental health problems, such as PTSD, depression, and anxiety, are comorbid with substance abuse, which in turn puts the individual at risk of (re-)victimization (Hill, 2009; Logan et al., 2002). The accumulation of strain may impact how individuals react to the world around them, thus putting them at risk of re-victimization.

In this context, it is interesting to consider the temporal aspect of re-victimization. While it is not clear why the risk of re-victimization diminishes with the passage of time, from the victim's perspective this temporal factor is important with respect to their recovery. If re-victimization occurs soon after the initial victimization, the person may not have an opportunity to fully recover from the initial event before he or she is re-victimized. How a person responds to victimization is, in part, determined by their well-being before the event (Hill, 2009). For someone who is already anxious or stressed because of prior victimization, a new victimization may be devastating. If, however, former victims have had a chance to recover from the initial victimization, they may be less vulnerable and, as a result, their risk of re-victimization may diminish.

According to Tillyer (2013), however, neither risk heterogeneity nor state dependence suggest that re-victimization would necessarily be limited to the few months or years following a victimization experience. Tillyer argues that one needs to consider re-victimization across the individual's lifetime. Using data from a national longitudinal study of adolescent health, she examined how well prevalence, onset, and persistence of violent victimization during earlier stages in the life course predict violent victimization risk in adulthood, while controlling for current violent offending by the individual. Like many others (Chu, 1992; European Union Agency for Fundamental Rights, 2014; Perreault, 2015), Tillyer finds that those who report early and persistent violent victimization are particularly vulnerable to subsequent victimization in adulthood. However, Tillyer also included current offending in her analyses and found that the relationship between prior violent victimization and subsequent victimization remains even when current offending is taken into consideration. Hence, her findings appear to suggest that it is not because of their delinquent behaviour that prior victims are at risk of re-victimization.

From a victimological perspective, strain theory and exposure theories are not incompatible but are complementary. Strain, including victimization, may render an individual an attractive target. According to rational choice theory, offenders carefully select their victims by looking for easy targets. Individuals who do not react to danger cues because of trauma, depression, or drug and alcohol use are attractive targets. Alternatively, individuals who have learned that they are unable to avoid negative events, or individuals who have learned

Heterogeneity (characteristics + behaviour) ⟶ Victimization

⟶ Boost (stress) ⟶ Re-victimization

FIGURE 5.4: Strain Theory, Risk Heterogeneity, and State Dependence

to deal with stress by offending, may increase their risk of re-victimization. Hence, personal and environmental or situational factors may interact and together enhance the probability of subsequent victimization.

With respect to risk heterogeneity and state dependence, according to strain theory the initial victimization may be due to exposure mechanisms and the dynamics of the victim–offender situation, but re-victimization is state dependent. In other words, victimization leads to re-victimization. Strain from prior victimization is thought to increase risk of re-victimization either by triggering criminal behaviour or by rendering the individual an attractive target. In the first case, victims' exposure and criminal lifestyle puts them at risk. In the second case, prior victimization boosts one's risk of re-victimization through the impact that it has on the individual's well-being, thus rendering the individual more vulnerable and, therefore, a more attractive target. Hence, both flag and boost processes are believed to be at work (see Figure 5.4). While further research is needed to better understand the impact of victimization across the individual's lifetime, multiple victimization highlights the importance of a developmental approach to victimology.

Developmental Victimology and Life Course

Multiple victimization means that we cannot understand victimization by studying individual victimization incidents and highlights the necessity of a longitudinal or developmental perspective. After a time, routines, including victimization, become part of our lives and our life course. *Developmental victimology* is the comprehensive study of childhood victimizations. Childhood is a broad category, since there are enormous differences between an infant and an adolescent. When studying the victimization of children, one has to keep their age or developmental stage in mind. Developmental victimology explores the developmental changes that influence children's risk of and reactions to different types of victimizations (Finkelhor, 1997, 2007).

Studying the victimization of children and youth, Finkelhor and colleagues (Finkelhor et al., 2005; Finkelhor et al., 2007) found multiple victimization to be the norm. Among the 71 per cent of children and youth in their sample who reported directly experiencing or witnessing at least one victimization in the preceding year, the average number of separate incidents experienced was three (Finkelhor et al., 2005). The finding that children and youth have high rates of multiple victimization appears robust (Chan, 2014; Cyr, Clément, & Chamberland, 2014; Radford et al., 2014).

Finkelhor and colleagues introduced the term *polyvictims* to refer to individuals who have experienced multiple types of victimization (Finkelhor, Ormrod, Turner, & Holt, 2009). In other words, they found that among youth who experienced victimization the average juvenile was victimized in three different ways in separate incidents over the course of the preceding year. Similarly in Canada, Cyr, Clément, and Chamberland (2014) found that, on average, children and youth between 2 and 17 years of age who experienced victimization reported experiencing 3.3 different types of victimization during their lifetime. As age increases, lifetime victimization increases as well, and the older youths in their study (15 to 17 years of age) who experienced victimization reported on average 4.3 different types of victimization. The emerging work on the polyvictimization of children and youth and victimization across the life course highlights the importance of understanding why multiple victimization occurs so that we can prevent it from happening.

If the life course of an individual seems to render them persistently vulnerable to comparatively frequent victimization from a variety of crimes, does this indicate that victims are prone to victimization, or does it suggest that they either objectively or subjectively cannot avoid high-risk situations in their everyday lives (Hope et al., 2001)? We need to determine the extent to which risk of re-victimization is caused by victim characteristics and behaviour and how much is caused by situational factors in their environment.

Exposure theories, which emphasize lifestyle factors such as going out at night, going out alone, and drug and alcohol use, do not adequately take into account characteristics that are specific to child victims. Young children, for example, are dependent on their caregivers, but as they grow older they become more independent, spending more time outside of the home. In terms of opportunity theory, one could argue that they are exposed to different opportunities for victimization. As a result of their situation, young children are at risk of dependency related types of victimization, such as neglect, family abduction, and psychological maltreatment, while teenagers are at risk of nondependency related types of victimization, such as homicide and stranger abduction (Finkelhor, 1997, 2007). According to Finkelhor (2007), when addressing the victimization of young children it is more appropriate to refer to "environmental factors" that expose or protect the child from victimization rather than their "lifestyle." Concepts such as guardianship, exposure, and proximity to a motivated offender are important with respect to children. As we saw, these are key determinants according to RAT.

Besides situational or environmental factors, target attractiveness is also a key element in exposure theories. According Finkelhor (2007), certain personal characteristics, such as gender and physical or mental disability, increase vulnerability in children. However, instead of target "attractiveness," Finkelhor prefers the term target "congruence," which is a broader concept and highlights the congruence between the victim's characteristics and the offender's preferences.

Given the importance of early developmental stages for the individual's personal growth, strain theory as well as social learning theory may also explain victimization and, in particular, re-victimization. The impact of strain during childhood, including criminal victimization, may be particularly strong and long lasting. Finkelhor (2007) notes that research on child sexual abuse suggests that children who suffer emotional deprivation or whose parents fight or are distant and punitive are vulnerable to the offers of attention and affection that sexual predatory offenders sometimes use to draw children into sexual activities. Prior victimization experiences (e.g., neglect, sexual abuse) may boost the person's vulnerability and risk of victimization, and this may carry through into adulthood (European Union Agency for Fundamental Rights, 2014; Fleming, Mullen, Sibthorpe, & Bammer, 1999; Perreault, 2015).

Pathways

Integrating elements of exposure and strain theories, Finkelhor and colleagues (Finkelhor, Ormrod, Turner, & Holt, 2009) propose four different pathways to polyvictimization: (1) dangerous community, (2) dangerous family, (3) family problems, and (4) symptomatic child.

The first pathway, *dangerous community*, suggests that some children and youth are at increased risk of victimization because of where they grow up—namely, in a dangerous environment. As we have seen, victimization, particularly violent victimization, is especially prevalent in certain disadvantaged areas (Lauritsen & Davis-Quinet, 1995; Outlaw, Ruback, & Britt, 2002). In addition to continuing exposure to motivated offenders, the dangers of living in such communities may place stresses on families, which in turn promote victimization and offending. These mechanisms might help explain family violence. Children in these situations are at risk of victimization or exposure to violence within the neighbourhood itself, in the schools populated with other children from the neighbourhood, and in their homes. Turner, Finkelhor, Hamby, and Shattuck (2013) examined community disorder and victimization in a national sample of 2,039 children and youth aged 10 to 17 years. They found that community disorder is strongly associated with victimization and in particular polyvictimization, which in turn is associated with distress. The researchers also found that family social support mediates the impact of community disorder on distress. In other words, a supportive family can lessen the impact of community disorder on individual distress.

The second pathway is the *dangerous family*. According to Finkelhor and colleagues, these polyvictim children are products of a particular developmental process that starts with victimization and violence inside the family, which in turn sets the child up for further victimization. Research suggests a link between violent victimization in the home and victimization in other settings such as school (Mohr, 2006; Perry, Hodges, & Egan, 2001; Tucker, Finkelhor, Turner, & Shattuck, 2014b; Wemmers, 2003). In their research with a nationally representative sample of 1,726 children aged 2 to 9 years, Tucker, Finkelhor, Turner, and Shattuck (2014a) found family dynamics to be predictive of sibling victimization. Young children's experiences with sibling victimization were linked to interparental conflict, exposure to family violence, and parenting quality. In a related study, they examined sibling and peer victimization in a nationally representative sample of 1,536 children aged 3 to 9 years and 1,523 adolescents aged 10 to 17 years (Tucker et al., 2014b). Consistent with the notion of the horizontal transmission of violence, they found that victimization by a sibling was predictive of peer victimization.

The third pathway identified by Finkelhor and colleagues is the *problem family*. These are families that are characterized by considerable chaos and multiple, ongoing problems that result in children being poorly supervised and exposed to victimization in different contexts. These children may live in single-parent or reconstituted families, which research suggests is associated with a higher risk of victimization (Finkelhor, Ormrod, & Turner, 2007; Radford et al., 2014). Similarly, when parents are unable to care for their children because of illness, psychiatric problems, or addiction, the children may be subject to additional caregivers. Essentially, because of the characteristics of the home these children are exposed to extraneous individuals circulating through their lives and households in the form of additional caregivers, partners, and stepsiblings. Higher rates of victimization have been found among children in single-parent families and step/cohabiting families relative to those living with two biological or adoptive parents (Lauritsen, 2003; Turner, Finkelhor, & Ormrod, 2007; Turner et al., 2013). Based on a representative sample of 4,046 children aged 2 to 17 years, Turner, Finkelhor, Hamby, and Shattuck (2013) found that children living in nontraditional family structures not only have a greater risk of victimization, they are also exposed to multiple forms of victimization. In line with earlier research on polyvictimization, the researchers also found elevated levels of distress symptoms among children in single-parent families and step/cohabiting families relative to youth living with both biological parents.

Finkelhor's fourth pathway, the *symptomatic child*, focuses less on the situational factors and more on the characteristics of the child. This group consists of children who have particular enduring behavioural patterns or emotional problems that make them prone to victimization. For example, Finkelhor refers to the work by Hodges and Perry (1999), who studied victimization among elementary school children over a two-year period. They found that children who are anxious or withdrawn and cry easily are at risk of victimization over time. The authors argue that these children's internalizing behaviours contribute to their victimization. However, they also found that victimization contributed to internalizing problems and peer rejection, suggesting an interaction effect. Hodges and Perry's study failed to measure prior victimization, so it is impossible to exclude the possibility that these children already experienced victimization at home, for example, and that their behaviour is symptomatic of their prior victimization.

In a more recent study, Turner, Vanderminden, Finkelhor, Hamby, and Shattuck, (2011) examined disability and victimization in a national sample of over 4,046 children and youth ages 2 to 17 years. They found that interpersonal and behavioural difficulties, such as attention-deficit disorder, developmental and learning disorders, and internalizing psychological disorders, are strongly associated with victimization risks. Similarly, survey data with individuals 15 years of age and older show that people who reported a mental or psychological disability have higher victimization rates (Perreault, 2015).

Finkelhor's work demonstrates that there is not one but several possible pathways that may lead to polyvictimization. Each pathway integrates situational and personal variables a little differently. Regardless of the precise pathway to polyvictimization, research shows that victimization during earlier stages of life is a risk factor for subsequent victimization (Finkelhor, Turner, Hamby, & Ormrod, 2011; Tillyer, 2013). The research findings regarding multiple victimization and, in particular, polyvictimization highlight the importance of early detection of violent victimization and intervention to prevent re-victimization.

Prevention

The findings regarding multiple victimization and polyvictimization mean that victims, especially victims of violence, should be a priority for crime prevention programs. In this chapter we focused on possible explanations for victimization and re-victimization. Following exposure theories, prevention should aim to reduce victims' exposure to situational and environmental risk factors. Preventative measures might focus on changing victims' environments by reducing exposure to potential offenders and increasing the presence of a capable guardian in their daily lives.

From a social learning perspective, early intervention with victims is vital. This approach highlights the importance of stopping the intergenerational transmission of violence through parent intervention and early childhood intervention programs (Widom, 1998). Rather than focusing on punishing the offender, the focus is on helping children and their families escape the cycle of violence.

Strain theory focuses on the impact of strain (such as prior victimization) on an individual's well-being. Following this approach, preventative measures aim to enhance the victim's psychological well-being, for example, by offering victims adequate and timely support and encouraging them to develop positive coping strategies. In other words, victim support is crime prevention. To counter the accumulation of strain, prevention efforts should prioritize the youngest and most frequent victims of violence. We will address the consequences of multiple and polyvictimization for victim support in Chapter 8.

Conclusion

In this chapter we examined theories explaining victimization and, in particular, re-victimization. Two processes shaping risk of victimization are risk heterogeneity (flag) and state dependence (boost). The available research is unable to rule out either risk heterogeneity or state dependence as a possible explanation for re-victimization (Hope et al., 2001; Tillyer, 2013). While these two opposing processes are in tension with one another, they may nevertheless interact over the life course of people's everyday lives. It may be that the initial victimization and all subsequent victimizations result from some enduring characteristics and behaviours that repeatedly place individuals at risk for victimization over their life course. Alternately, victimization, especially violent victimization during childhood, may lead to changes in people's characteristics and behaviours, which increase their future risk of victimization. Developmental victimology explores the developmental changes that influence children's risk for and reactions to victimization. It highlights the importance of studying victimization not as an isolated event but rather in the context of the person's life course. In the next chapter we will address the needs of victims.

CHAPTER 6

VICTIMS' NEEDS AND SECONDARY VICTIMIZATION

In the 1970s, research on victims' experiences in the criminal justice system began to emerge. These early studies showed that victims were more dissatisfied with their treatment in the criminal justice system than offenders (Junger-Tas & Zeefkens, 1978; Tufts, 2000). In other words, individuals who had come to the police seeking assistance following a crime were less satisfied than individuals who had been stopped involuntarily by the police. As we have seen, victim cooperation with police has been and continues to be an important concern for criminal justice authorities.

Victim cooperation with authorities—or, more accurately, the lack thereof—contributed to the introduction of victim-friendly policies in criminal justice in the 1980s (Goodey, 2005; Wemmers, 1996). Victims' unwillingness to cooperate was, in part, attributed to their poor treatment in the criminal justice system, and it was thought that victim policies, which aimed to improve how victims were treated in the criminal justice system, would improve victims' collaboration with police. Nowhere is this more obvious than in Canada and Quebec, where the federal government introduced a Canadian *Statement of Basic Principles of Justice for Victims of Crime* in 1988 and Quebec introduced the *Loi sur l'aide aux victimes d'actes criminels*. Both of these documents declared victims' rights to information, participation, reparation, and support while also reminding victims of their obligation to collaborate with authorities (Wemmers, 2003). However, according to Alan Young (2001), Canada's victim policies and legislation were not based on comprehensive research on victims' needs but on "stereotypical views of crime victims" (p. 65).

In this chapter we will examine the needs of crime victims as well as what happens when victims' needs are not met. As we saw in Chapter 4, the effects of crime reach far beyond the person who is the direct object of a crime. Besides the needs of those directly victimized, we will also consider the needs of indirect, secondary, and tertiary victims. Understanding victims' needs is a crucial first step toward meeting those needs and helping victims recover.

Secondary victimization is a key concept in victimolgy, and this chapter will examine how it affects victims individually as well as society as a whole. In later chapters (Chapters 8, 9, 10) we will discuss victims' services in relation to victims' needs.

Victims' Needs

What are victims' needs and what are the consequences, both for the individual victim and society, of not addressing victims' needs? Before we can identify a victim's needs, we must first know the consequences of his or her victimization (Parmentier & Weitekamp, 2007). Victimization surveys provide insight into the consequences of crime. As we saw in Chapter 4, victimization can impact the individual emotionally, socially, financially, and physically. While needs are related to the impact of crime, the two are not synonymous. Whether or not a consequence translates into a need depends on the individual's capacity to absorb the consequences of the victimization. For example, the theft of $100 may be a lot of money for a person who is living on welfare and has limited financial resources, but for someone who has a high income it might be considered a negligible loss. Similarly, a person who has a rich social network may have lots of people to talk to about the crime, whereas a person who lives alone and is socially isolated may not have a robust support network to fall back on and may need additional support. Also, a victim who is already mourning the recent death of a loved one from natural causes may find it especially difficult to handle additional stress from victimization. Hence, needs are tied to the consequences of the crime and the victim's resources.

Much of the research on victims' needs has focused on the needs that are expressed by victims. While the individual victim may well be able to identify his or her needs, it is important to bear in mind that this source of information is highly subjective because victims' expressed needs are culturally based (Maguire, 1985). They are related to victims' expectations about the potential effects of the offence and their knowledge of what remedies exist (Shapland, Wilmore, & Duff, 1985). Victims may be reluctant to express a particular need for fear of how others will react; others sometimes have strong expectations regarding how victims should react and can be judgmental of victims who react in unexpected ways (Van Dijk, 2009). To illustrate, research on restorative justice with victims of serious violent crimes revealed that victims were sometimes reluctant to express their interest in meeting their offender because of concerns about how others would react (Wemmers & Van Camp, 2011). Alternatively, victims may be in denial and think that they are able to cope with the consequences of victimization on their own, when in reality they are not.

In general, victims' needs fall into six categories: (1) support, (2) protection, (3) information, (4) reparation, (5) practical needs, and (6) need for recognition in the criminal justice system (Herman, 2005; Ten Boom & Kuijpers, 2012; Wemmers, 2003, 2006).

Support

Victimization can impact victims' health. Depending on the nature of their *physical injuries*, victims may require medical attention, medicine, and possibly hospitalization. Besides direct victims of crime, another category of victims who may suffer physical injuries is secondary victims who intervene to assist a direct victim. These include professionals such as police and firefighters or they may simply be bystanders.

Victimization also can impact the individual's psychological or mental health. As we saw, post-traumatic stress disorder (PTSD) can be diagnosed in direct victims, secondary victims, as well as indirect victims. The psychological effects of victimization can sometimes even be experienced by tertiary victims. Hence the need for psychological support is general and is not specific to direct victims.

Informal support is the most common form of support used by victims. Victims of violence are more likely to express a need to talk to someone than victims of property offences (Ten Boom & Kuijpers, 2012). Typically, victims turn to family or friends for support (AuCoin & Beauchamp, 2007). Most victims claim to have been able to find the support they needed in their own network of friends and family (Denkers, 1996; Wemmers & Cyr, 2006a). While 80 per cent of victims are emotionally impacted by their victimization, in most cases symptoms resolve rapidly (Perreault & Brennan, 2010; AuCoin & Beauchamp, 2007).

When symptoms persist, victims may require professional support such as that of a psychologist, psychotherapist, or psychiatrist. Victims who suffer from acute stress disorder (ASD), PTSD, depression, anxiety, or any other clinical disorder following their victimization will need professional help. Receiving timely support can prevent symptoms from worsening and possibly avoid ASD from developing into full-blown PTSD. Almost 1 in 10 victims of violent crime in Canada seek formal support of one kind or another (AuCoin & Beauchamp, 2007). Victim assistance is discussed in Chapter 8.

Protection

Following victimization, victims may feel fearful and be afraid of re-victimization. One in 10 victims in Canada reported that their victimization made them fearful (Perreault & Brennan, 2010). Victims often worry about their general risk of falling victim to a crime again in the future (AuCoin & Beauchamp, 2007).

However, victims' fears are sometimes more specific, as when they fear retaliation from their offender or others. Victims of violence, including domestic violence, more often express a need for safety than victims of property offences (Ten Boom & Kuijpers, 2012). Based on a systematic review of 33 empirical studies on victims' needs, Ten Boom and Kuijpers (2012) found that the need for safety or protection is one of the more frequently expressed needs of crime victims.

Besides fearing for their own safety, victims may fear for the safety of their family members. For example, victims of human trafficking may be threatened with violence against their family members to force them to comply with the demands of the trafficker (Aronowitz, 2009). Indirect victims may also experience fear following the victimization of a family member (Armour, 2002; Bowling, 1994). They may fear harm from perpetrators who are still at large, and in some cases indirect victims may require protection from intimidation (Armour, 2002).

Fear may keep victims from reporting to the police or, conversely, it may motivate them to contact authorities. One of the reasons why victims report their victimization to the police is because they seek protection from the offender (Dichter, Cerulli, Kothari, Barg, & Rhodes, 2011; Gannon & Mihorean, 2005). Hence, it is not unusual for victims to feel insecure and in need of protection when they enter into contact with the criminal justice system.

Once they enter into the criminal justice system, direct victims and secondary victims are often important witnesses in the criminal justice process, which may put added stress on them. They may be reluctant to act as a witness in court because of perceived or actual threats to their safety or that of their family (Verhoeven, Van Gestel, De Jong, & Kleemans, 2015). Just the thought of testifying in court in front of one's aggressor can be extremely stressful for the victim (Herman, 2003). Victim-witnesses could even be subject to questioning by the accused if the defendant chooses to represent him or herself before the court. We will discuss protective measures for victim-witnesses in Chapter 10.

Tertiary victims may also experience fear and require protection. Certain types of crimes that target a specific group, such as hate crimes, impact the entire community. In such cases, other group members may feel enhanced fear for their own safety and that of their family, neighbours, and friends (Bowling, 1994; Wemmers, Lafontaine, & Viau, 2008). For example, concern about the large number of missing and murdered Indigenous women in Canada has led to calls for their protection (Amnesty International, 2004; Native Women's Association of Canada, 2014). Terrorist acts are intended to spread fear or "terror" throughout a community (Schmid & Jongman, 1988). Hence, the impact of terrorism reaches far beyond direct, indirect, and secondary victims since it targets the entire community. Besides fear, terrorist acts can also lead to anxiety, stress, and depression (Danieli, Engdahl, & Schlenger, 2004; Marshall, Picou, & Gill, 2003). These concerns are reflected in public demands to increase protection of vulnerable locations.

Information

The need for information is one of the most common needs expressed by victims (Davis & Mulford, 2008; Maguire, 1985; Ten Boom & Kuijpers, 2012; Wemmers & Cyr, 2006a). The need for information may be experienced by all categories of victims. Information can empower victims because it provides them with a sense of control over their affairs (Spreitzer, 1995). Empowerment requires that people understand the goals of their role in the criminal justice system and how their role fits within the larger system (Cyr, 2008).

Information is a fundamental need because without it victims may not be able to access services to satisfy their other needs. For example, without information about available compensation programs, a victim who is in need of financial support may not be able to access the program. The need for information can include information about available services, information about the criminal justice system and the progress of their case (Wemmers, 1996; Wemmers & Cyr 2006a), or information about crime prevention (Davis, Taylor, & Titus, 1997; Van den Bogaard, 1992; Wemmers, 2011a; Winkel, 1987). Indirect victims of homicide may need information about support services, compensation programs, as well as the criminal justice system (Armour, 2002).

Yet victims often do not have the information they need. Victims are typically not legal experts and do not have essential knowledge about how the criminal justice system works, nor are they necessarily familiar with all the different services for victims that exist in their area. A study in Quebec found that 60 per cent of victims whose cases were before the provincial courts said that they did not know where to seek help or information (Wemmers & Cyr, 2006a). The absence of information about procedures and services leaves victims feeling powerless (Cyr & Wemmers, 2011). Information is empowering, and research with victims whose cases were handled by the courts shows that when victims are provided information, they are more likely to feel that they were treated fairly and less likely to suffer PTSD symptoms (Morissette & Wemmers, 2016).

Reparation

Reparation can take many different forms. It can be restitution of stolen property, financial compensation for the victim or the victim's family members, an apology by the offender, or recognition of guilt and responsibility for the victim's suffering (Wemmers, 2014). Individual victims (direct, indirect, secondary) and communities can be harmed by victimization and may seek reparation.

Financial compensation is perhaps the most familiar form of reparation. As we saw in Chapter 4, the financial impact of victimization may be devastating for victims, their families, as well as their communities. Victims of property crimes more often express a need for financial compensation than victims of violence (Ten Boom & Kuijpers, 2012), even though the financial costs of violent crime outweigh those of property crime (Leung, 2004). State compensation programs will be discussed in Chapter 9, and compensation orders within in the context of the criminal justice system will be discussed in Chapter 10.

Besides material (e.g., compensation) and immaterial forms of reparation (e.g., apology), other forms of satisfaction, such as the arrest and punishment of the offender, are also considered reparative (Manirabona & Wemmers, 2014; Van Camp & Wemmers, 2013; Wemmers & Manirabona, 2014). Reparation can also include repairing relationships with the offender or with the wider community; this is referred to as *reconciliation* (Van der Merwe, 2008; Wemmers, 2014). Victims of violence who know their offender often express a need to repair the relationship with the offender (Ten Boom and Kuijpers, 2012). Sometimes victims of sexual violence by a known offender express the need to repair their relationship with other family members or with the community at large (Koss, 2014; Van Camp, 2014). Surviving relatives of victims of homicides, for example, sometimes want to confront the offender and tell him or her how the crime affected them and ask questions about the details of the murder (Armour, 2002; Van Camp, 2014). We will address reparative justice for victims in Chapter 11.

Practical Needs

Practical needs include a variety of applied tasks that victims may require help with, such as repairing a broken lock, cleaning up the mess left following a burglary, replacing stolen documents, and so on. A greater proportion of victims of property offences than violent offences express the need for practical help, such as making emergency repairs, transportation, domestic tasks, assistance with paperwork, translation services, and contacting companies (Ten Boom & Kuijpers, 2012). Victims of domestic violence may need alternate housing to get away from their aggressor. Often these practical needs become manifest immediately after the victimization and need to be addressed in a timely fashion (Baril, 1984).

Indirect victims, in particular those bereaved after a homicide, often express practical needs such as crisis management, help sorting out their loved one's belongings, as well as help dealing with the media (Armour, 2002; Ten Boom & Kuijpers, 2012). Following a horrific crime like murder, families can find themselves swarmed by the media. They often have no prior experience with the media and do not know how to handle the demands made on them, and all of this happens at a time when they are already under duress because of the sudden and tragic loss of their loved one.

Community members, or tertiary victims, may also need help dealing with the media. Following particularly horrific crimes, such as school shootings, the media often targets community members. These victims have been found to experience distress at exposure to media (Norris, 2007).

Victims' practical needs are not limited to the crime itself and may also arise as a result of the criminal justice response. If the case goes to court, victims may have practical needs such as help getting to the court and access to child-care services so that they can be in court to testify.

Need for Recognition

As we have seen, a victim's role in the criminal justice system is limited to that of witness to a crime against the state, and as a result victims are sometimes referred to as the "forgotten party" (Kirchhoff, 1994; Wemmers, 2003). This is a major source of dissatisfaction for victims, who often expect and want to play a more substantial role (Kelly, 1984; Shapland et al., 1985; Wemmers, 2009c). When victims are asked what role they think they should play in the criminal justice system, most feel that they should be consulted by authorities throughout the process (Kilchling, 1995; Shapland et al., 1985). They do not want decision-making power and feel that the burden of decision making should lie with authorities (Shapland et al., 1985; Wemmers & Cousineau, 2005; Wemmers & Cyr, 2004). However, they do want to have a voice in procedures so that decision makers can bear their concerns in mind when deciding the case (De Mesmaecker, 2014; Laxminarayan, Henrichs, & Pemberton, 2012; Wemmers, 1996; Wemmers & Cyr, 2006b). Recognition and consideration of victims' views and concerns are empowering and allow the victim to regain a sense of control or self-efficacy following the victimization (Cyr & Wemmers, 2011).

Victims' need for recognition begins with the police. Victims want and need the police to be respectful, positive, and supportive, particularly in their initial contacts with them (Shapland et al., 1985; Wemmers & Cyr, 2006a). Should a suspect be apprehended, victims expect the prosecutor to inform them of this, out of courtesy and respect (Shapland et al., 1985; Wemmers, 1996; Wemmers & Cyr, 2006b). It is not uncommon for victims to mistakenly view the prosecutor as "their lawyer," which inflates their expectations and their disappointment with regard to the prosecution (Herman, 2005; Shapland et al., 1985; Wemmers, 2008a). In court, while they expect impartiality from the judge, they do want the judge to show them interest and respect (Wemmers, 1996; Wemmers & Cyr, 2004). Victims wish to be consulted by the prosecutor and the judge, and while they do not seek to control the decisions, they do wish to be included in the process (Booth, 2016; Laxminarayan et al., 2012; Wemmers & Cyr, 2004).

Victim-centred prosecutorial policies recognize victims and encourage their input. In contrast, mandatory prosecution eliminates all input from the victim. Mandatory prosecution in cases of domestic violence became popular in the 1990s in an effort to protect the victim from possible intimidation by the offender (Dempsey, 2009). However, many researchers argue that mandatory prosecution policies disempower women and ultimately discourage them from going to the police at all (Ford, 1991; Davis, O'Sullivan, Farole, & Rempel, 2008; Wemmers & Cousineau, 2005; Wemmers & Cyr, 2016). Instead these researchers tend to endorse victim-centred prosecutorial policies, which promote victim empowerment and encourage input from victims. Finn (2013) compared the impact of victim-centred prosecutorial policies with those of mandatory prosecution in cases of domestic violence and found that victims whose cases were prosecuted in the jurisdictions employing victim-centred policies were less likely to experience violence again than victims whose cases were prosecuted in jurisdictions employing mandatory prosecutorial policies. By allowing victim input without burdening them with the responsibility of decision making, criminal justice authorities recognize and validate victims, which in turn can build their self-confidence and empower them (Cyr, 2008).

The need for recognition is not limited to direct victims and is common across different types of victims (Ten Boom & Kuijpers, 2012). Research with family members of homicide victims reveals that they too seek recognition and wish to have a voice in the criminal justice process (Armour, 2002). Recognition allows the victim to regain a sense of control, which is often lost following victimization (Armour, 2002; Symonds, 1980). In some cases, the community may seek recognition in the criminal justice process. Community impact statements were developed with this in mind (see Chapter 10).

Basic Human Needs

Several authors have pointed out the similarities between victims' needs and basic human needs (Ten Boom & Kuijpers, 2012; Wemmers & De Brouwer, 2011; Wemmers & Manirabona, 2014). The human needs framework helps us understand the relative importance of these needs and highlights their significance for all victims—direct, indirect, secondary, and tertiary victims.

One framework that has been used to understand victims' needs is Abraham Maslow's hierarchy of needs (Wemmers & De Brouwer, 2011; Wemmers & Manirabona, 2014). Maslow distinguishes five basic needs: (1) physiological (things like food and shelter as well as medical care), (2) safety and security, (3) belonging and acceptance, (4) self-esteem, and (5) what Maslow refers to as self-actualization (Maslow, 1968). The hierarchy indicates that certain needs come first, and higher-level needs can only be addressed when a person's lower needs are satisfied. Hence, the needs experienced by any one victim can change over time. Only once a victim's basic physiological needs have been met will other, higher-level needs, such as the need for acceptance by others, become apparent.

Another possible framework that may be helpful to understand victims' needs is Ervin Staub's theory of human needs (2003, 2004, 2007). Building on the work of Maslow and other human needs theorists, Staub focuses on six needs that are fundamental and shared: (1) the need for security, (2) the need for positive identity, (3) the need for a sense of effectiveness and control, (4) the need for positive connections to other people, (5) the need for autonomy, and (6) the need for a comprehension of the world and one's place in it. In terms of the underlying order of these six basic human needs, Staub views them all as equal, the only exception being security, which needs to be fulfilled before other needs can be addressed. According to Staub, fulfillment of basic needs leads to optimal human functioning, caring relationships with others, and continued personal growth. Staub posits that once these needs have reasonably been satisfied, the need for transcendence will emerge or the need to go beyond one's own material concerns and beyond the self (2003). Frustration of these basic needs can promote violence and hostility.

Justice is considered a basic human need by some authors (Taylor, 2003; Ten Boom & Kuijpers, 2012). Following their review of 33 studies on crime victims' needs, Ten Boom and Kuijpers (2012) examined the overlap between the needs of victims and fundamental human needs. They propose eight basic human needs: (1) physiological needs; (2) safety needs; (3) love, security, positive relations with others; (4) self-realization, independence, autonomy; (5) self-esteem, positive identity; (6) comprehension of reality; (7) effectiveness and control; and (8) justice. Most of these needs are found in the works of Maslow and Staub described above. While Staub (2003) suggests that justice may be another basic need, Ten Boom and Kuijpers argue that in the context of victimization one must include a basic human need for justice. The need for justice is multifaceted and includes the need for reparation as well as the need for punishment, accountability, and vindication (Daly, 2011; Herman, 2005; Parmentier & Weitekamp, 2007; Ten Boom & Kuijpers, 2012).

Prioritizing Needs

When faced with limited resources and seemingly unlimited needs, it is important to consider which needs ought to be given priority. Using human needs as a framework can help prioritize victims' needs. In the following pages we will examine the overlap between victims' needs and human needs based on Ten Boom and Kuijpers's (2012) framework of basic human needs for crime victims. It is important to bear in mind that because these needs are fundamental human needs they apply to all victims.

The first or primary needs of victims are their physiological needs. Medical assistance is a first priority. Failure to respond to victims' physiological needs would jeopardize their health and could put their life at risk. Financial assistance or compensation can also be important since it can provide victims with access to food, shelter, and medical services such as medications, which they might otherwise not be able to afford when they can no longer work. Many studies identify victims' need for emergency financial aid (Baril, 1984; Shapland et al., 1985; Shapland & Hall, 2007).

Second, victims need safety and security. This corresponds to victims' need for protection, which was discussed above. Besides protection from their offender or others, providing victims with information about the criminal justice process and crime prevention can reduce their feelings of insecurity and enhance their sense of safety (Van Camp, 2014; Van den Bos & Lind, 2002). Not feeling safe can inhibit the individual's functioning. For example, a person may stop going out and stop socializing with others, which in turn can further deteriorate his or her well-being. Victimization, in particular polyvictimization, constitutes a threat to the individual's sense of safety.

Once their primary needs are satisfied, other higher-level needs emerge. Using the human needs framework for victims' needs helps us to understand how the needs expressed by victims can change over time. The remaining basic needs are not hierarchical but are equally important (Staub, 2004; Ten Boom & Kuijpers, 2012). They are also interrelated. For example, a positive identity makes people feel good about themselves and enhances their self-esteem. Similarly, feeling that one understands reality can enhance the individual's sense of control as well as their autonomy.

Belonging and acceptance are reflected in victims' need for emotional support from family and friends (i.e., informal support) as well as from professionals. More broadly, in all of victims' dealings with criminal justice authorities they may seek reassurance that they are valued members of society (Orth, 2002; Wemmers, 1996). The need for information may also be a manifestation of the individual's need for belonging and acceptance. Communicating information to victims about the criminal justice process and the developments in their case sends the message that authorities recognize the victim as a valued member of the group (Colquitt, 2001; Wemmers, 1996, 2010a). Victims' need for reparation may also reflect a basic human need for belonging and acceptance in that reparation can provide victims with a sense of validation, recognition of their suffering, and confirmation that they are a valued member of society (Feldthusen, Hankivsky, & Greaves, 2000; Wemmers, 2006, 2014).

The basic human need for autonomy or self-realization corresponds with victims' need for a recognized role in the criminal justice system. Victims want a voice in the criminal justice process (Bazemore, 1999; Davis & Mulford, 2008;

Erez & Roberts, 2007; Shapland et al., 1985; Wemmers & Cyr, 2004). While they do not seek control over decisions, they do want to have input into those decisions (Wemmers, 1996; Wemmers & Cyr, 2004). Within the limits of their narrow role in the criminal justice system, victims express agency through their compliance or defiance. Victims can choose whether to report the crime and collaborate with authorities or not (Greeson & Campbell, 2011). In other words, when victims' basic human needs are not satisfied by the criminal justice system, victims may choose to leave the system, which in effect would negatively impact the system's ability to react to crime.

People need to feel good about themselves and the groups they belong to. This basic human need for self-esteem and positive identity is reflected in victims' need for recognition throughout the criminal justice process. While the need for information may stem from a need for security and certainty, receiving information and notification provides victims with recognition, which can make them feel good about themselves (Erez & Tontodonato, 1992; Wemmers & Raymond, 2011). Notifying victims about the progress of their case recognizes their interest in it (Morissette & Wemmers, 2016; Shapland et al., 1985; Wemmers, 1996). Support can also help victims recover their self-esteem and provide them with positive feedback. Reparation can nourish victims' self-esteem and validate their importance or value to society (Feldthusen et al., 2000; Wemmers, 2006, 2014).

The basic human need for effectiveness and control may be reflected in victims' need for information. Providing victims with information about the criminal justice system reduces uncertainty about what will happen and allows victims the chance to regain a sense of control and understanding (Carr, Logio, & Maier, 2003; Gray, 2005; Wemmers, 1999). Information about crime prevention can also help victims regain a sense of control (Fattah, 1999; Wemmers, 2011a). Studying victim empowerment, Cyr (2008) reports that many victims expressed frustration with their ineffectiveness in the criminal justice system and, therefore, victims tried to regain a sense of effectiveness in other ways. The need to achieve a sense of effectiveness and control may be why so many victims get involved in activism and lead the fight for change. There are countless examples of former victims who have become leaders in their community and advocates for victims' rights (see Kenney, 2010).

Humans need to comprehend events in the world around them, and this includes victimization. Making sense out of victimization is a mechanism for coping with stress. Giving an event meaning restores the person's sense of purpose and agency and re-establishes his or her perception of order in the world (Neimeyer, 2000; Armour, 2002; Herman, 2003; Gray, 2005; Cyr & Wemmers, 2011; Van Camp, 2014). Early studies with victims revealed that victims often ask "why me" (Bard & Sangry, 1979; Baril, 1984). One of the reasons why victims participate in restorative justice programs, which include meetings with offenders (see Chapter 11), is because they can ask questions about why this happened to them (Umbreit, Bradshaw, & Coates, 1999; Van Camp, 2014; Wemmers & Cyr, 2004). Victims are sometimes relieved when they learn that they were not targeted because of who they are or what they did but simply because they were in the wrong place at the wrong time (Strang, 2002; Wemmers & Cyr, 2004). Providing victims with information about the criminal justice system and the justice process may satisfy their need to comprehend or understand the criminal justice system, how it works, what is happening to their case, and why it is happening.

Justice

The need for justice can be approached in terms of just outcomes as well as just procedures (Tyler, 1990, 2000; Tyler & Lind, 1992). In the context of criminal victimization, just outcomes might include punishment of the offender and reparation. Much research has been done on the fair distribution of outcomes, which is also known as *distributive justice* (Deutsch, 1975). Not surprisingly, the distribution of outcomes affects the well-being of those involved, and perceived injustice causes stress (Deutsch, 1985; Vermunt & Steensma, 2008). Deutsch (1975, 1985) identifies three different rules of the fair distribution of outcomes: equity, equality, and need.

- *Equity* or merit means increasing the distribution according to the value and contribution of the individual to his or her social group. It reflects the notion of proportional outcomes. For example, an offender is given more or less punishment depending on his or her contribution or responsibility for the crime.
- *Equality* means giving an equal outcome to everyone. Equality in sentencing implies that similar crimes should receive similar sentences.
- *Need* means providing resources based not on performance but on what a person requires for his or her well-being. This might mean providing reparation for victims based on their level of need.

According to Deutsch (1975), in any situation the rules governing fair distributions depend on the kind of social goods and resources being distributed as well as sociohistorical circumstances. Equity should be the main principle of distributive justice in cooperative relations in which the primary goal is economic productivity. If the goal is fostering or maintaining good social relations, the dominant principle should be equality. If, however, the primary goal is fostering personal development and personal welfare, then need should be the dominant principle of distributive justice.

Just procedures refer to how outcomes or decisions are reached (Thibaut & Walker, 1975; Tyler & Lind, 1992; Van den Bos & Lind, 2002; Wemmers, 2010a). Procedural justice is a crucial variable in understanding victims' evaluations of criminal proceedings (Bradford, 2011; Lind & Tyler, 1988; Orth, 2002; Tyler, 1990; Wemmers, 1996). It is argued that fair procedures have two dimensions: (1) quality of treatment (being treated with dignity and respect) and (2) quality of decision making (neutrality, honesty) (Blader & Tyler, 2003; Tyler, 2005; Wemmers, 1996, 2010a). These two components can be broken down further into formal rules and procedures (i.e., the rights of victims) and the informal treatment of victims by authorities (Blader & Tyler, 2003). Informal treatment is also referred to as *interactional justice*, or the interpersonal treatment people receive as procedures are enacted (Bies, 2008; Colquitt, 2001; Greenberg, 1993).

In general, research on procedural justice has revealed four important determinants or characteristics of fair procedures: (1) voice, (2) standing, (3) neutraility, and (4) trust (De Mesmaecker, 2014; Tyler, 2000; Tyler & Lind, 1992; Wemmers, 2010a; Wemmers, Van der Leeden, & Steensma, 1995). *Voice* or process control, as it is otherwise known, refers to the extent to which victims are able to present information throughout the criminal justice process (Folger, 1977; Thibaut & Walker, 1975; Tyler & Huo, 2002; Van den Bos, 1996, 2008). According to Thibaut and Walker (1975), process control allows those involved in decisions (i.e., victims) to maintain a certain measure of control over the decision-making process by providing input into information that was presented during the trial. As we have seen, research shows that victims seek a voice in the criminal justice process: They want to be consulted and have their concerns taken into consideration (Booth, 2016; Wemmers, 1996, 2010a).

Standing is defined as being treated with dignity and respect and showing respect for the rights of the individual (Tyler & Lind, 1992). Tyler and Lind's relational model of procedural justice is built on the notion of group value and assumes that people want to feel like valued members of the group. Fair procedures have a normative value and send a message to the individual about his or her value or standing in the group (Lind & Tyler, 1988). Showing respect includes considering victims and their interests, providing victims with information, and notifying them of the developments in their case (Carr et al., 2003; De Mesmaecker, 2014; Wemmers, 1996; Wemmers & Raymond, 2011). When victims are treated with dignity and respect, they feel better and suffer less stress symptoms (Orth & Maercker, 2004; Vermunt & Steensma, 2008; Wemmers, 2013). In other words, respecting victims' rights to information, participation, and reparation sends a message that they are important and respected by others.

Neutrality refers to honesty, the absence of bias, and making informed decisions based on the facts of the case. People want authorities such as the police and judges to be impartial and free from any bias (Leventhal, Karuza, & Fry, 1980; Orth, 2002; Wemmers, 1996; Wemmers & Cyr, 2004). Justice must be seen to be done (Lind & Tyler, 1988). As much as victims want authorities to find and punish their offender, and they complain about the length of time that trials take, they are not willing to sacrifice accuracy for speed and do not want an innocent person to be punished for a crime they did not commit either (Lind et al., 1989).

Trust is directed at the individual's concerns about the authority's intentions. Unlike voice, neutrality, and standing, trust can be both a determinant and a consequence of procedural justice (Tyler, 2003; Tyler & Huo, 2002; Van den Bos & Lind, 2002; Wemmers & Manirabona, 2014). In other words, when victims are treated fairly it enhances their trust in the criminal justice system. At the same time, when people trust authorities, they are more likely to think that they were treated fairly and will be supportive of authorities even when the authorities were not in fact objectively fair (Tyler & Lind, 1992; Jost & Banaji, 1994; Starzyck, Gaucher, Boese, & Neufeld, 2014). However, trust is not unwavering, and once it is lost it may be difficult for authorities to regain (Van den Bos & Lind, 2002). Providing victims with voice and a sense that their concerns are being heard enhances their confidence in the criminal justice system (Bradford, 2011; Wemmers, 1996, 1999).

The agreement between victims' expressed needs and basic human needs requires that we include the basic need for justice, which implies that when we respond to the needs of crime victims we are simply treating them fairly and with respect for their dignity. Failure to meet an individual's basic human needs results in frustration and conflict, while fulfillment of basic human needs fosters effective functioning and growth (Staub, 2003). Hence, the realization of victims' basic human needs is important for their well-being.

Table 6.1 provides an overview of basic human needs and the needs expressed by victims of crime.

Secondary Victimization

The notion of secondary victimization is a basic concept in victimology that is found in most introductory textbooks (see Davis, Lurigio, & Skogan, 1997; Doerner & Lab, 2005; Karmen, 2010; Wemmers, 2003). Martin Symonds (1980) first introduced the idea of secondary victimization, or "second injury" as he called it, in 1980. According to Symonds, following the loss of control that often accompanies criminal victimization, victims seek recognition and

TABLE 6.1: Overview of Basic Human Needs and Victims' Expressed Needs

BASIC HUMAN NEED	NEEDS EXPRESSED BY VICTIMS
Physiological	Support: medical needs; rehabilitation Reparation: compensation/restitution (food, shelter, medication)
Safety and security	Protection; information
Belonging and acceptance	Emotional support; information (notification); reparation
Autonomy/self-realization	Information; recognition (consultation, voice); reparation (compensation)
Self-esteem/positive identity	Recognition; information; reparation
Effectiveness and control	Information; recognition (voice, consideration of views)
Comprehension of reality	Support; information; reparation
Justice	Reparation; recognition; information

support. He claims that professional but distant reactions from authorities can leave victims feeling rejected and not supported, which as we have seen are basic human needs. Other authors emphasize the ill treatment of victims by authorities. For example, according to Williams (1984), secondary victimization results from negative, judgmental attitudes directed toward victims of crime. Similarly, Maguire (1991) describes secondary victimization as exacerbating victims' distress by unsympathetic reactions, including blame for inviting the incident. What these definitions all have in common is the idea that victims are injured once by the crime and a second time by the reactions of others— in particular criminal justice authorities and their failure to respond to the victim's needs. Since the 1970s, when the first studies on victims' experiences with the criminal justice system appeared, numerous studies report that victims often feel victimized a second time when faced with insensitive reactions by authorities (Holmstrom & Burgess, 1978; Goodrum, 2007; Orth, 2002; Parsons & Bergin, 2010; Veronen & Kilpatrick, 1980; Wemmers, 2014). Victims of property crimes (Kunst, Rutten, & Knijf, 2013; Maguire, 1985), violent crimes (Parsons & Bergin, 2010), as well as indirect victims (Amick-McMullan, Kilpatrick, Veronen, & Smith, 1989; Armour, 2002; Goodrum, 2007) have all been found to experience secondary victimization.

Victims who are traumatized by their victimization appear to be at greater risk of secondary victimization (Campbell & Raja, 1999, 2005). This may be because traumatized victims have greater needs, such as the need for validation and acceptance, and are therefore more vulnerable (Wemmers, 2013). According to Campbell (2005, 2008) the higher risk of secondary victimization found among traumatized victims may be due to traumatic memory or the way victims piece together their memories of the event following the trauma of victimization. Memories of traumatic events can come together slowly and emerge over time. Questioned by a police officer immediately after the crime, the victim may only recall fragments of the event. More might come back over time and, to an untrained police officer, it may appear that the victim is making it up.

Secondary victimization can occur at all stages of the criminal justice process, and negative experiences may accumulate over time. Victims' evaluations of the criminal justice system appear to worsen over time as their cases make their way through the courts (Shapland et al., 1985; Wemmers & Cyr, 2006a). Certain phases of the criminal justice process, such as the trial process, can be particularly upsetting for victims (Calhoun, Atkeson, & Resick, 1982; Epstein, Saunders, & Kilpatrick, 1997; Herman, 2003; Orth, 2002). Criminal justice workers' responsibility to build a strong case for the state leads them to place the state's interest ahead of victims' interests. Victims who are not a witness, such as bereaved victims who have lost a family member to homicide, are not a priority for criminal justice authorities and, as a result, victims may feel completely excluded and ignored (Goodrum, 2007).

Therapeutic Jurisprudence

The notion of secondary victimization in victimology resembles the work on therapeutic jurisprudence in legal academia. Therapeutic jurisprudence views legal rules, legal procedures, and the roles of legal actors (such as lawyers and judges) as social forces that produce behaviours and consequences, which are sometimes therapeutic and sometimes anti-therapeutic for the individuals affected by the law (Wexler & Winick, 1991, 1996; Winick, 1997, 2000). This approach draws our attention to the emotional and psychological side of law and the legal process. Therapeutic jurisprudence is not a theory, but a way of looking at the law. It calls for the study of these consequences to identify them and determine whether the law's anti-therapeutic effects (i.e., secondary victimization) can be reduced while enhancing its therapeutic effects without subordinating due process and other justice values (Winick, 1997).

According to therapeutic jurisprudence, lawmakers and those who apply the law must be aware of its effects on the mental health of those involved (Wexler & Winick, 1991; Winick, 2000). As Herman (2003, 2005) points out, a court of law is particularly effective for provoking intrusive post-traumatic symptoms.

However, fair procedures are considered to be therapeutic (Waldman, 1998; Wexler & Winick, 1991). In other words, when victims feel they have been treated fairly it helps their recovery from their victimization. Victims who are treated fairly in the criminal justice system tend to suffer less PTSD symptoms and recover more quickly than victims who feel they were treated unfairly (Angel et al., 2009; Orth, 2002; Morissette & Wemmers, 2016; Wemmers, 2013).

Lawmakers and those who apply the law must be aware of how the law affects the mental health of victims. Trauma-informed approaches to law avoid retraumatizing victims (Randall & Haskell, 2013). Satisfaction with the criminal justice system has been found to be positively associated with post-trauma adjustment among victims of violence (Armour, 2002; Byrne, Kilpatrick, Howley, & Beatty, 1999; Campbell et al., 1999; Campbell & Raja, 1999; Kilpatrick, Saunders, Veronen, Best, & Von, 1987; Kunst et al., 2013). While much of the available research on secondary victimization is correlational, which does not allow us to draw conclusions about the direction of the relationship between well-being and treatment, a few studies have used repeated measures and followed victims over time. These studies suggest that negative experiences with the criminal justice system can slow victims' recovery (Cluss, Boughton, Frank, Stewart, & West, 1983; Wemmers, 2013). Victims' satisfaction is positively correlated with policies favouring their inclusion and participation in the justice system (Erez, 1999; Wemmers, 1996). We will discuss victim participation in criminal justice in Chapter 10.

How authorities treat victims affects not only how victims cope with their victimization but also how they rebuild their view of society and, in particular, the criminal justice system. Victim collaboration is important for law enforcement. Without it, the detection and prosecution of crime becomes difficult. Moreover, for certain types of crime, such as sexual violence, it is important that victims report the crime to the police as soon as possible since it will impact the successful prosecution of the case (Patterson & Campbell, 2010). Yet, as we saw in Chapter 3, most victims do not report their victimization to police, and for some types of crime, such as sexual assault, the rate of nonreporting is extremely high. How victims are treated by the criminal justice system can impact their participation in the system in the future (Patterson & Campbell, 2010; Shapland et al., 1985). The more experiences individuals have as a victim, the less satisfied they are with the police and the less likely they are to report the crime (Van Dijk, 1999). Victims should be treated properly to prevent them from losing confidence in the police and becoming cynical about the rule of law (Bradford, 2011; Wemmers, 1996). Given the critical role that victims play in the criminal justice system as witnesses, authorities should aim to reduce the risk of secondary victimization by treating victims with dignity and respecting their rights.

Conclusion

In this chapter we examined victims' needs and secondary victimization. Many of the needs expressed by victims are essentially basic human needs. Failure to satisfy fundamental human needs results in frustration, stress, and secondary victimization, which ultimately undermines victims' collaboration with criminal justice authorities. Secondary victimization matters because it inflicts unnecessary suffering on people and hinders their recovery process. While it is not possible to satisfy all needs of all victims, and criminal justice cannot guarantee victims positive outcomes, efforts can and should be made to treat victims with dignity and respect. Justice is a process, not just an end. Procedural justice is important for victims' well-being and their satisfaction with justice. It is essential to consider how the law and legal authorities impact crime victims. Without subordinating due process and other justice values, every effort should be made to reduce the negative effects and enhance the positive effects of the criminal justice system on victims.

CHAPTER 7

VICTIMS' RIGHTS

Beginning in the 1980s, many Western countries, including Canada, decided to grant a more important status to victims of crime. As we saw in Chapter 1, since the Middle Ages the state has gradually come to replace the victim in the prosecution of the accused. Criminal liability, as currently perceived in Canada, views crime as an attack on social order rather than an attack on one victim in particular. Victims were the forgotten party in criminal justice (Waller, 2011). That began to change when an effort was made to improve the situation of victims within the criminal justice system. In this chapter we will look at the emergence of victims' rights, both nationally and internationally.

In Canada, criminal jurisdiction is shared between the federal government and the provinces under the *Constitution Act, 1867*. The federal government has legislative authority with respect to criminal law, whereas the provinces are responsible for the administration of justice through the courts. This is important with regard to victims' rights, since the two levels of government each have a responsibility toward victims. Hence, to understand victims' rights in Canada we need to consider federal as well as provincial and territorial laws.

In this chapter we will consider victims' rights using a human rights framework. Following a brief presentation of major victims' rights instruments, we will address the consequences of considering victims' rights as human rights. We will also examine jurisdictions that have made significant advances in recognizing victims as persons before the law.

The UN Declaration

A significant development both for Canada and the international community was the adoption in 1985 by the United Nations General Assembly of the *Declaration of Basic Principles of Justice for Victims of Crime and Abuse of Power* (hereinafter "the UN Declaration"). Some experts refer to it as the

Magna Carta of victims' rights legislation (McGonigle-Leyh, 2011; Waller, 2011). Incidentally, Canada was active in securing the adoption of the UN Declaration (Rock, 1986).

According to the UN Declaration, "'victims' means persons who, individually or collectively, have suffered harm" as a result of a crime or a criminal abuse of power (UN General Assembly, 1985, art. 1; see Appendix 1 for the complete text of the UN Declaration). This is a very broad definition. Besides direct victims, it includes indirect victims (i.e., immediate family of the direct victim) as well as secondary victims (e.g., good Samaritans) and tertiary victims. While the definition focuses on persons, thus excluding organizations or businesses that are victimized, it includes both individual and collective victimizations. Typically, Western criminology has focused on individual crimes and victimizations (Hagan, Rymond-Richmond, & Parker, 2005). However, in recent years criminology has (re)discovered certain crimes, such as genocide, crimes against humanity, and war crimes, which target entire groups and constitute a form of collective victimization (Hagan et al., 2005; Volhardt, 2012). The inclusion of collective victimization as well as victims of abuse of power constitutes innovative elements of the UN Declaration. We will return to the question of collective victimization in Chapter 12 when we discuss the International Criminal Court.

The UN Declaration reflects a human rights approach to victimology and includes both victims of crimes and victims of abuse of power. It is noteworthy that the Declaration refers to "basic principles . . . relating to victims," rather than to victims' rights. While this is a soft law instrument rather than a legal document spelling out detailed obligations, it nevertheless constitutes a basis for minimum standards in the treatment of victims that governments are bound to respect in their domestic legislation (Wemmers, 2003). It lists a series of principles of justice relating to victims: (1) access to justice and fair treatment, which includes information, participation, and protection; (2) a right to restitution; (3) access to compensation from the state; and (4) access to victim assistance services.

One of the most important advances achieved by the UN Declaration, however, consisted of the procedural rights described in article 6, which refers to "allowing the views and concerns of victims to be presented and considered at appropriate stages of the proceedings where their personal interests are affected, without prejudice to the accused and consistent with the relevant national criminal justice system." It is worth noting that this fundamental instrument for victims' rights was adopted unanimously by the United Nations General Assembly, despite the diversity of the legal systems of member states and the contradictions between them. In particular, there are significant differences between common law countries, where the victim is traditionally relegated to the role of a witness, and civil law countries, where victims are given more procedural rights, up to and including the status of a party at trial.

However, unanimous adoption was not achieved without compromise, and article 6(b) of the Declaration provides a perfect example. The introduction of the right to participate generated lively debate during the drafting of the Declaration, particularly on the part of the United Kingdom and the Netherlands, which argued for reducing the scope of the victim's right to participate through the addition of the second part of the provision relating to the right of the accused to a fair trial (McGonigle-Leyh, 2011). Hence, when a jurisdiction allows victims' views and concerns to be presented, it must also take into consideration the rights of the accused. Victims' rights, therefore, are not absolute, but are to be given their due proportion. Consequently, article 6(b) represents a compromise, drafted in terms that are broad enough to allow governments wide discretion in implementing the UN Declaration within their respective criminal justice systems (Bitti, 2011; McGonigle-Leyh, 2011; Wemmers, 2003).

Since the adoption of the Declaration in 1985, there have been attempts to anchor victims' rights in hard law by introducing an international convention of rights for victims of crime, abuse of power, and terrorism. Unlike a declaration, which is nonbinding, a convention is binding and includes provisions for monitoring its implementation. As a result, conventions require ratification by member states. However, to date such efforts have not been successful (Van Genugten, Van Gestel, Groenhuijsen, & Letschert, 2006; World Society of Victimology, 2010).

After the adoption of the UN Declaration, some member states made changes to their criminal justice system to grant certain rights—procedural, economic, or social—to the victims of crime (Groenhuijsen, 1999). In the following pages we will discuss how Canada modified its Criminal Code to accommodate the UN Declaration.

Canada's Reforms

As a member of the United Nations, Canada had an obligation to implement the UN Declaration. To this end, in 1988 the federal and provincial justice departments endorsed the Canadian Statement of Basic Principles of Justice for Victims of Crime (hereinafter "the Canadian statement"). They agreed to adopt this statement of victims' rights to provide guidance and establish a standard for any legislative or administrative initiative in the area of criminal justice in Canada.

By and large, the Canadian statement corresponds with the UN standards. It calls for victims of crime to be treated with courtesy, compassion, and respect; to receive prompt, fair reparation for any harm suffered; to be provided with information about available victim assistance services; and to have their views taken into consideration. Both instruments refer only to principles and do not give victims enforceable rights. Like the UN Declaration, the Canadian statement does not indicate in any precise or practical way who is required to abide by these principles. However, it is important to bear in mind that the ambiguity found in the UN Declaration was born of necessity: The Declaration had to be sufficiently abstract to apply to all of the different domestic criminal justice systems that exist within the almost 200 countries that are members of the United Nations. In contrast, Canada has only one Criminal Code that applies across the entire country. It would have been both possible and desirable to provide much more clarity and precision when interpreting the UN standards and norms to the Canadian situation. Who should inform victims? What information should they receive? When should they receive it? Without indicating who is responsible for what, the guidelines provide a lot of room for interpretation and offer little more than good intentions (Fattah, 2001). The failure to provide precise and practical information about who is required to abide by these principles is an obstacle for the coherent implementation of the guidelines (Brienen & Hoegen, 2000).

Some topics found in the UN Declaration were not included in the Canadian statement. For example, it did not contain a definition of "victim." The title seems to suggest that the Canadian statement relates to victims of crime, but without a clear definition it is impossible to know whether it applies to indirect, secondary, and tertiary victims as well. Unlike the UN Declaration, the Canadian statement excluded victims of abuse of power. It also did not specifically make mention of government-run compensation programs for victims, which is often fundamental for victims' successful recovery. The Canadian statement also did not include collective victimizations, which is part of the definition of "victim" in the UN Declaration. The Canadian statement did, however, add that victims are required to cooperate with judicial authorities, which is something not found in the UN Declaration.

The Canadian statement was introduced together with Bill C-89, which modified the Criminal Code. Specifically, this Bill introduced victim impact statements (art. 722) into the Criminal Code, and with it the word "victim" appeared in the Criminal Code for the first time (Laurin & Viens, 1996). We will discuss victim impact statements in Chapter 10 when we examine victims in the criminal justice process. However, it is important to mention Bill C-89 here because it also created the victim surcharge (art. 737), which carried important implications for the provinces and territories. The victim surcharge, which is sometimes referred to as a victim tax, imposes an additional fee on offenders, and the money it generates is supposed to pay for victim services in the provinces and territories. The victim surcharge allowed the government to introduce new services for victims at a time when government spending was undergoing cuts (Wemmers, 2003).

Fifteen years later, in 2003, the federal, provincial, and territorial ministers of justice endorsed a revised version of the statement. Essentially, the new Canadian statement matched the content of the previous one, except that it no longer contained the requirement for victims to cooperate with judicial authorities. It did not, however, contain any more details than the first statement did regarding who is responsible for implementing victims' rights, how they are to be implemented, and when or at what stages in the criminal justice process they should be implemented. It merely embodied a list of good intentions with respect to victims without providing victims any real rights.

Recently, the federal government introduced the *Canadian Victims Bill of Rights* (hereinafter "the Bill of Rights"). The Bill of Rights, which came into force on 23 July 2015, provides for statutory rights for victims of crime. In it, victims are defined as "an individual who has suffered physical or emotional harm, property damage or economic loss as the result of the commission or alleged commission of an offence" (s. 2). Section 3 (a–e) of the Bill of Rights specifies that if the direct victim is dead or incapable of acting on his or her own behalf, the victim's partner, relatives, dependents, or legal guardian may exercise the rights on behalf of their loved one. Together, this seems to suggest that only direct victims are considered victims unless they are unable to assume their rights, and then an indirect victim may do so on their behalf.

The Bill of Rights provides victims with a right to (1) information, (2) protection, (3) participation, and (4) restitution. A complete copy of the Bill of Rights can be found in Appendix 2. The Bill of Rights provides several specific rights with respect to information (s. 6–8). Victims have a right to information about the criminal justice system and their role in it; the services and programs available, including restorative justice programs; as well as notification about the status and outcome of the investigation and the proceedings. These rights are not new and can be found in the earlier Canadian statements as well. Victims are also entitled to certain information about the offender or the accused. However, the provision of information is not automatic, and the Bill of Rights clearly indicates that victims need to make a request for information and only when they request information do they have a right to receive it. This requires that victims know their rights and are aware of what they can ask for.

In addition, the Bill of Rights is no more specific than its predecessors in terms of identifying at what stages in the criminal justice process these rights apply and who is responsible for implementing them. One might argue that this is because the administration of justice is under provincial and territorial jurisdiction and the federal government has respected this division of powers.

However, these are statutory rights that have been written into Canada's laws; for example, the Criminal Code already contains extensive procedural law when it comes to matters such as arrests. The identification of victims' rights in federal law ensures a basic level of consistency and coherence with respect to the application of victims' rights across the country, but it would have been both possible and desirable for the Bill of Rights to have been more specific to ensure that all victims everywhere in Canada are treated equally (Manikis, 2015).

With respect to protection (s. 9–13), the Bill of Rights recognizes victims' right to have their security considered by appropriate authorities in the criminal justice system (s. 9) and for authorities to take reasonable and necessary measures to protect the victim from intimidation and retaliation (s. 10). Victims' right to privacy and protection of their identity as well as their right to request testimonial aids when appearing as a witness are recognized as well. Much of the legislation on which these rights are based has existed since the 1980s. For example, in cases of sexual assault and cases involving juvenile victims a publication ban is imposed automatically, which means that the media cannot publish victims' names in order to protect their privacy.

Concerning participation (s. 14–15), the Bill of Rights specifies that when victims' interests are affected they have the right to convey their views about decisions made by judicial authorities and to have those views considered. However, it does not indicate exactly when victims' interests are affected. One could argue that victims' interests are always impacted when it concerns their victimization. However, there is strong opposition to such a position, and opponents of victim participation would like to see victim participation limited to an absolute minimum (Blondel, 2008; Cassell, Mitchell, & Edwards, 2014). For example, in the United States and at the International Criminal Court there has been considerable debate concerning whether or not victims' right to participation applies during the criminal investigation stage or whether it only begins at the time of the criminal trial (Wemmers, 2010b; Cassell et al., 2014). Hence, the lack of specificity in the Canadian Bill of Rights is regrettable. We will return to the question of victim participation in the criminal justice system in Chapter 10.

Many of the legal provisions referred to in the Bill of Rights, including restitution, are not new and already existed within the Criminal Code. The Bill of Rights simply draws attention to these rights. Regarding reparation, the Bill of Rights specifies that victims have the right to have the court consider ordering the offender to pay restitution to the victim (s. 16–17). Unlike the UN Declaration, which includes provisions regarding restitution and compensation, the Bill of Rights does not make any mention of government-run compensation for victims. If the Bill of Rights is considered Canada's response to the requirements of the UN Declaration, then it falls short of the international standards regarding victim compensation. We will discuss compensation for victims in detail in Chapter 9.

Unlike previous Canadian statements, the Bill of Rights includes a section on remedies (s. 25–26). However, it stops short of providing victims with enforceable rights (Campbell, 2015). Instead, it ensures victims have the right to file a complaint when their rights have been infringed or denied by a federal department. When victims' rights have been infringed or denied by a provincial or territorial department, which as we will see is the case throughout most of the criminal justice process, they are referred to the laws of the province or territory.

Provinces and Territories

Following the adoption of the UN Declaration and introduction of the first *Canadian Statement of Basic Principles of Justice for Victims of Crime* in 1988, many of the provinces and territories passed their own legislation regarding victims of crime. In general, these laws consist of three parts: Part one describes victims' rights, part two establishes the creation of a central office or committee for victim services, and part three establishes the creation of a victim services fund for the victim surcharges. Today all provinces and territories have victims of crime legislation in one form or another.

The rights or services included in these documents largely correspond with those found in the UN Declaration and the subsequent Canadian statement, such as the right to information, protection, participation, and restitution. However, like the Canadian statement, these laws tend to exclude compensation, which is dealt with in separate legislation (see Chapter 9). The texts are so similar they often use the same vague wording; for example, emphasizing victims' right to be treated with "courtesy, compassion and respect" without specifying who is responsible for what. One exception is the Manitoba *Victims' Bill of Rights*, which breaks down victims' rights with respect to the different actors in the criminal justice system, namely law enforcement agencies, the prosecution division, the court division, and the corrections division (Manikis, 2015; Wemmers & April-Ménard, 2013). First adopted in 1999, Manitoba's *Victims' Bill of Rights* replaced the previous *Victims' Rights Act* and has since undergone several modifications. This *Victims' Bill of Rights* uses strong and clear language, avoiding the ambiguous language found in most other victims' rights laws. It states clearly that authorities "must" provide victims with certain information regarding their rights and available services, and it goes into considerable detail about what information must be provided by which authorities. When rights are written in clear and precise language it enhances the likelihood that they will be properly implemented (Brienen & Hoegen, 2000).

Many of the provincial and territorial laws are passive in their approach, emphasizing victims' right to request information rather than the justice authorities' responsibility to offer information. As described above, Manitoba's *Victims' Bill of Rights* obliges authorities to provide victims with information about their rights, but other information, such as notification about developments in their case, requires that the victim make a request. In contrast, Yukon's *Victims of Crime Act* (2011) takes a more proactive approach to the provision of information. Rather than emphasizing victims' right to request information, the act focuses on victims' right to receive information. It specifies that unless victims choose not to receive information, they should be informed (art. 8).

Many of these provincial and territorial laws include a definition of victims. In most cases, the word "victim" is reserved for the individuals who are the direct victims of crime and, in the case of death, their family, who can act on their behalf. Only Yukon and Quebec also allow indirect victims to act on the victim's behalf if he or she is unable to do so. In addition, the Northwest Territories and Nunavut (*Victims of Crime Act*, RSNWT 1988[7]) are unique in that they recognize as victims persons who individually or "collectively" have suffered harm. As we saw earlier, collective victimization is included in the UN Declaration, but it is not included in the Canadian Bill of Rights, which instead focuses on individual victims.

Regarding the enforcement of rights, the Canadian Bill of Rights refers to provincial and territorial laws (art. 26). However, none of the provincial and territorial laws provides enforceable rights for victims. They all contain escape clauses, limiting the rights of victims and explicitly specifying that the availability of resources may limit victims' rights. Most, like Ontario and Quebec, do not provide any information regarding remedies (see Box 7.1). At best, they include a complaints procedure. For example, Yukon's *Victims of Crime Act* creates a director of victim services within the Department of Justice. The director is tasked with receiving complaints from victims who feel that their rights, as outlined in the federal Bill of Rights, were not respected (art. 11.2.b).

Manitoba's *Victims' Bill of Rights* goes even further and includes a detailed complaints procedure. Victims who feel that their rights were not respected can make a complaint to the director of victims services who "must investigate each complaint" (art. 28.2) and provide the victim with a report on the investigation "within 30 days" (art. 28.3), although an extension of time is possible under certain conditions (art. 29). It specifies what information must be included in the report (art. 28.4) and that the victim must have an opportunity

....

7 In Nunavut, the *Victims of Crime Act* was adopted from the Northwest Territories after Nunavut became its own territory in 1999.

BOX 7.1: ONTARIO'S *VICTIMS' BILL OF RIGHTS*, 1995[8]

Principles

1. Victims should be treated with courtesy, compassion and respect for their dignity and privacy by justice system officials.
2. Victims should have access to information about,
    i. The services and remedies available to victims of crime,
    ii. The provisions of this Act and of the *Compensation for Victims of Crime Act* that might assist them,
    iii. The protection available to victims to prevent unlawful intimidation,
    iv. The progress of investigations that relate to the crime,
    v. The charges laid with respect to the crime and, if no charges are laid, the reasons why no charges are laid,
    vi. The victim's role in the prosecution,
    vii. Court procedures that relate to the prosecution,
    viii. The dates and places of all significant proceedings that relate to the prosecution, the outcome of all significant proceedings, including any proceedings on appeal,
    ix. Any pre-trial arrangements that are made that relate to a plea that may be entered by the accused at trial,
    x. The interim release and, in the event of conviction, the sentencing of an accused,
    xi. Any disposition made under section 672.54 or 672.58 of the Criminal Code in respect of an accused who is found unfit to stand trial or who is found not criminally responsible on account of mental disorder, and,
    xii. Their right under the Criminal Code to make representations to the court by way of a victim impact statement.
3. A victim should, if he or she so requests, be notified of,
    i. Any application for release or any impending release of the convicted person, including release in accordance with a program of temporary absence, on parole or on an unescorted temporary absence pass, and
    ii. Any escape of the convicted person from custody.

....
8 Note that this is an abridged version of Ontario's Bill of Rights; the complete text can be accessed at www.ontario.ca/laws/statute/95v06.

4. If the person accused of a crime is found unfit to stand trial or is found not criminally responsible on account of mental disorder, the victim should, if he or she so requests, be notified of,
    i.   Any hearing held with respect to the accused by the Review Board,
    ii. Any order of the Review Board directing the absolute or conditional discharge of the accused, and
    iii. Any escape of the accused from custody.
5. Victims of sexual assault should, if the victim so requests, be interviewed during the investigation of the crime only by police officers and officials of the same gender as the victim.
6. A victim's property that is in the custody of justice system officials should be returned promptly where the property is no longer needed for the purposes of the justice system.

Limitations

The principles set out above are subject to the availability of resources and information, what is reasonable in the circumstances of the case, what is consistent with the law and the public interest and what is necessary to ensure that the resolution of criminal proceedings is not delayed.

No new cause of action, right or appeal, claim or other remedy exists because of this section or anything done or omitted to be done under this section.

to comment on the report. The act further specifies that the director must publish an annual report regarding complaints (art. 31.1) and that the report must be tabled before the province's Legislative Assembly (art. 31.2).

The importance of victims' rights was made painfully clear in the case of Vanscoy and Even, two victims of violent crime in the province of Ontario who hired a lawyer to represent them as they pursued an action against the province for its failure to respect their rights as outlined in the Ontario *Victims' Bill of Rights*. Karen Vanscoy's young daughter had been shot and killed in 1996, and Linda Even was permanently crippled in a stabbing attack. The victims argued that their rights had been violated because they were not notified of pending court dates and not consulted with respect to plea resolution agreements. Justice Gerald Day of the Ontario Court of Justice dismissed the case, stating "I conclude that the Legislature did not intend for the Victims Bill of Rights to provide rights to the victims of crime" (*Vanscoy v. Ontario*, [1999]

OJ No 1661 (Ont SCJ)). In his decision, Judge Day argued that the precatory language used in the Bill of Rights meant that they were mere recommendations, which did not provide the victims any claim before the courts. According to Judge Day, rights without remedy are not rights.

Hence, for most victims in Canada, if their rights are not respected there is little they can do about it. By providing victims with a complaints procedure, provinces such as Manitoba recognize that victims' rights should be respected. However, without legal recourse, victims' rights are not real rights (Beloof, 2005; Manikis, 2015; Wemmers, 2012).

Rights and Human Rights

Throughout this chapter we have used the word "right" without examining the meaning of it. The above decision by an Ontario Court judge that the Bill of Rights was not meant to give victims rights raises the question "What is a right?" The word "right" has several different meanings. For instance, it has a moral and a political meaning: rectitude and entitlement (Donnelly, 2003). In the context of victims' rights, we are especially concerned with rights in the sense of entitlement or something that one may do. We typically speak of someone "having" a right. For example, a person has the right to freedom of speech. But more than just the ability to act, rights are enforceable. They bring with them an obligation to respect a person's right. For example, we are obliged to respect someone's freedom of speech, even if we do not agree with what they are saying. We can, however, impose limitations on rights—rights are not endless. It is generally accepted that one person's rights stop where another person's rights begin (Baril, 1985). To continue with the same example, a person has the right to freedom of speech, but they cannot abuse that right to transmit messages that are racist or sexist.

Human rights are basic rights, and it is generally believed that all people should have these rights since without them we are unable to live as humans and develop to our full potential. Human rights have four major characteristics: They are universal, inherent, indivisible, and inalienable (Donnelly, 2003). *Universal* means that they apply to human beings everywhere. *Inherent* refers to the fact that they are intrinsic to being human and do not rely on codification or some other external validation to exist. *Indivisible* means that these rights are interdependent and interrelated and therefore cannot be prioritized without affecting other rights. *Inalienable* means that no one can ever take away these rights.

Past abuses of power have led to the development of human rights instruments to protect the rights of individuals and groups. An important development was the creation of the Universal Declaration of Human Rights (UDHR) in 1948.

As a declaration, the UDHR is a nonbinding document. It was conceived as a statement of objectives to be pursued by governments. Following the horrors of World War II (1939–45) the international community pulled together to create the United Nations (UN). As one of its first tasks, the UN created the Commission on Human Rights, which wrote the UDHR. As Ignatieff (2001) writes, the UDHR is not about Western moral superiority but a warning by Europeans not to reproduce their mistakes and abandon individualism to collectivism. The core of the UDHR is moral individualism and respect for human dignity. It attempts to protect individual agency against the totalitarian state.

The UDHR contains some 30 rights in all. Although neither the word "victim" nor "offender" appears in it, several articles do refer to "everyone charged with a penal offence." The rights of the accused include the right to be presumed innocent, the right to a fair trial, freedom from torture, and the right to not be arrested or detained arbitrarily. Nevertheless, the UDHR does contain several substantive and procedural rights that are relevant for victims. Regarding substantive rights, crime can be viewed as a violation of the victims' right to life, liberty, and security of person (art. 3) or their right to property (art. 17). To treat victims with dignity and respect (art. 1), an individual must first be recognized as a moral and legal person. In turn, this requires certain basic personal rights, such as the right to recognition before the law (Donnelly, 2003). Article 6 of the UDHR states "Everyone has the right to recognition everywhere as a person before the law." This gives rise to the notion of victim participation and procedural rights for victims. It suggests that victims must not be treated as mere evidence, but instead must be regarded as a subject with personal, individual, and independent standing at the criminal trial (Walther, 2011; Wemmers, 2012).

In addition to international law, many national governments have their own legally binding civil rights. For example, in Canada the *Charter of Rights and Freedoms* (1982) outlines the rights of Canadians (hereinafter "the Charter"). The Charter is divided into sections and includes a section titled "legal rights." In the preamble of the *Canadian Victims Bill of Rights*, it is specified that victims of crime have rights that are guaranteed by the Charter (SC 2015, c.13, s.2). However, victims' rights are not mentioned in the Charter. The legal rights of Canadians ensure that they are protected against unreasonable search or seizure, they have the right to not be arbitrarily detained or imprisoned, and they have the right to not be subject to cruel and unusual punishment. Upon detention they have the right to information, counsel, and to have the validity of their detention tested. In criminal proceedings, the accused has several rights, including the right to information, to be presumed innocent, and to a fair and timely trial. These rights are the rights of those accused of a crime and not those of a person who is the victim of a crime. Individuals who feel that their Charter rights were not respected can seek recourse before the courts (art. 24). These legal rights reflect the spirit of the UDHR in that they place respect for the dignity of the individual before the interest of the state and protect against abuses of power by the state.

Why Not Victims?

It may seem odd that human rights instruments would include extensive rights for those accused of having committed crimes but not mention victims of crime. After all, victims are human too. To understand this apparent imbalance, it is important to recall the history of criminal law. As we saw in Chapter 1, over time criminal law evolved and the state replaced the victim in the legal process (Doak, 2008; Viau, 1996; Wemmers, 2003; Young, 2005). The result of this transformation is that today the criminal justice process in common law legal systems is founded on the state laying charges against the accused; victims are witnesses to crimes against the state.

Once the state ousted victims from the criminal justice process, there was an imbalance of power between the omnipotent state and the individual accused of a crime (Doak, 2008; Kirchengast, 2006). Abuses of power by tyrant kings led to calls from scholars such as Montesquieu and Cesare Beccaria for the introduction of limitations on the power of the state and the creation of rights for the accused. Today the rights of the accused are well entrenched in law. Victims did not need rights because their freedom was not at stake.

Across legal traditions, the focus of the trial is on proving the guilt of the accused. As we saw in Chapter 1, in common law countries that have an adversarial system there are only two parties: the state and the accused. If crimes truly were directed at the state and were not committed against people, then this dual-party configuration would make sense. However, in reality crimes are committed against people. And these people—the victims—seek recognition of the crimes committed against them. Recognizing victims' rights as human rights means recognizing victims as persons before the law, which as we saw is proclaimed in article 6 of the UDHR.

International Developments and Victims' Rights in Domestic Criminal Law

The European Union

There has been considerable progress in the recognition of crimes as violations of victims' rights in the European Union (EU). In 2012, the European Parliament and the Council of Europe adopted Directive 2012/29/EU, which established minimum standards on rights, support, and protection of victims of crime (herein after "the directive"). This directive replaced the Council's Framework Decision on the Standing of Victims in Criminal Proceedings from 2001, which set out basic rights for victims in the EU. Although the framework decision was a binding document on EU member states, there were serious shortcomings in its implementation, which led to the adoption of the directive (Groenhuijsen & Pemberton, 2009).

The directive represents a step forward in the struggle for victims' rights. Paragraph 9 of the directive clearly states that crimes are considered "an offence against society as well as a violation of the individual rights of victims." In the 2001 framework decision, which the directive replaced, crime was not explicitly defined as a violation of victims' rights. Instead, states were merely encouraged to recognize victims' "legitimate interest" in proceedings. The directive goes much further by recognizing crime as a violation of victims' human rights.

The directive requires that all EU member states adopt laws, regulations, and administrative provisions to provide state-wide effective, comprehensive, coordinated access to the rights and services contained in the directive. The directive covers three main areas: information and support, participation in the criminal justice process, and protection. Compensation is not included in the directive, but the EU has separate legislation dealing with state compensation (Council Directive 2004/80/EC). Victims are defined as the direct victims of crime and, in the case of death, their family members (art. 2). The directive provides considerable detail regarding what information EU member states need to give victims and when they are to receive it. Compared to the previous legal framework, it contains more concrete and comprehensive rights for victims and clearer obligations for member states.

However, the directive contains many escape clauses that allow member states to not respect victims' rights. Moreover, it does not institute mechanisms to monitor the actual provision of rights or provide a means by which victims who are denied their rights can enforce them. As we have seen, compliance mechanisms are vital to guarantee victims' rights, and their absence casts doubt on the ability of the directive to lead to real change for victims (Allegrezza, 2015; Groenhuijsen, 2014).

The United States

All 50 states in the United States have enacted statutory rights for victims, and over 30 have amended their state constitutions to reflect victims' rights (American Bar Association, 2006). However, according to the American legal scholar Doug Beloof (2005), the rights of victims of crime in state constitutions are often illusory because victims have no standing to enforce them and no access to a review or remedy for violation. Much like the provinces and territories in Canada, victims' rights in state constitutions do not always afford them real rights because of legislative wording, judicial discretion, or judicial interpretation.

Studying the impact of legal protection on crime victims' rights, Kilpatrick, Beatty, and Smith-Howley (1998) found that strong legislation, which they defined as being comprehensive and specific, made a difference. While victims' rights were more likely to be respected when strong rights legislation was in place, they found that the enactment of state laws and state constitutional amendments alone was not enough to guarantee the full provision of victims' rights. To guarantee that victims' rights are respected, they recommended that states institute a mechanism to monitor the provision of rights and provide a means by which victims who are denied their rights can have them enforced. Victims need enforceable rights.

In 2004, the US Congress adopted the *Scott Campbell, Stephanie Roper, Wendy Preston, Louarna Gillis, and Nila Lynn Crime Victims' Rights Act* (hereinafter "the CVRA"). The name of the act explicitly acknowledges several victims of federal crimes in the United States whose rights had not been respected and for which the CVRA constituted an act of reparation, since it was meant to prevent such travesties from occurring again (Kyl, Twist, & Higgins, 2005). The CVRA represents a revolution in criminal law and procedure and constitutes a "paradigm shift" in the way that crime victims are treated (Cassell et al., 2014, p. 103). The CVRA gives victims of federal crimes enforceable rights.

It is worth noting that the CVRA sprang from the failure to introduce victims' rights into the US Constitution. Throughout the 1990s, many states had modified their respective constitutions to include victims' rights and enacted numerous statutory rights for victims (Beloof, 1999). In 1996, victims' advocates proposed a victims' rights amendment to the US Constitution. Several attempts were made to modify the US Constitution, but they failed to obtain enough support. Finally, in April 2004 crime victims' rights advocates decided to focus on federal legislation protecting crime victims instead, and hence the CVRA was created (Cassell et al., 2014; Kyl et al., 2005; Tobolowsky, 2015).

Like many of the bills of rights discussed previously in this chapter, the CVRA provides victims in federal criminal cases with a right to protection, information, restitution, and participation (see Box 7.2 for the complete list of victims' rights). Granting procedural rights to victims of federal crime, the CVRA enables victims to participate in criminal trials. Specifically, it gives victims the right to not be excluded from court proceedings and to be heard, as well as the right to confer with the attorney for the government in the case.

In addition to setting out the rights of victims, the CVRA also provides for review mechanisms when those rights are not respected in judicial proceedings. Victims are recognized as participants in the trial and granted procedural

BOX 7.2: THE US *CRIME VICTIMS' RIGHTS ACT*

The US *Crime Victims' Rights Act* gives the following eight rights to victims in federal criminal cases:

1. The right to be reasonably protected from the accused.
2. The right to reasonable, accurate, and timely notice of any public court proceeding, or any parole proceeding, involving the crime or of any release or escape of the accused.
3. The right not to be excluded from any such public court proceeding, unless the court, after receiving clear and convincing evidence, determines that testimony by the victim would be materially altered if the victim heard other testimony at that proceeding.
4. The right to be reasonably heard at any public proceeding in the district court involving release, plea, sentencing, or any parole proceeding.
5. The reasonable right to confer with the attorney for the Government in the case.
6. The right to full and timely restitution as provided in law.
7. The right to proceedings free from unreasonable delay.
8. The right to be treated with fairness and with respect for the victim's dignity and privacy.

rights. In the event that their rights are not respected, victims can submit a *writ of mandamus* to an appellate court to ensure that the trial court follows the rule of law and respects their procedural rights (Tobolowsky, 2015). The court hearing the application must decide on it within 72 hours after the petition has been filed, thereby facilitating the administration of justice and preventing recognition of victims' rights from complicating or delaying proceedings. If the court of appeal does deny the relief sought, the reasons for the denial must be clearly stated in a written decision (Kyl et al., 2005).

This procedure has been the subject of several rulings. In *Kenna v. US District Court*, the victim filed a petition for a writ of mandamus when the trial judge declined to hear the victim at a sentencing hearing for the accused since he had heard from the victim during the trial of the co-accused. The court hearing the petition found that the trial judge had made an error in law by refusing to hear from the victim in court, thereby denying his right to be "reasonably heard" at a hearing. The appellate court argued that the statute was enacted to make crime victims full participants in the criminal justice system. However, a review of the use of writs of mandamus since 2004 reveals that victims' petitions are denied more often than they are granted (Tobolowsky, 2015).

Confusion around the implementation of the CVRA, and the writ of mandamus in particular, prompted the US Department of Justice to produce a memorandum in December 2010 stating that victims' rights under the CVRA did not apply until prosecutors formally initiate criminal proceedings. In other words, victims' rights do not apply during the criminal investigation. This position, which is not in line with the spirit of the UN Declaration, has been met with strong opposition (Cassell et al., 2014).

Once victims have rights with recourse, they can hire a legal representative to represent their interests and ensure that their rights are respected. Only an independent lawyer can adequately represent victims' interests because the prosecutor's job is to represent the state (Garvin & Beloof, 2015). Victims and their legal representatives may contest decisions of the state attorney and petition a district court and then an appellate court if they are not being accorded their rights (Blondel, 2008; Kirchengast, 2011). Victims' lawyers may also be present for certain pre-trial matters for federal offences in the United States (Kirchengast, 2013). To further facilitate the integration of victims' legal counsel into the criminal justice system while maintaining balance and fairness, the National Crime Victim Law Institute (NCVLI), a nonprofit legal education and advocacy organization, was established in 1997 by Professor Doug Beloof at Lewis & Clark Law School in Oregon. With enforceable rights and legal representation, victims are recognized as persons before the law. The emergence of private counsel for victims of crime in adversarial systems represents a substantial development and provides a new role for victims— namely that of a participant—in common law systems of justice (Kirchengast, 2013). Recognizing victims as persons before the law gives victims agency and empowers them (Garvin & Beloof, 2015). Victim participation in criminal justice will be discussed in Chapter 10.

Conclusion

Victims, who once had a place in laying charges against the accused, have been completely pushed out of the criminal justice process and replaced by the state (Kirchengast, 2006; Schafer, 1968). They have been rendered powerless against an omnipotent state that has the power to force them to testify as well as the power to shut them out. Victims' rights are intended to restore balance and recognize victims' legitimate interests in the criminal justice process. Crime is a violation of victims' human rights as well as an offence against society. Treating victims with dignity and respect means recognizing them as persons before the law with rights and recourse. The UN Declaration encourages member states to provide victims with basic rights, including information, participation, protection, assistance, restitution, and compensation. As a result, victims' bills of rights now exist in many regions. By and large these include the right to information, protection, assistance, participation, and restitution. However, the road to recognizing victims' rights has been slow and difficult. Rights without recourse are popular with governments, but they do little to improve the plight of victims. Until victims have real rights, they will not be acknowledged as persons before the law. However, as Beloof (2005) points out, the question is not *whether* victims will achieve real rights but *when*.

CHAPTER 8

VICTIM ASSISTANCE

The consequences of victimization can be far reaching and range from physical injuries to financial loss to psychological effects. Most victims will turn to family and friends for informal support following victimization (Perreault, 2015; Steinmetz, 1990). However, their family and friends are indirect victims and can also be impacted psychologically, socially, and financially. Sometimes victims will not be able to find the support they need from their own informal network. Victims suffering from shock, trauma, depression, anxiety, and so on may need more than informal support and require formal support services. The aim of victim assistance is to help victims with their healing process. When done properly, the individual transforms from victim to survivor of crime. Often short-term support may be enough, although sometimes long-term support services are necessary for victims to heal. The link between victimization and re-victimization highlights the significance of victim support for the prevention of multiple victimization (Wemmers, 2011a). In this chapter, we will examine international standards and norms regarding victim assistance and then use them as a framework for analyzing victim support services. After discussing access to services, we will address key issues for professionals working with victims of crime.

International Standards and Norms

Services for victims, which first emerged in the 1970s, experienced a period of consolidation during the 1980s (Van Dijk, 1997). Victim assistance has a prominent place in the 1985 UN *Declaration of Basic Principles of Justice for Victims of Crime and Abuse of Power*, which specifies that victims should receive support (see Appendix 1). The UN Declaration does not specify how support should be offered, but it does insist that victims receive any necessary material, medical, psychological, and social assistance (art. 14).

In addition, victims should be informed of the availability of services and be readily afforded access to them (art. 15). According to the UN Declaration, police, justice authorities, health care workers, and other professionals who may come into contact with victims should receive training to sensitize them to the needs of victims, and guidelines should be created to ensure proper and prompt aid (art. 16). In addition, the UN Declaration highlights the importance of services for victims with special needs that arise because of the nature of the harm inflicted (e.g., sexual violence), prior disability, or their social group (e.g., visible minorities) (art. 17).

Globally, the early 1980s was a time of economic recession, which made it difficult for governments to introduce new services that were accessible to the public and free of charge. Hence in many countries, including the United States, the Netherlands, Great Britain, and Canada, volunteers provided support to victims. The volunteer model usually includes a paid staff member who runs the office and a handful of volunteers who provide the actual support services to victims (Fattah, 1999). Victim support was, and to some extent still is, essentially a community-based, grassroots movement that relied on the goodwill and hard work of volunteers (Fattah, 2010). For example, in 2015, Victim Support Netherlands worked with 1,300 volunteers and had 460 paid staff (Slachtofferhulp Nederland, 2016). In Canada, most service providers (72 per cent) make use of volunteers, and many (62 per cent) do not have minimum education requirements for volunteers, although most (71 per cent) do offer some kind of formal training (Allen, 2014). The heavy reliance on volunteers has been criticized for its lack of professionalism and is thought to reflect an absence of any real interest in the needs of victims (Fattah, 2010).

Another model that emerged in the 1970s is the systems-based service model. Fattah (1999, 2010) reminds us that many of the early systems-based services were created to make victims better witnesses for the court. Assisting victims was a means to an end rather than an end in itself. For example, in the 1970s the US government provided funding to encourage the creation of court-based victim-witness support services. These victim-witness programs aimed to enhance victims' collaboration with the court by addressing their needs (NOVA, 1988). Similarly in Canada, early police-based programs aimed to encourage victim cooperation with the police in the prevention of crime (Fattah, 1999). A more recent example is the creation of the Victim Witness Protection Unit at the International Criminal Court, which offers victim-witnesses any support services they need to testify at the court. Victims will, for example, receive just enough counselling so that they will be able to testify, but they will not receive sufficient counselling to fully recover from their victimization (Wemmers, 2009b).

The European Union's *Directive establishing minimum standards on the rights, support and protection of victims of crime* (2012/29/EU) is more detailed than the

UN Declaration. Article 8 of the directive concerns the *right to access victim support services*. It specifies that throughout the European Union direct victims and their family members should have access to support services free of charge, and support should be available from the moment authorities are aware of the victim as well as throughout the criminal justice process (art. 8.1). The directive further specifies that vulnerable victims and their family members (e.g., victims of gender-based violence) should have access to specialized support services free of charge (art. 8.3). The directive indicates that victim support services can be set up as nongovernmental or public organizations and organized based on a professional or voluntary model (art. 8.4). However, the directive clearly states that the offer of support should *not* be contingent on victims making a complaint with regard to the criminal offence (art. 8.5).

In terms of what kinds of support victims should be offered, article 9 of the EU Directive indicates minimum services that should be provided to victims. At a minimum, victims should be offered the following:

- Information about rights and services
- Information about or direct referral to any relevant specialist support services (e.g., victim compensation programs)
- Emotional and, where available, psychological support; the directive does not require that victim support services provide extensive specialist and professional expertise themselves, but they should assist victims in calling on existing professional services
- Advice relating to financial and practical issues arising from the crime
- Advice relating to the risk and prevention of secondary and repeat victimization
- Specialized services, such as shelters, offering victims safe accommodation
- Targeted and integrated support for victims with specific needs, including trauma support and counselling

The EU Directive only applies to European countries that are members of the European Union. Nevertheless, it is useful for non-EU countries, like Canada, as an example of good practice. The UN Declaration, however, pertains to the 193 countries that are currently member states of the United Nations, including Canada.

Canada

The *Canadian Victims Bill of Rights* includes many rights for victims, such as information and protection, but it does *not* include a right to support (see Chapter 7). Victim services fall under provincial jurisdiction and, unlike the European Union, there are no minimum standards for victim support in Canada. Hence, there are large differences between the provinces and territories.

Since 2003, Statistics Canada has conducted the Victim Services Survey (VSS) biannually to maintain an overview of the provision and use of victim services in Canada. In 2011–12, 760 service providers participated in the VSS. On a given day (24 May 2012) these 760 services provided assistance to 10,000 victims. Almost half (49 per cent) were repeat clients who had previously used the service (Allen, 2014).

Victims can turn to a variety of services in Canada. They are offered through police departments (36 per cent), community-based not-for-profit organizations (24 per cent), sexual assault or rape crisis centres (14 per cent), the courts (10 per cent), or other systems-based organizations (7 per cent). The majority of service providers (65 per cent) offer services to victims of all kinds of crime. However, about one-third (35 per cent) are mandated to help victims of specific offences, such as sexual assault or domestic violence. In addition, many of the general service providers offer dedicated programs targeting specific populations, such as children or elderly victims (Allen, 2014).

Both the volunteer and professional model for victim support services can be found in Canada. In some places, reliance on paid staff has gradually increased and volunteers are being replaced with paid professionals. For example, in the province of Quebec the Centres d'aide victimes d'actes criminels (CAVAC) no longer work with volunteers since the provincial government increased their funding in 2003 following the introduction of a "victim tax" on fines for traffic offences. However, with increased funding the CAVAC has gradually moved away from their community-based roots toward an increasingly systems-based service model. In 2012, the CAVAC took over the responsibility of informing victims about developments in their case (which was previously the court's job). The CAVAC currently offers support to victims who are independent of the police and court systems as well as systems-based information and support services for victims whose cases are handled by the province's criminal courts.

The transformation of the CAVAC from a volunteer to a professional organization is evidence of the growing professionalism in victim assistance. Much like nursing, which has its early roots in volunteer work and today is a well-established profession, Waller (2011) argues that victim assistance is developing into a serious and respected vocation. The recent emergence of professional degrees in victimology (see Chapter 2) is another indication of the growing professionalism of victim assistance (Muscat, 2010; Waller, 2011).

Access to Services

Access to services is a key point in the UN Declaration, which affirms that victims should receive the necessary assistance as well as be informed of the availability of services and be readily afforded access to them. The *Canadian Victims Bill of Rights* also stresses that victims have a right to information about the services and programs available to them as a victim (art. 6b).

According to the 2011–12 VSS, the 760 victim service providers that participated in the survey served almost 460,000 direct and indirect victims (Allen, 2014). This may seem like a lot, but in 2014 5.6 million Canadians ages 15 years and older reported that they or their household had been the victim of at least one of the eight crimes measured by the national victimization survey in the 12 months preceding the survey (Perreault, 2015). This number was down from 2009, when 7.4 million Canadians reported at least one victimization (Perreault & Brennan, 2010). Only 14 per cent of victims of violence report having had contact with victim support services, and even fewer victims of property crime had contact with victim support services (Perreault, 2015). Similar findings are obtained in the United States, where among victims of violence who experienced socioemotional problems, 54 per cent reported the crime to the police and only 12 per cent received victim services (Langton & Truman, 2014). If we add to this the family and friends of direct victims, the indirect victims, it becomes obvious that relatively few victims are helped by formal victim support services.

What these numbers do not tell us is why most victims do not have contact with victim support services. If victims did not seek contact with support services because they did not want or need these services, then there would be no cause for concern. However, if most victims did not have contact with victim support services because they were unaware of available services or because services were unavailable to them then this is a problem. Research on victims of crime in Quebec suggests that victims are not always informed of the availability of services. In one study, the researchers found that 38 per cent of victims who reported their victimization to police were not informed about victim support services. Moreover, most of these victims (64 per cent) said that they would have liked to receive information about available support (Wemmers & Cyr, 2006a). Similar findings are reported in the International Crime Victims Survey, where globally 21 per cent of victims indicating a need for victim support received it. This percentage was 37 for Canada (Van Dijk, Van Kesteren, & Smit, 2007). Hence, not all victims who want support actually receive it, which is reason for concern regarding victims' access to support services.

Certain types of victims may be more likely to receive information about victim support than others. Most of the victims helped by support services were female (75 per cent), victims of violence (80 per cent), and in most cases the victims knew their offender (Allen, 2014). Research suggests that police are more likely to inform the victim of support services when the victim is female and when the offender is her (ex-)partner (Steinmetz, 1990). Hence, the fact that certain victims are more likely to make use of support may, at least in part, be the result of preselection by authorities who act as gatekeepers to information about available services. These findings highlight the importance of sensitizing police and other justice professionals to the needs of victims.

How information is presented to victims may also influence their willingness to contact victim support services. Victims who report their victimization to police are likely to come into contact with authorities when they are in a state of disorganization (see Chapter 4). The police officer who arrives at a crime scene will, therefore, likely be confronted with a victim who is confused and disoriented as he or she tries to figure out what just happened (Campbell & Raja, 1999; Campbell, Wasco, Ahrens, Sefl, & Barnes, 2001). In a controlled experiment, Steinmetz (1990) randomly assigned victims to one of three conditions: (1) victims were given a brochure containing information about victim support, (2) victims were called on the phone and told about victim support, and (3) victims were visited in person and told about victim support. Victims were most likely to actually make use of victim support services when they were visited in person (47 per cent) or when they were called (33 per cent) and were least likely to do so when they were simply given a brochure (12 per cent). These findings suggest that handing out a brochure may not be enough to encourage victims to make use of support services and that more active forms of notification may be warranted. Given victims' state of disorganization following victimization, they may forget about the brochure, making a more proactive victim-outreach strategy better suited to their needs.

Access to services may be particularly problematic in sparsely populated, hard-to-reach places. In rural regions of Canada, such as the far North, there are chronic gaps in access to health services, including mental health services, major trauma care, and dental health services. This means that people will either have to do without, likely worsening their condition, or travel great distances, often at their own expense, to access care (Hay, Varga-Toth, & Hines, 2006). The availability of culturally (e.g., Indigenous) and linguistically appropriate services (e.g., French or English) is also a challenge in remote areas, which impacts the effectiveness and the outcome of services (Hay et al., 2006). As much as 30 per cent of Canada's population lives in rural areas, which, according to the Organisation for Economic Co-operation and Development, are defined as areas with a population density of less than 150 people per square kilometre

(OECD, 2014). This is especially concerning given that, as we saw in Chapter 3, the rate of victimization is much higher in Canada's rural North than in the rest of Canada (De Léséleuc & Brzozowski, 2006; Perreault & Simpson, 2016). These findings raise concerns about whether victims in Canada, in accordance with the UN Declaration, are receiving the necessary medical, psychological, and social assistance they require.

Assistance

The UN Declaration does not give specific details about the type of assistance that should be available to victims other than broadly indicating that victims should receive material, medical, psychological, and social assistance. As we saw, the EU Directive provides more details, specifying that victims should have access to emotional and, where available, psychological support; information and advice about available compensation programs, specialist services, and crime prevention; as well as information, advice, and support regarding their rights and role in the criminal justice process. In Canada, victim service providers are not bound by minimum standards. The available victim support services offer a wide variety of services to victims.

Most victim support services provide victims with information and support within the criminal justice system. In Canada, 90 per cent of victim service providers supplied support to victims to help them participate in the criminal justice system. This includes court accompaniment, assistance with victim impact statements, and victim or witness preparation. In addition, most services (89 per cent) provided information to support victims within the system. This ranged from information about the criminal justice system to victim notification specific to their situation. About half of victim services also provided legal information to victims (Allen, 2014). We will return to this topic in Chapter 10, when we examine victim participation in the criminal justice system.

Many service providers give information and advice about available compensation programs. According to the VSS, 56 per cent of service providers offered victims help with claims for compensation. In addition, 30 per cent provided services related to reparative justice (Allen, 2014). Victim compensation and reparation are discussed in detail in Chapters 9 and 11.

Crime prevention is important for victims and, as we saw, almost half of the clients using victim services in Canada were repeat clients. Over 90 per cent of victim service providers offered services related to *protection*. Most providers offered immediate (80 per cent) or long-term (63 per cent) safety planning, and about 60 per cent provided risk assessment and prevention training (Allen, 2014).

With regard to emotional support, victimization throws the victim into a state of disorganization, after which the individual tries to adjust to the long-term emotional and other effects and starts to give meaning to his or her victimization. This is referred to as *transition*. The transition phase is vital for the successful recovery of the victim, and it is at this stage that the victim is likely to need the most help (Hill, 2009). Box 8.1 provides an overview by Hill (2009) of what topics to cover in an initial interview with a victim to properly assess the victim's needs.

Following traumatic events such as victimization, healing begins with the resolution of the crisis at hand. Almost all (92 per cent) victim service providers in Canada offered emotional support to victims, and 90 per cent offered crisis services. Crisis services include crisis intervention and response (75 per cent) and critical stress debriefing (64 per cent). Almost half of service providers (47 per cent) offered some form of counselling for victims (Allen, 2014).

Crisis intervention is a form of support that seeks to help the person develop adaptive ways of confronting challenges that have temporarily overwhelmed the individual's ability to cope (France, 2014). It seeks to limit the severity of crises and restore or improve coping. By focusing on existing problems in their early stages, crisis intervention aims to decrease their duration and severity.

BOX 8.1: WHAT TO COVER IN AN INITIAL INTERVIEW WITH A VICTIM

To properly assist victims and understand their needs, Hill (2009) suggests that an assessment interview should cover the following four main topics:

1. *Victim's history:* Previous victimization, previous PTSD and severity, personal and family psychiatric history, coping skills used in the past, etc.
2. *Current characteristics of the victim:* Demographics; drug and alcohol use; current coping strategies; risk of suicide, homicide, or retaliation; current mental health status; presence of dissociation; victim's perception of his or her needs; etc.
3. *Crime-related characteristics:* Seriousness of the crime, use of threats, use of a weapon, whether it was an isolated incident or part of a series of victimizations, the relationship between the victim and offender, etc.
4. *Victim's strengths and resources:* Victim's strengths, problem-solving skills, ability to manage emotions, communication skills, informal support network, cognitive abilities, etc.

While the specific nature of the intervention will vary depending on the type of crisis event that occurred, intervention generally consists of two phases. The first phase occurs within 48 hours after the traumatic event or crisis episode and is generally referred to as crisis management, emotional first aid, or crisis stabilization (Yeager & Roberts, 2015). The second phase is crisis intervention or crisis counselling. It takes place in the days or weeks after the event. While various intervention models exist, most focus on problem solving, which is accomplished by exploring thoughts and feelings, considering alternatives, and developing a plan, which, depending on the victim's needs, may involve referral to a specialist and providing information about what will happen next and why (France, 2014; Muscat, 2010; Yeager & Roberts, 2015). The important part of crisis intervention is being there for the victim and asking what he or she wants and needs (Muscat, 2010). As for its effectiveness, research shows that most victims are satisfied with crisis intervention and find it helpful. Crisis intervention is associated with a variety of short- and long-term positive outcomes, including a decrease in distressing emotions and an increase in adaptive problem solving (France, 2014).

Debriefing is a particular crisis intervention strategy. While there are several different models of debriefing, the most popular is *critical incident stress debriefing* (CISD), in which a group of individuals is interviewed soon after the traumatic event in a single session. In the session, participants are led through the different stages of the CISD, discussing what happened, their symptoms, and reflecting on what they have learned. Debriefing aims to decrease arousal and prevent the development of post-traumatic stress disorder (PTSD) using cognitive restructuring techniques (Mitchell, Sakraida, & Kameg, 2003; Raphael & Wooding, 2004). CISD was originally developed for disaster support workers, and it seems to work well when it is applied to groups that work as a team (Raphael & Wooding, 2004; Regel & Dyregrov, 2012). It has since been extended beyond disaster support workers and has become widely used in trauma counselling with affected populations.

An adaptation of CISD is *individual critical incident stress debriefing*, where victims are interviewed individually rather than in a group (Marchand et al., 2006). As we have seen, debriefing is popular among victim support services, and most services offer it (Allen, 2014). Individual CISD is associated with victim satisfaction, and they generally appreciate it and consider it helpful (Raphael & Wooding, 2004; Van Emmerik, Kamphuis, Hulsbosch, & Emmelkamp, 2002). However, clinical research suggests that debriefing is not effective in the prevention of PTSD and other disorders after trauma for crime victims (Van Emmerik et al., 2002; Joyce et al., 2016; Marchand et al., 2006; Raphael & Wooding, 2004).

Effective interventions for individuals at risk of developing PTSD as well as those who have developed PTSD include cognitive behaviour therapy (CBT), exposure therapies, and problem-focused programs (Joyce et al., 2016; Van Emmerik et al., 2002). There is strong evidence that CBT reduces stress, depression, and anxiety symptoms (Joyce et al., 2016). Brief CBT programs consisting of four to five weekly, individual sessions starting within a month after the traumatic event and with homework assignments have produced promising results in terms of reducing PTSD symptoms in victims (Van Emmerik et al., 2002). However, CBT requires professional intervention by a psychologist or a psychotherapist.

In Canada, health care, including mental health, falls under provincial and territorial jurisdiction. While psychiatric fees are covered by provincial and territorial health plans, drugs prescribed by a psychiatrist may not be (Health Canada, 2013). When a psychologist practices in the community, their fees are typically not covered by provincial health plans. Similarly, other therapists or counsellors are generally not covered by public health care (Canadian Mental Health Association, 2015). Private insurance may cover these fees, but not everyone has private insurance, so some victims may not have access to the services they need. Victim compensation programs will sometimes cover the cost of drugs and specialized therapies, but as we will see in Chapter 9 these programs are not available to all victims. A key feature of effective victim support services is that they are available to victims free of charge to ensure that they are accessible for everyone. Hence, if professionals such as psychologists or legal experts are not part of a team of specialists working to support victims, then victims might be unable to access these services free of charge.

Crises are distressing turning points in which the failure of the individual's usual problem-solving strategies can propel them toward growth, defensiveness, or withdrawal (France, 2014). Victim support services aim to assist victims in this transitional phase as they rebuild their view of the world and recover from their victimization. *Post-traumatic growth* refers to positive psychological changes experienced as a result of the struggle with highly stressful and challenging life events (Kunst, 2010; Tedeschi & Calhoun, 2004). That is not to minimize the devastating impact of victimization and its consequences. Rather, victims are able to redefine themselves as they integrate the experience in their lives and prevail despite their victimization (Anderson, Renner, & Danis, 2012). When outcomes following stressful encounters are satisfactory, individuals tend to view the difficult episodes as learning experiences (Janoff-Bulman, 2006).

However, people will sometimes cut themselves off emotionally from painful experiences, and over time this can evolve into mental health problems such as dissociation, depression, PTSD, and even substance abuse. These are negative coping strategies that confound the negative impact of crime. Events that seem uncontrollable, such as victimization, are more distressing than negative events, which people think they can influence (Brown & Siegel, 1988). Hence, regaining a sense of control is important for victims following victimization, and an important part of crisis intervention is providing options and letting the victim make the decision (Muscat, 2010). Victims are susceptible to reactions from others at this stage, and timely support can help victims develop positive coping strategies, enhance their sense of control, and reduce the risk of re-victimization (Hill, 2009; Wemmers, 2011a).

Many victim support programs work with volunteers who are not trained professionals. They might be able to provide information and practical assistance (e.g., help with filling out forms) as well as emotional support, but they cannot offer professional counselling and are instructed to refrain from acting like a psychologist or counsellor (Fattah, 1999). Instead, it is important that they recognize the limits of their abilities and refer victims in need to trained professionals who have the necessary expertise.

The effectiveness of the volunteer model for victim assistance is unclear because of a lack of solid empirical research (Fattah, 1999, 2010). There are few available studies, and those that have been published use a post-test-only design, which makes it impossible to attribute any observed differences to the availability of victim support. However, these studies do not find that victims who receive short-term support do better than victims who do not receive support (Jorg-Birol, 2010; Steinmetz, 1990). The absence of any observed differences may be due to several factors, such as the actual (short-term) treatment victims received and how long after their victimization they received it, or simply the fact that the groups were different before they were in contact with victim support services (Jorg-Birol, 2010). Nevertheless, the victims who used support services tended to be satisfied with them (Freeman, 2013). In particular, victims were satisfied with how they were treated by victim support workers and the emotional support that they received (Winkel, Spapens, & Letschert, 2006).

Special Protections

The UN Declaration and the 2012 EU Directive both highlight the importance of assistance for victims that need special protection. According to the EU Directive, vulnerable victims in need of special protection include victims of gender-based violence, children, and socially marginalized groups such as immigrants. Gender-based violence concentrates on violence against women, which is a global problem. Besides informing victims of their rights and available services, specialist support services sometimes offer shelter and safe accommodation, immediate medical support, referral to professional services such as psychological counselling and legal advice, and specific services for children.

Although the *Canadian Victims Bill of Rights* does not address victims with special needs or vulnerable victims, referrals to residential services and emergency shelters are among the most common referrals made by victim service providers in Canada (Allen, 2014; Munch, 2012). One in five (20 per cent) victim service providers in Canada offered emergency shelter or housing (Allen, 2014). The Transition Home Survey provides information on shelters for abused women in Canada (Beattie & Hutchins, 2015). In 2014, there were 627 shelters for abused women operating across Canada. These include various types of shelter facilities such as transition homes offering short- and moderate-term respite (37 per cent), second-stage housing offering long-term shelter (23 per cent), women's emergency centres offering short-term respite (13 per cent) and emergency shelters offering short-term shelter (21 per cent). Most of these shelters target abused women with or without children, with the exception of emergency shelters, which provide respite for a wide population.

The women using shelters are often marginalized, depressed, unemployed, and with few resources (McFarlane, Maddoux, Nava, & Gilroy, 2015). Research with abused women who have used shelters found that they consider the tangible supports offered by shelters, such as food and housing, financial assistance, and spiritual support, to be particularly helpful (Anderson et al., 2012; Postmus, Severson, Berry, & Yoo, 2009).

On 16 April 2014, a total of 7,969 women and children resided in these facilities. On that snapshot date, another 338 women and 201 accompanying children were turned away from shelters. The most common reason for turning away victims was the shelter was full (56 per cent). Other reasons included drug and alcohol issues (8 per cent) and mental health issues (6 per cent) (Beattie & Hutchins, 2015). These statistics highlight the importance of adequate resources for specialist victim support services. While the value of specialized services for victims is recognized, they often operate with inadequate funding and, as they struggle to meet victims' needs, the provision of services has overshadowed their advocacy role (Johnson & Dawson, 2011; Muscat, 2010).

Victims of sexual violence are particularly vulnerable. As we saw in Chapter 3, most victims of sexual violence do not contact police, and many do not contact any other organization either because of feelings of shame and embarrassment (European Union Agency for Fundamental Rights, 2014; Perreault, 2015; Wolitzky-Taylor et al., 2011). Special support services with trained staff who are sensitive to popular myths about sexual violence are required to address the needs of victims who suffer from these negative feelings in the aftermath of victimization (Ben-David, 2009; Campbell et al., 2001; Koss, 2014).

In Canada, about one-third of service providers are mandated to serve victims of sexual violence. Most rape and sexual assault crisis centres are community based (Allen, 2014). Their main focus is to provide 24-hour crisis telephone lines, crisis intervention, individual and group counselling, advocacy, prevention and public awareness, training for other agencies that come into contact with victims, and assistance to women navigating the legal and health care systems (Sauvé, 2009). Almost two-thirds (64 per cent) of providers offered medical-related services, such as hospital accompaniment (Allen, 2014). Most rape and sexual assault centres in Canada receive funding from provincial governments but operate with very limited resources (Johnson & Dawson, 2011).

The documentation of forensic evidence can be particularly difficult for victims. It was not until the 1970s, under pressure from women's groups, that specialized hospital-based programs were developed. Prior to that, rape victims in Quebec, for example, were sent to the local morgue for a forensic examination (Gravel, 2008). Hospital-based programs consist of a team of medical specialists who are on call 24/7 to provide victims with specialized medical and emotional care (Allen, 2014).

Child victims are also extremely vulnerable and often require special protections. Child protection services are governmental or private services that help protect children and promote family stability. These agencies deal with children's welfare in general, which is very broad and is not limited to criminal victimization. As we saw in Chapter 3, 76 per cent of children and youth between 2 and 17 years of age have experienced one or more criminal victimization events during their life (Cyr, Clément, & Chamberland, 2014). The prevalence of victimization is even higher among youth under the protection of child services (Cyr, Chamberland, Clément, & Lessard, 2014).

The criminal justice process can be particularly difficult for children and youth. In recent years, specialized services have been developed to improve children's experiences in the criminal justice system and reduce the risk of secondary victimization. Child advocacy centres (CAC) and child and youth advocacy centres (CYAC) help child and youth victims and their families navigate the criminal justice system. They provide a safe, child- and youth-friendly environment where a coordinated, multidisciplinary team of professionals works to meet the specific needs of each youth. The multidisciplinary team in a CYAC or CAC joins forces to reduce the emotional and mental harm to child and youth victims involved in the criminal justice system. Research with CACs suggests that children and their families are generally satisfied with the investigation experience and the multidisciplinary team interviews (MacDonald, Scrim, & Rooney, 2013).

In 2013, there were six CACs and CYACs operating across Canada, and one year later, in 2014, the number rose to 15 (Child Advocacy Centres Canada,

2014). This increase was due largely to the provision of funding by the federal government, and it is likely that this number will continue to rise in the future (MacDonald et al., 2013). In Quebec, the Centre d'expertise Marie-Vincent in Montreal is the only CAC in the province. It serves children aged 12 and under who are victims of sexual assault. The centre provides support to minimize the trauma children and youth can experience when they participate in the criminal justice system either as victims or witnesses by providing a single, child-friendly setting to encourage child and youth victims or witnesses and their families to seek services. It is victim centred in that it brings all necessary actors together in one place so that the child victim no longer has to travel back and forth between professionals and continually retell his or her story.

Training

According to the UN Declaration, police, justice authorities, health care workers, social service providers, and other personnel involved in supporting victims should receive training to sensitize them to the needs of victims. As we saw in Chapter 2, education and training in the field of victimology has come a long way over the past 40 years, and today many postsecondary institutions offer courses, certificates, and even diplomas in victimology (Muscat, 2010; Waller, 2011).

Research on trauma and PTSD has ensured that victims are represented in the area of mental health. *Traumatology* refers to professionals who study and treat people exposed to highly stressful and traumatic events, such as terrorist bombings, war disasters, fires, accidents, criminal and familial abuse, hostage taking, hospitalization, major illness, abandonment, and sudden unemployment (APA, 2016). Organizations such as the International Society for Traumatic Stress Studies, which publishes the *Journal of Traumatic Stress*, have done much to advance awareness of the needs of victims among health professionals. Like Benjamin Mendelsohn's general victimology (see Chapter 2), traumatology is not limited to victims of crime and includes individuals who are exposed to any kind of traumatic event, criminal or otherwise.

Despite the relevance of victimology for criminal law, however, it has not yet become fully integrated into the standard curriculum for professionals seeking degrees in law or policing. For example, most law schools in Canada do not teach victimology. This division is in part a consequence of the fact that, in North America, victimology is generally taught within criminology programs, which are typically framed as a derivative of sociology and, therefore, are part of the arts faculty rather than the law faculty. The situation is different in Europe, where criminology is typically part of the law faculty.

As a result, in North America many young lawyers know victims as "complainants" or "witnesses" and know little about victims' needs.

Outside of their basic training, these professionals can often take postgraduate courses on specific topics, which might address victims. While such ad hoc training can be highly relevant and informative, it does not ensure that, as a group, police and justice personnel are systematically sensitized to the needs of victims. The UN Declaration encourages this sensitivity to reduce the risk of secondary victimization. It is important that victimology become fully integrated in the basic training for police and justice professionals to sensitize them to victims' needs.

Vicarious Trauma

Any discussion of victim assistance would not be complete without addressing the topic of vicarious trauma. As we saw in Chapter 4, PTSD can occur when a person is indirectly exposed to the aversive details of traumatic events on a regular basis. Individuals working with crime victims are at risk of experiencing psychological distress as a result of their work. This is referred to as *vicarious trauma*. The distress can take many forms, including stress, burnout, fatigue, low empathy, or blurred boundaries whereby the person too closely relates to the victim's suffering (Muscat, 2010). Someone experiencing vicarious trauma may experience symptoms similar to those suffered by victims themselves, including nightmares, avoidance, agitation, and withdrawal (Hydon, Wong, Langley, Stein, & Kataoka, 2015; Muscat, 2010).

Like victims suffering from trauma, professionals suffering from vicarious trauma may use positive or negative coping strategies to relieve the distress. Negative coping strategies include the use of alcohol or drugs to self-medicate and avoid painful feelings (Hill, 2009; Muscat, 2010). It is important for anyone who works with victims to know about vicarious trauma, be able to recognize the signs of stress, and develop positive coping mechanisms. Anyone working with victims needs to know their own strengths, weaknesses, and vulnerabilities (Tabor, 2011). Positive coping mechanisms include having a balanced lifestyle, fixing limits, regularly taking breaks from work, focusing on what went well, and being able to count on the support of one's colleagues (Hill, 2009).

Conclusion

After the initial shock of victimization comes a period of transition in which the individual tries to adjust to the long-term emotional and other effects and starts to give meaning to the victimization (Hill, 2009). The transition stage is vital for healthy recovery, and it is at this point that victims often need assistance, either formal or informal, to successfully integrate the experience into their lives and evolve from victim to survivor. This requires, however, a substantial investment of resources to ensure that all victims, in accordance with the UN Declaration, receive the necessary medical, psychological, and social assistance they require. The volunteer model, with its heavy reliance on volunteer victim support workers, is limited in terms of the type of support it can offer. In addition, access to services requires that gatekeepers to these services, such as police and justice professionals, be sensitized to victims' needs through education. By ensuring that victims have access to the services they need to heal, governments invest in reducing the consequences of victimization for both victims and their communities.

CHAPTER 9

STATE COMPENSATION

As early as 1955, the British penal reformer and magistrate Margery Fry (1874–1958) concluded that civil tribunals, which permitted victims to obtain compensation from their offenders, were not an adequate remedy for crime victims and that the state should offer financial compensation to victims of crime (Drapkin & Viano, 1974; Waller, 2011). As we saw in Chapter 3, the impact of crime on victims can be devastating. Victims can suffer numerous financial consequences, such as a loss of income caused by an inability to work, medical fees for expenses not covered by insurance, and material losses for the repair and replacement of stolen or damaged property. While financial compensation can never fully repair the pain and suffering caused by victimization, it can provide victims with essential support.

In this chapter we will examine state compensation programs. After discussing the different underlying rationales for these programs, international legislation will be considered to understand the context in which national programs operate. Next we examine compensation programs in Canada within the framework of the international standards and norms of the UN *Declaration of Basic Principles of Justice for Victims of Crime and Abuse of Power*, as well as the extent to which programs address victims' needs. The chapter closes with a brief discussion of the Trust Fund for Victims, which can be viewed as a compensation program for victims of war crimes, crimes against humanity, and genocide.

Victim Compensation

Compensation refers to money given as reparation for loss or suffering incurred as a result of the offence. According to *Black's Law Dictionary* (2015), compensation is synonymous with indemnification or the payment of damages. Traditionally, victims of crime are able to try to obtain compensation from their offender. The state does not have a legal obligation to compensate the victim, but the offender does. However, as we saw in Chapter 1, victims of crime rarely claim civil damages from their offender. If the offender is unknown it is impossible to litigate. If the offender is known, then victims should be able to claim damages, but when offenders have no money it is not worthwhile trying to obtain compensation from them. If the offender has money, the victim may pursue civil litigation, but this is a long and costly process with no guarantee that the victim will be successful. Even when victims do successfully pursue their offender in civil court, there is no certainty that they will ever actually receive the money awarded (Goldscheid, 2004: Miers, 2014; Tobolowsky, 2001). As a result, victims risk being left carrying the costs of victimization.

If governments do not have a legal obligation to provide victim compensation, one could argue that they have a moral obligation to do so. Compensation can be justified under a social welfare theory based on the idea that the state has a humanitarian obligation to victims of crime (Goldscheid, 2004). Left with no income and many expenses, a civilized society cannot leave victims helpless in their misery. Hence, publicly funded compensation programs should be developed to provide humanitarian relief and to help victims recover from the devastating effects of victimization. Aimed at fostering personal development and personal welfare, a fair distribution of public compensation resources is one that is based on need (Deutsch, 1975).

An alternative rationale for victim compensation is to share the costs of crime (Goldscheid, 2004). This argument is found in the work of Margery Fry (1959), who believed that modern societies should share the risks resulting from crime, much like it shares in other risks, such as medical costs and unemployment. In this approach, compensation would be a public insurance program that citizens would make contributions to and receive compensation from following victimization. As a result, anyone who did not pay into the program (e.g., foreign tourists) would not be eligible for compensation. In this approach, the primary goal is to foster or maintain good social relations within society and, therefore, the main principle of distribution should be based on equality (Deutsch, 1975).

Yet another justification for compensation is to support the criminal justice system (Elias, 1993; Goldscheid, 2004). The rationale behind this approach is that the possibility of receiving compensation would encourage victim collaboration with police and consequently increase reporting. As we saw in Chapter 3, nonreporting is an important concern, especially for certain crimes like sexual assault. However, victims may have good reasons for not wanting to report their victimization to the police, and these victims would be penalized under this rationale.

Victims perceive compensation as a form of recognition and acknowledgement of the harm inflicted upon them (Feldthusen, Hankivsky, & Greaves, 2000; Manirabona & Wemmers, 2014). Victims often prefer that compensation be forthcoming from the individual or the organization responsible for their suffering, so depending on the context this may be their offender or in the case of abuse of power by an authority, an institution (e.g., the Catholic church), or the state. However, this is not always possible, and sometimes victims prefer to avoid confronting their offender. In these cases, victim compensation by a third party, such as the state, can provide victims with the recognition they seek (Feldthusen et al., 2000; Shapland, Wilmore, & Duff, 1985; Van Hecke & Wemmers, 1992).

Following the work of advocates such as Margery Fry, governments began to introduce compensation programs for victims of violence. The first country to do so was New Zealand, which adopted legislation in 1963 introducing a nationwide victim compensation program. One year later, in 1964, Great Britain introduced its Criminal Injuries Compensation Scheme, which provides financial compensation to victims of violence. In 1965, California became the first state in North America to introduce victim compensation (Miers, 2014). In Canada, Saskatchewan created the first victim compensation program in 1967 (Burns, 1992).

International Standards and Norms

The UN Declaration views state compensation as a safety net that should be available when compensation by the offender or other sources is not fully available (art. 12). It recommends that member states establish, strengthen, and expand national funds for programs providing financial compensation to victims who have sustained significant physical or mental injuries as a result of serious crimes. As we saw in Chapter 7, the UN Declaration's definition of "victim" includes direct as well as indirect victims who have suffered individually or collectively. In addition, the Declaration specifically recommends that the family, in particular the dependents of individuals who have died or become physically or mentally incapacitated as a result of victimization, have access to state compensation (art. 12b).

Besides the United Nations, the European Union also has clear standards for member states with respect to state compensation for crime victims. While Canada is not part of the European Union, it is worth noting how this union of sovereign nations has dealt with the question of state compensation. In 2004, the Council of the European Union adopted its Directive 2004/80/EC relating to compensation for crime victims. Many European countries had already established a national compensation program following the 1983 convention of the Council of Europe regarding the compensation of victims of violent crimes. However, not all EU states had programs, and the existing programs did not always accommodate foreign victims.

The 2004 directive was introduced to ensure the free and safe movement of individuals and services within the European Union. Hence, Chapter 1 of the directive addresses access to compensation in cross-border situations, where a resident of one member state is victimized in another member state. The directive requires that all member states offer compensation to victims of violent crimes committed in their territories (art. 12). To facilitate access for victims across linguistic borders, member states are required to indicate a second EU language that it can accept. The directive requires that EU residents be able to turn to an authority in their home state to ease any practical and linguistic difficulties following victimization in another state. To establish a degree of uniformity across member states and facilitate communication, the directive introduced a standard form for the transmission of applications and decisions (art. 14). The directive does not, however, contain any details regarding the actual benefits to which victims should have access.

Canada

In Canada, the federal government first reflected on compensation for crime victims in 1970 when, at the fifty-second annual meeting of the commission on the uniformity of regulations in Canada, the commission recommended the creation of compensation for victims. According to the commission, compensation programs should be created to offset the expenses actually and reasonably incurred by victims following injuries that resulted in an inability to work or their death. The commission also made specific recommendations regarding victims of rape, suggesting that the program should provide financial support to victims to assist with the costs of raising a child born as a result of the crime (Couture & Hétu, 1996; Wemmers, 2003).

Three years later, in 1973, the federal government created a cost-sharing program with the provinces to facilitate the creation of compensation programs for victims across the country. This cost-sharing program was effective, and by 1990 all provinces and territories in Canada had established compensation programs. However, the cost-sharing program was terminated by the federal government in 1992, after which many provinces modified or even abolished their programs to deal with the reduction in funding. In 1992, Newfoundland terminated its program, which had been created in 1968 (Couture & Hétu, 1996). One year later, in 1993, Yukon repealed its compensation plan, and soon after, in 1996, the Northwest Territories followed suit (Canadian Resource Centre for Victims of Crime, 2015). Having abolished their compensation programs, the Northwest Territories and Yukon now offer only restricted, short-term, emergency financial relief, and Nunavut has a travel support program for victims (Allen, 2014).

In recent years, the federal government has introduced limited programs for specific victims. In 2007 it introduced an emergency financial assistance program for Canadians who are victimized abroad. The program allows the direct victims of certain serious violent crimes in a foreign jurisdiction to obtain financial assistance. Regarding the type of victimization that falls under the program, only homicide, sexual assault, aggravated assault, and assault with serious personal violence committed outside of Canada qualifies. The program is intended as a safety net and may help cover expenses where the victim has no other source of financial assistance, up to a maximum of $10,000. Specifically, the program may help cover hospital and medical expenses, expenses to replace stolen official documents, and financial assistance for professional counselling upon returning to Canada. If the crime results in death, the victim's family may obtain help paying for funeral expenses. Assistance may also cover any out-of-pocket expenses resulting from being a victim of a violent crime. It does not compensate lost wages or legal fees, though (Department of Justice Canada, 2015b).

On 1 January 2013, the Federal Income Support for Parents of Murdered or Missing Children (PMMC) grant came into effect (Department of Justice Canada, 2012). This grant offers income support to parents and legal guardians who have suffered a loss of income from taking time off work to cope with the death or disappearance of their child or children as a result of a probable Criminal Code offence. It is important to note that the victim must be under 18 years of age at the time of the victimization. Hence, the parents of an adult child (i.e., 18 years of age and older) are not eligible for this program, even if their loss is equally painful. The program targets people who are working or employed, and eligible applicants must have a valid social insurance number. This requirement effectively disqualifies illegal workers. The program works as a safety net, and the applicant must not already be receiving other employment insurance benefits. In addition, the applicant must not have been charged with committing a probable Criminal Code offence that led to the death or disappearance of the child (Department of Justice Canada, 2015c). Under the program, parents can receive $350 a week (before taxes) of income support for up to 35 weeks ($12,250 maximum) during the year immediately following the crime.

The absence of victim compensation programs for victims of violent crime across the country is an important issue. Victimization rates in northern

Canada are higher than in the provinces (see Chapter 3), making the absence of compensation programs in the territories particularly concerning. Clearly Canada falls short of meeting its responsibility under the UN Declaration to ensure that victims have access to financial compensation. However, the Declaration is a nonbinding instrument, which means that the UN has no formal power to force Canada's compliance. More importantly, it means that many victims are left to deal with the consequences of criminal victimization on their own and without essential services.

Provinces and Territories

Nine of Canada's ten provinces offer government-run compensation programs for victims of crime. The UN Declaration recommends that states provide financial compensation to victims who have sustained significant bodily injury or impairment of physical or mental health as a result of serious crime. In the following section, the existing programs for those who are victimized in a region where compensation is available will be discussed within the framework of victims' needs. A detailed description of these provincial programs can be found in Appendix 3, and an overview is provided in Table 9.1.

In terms of who is recognized as a victim and, therefore, eligible for compensation, all of these programs target victims of serious violent crimes and exclude victims of property crime. However, not all violent crimes found in Canada's Criminal Code are eligible. The legislation for seven provincial programs includes a list of offences that are eligible for compensation. Only Ontario and New Brunswick accept applications for all violent crimes. The lists of eligible offences generally include many important violent crimes, such as homicide (s. 222 of the Criminal Code), sexual assault (s. 271), and robbery (s. 344). However, there are some surprises. For example, although Alberta is landlocked, its list of eligible offences includes section 78.1, which is seizing control of a ship. This is rather unusual given that all eligible crimes must have taken place in the province, thus making maritime victimization extremely unlikely in this province. Neither British Columbia nor Quebec, which have important international ports, include this crime in their list of eligible offences.

It is also interesting to note what is *not* included on the list of eligible offences. For example, terrorist activities (s. 83.01) are not included in the list of eligible offences (e.g., Alberta, Manitoba, British Columbia, Quebec, Saskatchewan, and PEI). Also, offences that were recently added to the Criminal Code, such as human trafficking, do not appear in many of the lists (e.g., Alberta, British Columbia, Quebec, Saskatchewan, and PEI). Regardless of the peculiarities of the different programs, it is not clear why a victim who suffers harm as a result of a violent crime recognized in the Criminal Code

TABLE 9.1: Overview of Victim Compensation Programs across Canada

PROVINCE/ TERRITORY	INCLUDES FAMILY MEMBERS	MAXIMUM AWARDS	LOST INCOME BENEFITS	LIST OF PRESCRIBED OFFENCES	DISQUALIFIED IF CRIMINAL RECORD	TIME LIMIT	REPORTING REQUIRED
Alberta	No	$110,000	No	Yes	Yes	2 yrs	Yes
British Columbia	Yes	No maximum provided	Yes	Yes	No	1 yr[b]	No[e]
Manitoba	No[a]	$100,000[d]	Yes	Yes	Yes	1 yr[b]	Yes
New Brunswick	No[a]	$10,000	No	No	No	1 yr	Yes
Newfoundland	No program available						
Northwest Territories	No program available						
Nova Scotia	No[a]	$2,000	No	No	No	1 yr[b]	Yes
Nunavut	No program available						
Ontario	No[a]	$25,000	No	No	No[c]	2 yrs	Yes
Prince Edward Island	No[a]	$15,000	Yes	Yes	No[c]	1 yr	Yes
Quebec	Yes	No	Yes	Yes	No[c]	2 yrs[b]	No[e]
Saskatchewan	No[a]	$100,000	Yes	Yes	No[c]	2 yrs	Yes
Yukon	No program available						

a Only if the victim dies are dependents eligible for services.
b Exceptions are made for certain groups of victims.
c A criminal record is not automatically a criteria for disqualification, but it will be taken into consideration and may result in exclusion if the victim is thought to have contributed to his or her victimization.
d In addition, a victim suffering a permanent impairment can receive a lump sum payment of up to $84,630.
e The victim is not obliged to report the crime to police, but cooperation with authorities is expected.

of Canada should be denied compensation because the particular charges against the assailant are not included in the province's list of eligible offences.

As we saw in Chapter 4, the effects of crime are far reaching. The UN Declaration uses a broad definition of "victim" that encompasses anyone who individually or collectively has suffered harm as a result of victimization. With respect to compensation, the UN Declaration specifies that in addition to the direct victims, the family, and in particular the dependents of individuals who have died or become physically or mentally incapacitated as a result of victimization, should have access to compensation programs. All the provincial programs use a narrow definition of "victim," limiting it to the direct victims of crime. Dependents of homicide victims are offered services in all provinces except Alberta, where support is limited to reimbursement for funeral expenses.

Victims in need of medical attention because of their physical injuries will have access to public health care across Canada. However, health care is under provincial jurisdiction, which means that not all provinces offer the same services to the public. Certain services, such as prescription drugs and dental work, are generally not covered by public health care. For victims requiring these services, compensation programs are important. All the provincial programs except Nova Scotia's offer victims financial compensation for physical injuries. Since 2009 Nova Scotia's Criminal Injuries Counselling Program (NS Reg. 270/2009) only offers counselling services to victims of serious violent crimes. Among the provinces that offer financial support for physical injuries there are vast differences in the level of compensation available, ranging from $10,000 in New Brunswick to $110,000 in Alberta to no maximum in Quebec. Many programs will cover prescribed drugs and therapies (e.g., physiotherapy) as well as dental work, although these expenses are sometimes capped (e.g., New Brunswick, Ontario, PEI). When financial assistance for these expenses is not available, victims may be left to pay these expenses themselves or simply not have access to the help they need.

With respect to mental health, all the provincial programs offer some counselling to direct victims. However, the emotional impact of criminal victimization can reach far beyond the direct victim. Family members who were not financially dependent on a deceased victim (e.g., parents of a child who is murdered) have less access to services than dependents. While several provinces will reimburse family members for funeral expenses, only Quebec, Nova Scotia, and Manitoba offer counselling services to these victims. If the deceased victim was an adult (e.g., parents of a 19-year-old child), then they are even less likely to have access to services. Only Nova Scotia offers counselling to all immediate family members of homicide victims regardless of their financial relationship with the victim or the age of the victim. Also, if the direct victim is not deceased, only two programs, British Columbia and Quebec, offer professional counselling services to family members. Hence, family members may have difficulty accessing professional counselling services. Community- and police-based victim assistance services are available free of charge throughout most of the country. However, family members suffering from PTSD or complicated grief following the victimization of their loved one require professional counselling, which goes beyond the ability of local, volunteer services (see Chapter 8).

Compensation programs are extremely important with respect to victims' financial needs. Victims who are temporarily or permanently unable to work following their victimization often rely on compensation programs to make ends meet. Yet not all programs offer lost income benefits to victims (e.g., Alberta, New Brunswick, Nova Scotia). Without help, victims may be pushed into poverty, which, as we saw in Chapter 3, is associated with a high risk of violent victimization. Five provinces offer lost income benefits. Sometimes the available financial support is limited (e.g., PEI, Ontario) or it is capped at minimum wage (e.g., British Columbia). However, in Quebec lost income benefits can reach up to 90 per cent of the person's net salary before the victimization, practically restoring his or her income to the pre-victimization situation.

Victims may also experience a need for protection. Protective measures such as security alarms or even moving away from the home where their victimization occurred bring added expenses. One of the few programs to offer victims compensation for protective measures is British Columbia. Victims in British Columbia who are at risk of additional harm from the perpetrator or are so traumatized by fear they cannot lead normal lives can apply for compensation for relocation expenses, security, or communication equipment and services (e.g., a cellphone) as well as courses for personal protection or security. While the need for protection is fundamental for crime victims, in most cases protective measures are not covered by the provincial compensation programs.

Access to information is crucial. All provinces have deadlines for applications for compensation ranging from one to two years. Without timely and adequate information, victims may not know about the available benefits and miss out on an opportunity to apply. Information must be easily available in a way that the victim can understand. Although there are two official languages in Canada, victim compensation falls under provincial jurisdiction, and not all provinces have bilingual websites. Bearing in mind vulnerable groups, such as new immigrants and Indigenous peoples, programs should offer information in many languages, yet none of the available programs offer multilingual websites.

One of the practical needs sometimes expressed by victims is the need for emergency financial assistance. Applying for compensation is a long process, and it may take several months before a victim's application is handled. To provide speedy relief to victims, several programs offer a quick response program (e.g., Ontario, Quebec). In cases where it is highly probable that the applicant will receive compensation, they are provided with some money right away, pending the final decision on the precise amount to be awarded.

While programs generally do not specify their underlying philosophy, most of the provincial programs in Canada appear to maintain a criminal justice philosophy. Seven of the nine provincial programs require that the victim report the crime to police and collaborate with authorities to be eligible. Only British Columbia and Quebec do not explicitly require victims to report to police. However, in practice, Quebec requires victims to demonstrate that a crime occurred, so the police report provides proof of criminal victimization (Lippel & Doyen, 2000). Mandatory reporting aims to advance the criminal justice system's essential functions of promoting prosecutions and convictions. Yet sometimes victims may have good reasons to not report a crime. For example, victims of sexual violence are often reluctant to report the crime and expose themselves to public scrutiny and the stress of the criminal justice process. To respect the victim's choice and not further penalize them, some programs have chosen to be flexible on this requirement.

Further evidence of the strong criminal justice philosophy underlying many programs is the offer of services to good Samaritans who are injured while trying to prevent the commission of a crime or while assisting a peace officer (Quebec, Manitoba, and Ontario have such laws). This group is offered the same services as direct victims of crime.

The strong criminal justice orientation of many programs is also reflected in their exclusion policies. All provincial programs exclude individuals who are thought to have caused or directly contributed to their victimization. For example, a parent who is responsible for the death of his or her child cannot apply for death benefits. The exclusion of victims who behave as offenders at the time of the offence is not controversial, but the exclusion of victims with a criminal history is highly disputed (Miers, 2014). In Manitoba and Alberta, people with a criminal record are excluded regardless of whether or not their past offence(s) is linked to their victimization. In Manitoba, if a victim has been convicted of certain serious offences in the 10 years before his or her victimization, this can result in the person being excluded from the program (*Victims' Bill of Rights*, art. 48.1(3)). In addition, if they are convicted of a crime *after* their victimization, their benefits may be reduced (art. 54.1(4)). In Alberta, if in the five years before the victimization the victim was convicted of a crime listed in the law (*Alberta Regulation* 63/2004, Schedule 2), they will receive less compensation. Interestingly, this list is much longer than the list of eligible offences (Schedule 1), and it includes minor offences such as vagrancy (s. 179 of the Criminal Code), common nuisance (s. 180.1), offences related to prostitution (s. 213), as well as more serious crimes such as terrorism (s. 83.19 to 83.231). Surprisingly, however, serious violent crimes such as sexual assault (s. 271) or homicide (s. 222) are not mentioned in the list of exclusions. Homicide in Canada has a mandatory life sentence, which may explain its absence from the list: An individual convicted of homicide five years ago would still be in prison. However, when tried as a summary conviction sexual assault is punishable by up to

18 months in prison. This raises the question why certain poverty-related crimes such as vagrancy are included in the list and other serious crimes are not. The case presented in Box 9.1 is an example of how these policies work against victims. Victims, and by extension their families, are effectively "outlaws" who are refused state benefits for which they would otherwise be eligible. As we saw in Chapter 3, victimization is related to income, and people with a low income are at a greater risk of violent victimization. Such exclusionary policies shut out the most vulnerable members of society, effectively increasing their suffering as well as their risk of further victimization.

More generally, while the relationship between victimization and offending is robust, it is not clear what explains this relationship. As we saw in Chapter 5, there are several possible explanations. If the link between victimization and offending is the result of a risky lifestyle, then perhaps it makes sense to hold

BOX 9.1: CLASS JUSTICE? THE EXCLUSION OF MARGINALIZED GROUPS

On 14 December 2014, Angela Poorman was stabbed to death in Manitoba. Angela was 29 years old at the time of her murder. She is one of hundreds of missing and murdered Indigenous women's cases that remain unsolved. Less than one month after her daughter's death, Angela's mother, Janett Poorman, found that she had to pay the $4,500 funeral bill. She applied to the province's compensation for victims of crime program to be reimbursed for her daughter's funeral expenses. Under the province's *Victims' Bill of Rights*, family members who have to pay for the victim's funeral costs are eligible for up to $5,400. However, Janett Poorman's application was rejected, and the victim services employee dissuaded the family from filing an appeal, saying there was no point in trying. Still grieving her daughter's violent death, Angela's mother learned that her daughter's life was not deemed worthy of victims' compensation.

Under Manitoba's *Victims' Bill of Rights*, compensation for funeral expenses may be reduced or even denied if the victim was convicted of an offence in the past 10 years. In Angela's case she had 10 convictions, the majority of which were for breaching conditions of release. Her original convictions were one count of driving while impaired and one count of identity theft, for which she was fined and put on probation. Manitoba's victim compensation laws end up excluding a large number of Indigenous people by virtue of their overrepresentation in the criminal justice system (Levasseur, 2015).

people accountable for their choices. However, if the link between victimization and offending is due to the criminogenic impact of victimization, then such exclusion policies may perpetuate the victims' suffering and the cycle of violence.

National Standards and Minimum Norms

There are tremendous differences in victim compensation across the country. Depending on where in Canada the victimization took place, victims may have access to a well-developed program (e.g., Quebec) or nothing at all. The lack of support experienced by many victims is concerning.

We began this chapter with a discussion of international and interregional standards and norms. Compared to the European Union, which is a union of sovereign states, Canada does not guarantee its citizens the same level of service across the country. Whereas the EU requires that all member states offer compensation to victims of violent crimes committed in their territories, Canada does not. Hence, Canadians who fall victim to a serious violent crime, other than the death of a young child, in the territories and Newfoundland fall into an abyss. They are neither covered by their provincial programs nor by the federal programs.

The introduction of minimum standards and norms would ensure that victims across the country have access to victim compensation and that Canada respects its obligation under the UN Declaration. The EU is an excellent example of what can be done when there is a will to help victims of crime. It has set out in legislation minimum standards and norms for member states to ensure a basic level of service across the union. When the federal government participated in cost sharing with the provinces, it succeeded in ensuring that victims of violence across the country had access to compensation programs. However, progress came to a grinding halt when the federal government stopped providing funding in 1993. This needs to change.

Prioritizing Victims

State compensation programs are an important resource for victims. Often they are the only resource available for victims in need, offering them access to vital resources that are indispensable for victims' recovery. When compensation programs provide victims with the support they need, they help victims heal and regain control over their lives (Feldthusen et al., 2000; Miers, 2014). As we saw in Chapter 3, victimization is associated with a high risk of re-victimization. It is crucial that victims receive adequate and timely assistance to reduce stress, heal from the effects of victimization, and reduce their vulnerability.

However, as we have seen, compensation programs often fail to meet the essential needs of many victims. This raises the question: If compensation programs are meant to help victims heal, then why do they shut out so many victims? What purpose do they serve? Some authors argue that the function of these programs is largely symbolic, to show that the government is concerned about victims but without making available the necessary financial resources to meet the real needs of victims (Elias, 1983; Maguire & Shapland, 1997). As we have seen, these programs often follow a criminal justice rationale rather than target more humanitarian goals such as the well-being of the individual victim and society. Maguire and Shapland (1997) argue that compensation programs are attractive for governments because they are reasonably easy to create and run. Governments control everything about the program: the available resources, the admission criteria, and the budget. To reduce costs, they exclude "bad" victims, such as those with a criminal record, and limit services to "good" victims who meet society's image of the innocent victim who is deserving of our help (Miers, 2014). Elias (1983, 1993) is cynical about the use of these programs. Rather than aiming to promote healing by targeting victims' needs, he concludes that they are a form of charity developed by the state to appease public opinion.

Compensation programs must give priority to the needs of victims. However, government resources are not endless either. A main challenge facing compensation programs is how to meet the needs of crime victims without increasing costs. This is why it is important to prioritize victims' needs (see Chapter 5). These issues are illustrated by the Trust Fund for Victims at the International Criminal Court.

Trust Fund for Victims

The Trust Fund for Victims (TFV) can be likened to a national state compensation program for victims. Established by the international community in 2002 together with the International Criminal Court, the TFV acts as a third party and offers reparation to victims of the most heinous crimes. Consequently, the TFV faces many of the same challenges discussed above with respect to government-run compensation programs (Mégret, 2009; Wemmers, 2006).

The legal basis for the TFV is article 79 of the *Rome Statute of the International Criminal Court*. The TFV was established for the benefit of victims of crimes, and their families, within the jurisdiction of the court. More specifically, the jurisdiction of the International Criminal Court is crimes against humanity, genocide, war crimes, as well as acts of aggression. The money entering the TFV may come from two different sources: (1) money and other property collected from offenders through fines or forfeiture imposed by the court, or (2) voluntary donations from member states who are signatory to the *Rome Statute* and, therefore, recognize the court.

Court-ordered compensation to victims can be managed by the TFV, which collects the money from the offender and ensures its proper distribution to victims, in accordance with the court's decision. Since this can only happen when an offender has been sentenced, it is not a common occurrence. Trials take many years to complete, and the court only issued its first conviction in 2012, 10 years after opening its doors.

Much of the TFV's money has come from voluntary donations from member states. Unlike money that comes from a court order, the TFV is at liberty to use this money as it sees fit. It must benefit victims and their families, but otherwise the TFV is free to determine who gets what. In this way, the TFV is confronted with many of the same questions facing national, government-run compensation programs: What to compensate? Who to compensate? Who not to compensate? What is the underlying philosophy of compensation?

The question of who to include and who to exclude is as fundamental as it is difficult to answer. As we have seen, national programs use exclusion criteria, and the notion of blame is inherent in all of these criteria. The question of "good" and "bad" victims is no less complicated for crimes against humanity and war crimes than it is for conventional crimes. It is possible that a person can be a victim at one time and an offender at another time. Child soldiers can commit horrible crimes, but because of their young age they are not considered responsible for their offences. These victims challenge popular stereotypes about what it means to be a victim (see Chapter 1).

Another important question facing the TFV is the question of collective versus individual compensation. By and large, domestic criminal law focuses on individual victims and offenders. In contrast, the International Criminal Court deals with crimes that typically involve mass victimization and entire communities of victims. This is a new challenge for criminal law, which focuses on individual responsibility and tends to disaggregate individuals from the group (Mégret, 2014).

There simply are not enough resources to satisfy the needs of all victims all of the time. The fair allocation of scarce resources is important for victims' justice judgments. Selection criteria must address issues of distributive and procedural justice. As we saw in Chapter 6, if the goal of compensation is to foster or maintain good social relations, then a fair distribution would be one based on equality. However, if the primary goal of compensation is to foster personal development and personal welfare, then need should be the dominant principle of distributive justice. Equity or merit means increasing the distribution according to the value and contribution of the individual to his or her social group. Equity should be the main principle of distributive justice in cooperative relations in which the primary goal is economic productivity (Deutsch, 1975). Injustices in the distribution of rewards constitute a form of secondary victimization (Feldthusen et al., 2000; Haynes, Cares, & Ruback, 2015; Jones, Parmentier, & Weitekamp, 2014). To this end, it is important to identify the goal of reparation and prioritize victims' needs.

From a victim-centred perspective, the focus of the TFV should not be the financial compensation of individual victims but the healing or rehabilitation of victims both individually and collectively. This aim is reflected in the TFV's vision of its purpose, which is to support programs that address the harm resulting from the crimes under the jurisdiction of the International Criminal Court by assisting victims to return to a dignified and contributory life within their communities (Trust Fund for Victims, 2016). This is consistent with social welfare theory and the idea that we have a humanitarian obligation to help victims recover from the devastating effects of victimization.

Conclusion

Compensation programs are the oldest available service for victims. However, despite their long existence, many victims do not have access to these programs. Existing programs are diverse in terms of the type and level of support provided. The introduction of national standards and norms would ensure that victims across Canada have access to compensation programs. Faced with high demands and limited services, all programs use strict criteria to define who is included and who is excluded from the program. Selection criteria must address issues of distributive and procedural justice. A humanitarian, needs-based approach aimed at encouraging healing and based on principles of justice allows difficult choices to be made while reducing the risk of secondary victimization. However, most programs appear to adhere to a criminal justice philosophy, and the distribution of resources is based on merit or equity, which may further victimize the most vulnerable members of society.

CHAPTER 10

VICTIM PARTICIPATION IN THE CRIMINAL JUSTICE PROCESS

Drawing attention to the plight of victims and their need for recognition in the criminal justice system, victimologists have studied ways to improve the treatment of victims. As we saw in Chapter 7, the importance of recognizing victims and allowing them to participate in the criminal justice process is reflected in the UN *Declaration of Basic Principles of Justice for Victims of Crime and Abuse of Power*. In particular, article 6(b) of the Declaration states that the responsiveness of judicial processes to the needs of victims should be facilitated by "allowing the *views and concerns* of victims to be presented and considered *at appropriate stages* of the proceedings where their *personal interests* are affected, *without prejudice* to the accused and consistent with the relevant national criminal justice system" (emphasis added). The UN Declaration was intended to promote victim participation while allowing flexibility for member states within the specific requirements of their domestic criminal justice systems. As a result, the Declaration leaves many questions unanswered: Just how and when should victims be allowed to present their views and concerns? Which victims should be allowed to participate? Are all views and concerns appropriate, and who decides what is and isn't appropriate?

In this chapter, we will examine victims' participation in the criminal justice system and its many forms. Special attention will be given to the victim impact statement (VIS), which is the main format through which victims are permitted to participate in Canada as well as in many other countries with a common law legal tradition. To understand the full range of experiences that are possible, other forms of victim participation will also be presented. After examining victim participation at the trial stage, victim participation post-sentencing will be addressed. Throughout the chapter research on victims' experiences in the criminal justice process and their satisfaction with the various forms of participation will be presented.

During the Trial

In common law jurisdictions, victim participation during the criminal trial is limited to that of a witness. As we saw in Chapter 1, the victim does not choose to be a witness: If they are subpoenaed they must testify, and if they are not called to testify as a witness they will not have an opportunity to speak during the trial. As a witness, they cannot speak freely and can only answer questions that are put to them before the court. Certain vulnerable victim-witnesses, such as victims of sexual assault and child victims, however, may have access to special protective measures during the trial. These include measures to protect their privacy as well as measures to protect them from intimidation from the accused (s. 486–486.5 of the Criminal Code).

Privacy protective measures include a publication ban for trials involving victims of sexual violence and child victims. A publication ban prohibits the media from publishing the name or any other information that could possibly identify the victim. Adult victims may ask the court to have the publication ban removed if they wish to speak publicly about their experience. In certain circumstances the public, including the press, can be banned from the courtroom.

Measures aimed at protecting the victim-witness to obtain a better testimony include testifying behind a screen so that the victim is not face-to-face with the accused and testifying via video link set up outside of the courtroom. In certain cases, such as child victims of sexual violence, a pretaped interview of the victim by police is presented in court to avoid the victim being interrogated repeatedly about the same events. In certain cases the accused cannot directly cross-examine the witness. If the victim-witness is a child or an adult victim of sexual violence, the accused must have a lawyer question the witness on his or her behalf. Vulnerable victim-witnesses may also bring a support person when testifying.

Victim Impact Statements

The limitations surrounding victim participation during the trial led to the introduction of the **victim impact statement (VIS)**. It consists of a written statement by the victim regarding the impact the crime has had on his or her life. In accordance with the UN Declaration, the VIS allows victims' "views and concerns" to be considered and gives them a voice in the criminal justice process. First introduced in California in 1974 (Sullivan, 1998), victim impact statements quickly spread to other states. By 1988, 48 states had passed legislation allowing input by victims at sentencing, and the American Bar Association had drafted a model statute for states considering developing such legislation (NOVA, 1988). That same year victim impact statements were introduced in South Australia (Erez, 1991) and Canada (Baril, Laflamme-Cusson, Boisvert, Boudreau, & Gravel, 1990).

The legal basis for the VIS in Canada is article 722 of the Criminal Code. In 1988, Bill C-89 introduced the VIS, and with it the word "victim" appeared in the Criminal Code for the first time. The VIS allows the victim to present information about the impact of the offence at the sentencing hearing, after an accused has been found guilty. However, it does not allow the victim to participate in the criminal justice process before the sentencing stage. Section 722(1) states that in determining the sentence to be imposed, or whether the offender should be discharged, the court "shall consider" the VIS (see Box 10.1). A copy of the written statement is to be provided to the offender. The victim may request to read the statement aloud in court. Choosing to read the statement aloud provides victims with an opportunity to ensure that their voice is heard in court.

BOX 10.1: VICTIM IMPACT STATEMENTS (CRIMINAL CODE S. 722)

(1) When determining the sentence to be imposed on an offender or determining whether the offender should be discharged under section 730 in respect of any offence, the court shall consider any statement of a victim prepared in accordance with this section and filed with the court describing the physical or emotional harm, property damage or economic loss suffered by the victim as the result of the commission of the offence and the impact of the offence on the victim.

(2) As soon as feasible after a finding of guilt and in any event before imposing sentence, the court shall inquire of the prosecutor if reasonable steps have been taken to provide the victim with an opportunity to prepare a statement referred to in subsection (1). . . .

(4) The statement must be prepared in writing, using Form 34.2 in Part XXVIII, in accordance with the procedures established by a program designated for that purpose by the lieutenant governor in council of the province in which the court is exercising its jurisdiction.

(5) The court shall, on the request of a victim, permit the victim to present the statement by

  (a) reading it;

  (b) reading it in the presence and close proximity of any support person of the victim's choice;

> (c) reading it outside the court room or behind a screen or other device that would allow the victim not to see the offender; or
>
> (d) presenting it in any other manner that the court considers appropriate.
>
> (6) During the presentation
>
> (a) the victim may have with them a photograph of themselves taken before the commission of the offence if it would not, in the opinion of the court, disrupt the proceedings; or
>
> (b) if the statement is presented by someone acting on the victim's behalf, that individual may have with them a photograph of the victim taken before the commission of the offence if it would not, in the opinion of the court, disrupt the proceedings.

A VIS can be submitted by the direct victims of crime. However, if for any reason a direct victim is unable to act on his or her own behalf (e.g., due to death or illness) their spouse, partner, or other family member may act on his or her behalf. As Smith (2011) points out, this definition does not put a limit on the number of people who can submit a VIS. For example, in the case *R. v. Lonechild*, the defendant was found guilty of the death of a young victim, Justin Sproat, at a house party in Saskatoon. At the sentencing hearing, the Crown prosecutor proposed to enter 50 victim impact statements. The sentencing hearing ran for two days, and some 20 VISs were read aloud in court by the victim's family members and friends, as well as friends of the victim's parents (Smith, 2011). The effects of crime can be far reaching, and this is recognized by a wide approach to the definition of "victim."

The Criminal Code requires judges to consider the VIS when determining the sentence. In 2015, the adoption of Bill C-32, which introduced the *Canadian Victims Bill of Rights*, brought with it the introduction of one standard form for the VIS that is used across Canada (Form 34.2; s. 722(4)). Prior to 2015, each province had its own form for the VIS. A copy of this new, federal form can be found in Appendix 4 of this book. It allows victims to indicate the emotional, physical, and economic impact of the crime and express any fears for their security. Victims are also invited to add a drawing, poem, or letter to their VIS. With the court's approval, an opinion or recommendation about the sentence may be included in the VIS as well. The introduction of the VIS put an end to a tendency in the case law to exclude victims' evidence concerning the harm they had suffered to avoid arbitrary testimony containing excessive emotional intensity (Roach, 1999).

However, not all views and concerns of victims are admissible, and there are limits on what a VIS may contain. On the form it is clearly indicated that victims must not include any unproven allegations or any information that is not relevant to the conviction. For example, it cannot contain opinion, new facts, or evidence from expert witnesses; criticisms of the accused; or recommendations as to the severity of the sentence (Ruby, 2012). If a VIS contains inappropriate information, it may be edited or even prohibited in its entirety.

Notably, the VIS is not free of consequences, because producing a VIS makes the victim subject to subsequent cross-examination by defence counsel (Manikis, 2015; Roach, 1999). While it is rare that a victim will be questioned about his or her VIS, it is a legal possibility. In her review of Canadian case law on victim impact statements, Campbell (2015) presents several cases, including *R. v. Bremner*, in which the VIS served as grounds for appeal. Campbell (2015) attributes the fact that victims are rarely cross-examined regarding their VIS to two factors. First, victim impact statements continue to be rarely presented by victims or their representatives in court (Roberts & Manikis, 2010). Furthermore, a vigorous cross-examination of a victim at a sentencing hearing regarding the harm suffered might do more harm to the defence's case than good (Campbell, 2015; Wemmers, 2008a). Defence will have had the opportunity to question witnesses during the trial, and to do so again after the accused has been found guilty is probably not worthwhile.

The administration of justice is under provincial jurisdiction in Canada, so how victim impact statements are dealt with administratively may differ from one province to the next. In Quebec, for example, victims are automatically sent a copy of the form for a VIS soon after their case has entered the office of the public prosecutor. If the victim chooses to submit a VIS, then they can fill in the form and send it to the clerk's office at the Court of Quebec. As many as 67 per cent of victims submit a VIS in Quebec (Wemmers & Cyr, 2006a). After submitting their VIS, the victim will often not hear anything back from the court. Unless they actually present their statement aloud before the court, they may never know for sure whether the judge actually read their VIS (Wemmers & Cyr, 2006a; Wemmers, 2008a). In other provinces, victims are not automatically sent the form, and statements appear in approximately 10 to 23 per cent of cases (Illingworth, 2016; Miller, 2014; Roberts & Edgar, 2006).

While it is clear that the courts must consider victim impact statements in sentencing, there is no evidence to show that authorities always read VISs, and the specific role of the VIS in sentencing remains unclear (Campbell, 2015; Roberts, 2009; Wemmers, 2008a). This recognition of a role for victims in criminal proceedings still does not give them the status of a participant or a party on the same basis as the prosecution and the accused. As Ruby (2012) points out, a criminal trial, including the sentencing hearing, is not a tripartite proceeding. Victims, or "complainants," as he calls them, do not have any special status under the law. As we saw in Chapter 1, victims have no status in criminal proceedings other than as witnesses for the Crown. As such, they do not have standing to make submissions for or against the offender. What the VIS gives victims is statutory permission to file a statement with the court describing the loss suffered or the harm done to them by the offender as a result of the commission of the offence, and nothing more. Presenting a VIS at a sentencing hearing is therefore not a right, but merely something victims are permitted to do (Wemmers & April-Ménard, 2013). In the remainder of the proceedings, victims act only in the capacity of witnesses. In other words, at all stages of the trial except the sentencing hearing, the status of "victim" is simply not recognized by the Criminal Code.

The VIS gives victims the opportunity, albeit a limited one, to take part in criminal proceedings, and victims have been found to use the VIS for many different reasons. Sometimes victims file a VIS without fully understanding what it is (Roach, 1999; Wemmers & Cyr, 2006a). For some victims, filling out a VIS allows them to express how their lives have been impacted by the crime (Erez, 1994; Lens, Pemberton, & Bogaerts, 2013; Sanders, Hoyle, Morgan, & Cape, 2001). Erez refers to this expressive function as therapeutic, since it is thought to provide the victim with psychological relief through the open expression of strong emotions (Erez, 1999; Erez, Ibarra, & Downs, 2011). It provides an opportunity for recognition of the victim, which, as we saw in Chapter 6, is a need of many victims. While some studies find that victims feel better after making a VIS (Erez & Tontodonato, 1992; Erez, Roeger, & Morgan, 1997), others find no effect (Davis & Smith, 1994), and yet others find mixed results (Sanders et al., 2001). In short, there is no clear evidence as to the therapeutic effects of the VIS (Lens et al., 2013; Roberts & Erez, 2004).

In particular, the VIS may allow the victim to send a message to the offender (Roberts & Erez, 2010). Victims suffering from PTSD may find it particularly difficult to meet their offender fact to face, and through the VIS they can still communicate what it is they want to say to the offender (Cheon & Regehr, 2006). Studies suggest that victims who are strongly impacted by the crime (e.g., those suffering from PTSD) are more likely to deliver a VIS (Lens et al., 2013; Roberts, 2009).

Another reason why victims make a VIS is in the hope of influencing the sentence (Lens at al., 2013; Sanders et al., 2001). Knowing the consequences of the crime, the judge can tailor the sentence to fit the situation. For example, victims may have concerns about their safety and wish to have specific conditions included in the sentence, such as a noncontact order (Lens et al., 2013). Victims may have financial damages for which they would like to obtain compensation from the offender (Baril, 2002). Victims' need for protection and reparation are highly relevant for sentencing decisions. However, there is no evidence that the VIS systematically impacts sentences, either making them tougher or more lenient in Canada or internationally (Baril et al., 1990; Erez & Roeger, 1995; Roberts, 2009; Sanders et al., 2001).

Victims' expectations are important because they help shape their satisfaction with the justice system. For example, victims who enter a VIS in the hope of influencing the sentence are disappointed when this does not happen (Erez, Roeger, & Morgan, 1994). Victims who submit a written statement without reading it aloud in court will often have no idea what was actually done with their VIS. This lack of knowledge, combined with cynicism about the criminal justice system, often leaves victims feeling dissatisfied (Erez & Tontodonato, 1992; Gilberti, 1991; Sanders et al., 2001). One study randomly assigned victims' cases to various treatments and found that victim impact statements had no effect on victims' feelings of involvement or satisfaction with the criminal justice process or its outcome (Davis & Smith, 1994). Nevertheless, many victims say that they would submit a VIS in the future if they were victimized again (Hoyle, Cape, Morgan, & Sanders, 1998; Meredith & Paquette, 2001).

How the VIS is administered may also play a role in determining victims' satisfaction. For example, Baril and colleagues (1990) found high levels of victim satisfaction following a pilot project with victim impact statements in Montreal. For this project, the court had set up a special office and hired staff to answer victims' questions about this new tool. After the VIS came into practice, however, this office was dismantled, and victims often reported not being able to reach the court with their questions (Wemmers & Cyr, 2006b). Roberts (2009) argues that many programs are poorly operationalized, which might explain why so many studies report finding no difference in satisfaction ratings between victims who made a VIS and those who did not.

Problems with the VIS

The opportunity to present a VIS at sentencing has now been in place for many years, yet the VIS continues to be a source of debate among legal scholars both in Canada and internationally (Ashworth, 1993; Campbell, 2015; Erez, 1994; Erez & Roberts, 2007; Manikis, 2012; Roach, 1999; Sanders et al., 2001; Smith, 2011). According to Edwards (2004), much of the debate surrounding victim participation has focused on balance, in particular balancing the rights of victims and the rights of the accused. In the United States, defence lawyers tried to ban the use of victim impact statements in cases where there was a risk that the accused might be sentenced to death. In *Payne v. Tennessee* (111 S.Ct. 2597 (1991)), lawyers for the accused argued that allowing victims to speak at the sentencing hearing and, hence, possibly influence the sentence introduced an arbitrary element into the proceedings. It was argued that a victim who gave a strong and touching victim impact statement versus a victim who was not as articulate could make the difference between life and death for the accused. The US Supreme Court did not agree and upheld the possibility for victims to make a VIS in all cases, including capital sentencing hearings (Erez, 1999). Crime is a violation of the victim's rights as well as an offence against the state, and victims have a legitimate interest in the sentencing of their offender.

Nevertheless, the emotional and highly subjective nature of the VIS is considered problematic by some legal practitioners and antithetical to the legal goals of the hearing (Rock, 2010; Wemmers, 2008b). As Rock (2010) aptly points out, courtrooms are embedded in long-standing traditions and rituals that are very different from the highly emotional rituals of victim impact statements and do not sit well with many lawyers. From a legal perspective, the principle of a fair hearing entitles the offender to be heard in his or her defence and have his or her penalty determined in a neutral and objective forum (Booth, 2016). Authors such as Roach (1999) and Smith (2011) consider the VIS a threat to the rights of the accused that undermines the bipartite (i.e., the state versus the defendant) nature of the sentencing hearing.

Besides a potential clash between the rights of the accused and those of the victim, there is also a possible conflict between the interests of the victim and those of the state. According to Roach (1999), victim impact statements are often used to serve the interests of Crown prosecutors rather than the interests of the victim. For example, a study done in British Columbia found that victim impact statements were most likely to be used in cases where prosecutors believed them to be important. Sometimes they were even filled out by the police, without the victim understanding that he or she was making a VIS (Roach, 1999). It is important to keep in mind that public prosecutors represent the state, not the victim. While prosecutors will consider the impact of crime on the victims, this is not the only factor they must consider when deciding how to handle a case (Wemmers, 2011b). Problems may arise when the interests of the prosecution are contrary to those of the victim. The VIS is not intended as a tool for the prosecution but as a tool for victims. It is supposed to allow their views and concerns to be presented and considered where their personal interests are affected. Any other use of the VIS is contrary to the principles of justice for victims outlined in the UN Declaration.

This divergence of interests is particularly striking in connection with plea bargaining between the Crown prosecutor and counsel for the defence. The case of *Vanscoy v. Ontario*, discussed in Chapter 7, is illustrative of this deep sense of dissatisfaction that victims feel when they are shut out of plea negotiations.

Research with victims who submitted a VIS shows that they found it particularly frustrating that the sentences in their cases had been negotiated between the Crown and the defence before their statements had even been prepared. Not only were these victims dissatisfied with the sentence given, they felt that the process had abused their time and fragile emotional state, knowing that their statements would be given no weight (Meredith & Paquette, 2001). While victims have no legal standing in plea negotiations, at the very least their VIS should be heard before entering into such negotiations. This does not happen because it is only after the defendant has pleaded guilty or is found guilty by the court that the VIS is presented.

There is, therefore, a risk that victims will be victimized a second time when they come into contact with the judicial process. Manikis (2012) argues that the VIS is merely symbolic in the context of a sentencing hearing. She therefore advocates for an improved framework for the plea-bargaining process in Canada that enables victims to play a greater role as participants. The VIS enters late in the criminal justice process, and research suggests that victims' involvement in the early stages of the criminal justice process is important for victims' sense of justice and their support for sentencing (Wemmers, 1999; Morissette & Wemmers, 2016). While there are problems with the VIS, it does nevertheless represent a step forward in the recognition of the procedural rights of victims (Roach, 1999).

Community Impact Statements

The effects of crime can be far reaching. As we saw in Chapter 4, an offence can affect not only an individual but an entire community. **Community impact statements (CIS)** (Criminal Code s. 722.2) were announced as part of Bill C-32, which introduced the *Canadian Victims Bill of Rights*. As of 23 July 2015, individuals can submit a statement on behalf of a community that has been affected by crime. The CIS focuses on the harm or loss suffered by the community as a result of the crime. Other than being open to community members, the CIS resembles the VIS in terms of what it can contain and how it works.

To submit a CIS, community members must fill in a form and submit it to the court. Like the VIS, there is now one form that is used nationally, which is included in Part XXVIII of the Criminal Code (Form 34.3, s. 722.2(2)). The CIS may include information about the emotional, economic, and physical impact of the crime on the community. These might include things like changes in lifestyle or activities of community members, loss of revenue from tourism, or the ability of members of the community to access services. Like the VIS, the CIS allows the community member to address any fears within the community about security, in particular regarding contact with the offender. There is also a possibility for the community member to include a drawing, poem or letter.

A CIS *cannot* contain certain information, such as unproven allegations or other statements about the offence or the offender that are not relevant to the harm or loss suffered by the community. Nor should it include an opinion or recommendation about the sentence without the court's approval.

According to the Department of Justice's website, community impact statements "allow the community to take part in the *sentencing* of the offender by explaining to the Court and the offender how the crime has affected the community" (2016). This is noteworthy for two reasons. First, the emphasis on sentencing seems misplaced because impact statements were introduced to promote victim participation in the criminal justice process (art. 6b of the UN Declaration), not just sentencing. Second, in our adversarial system the prosecutor is supposed to represent the interests of society or the state. The prosecutor is directly involved in the sentencing process, presenting the sentencing judge with a recommendation for the sentence. Hence, the CIS must refer to the local community in which the crime occurred. Therefore, while it is welcoming to see recognition of the wider impact of crime beyond direct victims, it is disappointing that this recognition is limited to sentencing.

Statement on Restitution

Both the VIS and CIS focus on the sentencing hearing and, as we have seen, much of the debate around victim input at sentencing focuses on the principles of sentencing. The purpose and principles of sentencing are specified in article 718 of the Criminal Code, according to which the fundamental purpose of sentencing is to protect society and to contribute, along with crime prevention initiatives, to respect for the law and the maintenance of a just, peaceful, and safe society. This is achieved by imposing just sanctions that have one or more of the following objectives: denunciation of the crime, deterrence of the offender, isolation or separation of the offender from society, rehabilitation of the offender, promotion of a sense of responsibility in offenders, and reparation for the harm done to victims and the community. Thus, the harm suffered by the victim is considered by judges at sentencing, and victims may present specific needs that should be considered at sentencing, such as the need for protection or reparation.

Judges may order offenders to compensate their victims. Specifically, **restitution orders** (s. 738.1 of the Criminal Code) involve the financial reimbursement of the victim by the offender for any damage to or loss of property and can be imposed on a convicted or discharged offender, in addition to any other measure imposed on the offender. Bill C-32, which came into effect in 2015, introduced the Statement on Restitution (SOR), hence putting new emphasis on reparation for victims by the offender at sentencing. The SOR is a new form (Form 34.1, s. 737.1(4)) that victims can use if they wish to be reimbursed for damages by the offender.

Restitution orders are, however, not new in the Criminal Code. They were always possible, and victims could identify any damages for which they desired reparation on the VIS. Evidence from victims suggests that restitution orders are not often imposed (Wemmers & Cyr, 2006a). This may be for many reasons: victims may not know that they can ask for restitution, or they may not be informed of the status of their case and miss their chance. However, not all judges are fond of restitution at sentencing and view it as a contamination of criminal law with civil law (LaPrairie Associates, 2004). The amount requested must be clear and not in dispute or the request will exceed the competence of the court and the victim will have to take the request to a civil court. Moreover, if the financial restitution is ordered it will be entirely up to the victim to obtain the money, which is often problematic. The topic of reparation will be discussed in detail in Chapter 11.

Victims' Preferred Role

The VIS is just one possible form of victim participation. It gives victims an opportunity to express to the court how they were impacted by the crime. Edwards (2004) identifies four different forms of participation: (1) expression, (2) provision of information, (3) consultation, and (4) control. Each role has specific implications for the victim and his or her relationship with the criminal justice system.

Expression involves offering victims the option to supply information or express their emotions during the trial. While authorities are obliged to provide victims with an opportunity for expression, victims are not obliged to act on that offer. This one-directional flow of information from the victim to the court resembles the VIS. Victims can choose whether they wish to make a VIS. In turn, the VIS does not impose any obligations on judges, who maintain their independence.

The second type of participation, the provision of information, requires courts to seek and consider information from victims. In turn, victims are obliged to supply information to criminal justice authorities and have no choice but to do so (Edwards, 2004). This role strongly resembles the role of witness, which, of course, is the traditional role reserved for victims in criminal justice. Victims provide vital information to police, often alerting them to crimes that would otherwise go undetected. As witnesses, victims can be subpoenaed to appear in court to testify. Victims cannot, however, choose whether or not to testify and, as witnesses, they have no control over what information they present since they must answer the questions that are put to them before the court.

The third type of participation, consultation, obliges authorities to seek and obtain information about victims' preferences. However, authorities are not obliged to follow the victims' directions and victims are not obliged to participate (Edwards, 2004). Unlike expression, this is a bidirectional flow of information. For example, in some countries victims of serious violent crimes have the right to meet and consult with the officials handling their case before offers of pleas are made or the defendant is released from custody (Davis & Mulford, 2008; Wemmers, 1996).

The fourth type of participation is control. It goes further than all other types of participation in that it gives victims control over decisions. Criminal justice authorities would be obliged to seek and obtain information as to the victim's preference and then follow that preference. In turn, the victim would be obliged to make his or her preference known to authorities (Edwards, 2004). This is the most extreme form of participation possible according to Edwards. Sharia, or Islamic, law is an example of such a system, where under certain circumstances victims are asked for their preferences regarding punishment and the court is obliged to follow the victims' wishes (Bassiouni, 1982).

As we saw in Chapter 6, research on the role that victims would like to have in the criminal justice system consistently shows that victims generally seek consultation. Victims do not generally want to control decisions (Shapland, Wilmore, & Duff, 1985; Wemmers & Cyr, 2004). For example, Michael Kilchling (1995) asked German victims what kind of role they would like to have in the criminal justice system and found that most expressed the desire to fulfill an "in-between" role: neither full exclusion nor full control. Few victims want to participate directly in trial proceedings, and what they seem to want most is to be consulted throughout the criminal justice process (Human Rights Centre, 2015; Sanders et al., 2001).

The VIS neither offers victims opportunities for consultation nor allows them to express their views and concerns during the trial. However, other models for victim participation can be found in domestic criminal law, and in the following section some of these models will be presented.

Other Forms of Participation

There exist many different models in which the victim may either personally intervene or have a legal representative act on his or her behalf during the trial stage. These models allow victim participation during the criminal trial. This is particularly important when victims and the state (represented by the prosecutor) have different priorities or interests. It allows the victim's voice, one that is often silenced in the court, to be heard. However, participating directly in the trial process may be traumatizing for some victims, particularly in an adversarial setting (Danieli, 2014; Herman, 2005; Stover, Balthazard, & Koenig, 2011). Allowing victims to be represented at trial relieves them of this burden and changes the dynamics of their participation (Wemmers, 2008b). Instead of highly subjective and emotional participation, which is in conflict with legal goals, victim participation is based on legal argumentation and representation (Rock, 2010). This changes the dialogue before the court, opening up the legal discourse to include the interests of the victim (Wemmers, 2008b). At the same time, it is in line with victims' preferences since it offers them the recognition they seek without burdening them with too much responsibility (Wemmers, 2005).

The Civil Party

Also known as the adhesion procedure, the civil party can be found in many European countries, such as France and Belgium (Brienen & Hoegen, 2000). It can be viewed as a bit of civil law tied onto the criminal justice process. Originally the civil party allowed victims to claim damages from the offender without having to go through the added bother and expense of a separate civil trial (Wemmers, 2005). More importantly, perhaps, it provides victims with formal rights to participation in criminal justice proceedings that are not found in most adversarial systems. Victims' participatory rights in the trial may include the right to legal representation, the right to make opening and closing statements, the right to present evidence, and the right to cross-examine witnesses (Brienen & Hoegen, 2000; Maguire & Shapland, 1997; Redress, 2015). To exercise their rights, victims will often have access to their case files and will be informed about the progress of their case (Wemmers, 2005). Because the civil party involves formal rights for victims, in some countries failure by the state to give victims a chance to make a request as a civil party leads to an obligation of the state to reimburse the victim for damages (Brienen & Hoegen, 2000).

The Auxiliary Prosecutor

The auxiliary prosecutor exists in countries such as Poland and Germany, where it is known as the *Nebenkläge* (Brienen & Hoegen, 2000). Although the prosecution is still led by the public prosecutor, the victim's legal representative has extensive participatory rights in the trial. As a *Nebenkläge*, victims have the right to be represented by a lawyer, they have access to the prosecutor's investigatory files, and they have the right to be heard at the trial, to be present throughout the trial, to file evidentiary motions, to bring challenging motions against judges or experts, to ask questions and make objections and statements (including closing statements), and to appeal an acquittal (Redress,

2015; Wemmers, 2005). However, victims cannot make sentencing recommendations, and decision making at sentencing is left entirely up to the judge (Walther, 2000). Research on victim participation in Germany found that victims with legal representation experienced fewer difficulties in obtaining information about case developments and were more satisfied with their overall treatment throughout the legal process than victims without legal representation (Bacik, Maunsell, & Grogan, 1998, cited in Doak, 2005). By providing victims with the recognition they seek and giving them, through legal counsel, a clear understanding of how the criminal justice system works, victim participation in the criminal justice process can help empower victims and combat the sense of powerlessness that many victims feel during criminal proceedings (Wemmers, 2009c).

These models illustrate the variety of ways in which domestic criminal justice systems allow the views and concerns of victims to be presented and considered at different stages throughout the criminal justice process.

Postsentencing

After sentencing, victims' personal interests may continue to be impacted by decisions regarding the offender. As we saw, sentencing has many objectives, and there are many different factors that need to be considered by the judge. While most offenders remain in the community, the most serious offenders who have committed violent crimes will generally be sentenced to prison. Eventually, however, almost all offenders will return to the community. *Parole* is the early release of an offender from a correctional facility to the supervision of a parole officer in the community. Parole boards deal with prisoners serving time for the most serious offences, and the victims of these offenders are therefore victims of serious crimes, often suffering long-term trauma (Padfield & Roberts, 2010). Sometimes these victims want to be kept informed of their offender's possible release into the community and participate in parole hearings, even though this may occur some years after the trial. As a result, many countries, including the United States, England, New Zealand, and Canada, provide victim information postsentencing and allow victim participation at parole hearings (Roberts, 2009).

In Canada, correctional services have developed programs for victims. Federal prisons house offenders who have been sentenced to two or more years of prison. Shorter custodial sentences (less than two years) fall under provincial jurisdiction. Approximately one in three adult offenders are given a custodial sentence (Maxwell, 2015), and it is less than one in five for young offenders (Alam, 2015). Among the adult offenders given a custodial sentence, less than

10 per cent are given sentences of two years or more (Maxwell, 2015). After discussing victims' postsentencing rights at the federal level, we will discuss their rights at the provincial level.

Federal Programs

The *Corrections and Conditional Release Act* (CCRA) regulates parole for federally sentenced offenders. When the CCRA was enacted in 1992, it introduced several rights for victims, such as the right to information about the offender and the right to observe national parole board meetings. Later, in 2000, victims were permitted to read aloud a prepared statement at parole hearings (Public Safety Canada, 2013). Over the years, victims' rights have been modified and expanded, most recently in 2015 by Bill C-32, which extended the definition of "victim" to include a person who has suffered property damage or economic loss as a result of an offence as well as physical or emotional damage. Victims may also authorize another person to represent them if they so wish. If the direct victim is dead or incapable of acting on his or her own behalf, someone else, such as a family member, may act on the victim's behalf.

Victim Notification

Victims may request and receive information regarding a federal offender. According to Public Safety Canada, some victims prefer not to receive any further information about the offender, so victims must register with the National Office for Victims at Public Safety Canada if they want information. They are *not* automatically contacted and informed of their rights by Correctional Service Canada (CSC) or by the Parole Board of Canada (PBC). Approximately 17 per cent of all federal prisoners have registered victims (Public Safety Canada, 2015). Most (86 per cent) of the victims who register with CSC are victims of violence, and the most common type of information requested is information about the release of the offender (Allen, 2014). Only certain information is always available to registered victims, such as the name of the offender and the sentence, and victims will often already have this information from the criminal trial. However, some information, such as release dates, will only be given if it is felt that the victim's interest outweighs the offender's right to privacy and does not pose a risk to public safety (CCRA s. 26(1)). Human rights are inalienable, and offenders do not lose their human rights when they enter prison. Box 10.2 provides an overview of the types of information victims can request.

BOX 10.2: DISCLOSURE OF INFORMATION TO VICTIMS OF FEDERALLY SENTENCED OFFENDERS (CCRA 26(1))

The following information must be provided to victims if requested:

- The offender's name
- The offence the offender was convicted of and the court that convicted the offender
- When the sentence began and the length of the sentence
- The eligibility and review dates applicable to the offender for temporary absences or parole

The following information may be released if the commissioner of the CSC or the chairperson of the PBC determines that the interest of the victim clearly outweighs an invasion of the offender's right to privacy:

- The offender's age
- The name and location of the penitentiary in which the sentence is being served
- If the offender is transferred, a summary of the reasons for the transfer and the name and location of the penitentiary in which the sentence is being served, including advance notice, whenever possible, of transfers to minimum-security institutions
- The programs in which the offender is participant or has participated
- The serious disciplinary offences the offender has committed
- Information pertaining to the offender's correctional plan, including information regarding the offender's progress toward meeting the objectives of the plan
- If the offender is removed from Canada under the *Immigration and Refugee Protection Act* before the expiration of the sentence
- The date, if any, on which the offender is to be released on temporary absence, work release, parole, or statutory release
- The date of any hearing for the purposes of a PBC review
- Whether the offender is in custody and if not, why
- Whether or not the offender has appealed a decision of the PBC and the outcome of that appeal
- The reason for a waiver of the right to a hearing

The following information may be released if the commissioner of the CSC or the chairperson of the PBC determines that disclosure would not have a negative impact on public safety:

- The date, if any, on which the offender is to be released on temporary absence, work release, parole, or statutory release
- The conditions attached to the offender's unescorted temporary absence, work release, parole, or statutory release and the reasons for any temporary absence
- The destination of the offender when released on any temporary absence, work release, parole, or statutory release and whether the offender will be in the vicinity of the victim while travelling to that destination
- A photograph of the offender

Parole Hearings

In addition to receiving information, victims may give information to the CSC or the PBC. The aim of parole is to support the successful rehabilitation of the offender as he or she transitions back into the community. However, the parole board must also protect society, including the victim. In Canada, most prisoners become eligible for day parole after having served one-sixth of their sentence and full parole at the one-third point. The PBC may grant, deny, or revoke the parole of all offenders except those serving less than two years in Ontario and Quebec, which have their own provincial parole boards.

Victims may wish to share with the PBC any concerns they have for their safety or that of others. They may provide a victim statement (VS) at any time. Like a VIS, a VS is a form on which victims can indicate the physical, emotional, or financial impact of the offence on them, their families, and their community. They may also request that special conditions be imposed on the offender upon conditional release. Victims may also present their VS in person at the offender's parole board hearing. Victims who choose to present an oral statement at parole hearings tend to be victims of serious crimes involving fatalities, such as murder, manslaughter, or impaired driving causing death (Padfield & Roberts, 2010).

Victims may apply to the Victims Fund, a federally administered fund, for financial assistance to attend PBC hearings of the offender who harmed them. It can be stressful for the victim to present his or her VS to the PBC, so it is possible for the victim to be accompanied by a support person. Financial assistance is also available for a support person to accompany the victim at PBC hearings (Public Safety Canada, 2013).

Sometimes victims worry about possible retaliation from the offender. They may have concerns about whether their information will be shared with the offender. It is always important to balance victims' rights (e.g., safety) and offenders' rights (e.g., privacy). Victims too have a right to privacy and offenders do *not* have a right to be notified if a victim registers with the CSC or PBC for information and notification. However, the law requires that these organizations disclose to the offender any information that will be considered by the CSC or PBC in making a decision. For example, if a victim submits a VS and this information is included in the decision making regarding the offender's parole application, then the offender has a right to obtain a copy of the VS. Victims' personal information, such as their addresses and phone numbers, however, are *never* shared with offenders.

Provincial Programs

Ontario and Quebec have established provincial parole boards that grant, deny, or revoke parole for offenders serving sentences of less than two years. Like their federal counterpart, the provincial parole boards aim to protect society and promote the successful reintegration of the offender into society.

Ontario

Victims wishing to receive notification about a provincially sentenced offender may register with the province's Victim Notification System. This is an automated voice messaging system that phones the victim any time there is a change in the status of the offender. The province offers a toll-free victim support line that victims may call to speak with someone about their case.

The Ontario Parole Board (OPB) allows victims to present an impact statement at parole hearings. Specifically, the board invites victims to describe the physical, financial, and emotional impact of the crime, including the ongoing impact and any conditions the victim would like the board to impose if the offender is granted release (Ontario Parole Board, n.d.). Victims may provide a written submission or attend the offender's parole hearing and give an oral statement. However, because this information can be used in deciding whether or not parole will be granted, the offender may have access to it and will be present if an oral statement is given at a hearing. Victims may also attend to observe a hearing and are encouraged to bring a support person with them. Victims may apply to the provincial government to receive financial assistance to attend parole hearings in Ontario (Ontario Parole Board, n.d.).

Quebec

The Commission québécoise des libérations conditionnelles (CQLC) handles parole for provincially sentenced offenders in Quebec. The rules governing parole for these offenders are found in the *Loi sur le système correctionnel du Québec* (RLRQ c. S-40.1). The province has put in place a comprehensive information system for victims.

Like the other programs, victims can register if they wish to receive information. In 2014–15, the CQLC received 278 requests for information from victims (CQLC, 2015). However, unlike other programs, the CQLC *automatically* contacts the victims of certain serious crimes. The CQLC established a distinct, proactive program for the victims of domestic violence, sexual assault, and crimes related to pedophile behaviour. The victims of these crimes do not have to register to be informed. The CQLC works together with the province's ministries of transportation (driver's licences) and health (public medical insurance) to locate victims. The CQLC is able to reach almost all victims of these serious crimes: In 2013–14, 92.8 per cent of these victims were reached (CQLC, 2014). In 2016, the CQLC reached an agreement with the province's victim support services (Centres d'aide aux victimes d'actes criminels, CAVAC), effectively delegating the communication with victims to the CAVAC. Under this agreement, the CAVAC's trained victim support workers contact victims on behalf of the CQLC.

Victims can also submit a written VS at parole hearings. However, contrary to other programs, victims are not permitted to present their VS in person. The offender must have access to all information that will be considered in the decision-making process, so victims must submit their VS in advance of the hearing. In 2014–15, the CQLC received 255 victim statements, while that same year they handled 4,550 cases (CQLC, 2015). One case may involve several victims, so it is impossible to say exactly what percentage of cases included a VS. However, it is safe to conclude that this occurs in only a minority of cases.

Punitive Rights or Informed Decision Making?

Victim participation postsentencing is highly controversial. Roberts (2009) argues that while victim input at sentencing is legitimate, victim input at corrections is an example of "punitive victim rights" (p. 347). According to Roberts and his colleagues, victims seldom possess information relevant to the parole decision, and allowing them to have input is inconsistent with the principles of justice (Padfield & Roberts, 2010; Roberts, 2009). In this view, the ongoing impact of victimization or the possible impact of release on the victim and his or her family are not part of the parole board's mandate and should be excluded from parole hearings. Roberts argues that this type of victim input constitutes "an example of punitive victim rights trumping sound correctional practices" (Roberts, 2009, p. 391). Moreover, unlike victim impact statements, which have not been found to lead to more severe sentencing, victim statements at parole hearings have been found to impact the likelihood of release (Caplan, 2007; Morgan & Smith, 2005; Smith, Watkins, & Morgan, 1997).

However, while some consider the VS to be punitive, others see it as a tool for informed decision making. Authors such as Herman and Wasserman (2001) argue that victim participation postsentencing leads to better-informed decisions and the achievement of re-entry goals. Victim input can highlight the need for strict supervision or special conditions such as protection orders, mandated treatment to address substance abuse or violent behaviour, and restrictions on where offenders can work or live. As we saw in Chapter 3, victims of violent crime often know their offender: They may be family or a former partner, colleague, or friend. In addition, crime does not affect all members of society equally, and some people and communities are more at risk of victimization than others. Hence, victims sometimes do have information relevant to the parole decision, and through dialogue with victims decision makers can make better-informed decisions.

This relationship between victims and victimizers reminds us that victims are not always diametrically opposed to offenders. Furthermore, the distinction between victim and victimizer is not always clear, and someone may be a victim as well as an offender (Cuevas, Finkelhor, Turner, & Ormrod, 2007; Van Dijk & Steinmetz, 1983). As we saw in Chapter 5, studies suggest a possible link between childhood victimization and later violence (Widom, Schuck, & White, 2006; Williams & Herrera, 2007). Bearing in mind the relationship between victims and offenders, victim participation in the planning, management, and implementation of offender re-entry policies and programs can contribute positively to parole decisions and the successful re-entry of offenders into the community (Herman & Wasserman, 2001). Moreover, as we saw earlier, because some victims miss out on the opportunity to prepare a VIS because of plea bargaining, the parole hearing might be one of the few opportunities a victim has to present an impact statement (Petersilia, 2000).

Besides contributing to the successful re-entry of offenders, victims' participation postsentencing can empower victims, providing them with a voice in the process that determines when and under what conditions offenders are to be released as well as reduce their risk of re-victimization (Herman & Wasserman, 2001). However, it may also contribute to re-victimization, as victims are forced to relive the crime when telling their story (Morgan & Smith, 2005). Further research is needed to better understand the impact of victim participation postsentencing on victims.

Conclusion

Victim participation in the criminal justice process is important for victims whose primary function in criminal law is that of a witness. Since the adoption of the UN Declaration, many countries, including Canada, have introduced measures aimed at giving victims an opportunity to present their views and concerns at appropriate stages of the proceedings where their personal interests are affected and to have their views and concerns considered by criminal justice authorities.

While victim participation in criminal justice may take many forms, in countries with a common law legal tradition the victim impact statement is a popular vehicle for victim participation. The VIS, however, does not provide victims with a status or procedural rights in criminal proceedings. In comparison to other modes of participation, the VIS offers victims a highly emotional and limited role that only occurs late in the criminal justice process. It is only at the sentencing stage that victims have permission to file a statement with the court describing the impact of the crime. At least in Canada, expanding victim participation in criminal justice has meant broadening the definition of who can give an impact statement to include community members (the CIS), the introduction of restitution statements at sentencing, as well as the possibility for victim statements postsentencing.

A key issue with respect to victims' right to participation is the balance of justice and the rights of the offender. As specified in the UN Declaration, victims' participation must be accomplished without prejudice to the accused. Human rights are inalienable, and defendants do not lose their human rights during criminal proceedings nor when they enter prison. However, respecting the rights of the accused does not mean shutting out victims. Many rights, such as the right to information and notification, do not interfere with the rights of the accused or the offender. Research on the preferred role of victims indicates that victims want to be consulted but not control decision making in criminal justice proceedings. We need to ensure that victim participation is therapeutic and does not inflict further harm on the victim or the offender.

Victims are relevant in the criminal justice process. Without victims there would often be no criminal trial. They possess information that can be valuable to decision makers in the criminal justice system. At the same time, criminal justice is important for victims and their need for recognition, protection, and reparation. However, criminal justice has its limitations and cannot meet the needs of all victims. In the next chapter reparative justice will be discussed.

CHAPTER 11

REPARATIVE JUSTICE

Victims' frustration with criminal justice has led some to argue for the need to rethink justice. As we saw, the criminal justice system serves many objectives, including reparation of the victim and the community. The word "reparation" refers to repairing or making amends for a wrong that one has done (*Oxford Dictionary*, 1989). Victims often express a need for reparation (see Chapter 6). In this chapter, reparative justice is presented as a form of victim-centred justice that takes into account victims' needs and, in particular, their need for reparation, while also respecting the rights of the accused. After considering the meaning of victim-centred reparation, the research on victims and restorative justice will be discussed to arrive at a concept of reparative justice that can meet the needs of victims while respecting the rights of the accused.

Reparation for Victims

Victims' rights are human rights, and from a human rights perspective reparation can be viewed as a means aimed at promoting justice by redressing violations of the law. This definition comes from *Basic Principles and Guidelines on the Right to a Remedy and Reparation for Victims of Gross Violations of International Human Rights Law and Serious Violations of International Humanitarian Law* (hereafter referred to as "Basic Principles and Guidelines"), which were adopted by the General Assembly of the United Nations in 2005. The Basic Principles and Guidelines provide a comprehensive overview of what reparation is from a victim's perspective. While this document pertains to victims of international crimes, it is inspired by research with victims of crime (Danieli, 2014). Its victim-centred approach makes it particularly interesting and relevant for victims of all types of crime, both domestic and international. After all, from the victims' perspectives there may be little difference between the murder of a loved one that happens in the context of a war crime and one that occurs in the context of gang violence.

A key feature of the Basic Principles and Guidelines is the explicit recognition of the many different forms that reparation can take. It specifies that reparation includes restitution, compensation, rehabilitation, satisfaction, and guarantees of nonrepetition. *Restitution* refers to restoring property or rights to their proper owner, or restoring the victim to his or her original state. *Compensation* refers to financial reparation. *Rehabilitation* refers to medical, psychological, social, as well as legal services for victims. *Satisfaction* includes a variety of measures that recognize the victimization, promote the truth, and denounce the crime. These include public apologies as well as sanctions against the offender(s). *Guarantees of nonrepetition* are any measures that contribute to crime prevention and deterrence. This could be changes to the law to ensure that in the future it becomes more difficult for a particular type of victimization to occur, or specific measures aimed at reducing the offender's risk of reoffending.

These different forms of reparation reflect its flexibility as a response to victimization, which is critical given the diversity of victims' needs. A significant contribution of the Basic Principles and Guidelines is its recognition that reparation is something more than just the return of property and monetary payment. Historically, legal definitions of reparation have largely focused on restitution and compensation (Goetz, 2014; Manirabona & Wemmers, 2014). For example, as we saw in Chapter 10, the Canadian Criminal Code allows victims to seek financial reimbursement from the offender at sentencing with what is called a "restitution order" (s. 737.1). Here the word "restitution" is used to mean compensation from the offender rather than the return of property. This focus on financial reparation is also reflected in the *Canadian Victims Bill of Rights*, which specifies that every victim has the right to have the court consider making a restitution order against the offender, and if the offender fails to pay the victim he or she can have the order entered as a civil court judgment that is enforceable against the offender (s. 16–17). Hence, restitution orders are akin to civil law, like the civil party procedure described in Chapter 10.

But a limited definition of reparation does not correspond with the range of victims' needs found in the research (see Chapter 6). Victims' need for reparation goes beyond financial compensation and includes the need for recognition, support, information, and protection. The Basic Principles and Guidelines are victim centred because they define reparation in terms of what it offers victims. In doing so, they recognize a wide range of forms of reparation for victims. Thus, the Basic Principles and Guidelines promote the view that justice should be defined in terms of reparations for victims (Manrique-Rueda, 2014).

Restorative Justice

The criminological literature refers to "restorative justice"[9] rather than "reparative justice." Restorative justice is generally defined as a process whereby all parties with a stake in a specific offence come together to collectively resolve how to deal with the aftermath of the offence and its implications for the future (Marshall, 1999). This view is also reflected in the *Basic Principles on the Use of Restorative Justice Programmes in Criminal Matters*, which was supported by the Economic and Social Council (ECOSOC) of the United Nations in 2002 (see Box 11.1). A similar definition is found in the Canadian *Values and Principles of Restorative Justice in Criminal Matters*, published by Department of

BOX 11.1: ECOSOC RESOLUTION 2002/12: *BASIC PRINCIPLES ON THE USE OF RESTORATIVE JUSTICE PROGRAMMES IN CRIMINAL MATTERS*

I. Use of terms

1. "Restorative justice programme" means any program that uses restorative processes and seeks to achieve restorative outcomes.
2. "Restorative process" means any process in which the victim and the offender and, where appropriate, any other individuals or community members affected by a crime, participate together actively in the resolution of matters arising from the crime, generally with the help of a facilitator. Restorative processes may include mediation, conciliation, conferencing and sentencing circles.
3. "Restorative outcome" means an agreement reached as a result of a restorative process. Restorative outcomes include responses and programmes such as reparation, restitution and community service, aimed at meeting the individual and collective needs and responsibilities of the parties and achieving the reintegration of the victim and the offender.
4. "Parties" means the victim, the offender and any other individuals or community members affected by a crime who may be involved in a restorative process.
5. "Facilitator" means a person whose role is to facilitate, in a fair and impartial manner, the participation of the parties in a restorative process.

....

9 It is noteworthy that in the French literature on restorative justice the term "*justice réparatice*" is used rather than "*justice restauratice*" (see Wemmers, 2002).

Justice Canada (2004). Restorative justice approaches crime as an injury or wrong done to another person rather than solely as a matter of breaking the law or offending against the state and is primarily oriented toward repairing the individual relationship and the social harm caused by the offence (Jones, Parmentier, & Weitekamp, 2014; Wemmers & Canuto, 2002). Accordingly, it is concerned with reparation, either materially or symbolically, and it encourages the victim and the offender to play active roles in finding a solution through discussion and negotiation. This could be anything from an apology by the offender to the payment of compensation. The only criterion is that both the victim and offender agree.

While restorative justice recognizes the harm suffered by the victim as a result of the offence, it takes a broad, criminological approach to harm. Accordingly, some authors have criticized restorative justice for being offender oriented and using victims to promote the rehabilitation of offenders (Green, 2006; Reeves & Mulley, 2000; Wemmers, 2002). Many of the first restorative justice programs have their roots in probation work. They were developed as a means to further the successful rehabilitation of the offender and not as a way to better meet victims' needs (Wemmers & Canuto, 2002). For example, one of the first restorative justice programs to receive international recognition is the victim–offender reconciliation program (VORP), which was established in Kitchener-Waterloo, Ontario (Vanfraechem & Bolivar, 2015). In 1974, Mark Yantzi, a probation officer and a volunteer with the Mennonite Central Committee, together with another volunteer, Dave Worth, and in coordination with the courts arranged for two young offenders to meet with their victims to apologize, to hear their victims' statements, to ask forgiveness of their victims, and to determine compensation. This was the start of what flourished into a successful and widely respected program (Yantzi, 2005).

Moreover, many of the early advocates of restorative justice, such as Fattah (1998) and Weitekamp (1999), follow an abolitionist approach, which supports the abolition of criminal justice (see Chapter 2). Victim–offender mediation is a model that conforms to Nils Christie's contention that crimes are essentially conflicts between people that should be given back to the parties. Instead of "stealing" the conflict from victims and pushing them to the sidelines, as the criminal justice system does, mediation allows victims to actively participate in finding a solution (Christie, 1977; Sherman & Strang, 2003). In the context of restorative justice, victim and offender participation is voluntary. It brings victims and offenders together under the watchful eye of a trained mediator to discuss the offence and find a mutually satisfying response. The word "mediation," however, is also used in other contexts where participation is obligatory, such as divorce courts. To make a clear distinction between voluntary and obligatory mediation, Koss (2014) uses the term "victim–offender dialogue" in the context of restorative justice.

Abolitionism gave rise to alternative measures and diversion programs in which criminal cases, particularly those of young offenders, are diverted out of the criminal justice system and into alternative, restorative justice programs. In Canada, extrajudicial measures with young offenders are an example of diversion. They allow young offenders to be diverted out of the criminal justice process provided they participate in alternative programs, such as community service or victim–offender mediation programs. New Zealand made restorative justice central to its response to young offenders when, in 1989, it adopted the *Children, Young Persons and Their Families Act*. This act introduced a particular form of restorative justice: the family group conference (FGC). It meant that young offenders who committed less serious offences were systematically diverted out of the criminal justice system and into an FGC. These are meetings in which the young offender, accompanied by a support person (e.g., a family member), meets with the victim(s) or a representative of the community to discuss what happened and find a satisfying solution. In practice, however, victims rarely attended FGCs, bringing into question the importance it placed on victims and its ability to provide reparation (Morris & Maxwell, 1998). Critics saw this as proof that these programs focused on the rehabilitation of the offender and had no real interest in victims (Reeves & Mulley, 2000; Wemmers & Canuto, 2002). To see an interesting example of how restorative justice is sometimes criticized by victim advocates, see Box 11.2.

As these examples illustrate, restorative justice can take many different forms. Essentially, any program that uses restorative processes is considered a restorative justice program (ECOSOC, 2002). In addition to VORP, mediation, and FGCs, another common form of restorative justice is *circle sentencing*. This particular approach is accredited to Barry Stuart, a former judge of the Yukon Territorial Court. As we saw earlier, in common law systems the criminal justice process has two phases: (1) the criminal trial, which determines whether or not the accused is guilty, and (2) the sentencing phase, which establishes the sentence imposed on the offender. Circle sentencing follows the normal criminal justice process up until the offender has been found guilty of the offence, at which point the sentencing is conducted in a circle rather than in a regular sentencing hearing. The circles involve the offender, the victim, the friends and families of each, and community members, and the goal is to provide sentencing consultation to the courts. In other words, while the judge still decides the sentence, this decision is made in consultation with those who participated in the circle (Stuart, 1996; Zehr, 2015).

Yet another restorative justice program is victim–offender encounters (VOE) in which victims meet with sentenced offenders who committed a

BOX 11.2: THE DALHOUSIE FACEBOOK INCIDENT

In December 2014, Dalhousie University in Halifax made national headlines. Some of the male dentistry students had created a private Facebook group, ironically called the "Class of DDS 2015 Gentlemen," on which they had posted inappropriate comments about female students in the program, including a poll asking members which classmates would they have "hate sex" with. When the female students who were targeted by these comments learned about them they were shocked. However, their response was to turn this into a matter of education, not punishment. The university enlisted the help of Jennifer Llewellyn, an expert in restorative justice and professor at Dalhousie's Schulich School of Law.

The decision to respond to this incident using restorative justice was widely criticized. Critics argued that the university should expel the men involved and that victims were being forced to participate in the restorative process. The female students were shocked by the negative, unsupportive reactions from others. They felt that the university had given them choices, and they did not want to see the men expelled and learn nothing about why what they wrote was wrong. In particular, the women were concerned about preventing this from carrying over into the professional setting, where these men would eventually work with women, often in the role of auxiliary staff, who might not feel able to stand up to them (Llewellyn, Demsey, & Smith, 2015).

Thanks to the courage of these women, the restorative process not only confronted the male students with the consequences of their behaviour, it also uncovered a culture of misogyny and sexism throughout the university that had enabled the creation of the Facebook group. This example not only illustrates the positive effects of restorative justice, it also shows how others will sometimes react negatively to victims when they do not respond to their victimization as others think they should.

crime similar to the one they experienced but who are not *their* offender. In this model, meetings will often include several victims and several offenders, guided by two or three trained facilitators. It is also possible for victims to meet with their offender postsentencing, which is referred to as "victim–offender dialogue" (VOD) (Koss, 2014). In both VOE and VOD, victims will participate in preparatory sessions before meeting with the offenders as well as followup meetings to guide the victim's healing process (Koss, 2014; Van Camp, 2014). Unlike diversion programs, VOE and VOD are not an alternative to the criminal justice system. Participating offenders have already been sentenced. Their participation is fully voluntary and has no impact on their sentence. However, it does allow dialogue between victims and offenders and recognition of the harm caused by the offence.

Thus, a wide variety of programs can be considered restorative justice, as long as they use restorative processes and are consistent with restorative values: respect, compassion, dignity, honesty, inclusion, reparation, and growth (Department of Justice Canada, 2004; Correctional Service Canada, 2012). These values apply to everyone affected by the crime—victims, offenders, and the community.

Restorative versus Retributive Justice

The relationship between retributive and restorative justice has been a point of contention for opponents of restorative justice who see it primarily in terms of abolitionism and reform of the penal process (Green, 2006; Groenhuijsen, 1999). Many of the early advocates of restorative justice saw it as a distinct approach that was in conflict with criminal justice (Walgrave, 2006). For example, Fattah (1998) contrasts restorative justice with retributive justice and concludes that restorative justice is not only incompatible with retributive justice, it is also superior to it. Restorative justice, he argues, looks forward, focusing on dealing with the aftermath of the crime, while retributive justice looks backward, focusing on punishing the offence. Furthermore, retributive justice designates the state and society as the "victims" of the offence, while restorative justice recognizes the harm done to the victim and the community.

Similarly, Roach (1999) considers the active participation of victims, which is characteristic of restorative processes, impossible in the criminal justice system because of its retributive nature. In his view, if victims want to participate they must do so in the restorative justice programs outside of the criminal justice process. However, even if victims are generally unhappy with their role as a witness in the criminal justice system, that does not make them abolitionists (Wemmers, 2009c). The complete abolition of the criminal justice system is a highly controversial idea and one that does not have the unequivocal support of crime victims. Moreover, victims' rights include participation, which means that victims should be able to participate in criminal justice procedures and they should not be obliged to exit the criminal justice system to express their views and have their concerns considered (see Chapter 7).

However, most supporters of restorative justice view it as an approach within the criminal justice system (Marshall, 1999). Even Fattah and Roach, who consider restorative justice distinct from retributive justice, view it in relation to the conventional criminal justice process. It is only after the victim has made a formal complaint to police that the case may be diverted into a restorative justice program. The police are the gatekeepers of the criminal justice system, and they are the ones who divert cases away from conventional prosecution toward an alternative restorative justice track (Johnstone, 2011).

Victims tend to support the criminal justice model, even if they are dissatisfied with their role as a witness to a crime against the state. As we saw in Chapter 10, victims express a need for recognition in the criminal justice system. They want to participate in procedures and be consulted. However, they also need protection and support, and they do not want the burden of decision-making power (Kilchling, 1995; Shapland, Wilmore, & Duff, 1985; Wemmers & Cyr, 2004; Wemmers, 2009c). Victims stress the criminal nature of the act committed against them and do not agree with the abolitionist terminology that talks about "conflicts" instead of "crimes" (Shapland, 1985; Wemmers & Cyr, 2005). Restorative justice lacks the necessary language to conceptualize the victim in a way that distinguishes him or her from other "interested parties" (Green, 2006). Hence, a different approach to restorative justice with its own terminology is needed for victims.

Furthermore, while the diversion of offenders out of the criminal justice system and into restorative justice programs may be acceptable for young offenders who commit minor offences, it is highly controversial for cases involving serious violent crimes and repeat offenders (Koss, 2014; Van Camp, 2014). Despite criticism of the criminal justice system for ignoring victims' interests and focusing exclusively on society's interests, society does have an interest in how offenders are dealt with. To illustrate this point, consider the example of homicide. If the victim's family and the offender were to agree on monetary compensation for the family instead of prison, many of us would feel that this was wrong. This would be seen by many as a distasteful buyout—putting a dollar value on a human life. The only reason we can justify diversion programs for minor offences is because in these cases, once reparation has been made to the victim, the debt owed to society is negligible. When it comes to serious crimes, it is not enough that the victim and the offender come to an agreement: The offender has a debt to society as well (Cavadino & Dignan, 1997; Wemmers, 2009c).

Prison-based programs illustrate that restorative justice is not just an alternative to retributive justice but can also be complementary to it. These programs combine different interests in a dual-track model of restorative justice, which relies on the restorative approach for dialogue and voice and on the criminal justice proceedings for a formal outcome and denunciation (Van Ness, 2003). The Restorative Opportunities Program at Correctional Service Canada is another example of a prison-based program. It offers direct and indirect victims a chance to communicate with the offender who caused the harm. In this VOD program, serious violent crimes are tried and sentenced in the criminal justice system and only after sentencing, perhaps years after the offence was committed, will parties voluntarily engage in restorative justice. Since the offenders have already been sentenced, the restorative opportunities program is not focused on reaching a settlement, but rather on meeting the needs of the participants and addressing the harms caused while protecting against re-victimization. The program is flexible and explores opportunities to use various victim–offender mediation models that best suit the needs of the participants, as defined by the participants with the help of a professional facilitator (Correctional Service Canada, 2012). Victims of serious violent crime are likely to experience many different needs in addition to reparation, such as the need for protection and support. The flexibility of the program allows it to tailor the response to meet the victim's safety concerns and work within the parameters of his or her healing process.

In addition to diversion and dual-track models, a third option exists that weaves restorative values into the existing criminal justice system (Smith, 2015; Wemmers, 2009c). In line with victims' preferences, this option retains the criminal justice model as a framework for dealing with crime. Rather than replacing the criminal justice system or adding restorative programs to it, restorative values are incorporated into the criminal justice system. In other words, restorative values such as respect for the dignity of the victim are woven into the criminal justice process. Instead of having to exit the criminal justice system to be treated with respect and dignity, victims are treated this way within the criminal justice system. This approach gives victims participatory rights, thereby providing them with a formal and recognized role in the criminal justice process. Hence, it meets victims' need for recognition in the criminal justice system. That is not to say that victims necessarily have all of the same rights as the accused or even that they are considered an equal party, but they do have a formal status. As we have seen throughout this book, this is currently not the case in most common law criminal justice systems in which victims are considered witnesses to a crime against the state. However, victim participation does exist in various forms in countries with a civil legal tradition, as well as at the International Criminal Court and, since the adoption of the *Crime Victims' Rights Act* in 2004, in the United States. We will return to this point in Chapter 12.

Effects on Victims

While victims complain about being shut out of the criminal justice process, there are many good reasons to shield victims from their offenders. Victims may be frightened of their offender and need protection. Opponents of restorative justice have tended to emphasize its potential to re-victimize (Laroche, 2002; Pemberton, 2015; Reeves & Mulley, 2000; Stubbs, 1995, 2010; Van Camp, 2014). Besides protection, victims also need support. As we saw in Chapter 4, as many as one out of every three victims of violent crime may suffer from post-traumatic stress disorder (Kilpatrick, Saunders, Veronen, Best, & Von, 1987). Traumatized victims may not be ready to face their offender (Noll & Harvey, 2008). Responsibility for decision making is considered by many victims to be an unwanted burden (Shapland et al., 1985; Wemmers & Cyr, 2004). These concerns have led to a protective approach regarding the offer of restorative justice in cases of serious violent crime. In this approach authorities do not inform victims of the availability of programs unless victims explicitly ask for it (Van Camp & Wemmers, 2016; Wemmers & Van Camp, 2011).

Paradoxically, the greater the degree of trauma and injustice suffered by the victim, the more important reparation becomes (Jones, Parmentier, & Weitekamp, 2014; Pemberton, 2015). Despite reluctance among those working with victims to embrace restorative justice, victims want reparation because it acknowledges the victimization, recognizes the victim, and contributes to the healing process (Koss, 2014; Wemmers & Canuto, 2002; Wemmers & Cousineau, 2005). Research has repeatedly shown that victims are interested in reparations, and when they participate in restorative justice programs they tend to be satisfied with it (Shapland, 2014; Van Camp, 2014). Victim surveys reveal that when respondents are informed about restorative justice programs such as mediation, many victims of all types of crime, including sexual violence, express an interest in it (Mattinson & Mirrlees-Black, 2000; Mihorean, et al., 2001; Strang et al., 2006; Tufts, 2000; Wemmers & Canuto, 2002).

Independent evaluative research, including randomized control trials in which cases are randomly assigned to a form of restorative justice or remain in the criminal justice system, reveals that restorative practices often outperform criminal justice proceedings in terms of meeting victims' needs for information and participation (Poulson, 2003; Rugge & Scott, 2009; Shapland, 2014; Shapland et al., 2006; Sherman et al., 2005; Sherman & Strang, 2007; Van Camp & De Mesmaecker, 2014; Wemmers & Cyr, 2004). Victims often feel better afterwards, feeling less fearful, anxious, and distressed (Angel, 2005; Angel et al., 2009; Strang, 2002; Wemmers & Cyr, 2005).

However, in order to gain victims' support, programs must meet certain conditions that respect the needs of victims. To begin with, participation in restorative justice must always be voluntary. Second, programs must recognize victims' need for support and should provide professional support to victims before, during, and after their dialogue with the offender. Victims may experience a need for protection following victimization, and any dialogue with the offender must take place in a safe and neutral setting (Shapland, 2014; Van Camp, 2014). Provided these needs are met, restorative justice can be empowering for victims as they regain a sense of control over their lives (Cyr, 2008; Johnstone, 2011; Koss, 2014; Shapland, Robinson, & Sorsby, 2011; Wemmers & Cyr, 2005).

Victim-Centred Justice

Victim-centred justice is based on a human rights approach and focuses on the needs and rights of victims, including their need for reparation (Finn, 2013; Goodey, 2005). Contrary to restorative justice, which is a criminological notion, reparative justice is victim centred and can be considered a victimological notion with its own terminology. Its focus is on victims of crime and their needs, perceptions, and dignity. According to Goetz (2014), reparative justice is based on three components: reparation, victims' procedural rights, and victims' experiences in the justice process. These components are interrelated since victims' rights shape their experiences and expectations, which in turn affect their recovery from crime.

The first component of reparative justice is reparation. As we saw at the beginning of this chapter, reparation encompasses a variety of forms, including restitution, compensation, rehabilitation, satisfaction, and guarantees of nonrepetition. It is flexible and able to offer a solution tailored to fit victims' needs and the situation. Compensation, restitution, and apologies are forms of reparation, which are often found in restorative justice programs (Wemmers & Canuto, 2002; ECOSOC, 2002). Reparative justice, however, encompasses many more forms of reparation than these, including satisfaction, guarantees of nonrepetition, and rehabilitation (Letschert & Van Boven, 2011).

Satisfaction includes a variety of measures that recognize the victimization, promote the truth, and denounce the crime. Criminal prosecution offers satisfaction to victims when it recognizes victimization and denounces the crime. However, there is of course no guarantee in criminal justice that the accused will be found guilty, and this can be difficult and frustrating for victims who seek recognition in the criminal justice system. Even if the offender is found guilty, victims may be frustrated with the criminal justice process because of their exclusion from it (see Chapter 6). Victims turn to restorative justice programs because these programs meet needs that were not met in the criminal justice process (Koss, 2014; Van Camp, 2014). Restorative justice offers victims an opportunity to ask questions (information) and to tell their story (truth telling) as well as empowerment as they reclaim their strength (Zehr, 2015). This is why it is important to recognize that reparation for victims is more than criminal prosecution and punishment. Regardless of whether or not criminal justice is available for victims—and it often will not be—they may be able to obtain reparation in other ways.

Guarantees of nonrepetition refer to crime prevention and deterrence. This includes specific measures aimed at reducing the offender's risk of reoffending, such as punishment. However, it can also include more general measures, such as legislation aimed at preventing a particular situation from happening again. The victims' movement is full of examples of victims fighting to change laws to prevent what happened to them from happening to others (Garland, 2001). For example, in 1992 Priscilla de Villiers fought to have the *Bail Reform Act* and the *Parole Act* modified after her daughter was abducted and murdered by a man who was out on bail. Knowing that they cannot change the past, victims may find solace in knowing that such a tragedy will not happen again. This allows them to give meaning to what is otherwise a pointless crime and regain a sense of control, all of which are important to the healing process (Cyr & Wemmers, 2011; Hill, 2009).

Rehabilitation, which includes medical, psychological, social, as well as legal services for victims, is also a form of reparation. These services are sometimes available to victims through government-run compensation programs or through victim support services (see Chapters 8 and 9). Yet theses services are not forms of restorative justice since they do not adhere with its definition. They do, however, acknowledge victims and their victimization, so they are important for reparation. As we saw in Chapter 4, victims' recovery relies on recognition of harm and a process of integrating fragmented experiences at several levels. Even if acknowledgement is not possible in the criminal justice system, it is possible in other ways, such as through victim support. As Danieli (2014) observes, it is what happens after the trauma that is crucial in the long term. Following the trauma of victimization, victims need to deal with their individual healing process while at the same time dealing with societal reactions to victimization, which can help or hinder victims' healing process (i.e., secondary victimization) (Koss, 2014; Mercer & Sten-Madsen, 2011). Before they can make sense of their suffering, victims' suffering first has to be acknowledged (Hill, 2009).

Victims' healing is about giving meaning to their victimization as they integrate the experience into their lives and find a new balance (Hill, 2009). Victim services help victims deal with the aftermath of their victimization. In doing so, victim support programs may incorporate victim–offender dialogue as part of their repertoire of services (Julich et al., 2011; Koss, 2014). Van Camp (2014) describes a program with victims of sexual assault (specifically incest) in which, depending on the victim's progress, therapists may suggest VOD to victims as part of their healing process. She reports that victims who partici-pated in this program were pleased that their therapist felt they had advanced enough to be able to participate in a dialogue with their offender. In a victim-centred approach, the focus is on the needs of the victim, and the only question is whether confronting the offender would be helpful for the victim.

This does not mean that the rights of the offender are unimportant. Offenders' participation must also be fully voluntary. If, for any reason, the offender is not available for dialogue, the victim can still practise confronting his or her offender. For example, by writing a letter to the offender (which may never actually be given to the offender) or participating in VOE with a surrogate offender. Confronting one's aggressor, even if only figuratively, can be empowering for victims (Cyr & Wemmers, 2011; Koss, 2014; McGlynn, Westmarland, & Godden, 2012; Wemmers, 2002).

The second component of reparative justice concerns procedural rights that facilitate and enable victims to effectively seek and obtain justice. These include practical rights, such as victims' rights to information and participa-tion, protection, support, and legal assistance (Goetz, 2014). For victims, the criminal justice system can be disempowering (Cyr & Wemmers, 2011). As we saw earlier, treating victims with dignity and respect means recognizing them as persons before the law with rights and recourse. Procedural rights are important for victims' perceptions of fairness and, as we saw in Chapter 6, formal rules and procedures contribute to victims' sense of fairness (Blader & Tyler, 2003). This highlights the importance of enforceable rights for victims in the criminal justice process and recognition of victims' legitimate interests in the criminal justice process through the integration of restorative values in what is essentially a retributive justice model (Wemmers, 2009c; Smith, 2015).

Procedural rights go beyond criminal prosecution and embrace all forms of reparation, including rehabilitation. Victim services that offer support and victim compensation programs must also provide procedural rights to victims. While victims need protection and support, one has to be careful not to patron-ize them. Victims have a right to information and want information about available programs and services so that they can be in control and make their own decisions (Cyr & Wemmers, 2011; Herman, 2003). Research with victims of serious violent crimes suggests that they prefer a proactive approach in which they are offered information about available services, including restor-ative justice programs, rather than a protective approach in which they are only given information if they explicitly ask for it (Van Camp & Wemmers, 2011; Wemmers & Van Camp, 2016). In terms of how information is given to victims, while written information is perhaps the most common method used to inform victims of available services, the transmission of information is more effective in terms of retention and the use of services when it is done in person (Steinmetz, 1990; Van Camp, 2014; Van Camp & Wemmers, 2016). Moreover, victims must be properly supported by trained personnel, and this can be achieved if information is provided in person (Shapland, 2014).

The third component of reparative justice relates to victims' experiences with the justice process. These include perceptions of fairness and trust as well as empowerment and healing (Goetz, 2014). Procedural justice emphasizes that justice for victims is not just about sentencing—it is also about how an outcome was reached (Bradford, 2011; Lind & Tyler, 1988; Orth, 2002; Wemmers, 1996; Wemmers, 2010a). As we saw in Chapter 6, victims evaluate the fairness of procedures based on two dimensions: (1) the quality of the decision-making process (i.e., what rights are allotted to victims), and (2) the quality of the treatment. Victims' experiences in the criminal justice system and their perceptions of fairness are important with respect to secondary victimization. Procedural justice explains a large part of victims' satisfaction with restorative processes (Van Camp & Wemmers, 2013).

Determinants of procedural justice include voice and standing, which refer to victims' rights in the criminal justice process and shape their experiences in the criminal justice system, as well as neutrality and trust. As we saw in Chapter 6, victims need recognition in the criminal justice system. Voice and standing provide victims with recognition in the criminal justice process, which allows them to regain a sense of control following their victimization (Cyr & Wemmers, 2011). Victims expect criminal justice authorities as well as mediators to be neutral (Wemmers & Cyr, 2004). The importance placed on neutrality by victims highlights that "victim-centred approaches" are not synonymous with "one-sided approaches," and reparative justice must never lose sight of the rights of the accused.

Trust is a determinant of procedural justice as well as a product of it (Tyler & Lind, 1992; Van den Bos & Lind, 2002; Wemmers & Manirabona, 2014). When we believe that someone is trustworthy, we are more likely to feel they treated us fairly (Tyler & Lind, 1992). Trust, however, cannot be taken for granted. To establish the trustworthiness of an offender or an authority, victims will look for information about fairness, such as procedural justice (Huo, Smith, Tyler, & Lind, 1996; Wemmers & Manirabona, 2014). Having been victimized by the offender, it is logical for victims to question the trustworthiness of the offender. Screening offenders is one way to ensure their motives for participation in restorative justice are sincere (Strang, 2002; Wemmers & Cyr, 2005). Victims tend to attribute the success or failure of programs like VOD to the offender, while procedural fairness is attributed to the facilitator and how the program was carried out (Pruitt, Peirce, McGillicuddy, Welton, & Castrianno, 1993; Van Camp & Wemmers, 2013). By recognizing victims' rights and providing them with an opportunity to voice their views and concerns, programs like VOD enhance their trust in the justice system (Strang, Barnes, Braithwaite, & Sherman, 1999; Wemmers, 2009c). Trust in the criminal justice system and criminal justice authorities is important because it can influence whether or not victims report crimes to the police (Hough, 2012; Sherman & Strang, 2007; Strang et al., 1999).

Conclusion

Reparative justice is victim centred and, as such, it looks at justice and reparation differently than restorative justice. While it shares the same values as restorative justice, it gives victims a distinct status and recognizes them as more than just an "interested party." Its focus is on victims and their needs. However, "victim centred" does not mean that offender rights are to be neglected or ignored. Following a human rights perspective, the rights of all individuals are important. Reparative justice recognizes that reparation can take many forms, including rehabilitation, satisfaction, and guarantees of nonrepetition, and it offers more to victims than financial compensation. Reparative justice is a broader concept than restorative justice. The latter exists within the conventional criminal justice system, whereas reparative justice focuses on the reparation of the victim and, as a result, it is not limited to the criminal justice system. While certain forms of reparation occur within the context of the conventional criminal justice system, other forms, such as rehabilitation, exist independent of it. This gives it the flexibility to do more to meet victims' needs than what is possible under restorative justice or through criminal justice prosecution.

CHAPTER 12

INTEGRATING VICTIMS IN CRIMINAL JUSTICE

Having completed our overview of victimology, this final chapter looks toward the future. Throughout this book we have purported a human rights–based approach in which victims are viewed as persons before the law. Crime is considered a violation of the human rights of the victim as well as an offence against society. Victims' rights should not be sacrificed to obtain a conviction when it serves the interests of society. The secondary victimization endured by victims means that we cannot continue to offer up victims for the greater good. In the end, victims' suffering and multiple victimization do not serve the interests of society. Victims' needs are human needs and, as such, it is essential for the individual as well as society to ensure that people's basic human needs are met. This includes their need for justice. It is important to bear in mind that justice is not unique to the criminal justice system. Reparative justice emphasizes that victims can achieve a sense of justice in many different ways. Nevertheless, both victims and society consider criminal justice a key mechanism for doing justice. In this chapter we will discuss the integration of victims in criminal justice from a human rights perspective.

Changing Legal Theory

Traditional legal theories are unable to accommodate victims (McGonigle-Leyh, 2011; Moffett, 2014). Theories of punishment can be divided into two general philosophies: retributivism and utilitarianism. *Retributivism* focuses on the proportional distribution of punishments, and the due process rights afforded to the defendant ensure that only those who are responsible for crimes are punished (Bedau, 1978). It is backward-looking because it looks at the wrong committed to justify the punishment (McGonigle-Leyh, 2011; Moffett, 2014). *Utilitarianism* is a form of distributive justice that seeks to ensure the maximum benefit to the majority through the imposition of punishment (Moffett, 2014). Punishment is not used to torment the offender or to nullify the crime but to achieve its aims of deterrence, incapacitation, and rehabilitation. It is forward-looking in that it seeks to reduce the occurrence of crime in the future (McGonigle-Leyh, 2011; Moffett, 2014). Neither retributivism nor utilitarianism recognizes victims as persons before the law (McGonigle-Leyh, 2011). In retributive theory, victims are considered objects used to justify punishment. Utilitarian theory is indifferent to victims' needs and interests, focusing instead on the collective interests of society (Moffett, 2014).

Theoretical work on the criminal process is similarly unable to accommodate victims. For over 50 years Herbert Packer's work on the crime control and due process models has dominated criminal law (Beloof, 1999; Kirchengast, 2013; McGonigle-Leyh, 2011; Roach, 1999). The crime control model values efficiency and the suppression of crime and sacrifices individual rights for the benefit of society. In contrast, the due process model values the rights of the accused and, accordingly, limits the powers of the state in the suppression of crime (Packer, 1964). Packer published his work on models of justice over 50 years ago. At that time, victimology was in its infancy, and victims' rights were unheard of. Hence, it is not surprising that victims and victims' rights do not fit in either criminal process model.

Yet victims have a legitimate interest in participating in the justice process (Beloof, 1999; McGonigle-Leyh, 2011; Roach, 1999). A lot has happened during the past 50 years. The victims' movement has drawn attention to the plight of the victim and excluding victims today from criminal justice procedures is no longer possible. Legal theories that fail to accommodate victims are incomplete and are unacceptable in the current context (McGonigle-Leyh, 2011; Moffett, 2014). Instead of suggesting that victims abandon criminal justice because the classical process models cannot accommodate them, we need to develop new models that respect the human rights of victims and recognize them as persons before the law.

Therapeutic jurisprudence is an interdisciplinary scholarly approach in which law is considered an instrument of healing and rehabilitation (Wexler & Winick, 1996; Winick, 2011). As we saw in Chapter 6, therapeutic jurisprudence focuses attention on the emotional well-being of all those who come into contact with the law and the legal system—both victims and offenders. It draws our attention to the emotional and psychological side of the law and legal processes. Therapeutic jurisprudence has a law reform agenda. It suggests that the negative effects of law should be minimized and, when consistent with other justice values, the potential of the law for increasing the emotional well-being of the individual victim and offender as well as society as a whole (Wexler, 1993; Winick, 1997, 2011).

Legal reform tactics with respect to victims can be broken down into three general approaches: (1) improving the plight of victims without changing the system, (2) changing the status of victims before criminal courts by granting them procedural rights, and (3) noncriminal proceedings (McGonigle-Leyh, 2011). Up until now, the first approach has been the most popular with governments. However, as we saw in Chapter 6, this approach has failed to alleviate secondary victimization. The third approach resembles the restorative justice movement discussed in Chapter 11. While restorative justice can accommodate victims, it is not a panacea. The interest of society in serious crimes means that some cases will always remain in the criminal justice system. It is unacceptable that the victims of these crimes face secondary victimization and exclusion from the criminal justice process. Therefore, the status of victims before the court needs to change.

The inclusion of the victim as a participant in adversarial systems constitutes a major shift. As we have seen in Chapter 10, changing the status of victims is a highly controversial approach. Efforts to change the status of victims tend to follow one of two methods (McGonigle-Leyh, 2011). One method is to pit the rights of victims against the rights of the accused, limiting the rights of defendants (Roach, 1999; Wemmers, 2009c). The second method is to make the criminal justice system more victim friendly without sacrificing the rights of the accused (McGonigle-Leyh, 2011; Wemmers, 2009c). Therapeutic jurisprudence corresponds with this second method.

Theoretical arguments may seem to have little practical relevance and be far removed from the reality of crime victims, but in fact that is not the case. Changing legal culture is difficult, and the inability of criminal justice theories to accommodate victims is consistently used to justify victims' exclusion from criminal justice procedures (Cassell, Mitchell, & Edwards, 2014; McGonigle-Leyh, 2011; Roach, 1999). This is no longer acceptable. Just because legal theories cannot accommodate victims does not mean that law cannot accommodate them. Victims have a legitimate interest in participating in the criminal justice process. In the following pages we will consider how criminal law can accommodate victims while respecting the rights of the accused.

Party versus Participant

Victims' participation in the criminal justice system was discussed in Chapter 10. There we saw different forms of victim participation in the criminal justice process, such as the civil party and the auxiliary prosecutor. The civil party gives victims procedural rights, allowing them to join criminal proceedings. This form of participation exists in various forms in countries with a civil legal tradition, which have an inquisitorial model of justice, but it does not exist in countries with a common law legal tradition, which have an adversarial model. The adversarial and inquisitorial models differ fundamentally in terms of who controls the proceedings. In the inquisitorial model, the judge actively directs the case. Judges initiate proceedings, collect evidence, and determine the procedure. In contrast, parties in adversarial systems are much more active, while the judge is more like a neutral umpire who ensures that the rules are properly followed. Parties initiate proceedings, develop evidence, and choose how they want to develop their arguments (Blondel, 2008).

The civil party is possible in countries with inquisitorial systems because the direction of communication in the court is vertical rather than horizontal. In other words, in inquisitorial systems parties do not communicate with one another; instead, they communicate with the judge. Vertical communication allows more flexibility because parties can be added without changing the dynamics of the court. In contrast, in common law or adversarial procedures communication is horizontal, between parties. As a result, adding parties in adversarial systems is impossible since it would fundamentally change the dynamics of the court (Kury & Kilchling, 2011). Victim impact statements are allowed in common law systems because they do not enter into the court until *after* a conviction has been reached, so they leave the structural exclusion of victims untouched (Doak, 2008; Kirchengast, 2011; Kury & Kilchling, 2011).

The fact that victims cannot be parties in adversarial criminal justice systems means that one cannot simply import this model into common law. But it does not mean that victims in common law countries can never be satisfied with their treatment in the criminal justice system. It is possible for victims to receive information, be notified, and even consult with the prosecution in the adversarial criminal justice systems (Doak, 2008; Roach, 1999). As we saw earlier, research on the role victims want to play in criminal justice reveals that while victims do not want to be mere witnesses to a crime against the state, they do not want to be a full party with active, decision-making power either (Kilchling, 1995; Wemmers & Cyr, 2004). They seek an in-between role in which they are consulted and included throughout the criminal justice process without the burden of decision making. They want to participate in procedures and be recognized as persons before the law with rights and recourse (Herman, 2005; Wemmers, 1996). Information, notification, and consultation by criminal justice authorities facilitate victim empowerment and healing (Cyr, 2008; Herman, 2003; Morissette & Wemmers, 2016; Parsons & Bergin, 2010; Wemmers, 2013). Consequently, this inability to be a party in the criminal justice process is not a problem. Victims want to be acknowledged as a participant in the criminal justice system, but not necessarily as a party (Beloof, 1999, 2005).

Victims and the International Criminal Court

The International Criminal Court (ICC) provides an excellent example of how victims can be integrated as participants in what was originally an adversarial model (Doak, 2015b). Victim participation is a distinguishing feature of the ICC, which opened its doors on 1 July 2002. The ICC deals with some of the most serious human rights violations, including genocide, torture, rape, and slavery. While there have been other international courts formed for the purpose of dealing with specific cases, such as the Nuremberg Tribunal following World War II or, more recently, the International Criminal Tribunal for the Former Yugoslavia and the International Criminal Tribunal for Rwanda, these are all ad hoc tribunals. The ICC is a permanent court and as such it can deal with almost any case involving crimes against humanity, genocide, and war crimes, provided they occurred on or after 1 July 2002.

To automatically fall under the jurisdiction of the ICC, a country must first recognize the authority of the ICC, which is done by ratifying the Rome Statute of the ICC. The Rome Statute is the UN treaty that established the court. As of December 2016, 124 of the 193 member states of the United Nations had ratified the Rome Statute. Canada ratified the Rome Statute in 2000 when it adopted the *Crimes Against Humanity and War Crimes Act* (SC 2000, c.24). While most countries do recognize the ICC, some important nations have not yet recognized it, including the United States, Israel, China, and Russia.

If a country has not ratified the Rome Statute, it may still be subject to the ICC following a decision by the UN Security Council. The council is composed of 15 members, including five permanent members. These five permanent members are China, France, Russia, the United Kingdom, and the United States. As permanent members they have veto power, which enables them to prevent the adoption of any substantive resolution. Hence it is extremely unlikely that the ICC will ever prosecute individuals from China, Russia, or the United States.

However, it is important to note that the ICC is intended to be complementary to national jurisdiction. Only if a country is unable or unwilling to prosecute alleged crimes will a case possibly come before the ICC. In other words, if, for example, Canadian peacekeeping troops were suspected of having committed war crimes in another country, they would not automatically be tried by the ICC. Instead, Canada (or more accurately the Canadian courts) would retain priority over the prosecution. Victims of these cases would thus be subject to Canadian law and the *Canadian Victims' Bill of Rights*. Only if Canada failed to prosecute the case would it go to the ICC.

Perhaps the most important innovation of the ICC is the integration of victims into the criminal justice process. The Rome Statute and the Rules of

Procedure and Evidence, which provide the legal foundation for the court, contain specific references regarding the role of victims, including reparation and participation. In the ad hoc criminal tribunals for Nuremberg, the former Yugoslavia, and Rwanda, victims only role was one of witnesses for the prosecution. These early UN tribunals were strongly influenced by American criminal law and, as a result, were essentially adversarial in nature (Karstedt, 2010; Tochilovsky, 1999). The ICC added elements from inquisitorial systems to a fundamentally adversarial legal system and created what is considered a *hybrid* court (Bitti, 2011).

Whereas these ad hoc tribunals did not respect the standards and norms outlined in the UN *Declaration of Basic Principles of Justice for Victims of Crime and Abuse of Power*, the ICC does (Bitti, 2011; Wemmers, 2009b). The ICC recognizes victims as more than just witnesses and introduces a victim-oriented notion of justice (Moffett, 2014). Specifically, it gives victims formal rights in the criminal trial process. This major innovation and shift in the status of victims before the court is due, in part, to pressure from nongovernmental organizations that saw the exclusion of victims as a major problem affecting the ad hoc tribunals (FIDH, 2007; Stover, 2005).

Hence, for the first time in the history of international criminal law, the ICC allows victims to participate in criminal justice procedures. Regarding who is a victim, the ICC defines victims as persons who have "suffered harm as a result of an offence" (Rule 85). Generally, this is taken to mean the direct victims of crime (Ferstman, 2012; Hébert-Dolbec, 2014). If victims are unable to act on their own behalf, because they are deceased or because they are under 18 years of age, then they may be represented by another adult (Rule 89.3).

Victims' legal right to participate in cases brought before the ICC is based on article 68.3 of the Rome Statute. It states that victims can present their "views and concerns" to the court at "appropriate" stages and "in a manner which is not prejudicial to or inconsistent with the rights of the accused." This text is very similar to the language used in the 1985 UN *Declaration of Basic Principles of Justice for Victims of Crime and Abuse of Power.* However, as we saw earlier, the UN Declaration does not discuss when and how victims may participate. Sticking close to the text of the UN Declaration, the Rome Statute and the Rules of Procedure and Evidence do not specify how victim participation is to be put into practice. Hence, this is left up to the court to determine. Victim participation at the ICC is new and faces many challenges (Hébert-Dolbec, 2014; Pena & Carayon, 2013). Nevertheless, victims have a legal right to participate in the criminal trial process, and they can participate *throughout* the criminal trial process, which represents a major shift (Pena & Carayon, 2013; Wemmers, 2010b).

The Rules of Procedure and Evidence further specify that victims be represented by a lawyer (Rule 90). Unlike the victim impact statement (VIS), which, as we saw in Chapter 10, is commonly used in domestic criminal law to allow victims to communicate directly with the court, at the ICC victims themselves do not intervene before the court. The kinds of crimes that the ICC deals with involve mass victimization, so any one case may involve hundreds or thousands of victims. A legal representative may act on behalf of one victim or an entire group of victims. Entire communities of victims may be represented by one or two lawyers, thus emphasizing collective needs shared by victims (Mégret, 2014; Wemmers & De Brouwer, 2011). This leads to a different type of participation by victims than the VIS (Wemmers, 2008b). Whereas the VIS limits victims to giving an emotional presentation of the effects of the crime at sentencing, at the ICC legal representatives defend victims' legal interests throughout the trial.

Meanwhile, the rights of the accused always have to be considered as well. Balancing the rights of victims with those of the accused, the prosecutor and the defence at the ICC are allowed to reply to any oral or written observation by the legal representative for victims (Rule 89). Justice is transformed at the ICC not by taking away rights or moving decision-making power, but by giving victims a voice in the criminal trial process. Victims' legal representatives are mandated to bring victims' interests to the attention of the court. Thus, victims are no longer silenced and become part of the legal discourse within the court (Wemmers, 2008b).

Reparation is another right that is accorded to victims under the Rome Statute. Article 75.1 specifies that "the court shall establish principles relating to reparations to, or in respect of, victims, including restitution, compensation and rehabilitation." To this end, the court may make an order directly against a convicted person specifying appropriate reparations (art 75.2). Reparation may be made directly to the victim(s) or may be made through the Trust Fund for Victims (TFV; see Chapter 9). Before deciding on reparation, the court may hear representations from or on behalf of victims (art 75.3). The TFV can take a broad approach to reparations, promoting other forms of reparation than criminal prosecution, such as victims' rehabilitation and satisfaction of (Mégret 2009, 2014; Wemmers, 2006).

Adversarial Systems and Victim Participation

While the ICC provides an interesting example of how victims' rights can be integrated into the criminal trial process, it is not the only example of how an essentially adversarial system has accommodated victims. As we saw in

Chapter 10, the introduction of victim impact statements was the first step in the recognition of procedural rights for victims in the criminal justice process in many common law systems. In the United States, the *Crime Victims' Rights Act* (CVRA) went a step further and introduced procedural rights for victims in the criminal trial (see Chapter 7). The CVRA extended broad rights to crime victims and contained specific enforcement mechanisms, making these enforceable rights for victims. The CVRA aimed to change the system's obliviousness to crime victims and allow them to be participants in the criminal justice process (Beloof, 2005; Kirchengast, 2011; Cassell et al., 2014).

The CVRA shows how victim participation can be included in adversarial criminal justice systems without sacrificing the fundamental principles of fairness or the rights of the accused. To be real and meaningful, rights must be accompanied by recourse, and the ICC and CVRA illustrate how enforceable rights for victims can be achieved (Beloof, 2005; Doak, 2015a). By recognizing victims' procedural rights, they are concrete examples how one might integrate victims in the criminal trial process.

The ICC and the CVRA are evidence of an international trend toward the inclusion of victims. Internationally, there is growing consensus surrounding the rights of the victim within the criminal justice process (Doak, 2015b). For example, the Australian state of Victoria has conducted a lengthy review of the role of victims in the criminal trial process and recommends that the role of victims be recognized as that of a participant (Victorian Law Reform Commission, 2016). In Canada, the recent adoption of the *Canadian Victims Bill of Rights* (see Chapter 7), which provides for statutory rights, can also be viewed as another step toward the recognition of victims as persons before the law. According to Beloof (2005), it is not *whether* victims will achieve real rights but *when*.

Reparative Justice

The ICC and its focus on victims has been likened to restorative justice for victims (Pena & Carayon, 2013; Smith, 2015; War Crimes Research Office, 2007). The ICC integrates restorative values such as inclusion and respect for the dignity of the individual by weaving them into the criminal justice process (Wemmers, 2009c). Similar values underlie the victim participation model, which emphasizes fairness, respect, and human dignity (Beloof, 1999). Criminal prosecution is, however, only one form of reparation. While victims have a need for justice and support within the criminal justice model, criminal prosecution will not always be available or desirable for victims.

Reparation can take many different forms, including victim satisfaction and rehabilitation, and offers more to victims than financial compensation.

Reparative justice is victim centred. It focuses on reparation of the victim and is not limited to the criminal justice system (see Chapter 11). When we consider victims' procedural rights at the ICC together with the TFV, with its emphasis on different forms of reparation, including rehabilitation and satisfaction, it provides an example of reparative justice. The TFV gives the court the flexibility to do more to meet victims' needs than what is possible under restorative justice or criminal justice prosecution.

In reparative justice, the healing or rehabilitation of victims is a priority. Victims' experiences can either help or hinder the healing process, which is why it is important to treat victims with dignity and respect, both inside and outside of the criminal justice system.

Criminal justice is not always possible or desirable for victims. No one can guarantee victims that their offender will face prosecution as many cases go unsolved and, even if the case is prosecuted, the offender may not be convicted because of a lack of evidence. Whether they are inside or outside of the criminal justice system, services for victims must be available to meet victims' basic human needs, including their need for justice. Currently, not all victims have access to even the most basic services, such as medical care and counselling. Procedures providing access to services, including compensation programs, must be based on dignity and respect for the victim. A civilized society cannot leave victims helpless in their misery and must offer victims humanitarian relief to help them recover from the devastating effects of victimization.

Conclusion

The role of the victim in criminal justice is changing. Victim healing has gained importance as the negative impacts of victimization and secondary victimization have become increasingly well known. To improve on the treatment of victims, we need a new approach in which we cease to view crime exclusively as an offence against the state and begin to recognize that crime also constitutes a violation of victims' human rights. Respecting victims' human rights requires that criminal justice systems recognize victims as persons before the law. The victims' movement has made considerable progress, bringing attention to the plight of victims. However, further research is needed, and victimology can help us in our efforts to better understand victims and victimizations. The voice of victims should inspire and guide us in our efforts to prevent further suffering.

APPENDIX 1

UN DECLARATION OF BASIC PRINCIPLES OF JUSTICE FOR VICTIMS OF CRIME AND ABUSE OF POWER

United Nations
A/RES/40/34
29 November 1985
96th plenary meeting

The General Assembly,

Recalling that the Sixth United Nations Congress on the Prevention of Crime and the Treatment of Offenders recommended that the United Nations should continue its present work on the development of guidelines and standards regarding abuse of economic and political power,

Cognizant that millions of people throughout the world suffer harm as a result of crime and the abuse of power and that the rights of these victims have not been adequately recognized,

Recognizing that the victims of crime and the victims of abuse of power, and also frequently their families, witnesses and others who aid them, are unjustly subjected to loss, damage or injury and that they may, in addition, suffer hardship when assisting in the prosecution of offenders,

1. Affirms the necessity of adopting national and international measures in order to secure the universal and effective recognition of, and respect for, the rights of victims of crime and of abuse of power;
2. Stresses the need to promote progress by all States in their efforts to that end, without prejudice to the rights of suspects or offenders;
3. Adopts the Declaration of Basic Principles of Justice for Victims of Crime and Abuse of Power, annexed to the present resolution, which is designed to assist Governments and the international community in their efforts to secure justice and assistance for victims of crime and victims of abuse of power;

4. Calls upon Member States to take the necessary steps to give effect to the provisions contained in the Declaration and, in order to curtail victimization as referred to hereinafter, endeavour:

(a) To implement social, health, including mental health, educational, economic and specific crime prevention policies to reduce victimization and encourage assistance to victims in distress;

(b) To promote community efforts and public participation in crime prevention;

(c) To review periodically their existing legislation and practices in order to ensure responsiveness to changing circumstances, and to enact and enforce legislation proscribing acts that violate internationally recognized norms relating to human rights, corporate conduct and other abuses of power;

(d) To establish and strengthen the means of detecting, prosecuting and sentencing those guilty of crimes;

(e) To promote disclosure of relevant information to expose official and corporate conduct to public scrutiny, and other ways of increasing responsiveness to public concerns;

(f) To promote the observance of codes of conduct and ethical norms, in particular international standards, by public servants, including law enforcement, correctional, medical, social service and military personnel, as well as the staff of economic enterprises;

(g) To prohibit practices and procedures conducive to abuse, such as secret places of detention and incommunicado detention;

(h) To co-operate with other States, through mutual judicial and administrative assistance, in such matters as the detection and pursuit of offenders, their extradition and the seizure of their assets, to be used for restitution to the victims;

5. Recommends that, at the international and regional levels, all appropriate measures should be taken:

(a) To promote training activities designed to foster adherence to United Nations standards and norms and to curtail possible abuses;

(b) To sponsor collaborative action-research on ways in which victimization can be reduced and victims aided, and to promote information exchanges on the most effective means of so doing;

(c) To render direct aid to requesting Governments designed to help them curtail victimization and alleviate the plight of victims;

(d) To develop ways and means of providing recourse for victims where national channels may be insufficient;

6. Requests the Secretary-General to invite Member States to report periodically to the General Assembly on the implementation of the Declaration, as well as on measures taken by them to this effect;

7. Also requests the Secretary-General to make use of the opportunities, which all relevant bodies and organizations within the United Nations system offer, to assist Member States, whenever necessary, in improving ways and means of protecting victims both at the national level and through international co-operation;

8. Further requests the Secretary-General to promote the objectives of the Declaration, in particular by ensuring its widest possible dissemination;

9. Urges the specialized agencies and other entities and bodies of the United Nations system, other relevant intergovernmental and non-governmental organizations and the public to co-operate in the implementation of the provisions of the Declaration.

ANNEX

Declaration of Basic Principles of Justice for Victims of Crime and Abuse of Power

A. Victims of Crime

1. "Victims" means persons who, individually or collectively, have suffered harm, including physical or mental injury, emotional suffering, economic loss or substantial impairment of their fundamental rights, through acts or omissions that are in violation of criminal laws operative within Member States, including those laws proscribing criminal abuse of power.

2. A person may be considered a victim, under this Declaration, regardless of whether the perpetrator is identified, apprehended, prosecuted or convicted and regardless of the familial relationship between the perpetrator and the victim. The term "victim" also includes, where appropriate, the immediate family or dependents of the direct victim and persons who have suffered harm in intervening to assist victims in distress or to prevent victimization.

3. The provisions contained herein shall be applicable to all, without distinction of any kind, such as race, colour, sex, age, language, religion, nationality, political or other opinion, cultural beliefs or practices, property, birth or family status, ethnic or social origin, and disability.

Access to Justice and Fair Treatment

4. Victims should be treated with compassion and respect for their dignity. They are entitled access to the mechanisms of justice and to prompt redress, as provided for by national legislation, for the harm that they have suffered.

5. Judicial and administrative mechanisms should be established and strengthened where necessary to enable victims to obtain redress through formal or informal procedures that are expeditious, fair, inexpensive and accessible. Victims should be informed of their rights in seeking redress through such mechanisms.

6. The responsiveness of judicial and administrative processes to the needs of victims should be facilitated by:

    (a) Informing victims of their role and the scope, timing and progress of the proceedings and of the disposition of their cases, especially where serious crimes are involved and where they have requested such information;

    (b) Allowing the views and concerns of victims to be presented and considered at appropriate stages of the proceedings where their personal interests are affected, without prejudice to the accused and consistent with the relevant national criminal justice system;

    (c) Providing proper assistance to victims throughout the legal process;

    (d) Taking measures to minimize inconvenience to victims, protect their privacy, when necessary, and ensure their safety, as well as that of their families and witnesses on their behalf, from intimidation and retaliation;

    (e) Avoiding unnecessary delay in the disposition of cases and the execution of orders or decrees granting awards to victims.

7. Informal mechanisms for the resolution of disputes, including mediation, arbitration and customary justice or indigenous practices, should be utilized where appropriate to facilitate conciliation and redress for victims.

Restitution

8. Offenders or third parties responsible for their behaviour should, where appropriate, make fair restitution to victims, their families or dependents. Such restitution should include the return of property or payment for the harm or loss suffered, reimbursement of expenses incurred as a result of the victimization, the provision of services and the restoration of rights.

9. Governments should review their practices, regulations and laws to consider restitution as an available sentencing option in criminal cases, in addition to other criminal sanctions.

10. In cases of substantial harm to the environment, restitution, if ordered, should include, as far as possible, restoration of the environment, reconstruction of the infrastructure, replacement of community facilities and reimbursement of the expenses of relocation, whenever such harm results in the dislocation of a community.

11. Where public officials or other agents acting in an official or quasi-official capacity have violated national criminal laws, the victims should receive restitution from the State whose officials or agents were responsible for the harm inflicted. In cases where the Government under whose authority the victimizing act or omission occurred is no longer in existence, the State or Government successor in title should provide restitution to the victims.

Compensation

12. When compensation is not fully available from the offender or other sources, States should endeavour to provide financial compensation to:
    (a) Victims who have sustained significant bodily injury or impairment of physical or mental health as a result of serious crimes;
    (b) The family, in particular dependents of persons who have died or become physically or mentally incapacitated as a result of such victimization.

13. The establishment, strengthening and expansion of national funds for compensation to victims should be encouraged. Where appropriate, other funds may also be established for this purpose, including those cases where the State of which the victim is a national is not in a position to compensate the victim for the harm.

Assistance

14. Victims should receive the necessary material, medical, psychological and social assistance through governmental, voluntary, community-based and indigenous means.

15. Victims should be informed of the availability of health and social services and other relevant assistance and be readily afforded access to them.

16. Police, justice, health, social service and other personnel concerned should receive training to sensitize them to the needs of victims, and guidelines to ensure proper and prompt aid.

17. In providing services and assistance to victims, attention should be given to those who have special needs because of the nature of the harm inflicted or because of factors such as those mentioned in paragraph 3 above.

B. Victims of Abuse of Power

18. "Victims" means persons who, individually or collectively, have suffered harm, including physical or mental injury, emotional suffering, economic loss or substantial impairment of their fundamental rights, through acts or omissions that do not yet constitute violations of national criminal laws but of internationally recognized norms relating to human rights.

19. States should consider incorporating into the national law norms proscribing abuses of power and providing remedies to victims of such abuses. In particular, such remedies should include restitution and/or compensation, and necessary material, medical, psychological and social assistance and support.

20. States should consider negotiating multilateral international treaties relating to victims, as defined in paragraph 18.

21. States should periodically review existing legislation and practices to ensure their responsiveness to changing circumstances, should enact and enforce, if necessary, legislation proscribing acts that constitute serious abuses of political or economic power, as well as promoting policies and mechanisms for the prevention of such acts, and should develop and make readily available appropriate rights and remedies for victims of such acts.

APPENDIX 2

CANADIAN VICTIMS BILL OF RIGHTS

SC 2015, c. 13, s. 2

[Enacted by section 2 of chapter 13 of the Statutes of Canada, 2015, in force July 23, 2015.]

Published by the Minister of Justice at the following address: http://laws-lois.justice.gc.ca

An Act for the Recognition of Victims Rights

Preamble

Whereas crime has a harmful impact on victims and on society;

Whereas victims of crime and their families deserve to be treated with courtesy, compassion and respect, including respect for their dignity;

Whereas it is important that victims' rights be considered throughout the criminal justice system;

Whereas victims of crime have rights that are guaranteed by the *Canadian Charter of Rights and Freedoms*;

Whereas consideration of the rights of victims of crime is in the interest of the proper administration of justice;

Whereas the federal, provincial and territorial governments share responsibility for criminal justice;

Whereas, in 1988, the federal, provincial and territorial governments endorsed the *Canadian Statement of Basic Principles of Justice for Victims of Crime* and, in 2003, the *Canadian Statement of Basic Principles of Justice for Victims of Crime, 2003*;

Now, therefore, Her Majesty, by and with the advice and consent of the Senate and House of Commons of Canada, enacts as follows:

Short Title

1   This Act may be cited as the *Canadian Victims Bill of Rights*.

Interpretation

Definitions

2   The following definitions apply in this Act.

offence means an offence under the *Criminal Code*, the *Youth Criminal Justice Act* or the *Crimes Against Humanity and War Crimes Act*, a designated substance offence as defined in subsection 2(1) of the *Controlled Drugs and Substances Act* or an offence under section 91 or Part 3 of the *Immigration and Refugee Protection Act*. (*infraction*)

victim means an individual who has suffered physical or emotional harm, property damage or economic loss as the result of the commission or alleged commission of an offence. (*victime*)

Acting on victim's behalf

3   Any of the following individuals may exercise a victim's rights under this Act if the victim is dead or incapable of acting on their own behalf:
   (a) the victim's spouse or the individual who was at the time of the victim's death their spouse;
   (b) the individual who is or was at the time of the victim's death, cohabiting with them in a conjugal relationship, having so cohabited for a period of at least one year;
   (c) a relative or dependent of the victim;
   (d) an individual who has in law or fact custody, or is responsible for the care or support, of the victim;
   (e) an individual who has in law or fact custody, or is responsible for the care or support, of a dependent of the victim.

Exception

4   An individual is not a victim in relation to an offence, or entitled to exercise a victim's rights under this Act, if the individual is charged with the offence, found guilty of the offence or found not criminally responsible on account of mental disorder or unfit to stand trial in respect of the offence.

Criminal justice system

5 For the purpose of this Act, the criminal justice system consists of

    (a) the investigation and prosecution of offences in Canada;

    (b) the corrections process and the conditional release process in Canada; and

    (c) the proceedings of courts and Review Boards, as those terms are defined in subsection 672.1(1) of the *Criminal Code*, in respect of accused who are found not criminally responsible on account of mental disorder or unfit to stand trial.

Rights

Information

General information

6 Every victim has the right, on request, to information about

    (a) the criminal justice system and the role of victims in it;

    (b) the services and programs available to them as a victim, including restorative justice programs; and

    (c) their right to file a complaint for an infringement or denial of any of their rights under this Act.

Investigation and proceedings

7 Every victim has the right, on request, to information about

    (a) the status and outcome of the investigation into the offence; and

    (b) the location of proceedings in relation to the offence, when they will take place and their progress and outcome.

Information about offender or accused

8 Every victim has the right, on request, to information about

    (a) reviews under the *Corrections and Conditional Release Act* relating to the offender's conditional release and the timing and conditions of that release; and

    (b) hearings held for the purpose of making dispositions, as defined in subsection 672.1(1) of the *Criminal Code*, in relation to the accused, if the accused is found not criminally responsible on account of mental disorder or unfit to stand trial, and the dispositions made at those hearings.

Protection

Security

9 Every victim has the right to have their security considered by the appropriate authorities in the criminal justice system.

Protection from intimidation and retaliation

10 Every victim has the right to have reasonable and necessary measures taken by the appropriate authorities in the criminal justice system to protect the victim from intimidation and retaliation.

Privacy

11 Every victim has the right to have their privacy considered by the appropriate authorities in the criminal justice system.

Identity protection

12 Every victim has the right to request that their identity be protected if they are a complainant to the offence or a witness in proceedings relating to the offence.

Testimonial aids

13 Every victim has the right to request testimonial aids when appearing as a witness in proceedings relating to the offence.

Participation

Views to be considered

14 Every victim has the right to convey their views about decisions to be made by appropriate authorities in the criminal justice system that affect the victim's rights under this Act and to have those views considered.

Victim impact statement

15 Every victim has the right to present a victim impact statement to the appropriate authorities in the criminal justice system and to have it considered.

Restitution

Restitution order

16 Every victim has the right to have the court consider making a restitution order against the offender.

Enforcement

17 Every victim in whose favour a restitution order is made has the right, if they are not paid, to have the order entered as a civil court judgment that is enforceable against the offender.

General Provisions

Application

18 (1) This Act applies in respect of a victim of an offence in their interactions with the criminal justice system

(a) while the offence is investigated or prosecuted;

(b) while the offender is subject to the corrections process or the conditional release process in relation to the offence; and

(c) while the accused is, in relation to the offence, under the jurisdiction of a court or a Review Board, as those terms are defined in subsection 672.1(1) of the *Criminal Code*, if they are found not criminally responsible on account of mental disorder or unfit to stand trial.

Reporting of offence

(2) For the purpose of subsection (1), if an offence is reported to the appropriate authorities in the criminal justice system, the investigation of the offence is deemed to begin at the time of the reporting.

National Defence Act

(3) This Act does not apply in respect of offences that are service offences, as defined in subsection 2(1) of the *National Defence Act*, that are investigated or proceeded with under that Act.

Exercise of rights

19 (1) The rights of victims under this Act are to be exercised through the mechanisms provided by law.

Connection to Canada

(2) A victim is entitled to exercise their rights under this Act only if they are present in Canada or they are a Canadian citizen or a permanent resident within the meaning of subsection 2(1) of the *Immigration and Refugee Protection Act*.

Interpretation of this Act

20 This Act is to be construed and applied in a manner that is reasonable in the circumstances, and in a manner that is not likely to

(a) interfere with the proper administration of justice, including

(i) by causing interference with police discretion or causing excessive delay in, or compromising or hindering, the investigation of any offence, and

(ii) by causing interference with prosecutorial discretion or causing excessive delay in, or compromising or hindering, the prosecution of any offence;

(b) interfere with ministerial discretion;

(c) interfere with the discretion that may be exercised by any person or body authorized to release an offender into the community;

(d) endanger the life or safety of any individual; or

(e) cause injury to international relations or national defence or national security.

Interpretation of other Acts, regulations, etc.

21 To the extent that it is possible to do so, every Act of Parliament enacted—and every order, rule or regulation made under such an Act—before, on or after the day on which this Act comes into force must be construed and applied in a manner that is compatible with the rights under this Act.

Primacy in event of inconsistency

22 (1) If, after the application of sections 20 and 21, there is any inconsistency between any provision of this Act and any provision of any Act, order, rule or regulation referred to in section 21, the provision of this Act prevails to the extent of the inconsistency.

Exception—Acts and regulations, etc.

(2) Subsection (1) does not apply in respect of the *Canadian Bill of Rights*, the *Canadian Human Rights Act*, the *Official Languages Act*, the *Access to Information Act* and the *Privacy Act* and orders, rules and regulations made under any of those Acts.

No adverse inference

23 No adverse inference is to be drawn against a person who is charged with an offence from the fact that an individual has been identified as a victim in relation to the offence.

Entering or remaining in Canada

24 Nothing in this Act is to be construed so as to permit any individual to

(a) enter Canada or to remain in Canada beyond the end of the period for which they are authorized to so remain;

(b) delay any removal proceedings or prevent the enforcement of any removal order; or

(c) delay any extradition proceedings or prevent the extradition of any person to or from Canada.

Remedies

Complaint—federal entity

25 (1) Every victim who is of the opinion that any of their rights under this Act have been infringed or denied by a federal department, agency or body has the right to file a complaint in accordance with its complaints mechanism.

Complaint to authority

(2) Every victim who has exhausted their recourse under the complaints mechanism and who is not satisfied with the response of the federal department, agency or body may file a complaint with any authority that has jurisdiction to review complaints in relation to that department, agency or body.

Complaints mechanism

(3) Every federal department, agency or body that is involved in the criminal justice system must have a complaints mechanism that provides for

(a) a review of complaints involving alleged infringements or denials of rights under this Act;

(b) the power to make recommendations to remedy such infringements and denials; and

(c) the obligation to notify victims of the result of those reviews and of the recommendations, if any were made.

Complaint—provincial or territorial entity

26 Every victim who is of the opinion that their rights under this Act have been infringed or denied by a provincial or territorial department, agency or body may file a complaint in accordance with the laws of the province or territory.

Status

27 Nothing in this Act is to be construed as granting to, or removing from, any victim or any individual acting on behalf of a victim the status of party, intervenor or observer in any proceedings.

No cause of action

28 No cause of action or right to damages arises from an infringement or denial of a right under this Act.

No appeal

29 No appeal lies from any decision or order solely on the grounds that a right under this Act has been infringed or denied.

VICTIM COMPENSATION PROGRAMS ACROSS CANADA

Federal Programs

Canadian Victims Abroad

In 2007, the federal government introduced a financial assistance program to help Canadians who are victimized outside of the country. The program allows the direct victims of certain serious violent crimes in a foreign jurisdiction to obtain financial assistance. If the victim is dead, ill, or incapacitated because of their victimization abroad, a family member of the victim can apply for assistance. If the victim is a child, a parent or the person responsible for the care and support of the child can apply to the program for financial assistance.

Regarding the type of victimization that falls under the program, only homicide, sexual assault, aggravated assault, or assault with serious personal violence committed in a foreign jurisdiction may be eligible for financial assistance.

The program may help cover expenses where the victim has no other source of financial assistance, up to a *maximum of $10,000*. Specifically, the program may help cover hospital and medical expenses that arise from being victimized, expenses to replace stolen official documents, and, upon return to Canada, financial assistance for professional counselling. If the crime resulted in death, the victim's family may obtain help paying funeral expenses. Assistance may also cover any out-of-pocket expenses that arise from being a victim of a violent crime.

The program is intended to be a safety net, so it does not replace any expenses covered by the applicant's insurance. Nor does it compensate lost wages, legal fees, or losses incurred because of the victim's own criminal behaviour. In addition, it only applies to crimes that took place on or after 1 April 2007.

In order to apply, the victim must first contact the Canadian embassy or consulate. They must also contact local police to report the crime. With the police report in hand, they then contact the Department of Justice for financial assistance (Department of Justice Canada, 2015b).

Parents of Murdered and Missing Children

On 1 January 2013, the Federal Income Support for Parents of Murdered or Missing Children (PMMC) grant came into effect (Department of Justice Canada, 2012). This grant offers income support to parents and legal guardians who have suffered a loss of income from taking time off work to cope with the death or disappearance of their child or children as a result of a probable Criminal Code offence. It is important to note that the child must be under 18 years of age at the time of their victimization. Hence, the parents of an adult child (i.e., someone over 18 years of age) are not eligible for this program even if their loss is equally important.

The program targets people who are working or employed. To be eligible for the PMMC grant, applicants must prove that they have $6,500 in earnings in either the 52-week period immediately preceding the incident or the calendar year immediately preceding the date of the victimization. Eligible applicants must have a valid social insurance number. This requirement effectively disqualifies illegal workers. In addition, the applicant must not be receiving employment insurance benefits or Quebec parental insurance plan benefits, which provides an income supplement to new parents on parental leave following the birth or adoption of a new child. More importantly, the applicant must not have been charged with committing a probable Criminal Code offence that led to the death or disappearance of the child (Department of Justice Canada, 2016).

Under the program, parents can receive $350 a week (before taxes). Applicants may receive up to 35 weeks of income support. However, income support will only be paid during the 52-week period (i.e., one year) immediately following the crime.

Provincial and Territorial Programs

Nine of Canada's ten provinces offer government-run compensation programs for victims of crime. Newfoundland terminated its program, which was created in 1968, when the federal government terminated its cost-sharing program in 1992, and many of the other provinces modified their programs in response to the cut in federal funding (Couture & Hétu, 1996). One year later, in 1993, Yukon repealed its compensation plan, and soon after, in 1996, the Northwest Territories followed suit (Canadian Resource Centre for Victims, 2015). Regarding the territories, neither Yukon nor Nunavut currently have a compensation program, whereas the Northwest Territories offers an emergency fund for victims. In the following pages, the various programs that exist across the country will be presented.

Provincial Programs

Alberta

Alberta first created its compensation program, the *Criminal Injuries Compensation Act*, in 1969 (Canadian Resource Centre for Victims, 2015). However, the program underwent several modifications and was finally repealed. Victim compensation is currently included in the province's *Victims of Crime Act* and is regulated by the *Victims of Crime Regulation* (AR 63/2004). This is a financial benefits program that offers limited financial assistance to three groups of victims: (1) direct victims who have suffered injuries as a result of a violent crime, (2) secondary victims who have witnessed the death of a loved one, and (3) individuals who have paid for the funeral expenses of a victim of homicide, to a maximum of $12,500.

Eligibility Victims must apply within two years after the date of the incident. However, if the victim was a minor at the time of the victimization, he or she has 10 years to apply.

Schedule 1 of the regulation includes a list of eligible offences. In other words, to be eligible the individual must have experienced one of the crimes listed in Schedule 1, and the crime had to take place in Alberta. While the list includes many important violent crimes such as homicide (s. 222 of the Criminal Code), sexual assault (s. 271), and robbery (s. 344), it does not include all violent crimes that are found in the Criminal Code. For example, terrorist activity (s. 83.01) is not included in the list of eligible offences. The list also contains some surprises. Although Alberta is landlocked, Schedule 1 includes section 78.1, which is seizing control of a ship. This is rather unusual given that all eligible crimes must have taken place in the province, thus making maritime victimization extremely unlikely. In addition, victims of a motor vehicle accident caused by impaired driving or property damage caused by break and enter crimes are not eligible. The victim must also have reported the crime to the police and cooperated with the investigation. The victim must apply for compensation within two years following the victimization, although more time may be granted if the victim was a minor at the time of the offence.

Awards The program is based on a points system. Schedule 3 of the regulation is a long and detailed list of physical as well as psychological injuries, each rated in terms of its severity. For example, irritation of the airway has a severity rating of 1.408, which is not so severe, while amputation of a lower limb above the knee is rated 80.103 and a spinal cord injury with no motor or sensory function preserved is rated 217.299, which is very severe. Psychological injury has a score of 19.23, but this may increase depending on certain factors such as the age of the victim or whether multiple aggressors were involved. The amount the victim receives is contingent on the total number of points accumulated as a result of the injuries suffered.

Schedule 4 contains a list of financial benefit awards. The lowest possible award granted is $500, for which the recipient needs to have a severity score of 2.5 to 4.999. The highest possible award is $110,000 for which the individual must have a score of 210 or higher. Returning to our example of a victim suffering from irritation of the airway, this person would have too few points to receive any compensation, while a victim with a lower limb amputation would receive $40,000, and a victim suffering spinal cord injury with no motor or sensory function would receive the maximum award of $110,000. Compensation is entirely determined by the severity of the injury and, consequently, there is no compensation paid for medical expenses, loss of wages, pain and suffering, or property damage. Awards are paid out in one lump sum payment.

Limitations If the victim's behaviour is thought to have contributed to the victimization, then he or she will have his or her benefits reduced or may even be denied financial benefits (Part 1, Schedule 4). Likewise, secondary victims will either be denied benefits or will have their benefits reduced if the victim contributed to his or her death.

In addition, if the victim has a criminal record he or she may be penalized. If in the five years prior to the victimization the victim was convicted of a crime listed in Schedule 2, he or she will be penalized accordingly. Five points will be deducted for each conviction during that time. If a victim has served a sentence in the last five years, one point per year or portion of a year for each custodial sentence served will be deducted (art. 7(2)). This list, which is much longer than the list of eligible offences (Schedule 1), includes minor offences such as vagrancy (s. 179), common nuisance (s. 180.1), and offences in relation to prostitution (s. 213), as well as more serious crimes such as terrorism (s. 83.19 to 83.231). Surprisingly, however, Schedule 2 does not include serious violent crimes such as sexual assault (s. 271) or homicide (s. 222). In other words, a victim who was homeless for a little while four years prior to the victimization and was convicted twice of vagrancy, but who has since gotten his or her life back on track, would be docked 10 points and, therefore, will receive less compensation even though the victimization has nothing to do with his or her prior homelessness. However, a person who was convicted of sexual assault four years prior to the victimization would not be penalized.

Recourse If applicants are unhappy with a decision they can make a request for a review to the Criminal Injuries Review Board. The request for a review must be made in writing, and the applicant must state the grounds for the review. Application for a review must be made within 30 days after the decision is received. It is possible that the review be held in public and may proceed with or without the applicant. The proceedings must be recorded, and the board's decision must be in writing.

An appeal may be made of the decision of the Review Board at the Court of Appeal.

British Columbia

In British Columbia, the Crime Victim Assistance Program offers financial assistance to victims of crime. First introduced in 1972, the program was drastically modified following cuts to federal funding in the 1990s (Canadian Resource Centre for Victims, 2015). The current program is based on the *Crime Victim Assistance Act*, which was assented to in 2001. The program targets (1) direct victims, (2) their immediate family members, and (3) witnesses dealing with the effects of violent crime. It offers financial assistance to help with some of the costs and services needed to assist in recovering from or coping with the effects of violent victimization. Benefits are subject to approval by the director of Crime Victims Assistance.

Eligibility The crime must have occurred in British Columbia after 1 July 1972. Victims must apply within *one year* following the victimization. Exceptions are made, however, for sexual offences (no time limit), minors (must apply before turning 20), and exceptional circumstances. Schedule 1 of the act contains a list of eligible offences. Only if the victim experienced one of these crimes will he or she be eligible for compensation.

Awards Counselling services or expenses are available to all victims as well as others who support the victim. Direct victims may receive up to 48 one-hour sessions. Victims under 18 years of age may be granted more than 48 sessions, if needed. Immediate family members may also receive counselling services (up to 36 one-hour sessions) to recover from the psychological injury caused by the crime. Witnesses who need counselling to recover from the psychological injury caused by witnessing the crime may receive up to 12 one-hour counselling sessions.

Victims who need health care, including dental care, because of their injuries from the crime may be reimbursed for eligible medical and dental expenses, including the cost of prescription drugs and disability aids. Immediate family members and witnesses who need prescription drugs to recover from the psychological injury caused by the crime may also receive reimbursement. The program does not provide benefits for pain and suffering.

Crime scene cleaning is available when the victim was injured in his or her home or vehicle and the crime scene requires specialized cleaning because of the nature of the crime. This includes the replacement of contaminated flooring, wall coverings, or other built-in features. If the victim is deceased, the immediate family members may receive help cleaning the crime scene. Similarly, witnesses who need specialized cleaning of their home or vehicle because the crime was committed there may receive help from victim assistance benefits. For all three groups, the maximum benefit is $2,500.

Victims who are at risk of additional harm from the perpetrator or who are so traumatized by fear they cannot lead normal lives may receive financial assistance regarding protective measures. For example, the victim may purchase security or communication equipment and services or take self-defence courses (maximum $3,000). If a victim needs to relocate for safety reasons, compensation is available to cover moving costs as well as a relocation allowance to help the victim get by in the beginning until he or she finds a job (maximum three months; $7,000).

Victims whose injuries have short-term or long-term effects on their ability to work and who had a job when the crime occurred may receive monthly payments to assist with financial support until the victim can return to work. Income support following a temporary or permanent lost earning capacity is calculated based on minimum wage and, depending on the victim's income prior to the offence, he or she can receive the equivalent of up to 40 hours at minimum wage. However, if the victim receives any other income (e.g., Canada Pension Plan) this will be subtracted from their income support benefits. If the victim did not have a job at the time of the crime but because of injuries sustained he or she is not able to work, the victim may receive monthly payments to assist with financial support. Thus, while many of the different benefits are capped, there is not one absolute maximum total that any victim can obtain.

The immediate family members of deceased victims who lose earnings from taking time off work or paying for the funeral or other matters related to the victim's death may also obtain reimbursement. Spouses and children of deceased victims who were financially dependent on the victim may also receive monthly payments to assist in financially supporting the family members. The spouse of a deceased victim may receive up to 75 per cent of the maximum amount of income support benefit (i.e., the equivalent of up to 40 hours at minimum wage) based on the deceased's income prior to the victimization, and payments may continue for up to five years following the death. Children who were under 19 years of age when their parent was killed receive a set amount of $3,000 as a contribution toward the loss of parental guidance. In addition, dependent children of the deceased victim may receive up to 15 per cent of the maximum amount of income support benefit.

Vocational services or expenses are available to victims whose injuries prevent them from returning to their job and who need training or education to re-enter the workforce. Spouses of deceased victims who need training or education to prepare for employment or improve their earning capacity and who are eligible for income support can also receive vocational services or have such expenses reimbursed.

If the victim sustained a disability because of the crime and requires help with childcare (maximum $800 per month) or household tasks (maximum $400 per month) such as cleaning, cooking, and shopping or home maintenance ($100 per month), they may receive services or be reimbursed for expenses. Spouses of deceased victims are also eligible for assistance in paying for childcare and homemaker services. Personal care services may also be available if the victim is no longer able to manage his or her personal care and needs help bathing or dressing because of injuries sustained (maximum $1,600 per month). Victims who have suffered a disability because of the crime and need modifications made to their home to assist them in daily activities may be reimbursed for home modification expenses. They may also receive assistance with vehicle modification or acquisition. If their home is no longer suitable because of their long-term disability they can receive help with moving expenses (maximum $2,000).

Transportation expenses to medical, dental, counselling, childcare, or vocational services provided as crime victim assistance benefits are covered (up to $200/month) for victims and their immediate family members. Witnesses who have to travel some distance to obtain counselling services provided as crime victim assistance benefits may be reimbursed for travel expenses, meals, accommodation, and childcare while attending appointments.

While the program targets victims of violent crime and excludes property crimes, limited funding is available for the repair or replacement of damaged or destroyed personal property, such as eyeglasses, disability aids, or articles of clothing that were damaged or destroyed because of the crime (maximum $150).

Victims of sexual assault who conceived a child as a result of the crime and are financially supporting the child may receive monthly payments (up to $300 per month) to assist with financial support.

Funeral expenses and related costs may be reimbursed for immediate family members of deceased victims who have to pay for the costs involved in the funeral service, burial, cremation, or related ceremony.

Assessment takes time, and for a victim with immediate needs and without any revenue this can pose a serious problem. If it is likely that the applicant will be awarded compensation, it is possible to make an interim payment while waiting for the final decision (art. 7).

Limitations If the applicant was party to the offence or contributed in any way to the victim's death, the application will be refused. Victims are not obliged to report to the police, but if the victim fails to comply with criminal justice authorities the director may refuse their application or reduce their benefits (art. 9.3). The program is intended to be a safety net. Any compensation that the victim received from other sources will be deducted from their benefits.

Recourse If the applicant's request is refused or if he or she is unhappy with the award, the applicant has the right to ask the director to reconsider the request. These applicants have 60 days to file their request. Reconsideration must be done by the director, if he or she did not participate in the original decision or, alternatively, he or she can delegate it to another person, provided that that person did not participate in the original decision (art. 14). Essentially, the procedure ensures a fresh look at the person's application. The director must then inform the applicant of the final decision and provide the reasons for this decision. Decisions are then final and not open to judicial review, except on a question of law or if the director is thought to have acted beyond the limits of his or her power (excess of jurisdiction). In this case, the applicant has 60 days to apply for juridical review.

Manitoba

In 1970 Manitoba first adopted compensation for victims of crime, but this was later modified and eventually replaced with comprehensive legislation for victims (Burns, 1992; Canadian Resource Centre for Victims, 2015). In 1998, the province adopted the *Victims' Bill of Rights* (CCSM c.V55; hereinafter "VBR"), together with the *Victims' Rights Regulation* (214/98), which replaced the *Victims' Rights Act*. This new legislation integrated the existing laws regarding victims' rights, the victims' surcharge, and the compensation program into one comprehensive piece of legislation on victims of crime. As mentioned in Chapter 7, the VBR provides detailed rights to victims. Part 5 of the VBR and Part 3 of the regulation address compensation for victims of crime.

The program gives compensation to (1) victims who have been injured as a result of a violent crime, (2) the families and dependents of victims who died in a crime, and (3) eye-witnesses.

Eligibility In order to be eligible to the program, there must be a victim—that is, a person who is injured or dies as a result of a violent crime that occurred in Manitoba. The victim, however, does not have to be a resident of Manitoba. Victims also include so-called good Samaritans, namely a person who is injured or dies as a result of attempting to lawfully arrest a person or preserve the peace, assist a peace officer, or lawfully prevent the commission of an offence or suspected offence under the Criminal Code.

Eligibility does not require that the offender be charged or convicted. However, the crime does have to be reported to the police within a reasonable time after it occurred (VBR, art. 54.a) and the applicant must cooperate with police during the criminal investigation (art. 54.b). Furthermore, the offence must be a crime under the Criminal Code of Canada and listed in Schedule A of the regulation. The list of recognized offences includes many standard violent crimes, such as sexual assault, manslaughter, assault, and robbery. However, it does not include all violent crimes found in the Criminal Code. For example, homicide (s. 222) and terrorist acts (s. 83.01) are heinous crimes, but neither is included in Schedule A. Victims of crimes that are not listed in Schedule A are not eligible for compensation. If the victim's death was caused by a motor vehicle incident they are also ineligible.

Awards The province's compensation is meant to be a safety net. If victims are entitled to benefits from another source, they should seek compensation from that source first and their compensation may be reduced. However, if, for example, they have exhausted their entitlement under their insurance, the director of the program may consider covering the cost of additional eligible products or services for that person (*Regulation* 7.1(2)).

The maximum amount of compensation payable as a result of an incident is $100,000. This includes compensation paid for lost wages or earnings, the costs of a rehabilitation program, the costs of retraining services, compensation for certain items damaged in the incident, and compensation in respect of eligible products or services or other expenses paid. Victims can receive 55 per cent of their gross reported wages or earnings for the year prior to their victimization to a maximum of $468 per week; they can receive this until they are able to return to work or until they reach 65 years of age. However, their compensation can be terminated by the director if, for example, the victim fails to attend a required examination or does not cooperate with health care providers.

If the victim suffers permanent impairment as a result of the crime, he or she will receive compensation in accordance with the degree of impairment suffered. In addition to the $100,000 maximum compensation, a victim suffering a permanent impairment can receive a lump sum impairment award. This award is calculated by determining the percentage of impairment as it relates to the whole body. Accordingly, if a victim suffers an impairment of 100 per cent, he or she would receive an additional lump sum of $84,630 (Elliott, 2016). If a victim of sexual assault becomes pregnant and has the baby, she is entitled to $270 for each month that the child lives with her until the child reaches 18 years of age.

Various medical and dental expenses are covered, including cosmetic surgery, prescription drugs, physiotherapy, and massage therapy. If victims have to travel to receive medical treatment or are unable to drive or use public transportation because of their injury, they can receive compensation for travel and accommodation expenses. If they require an attendant to help perform certain activities, such as bathing and dressing, because of a disability directly resulting from the crime, this can also be covered. Certain modifications to the home or vehicle of an injured victim may also be compensated.

Victims may receive compensation for certain items damaged during the crime, such as prescription eyewear, clothing (maximum $500), and disability aids (e.g., canes or hearing aids). However, in general material damage to property is excluded from the program. In certain circumstances the victim may obtain compensation for specialized cleaning of the crime scene (e.g., removing blood stains).

In the case of death, certain family members of the victim are also eligible for the maximum $100,000 compensation. This includes money for lost income, counselling, and funeral expenses. The spouse or common law partner who was financially dependent on the deceased victim is eligible to receive the above mentioned compensation for lost income: 55 per cent of their last income to a maximum of $468 a week until the victim would have reached the age of 65. If the victim had children under the age of 18 years they too may receive compensation for lost income if the victim had no spouse or common law partner at the time of his or her death, or if the spouse or partner was not the child's parent. In either of these two cases, each child of the victim who is under 18 years of age is entitled to $270 per month until the age of 18. If, however, there are more than four children under 18, each child is entitled to a pro rata share of $1,080 each month. Other family members may also be eligible for compensation for lost income if the victim has no spouse or common law partner at that time and they were financially dependent on the victim. In the case of individuals who were dependent because of mental or physical disability, they will receive $270 per month until they are either no longer disabled or until the date the victim would have reached 65 years. Compensation for counselling is available for family members to a maximum of $2,000. They may also be reimbursed for travel and accommodation expenses incurred to attend the funeral or counselling sessions. Compensation is payable to the person who paid for the victim's funeral to a maximum of $5,400.

Witnesses are entitled to compensation for costs to clean or replace any clothing that was damaged in the incident. Counselling services required as a direct result of witnessing the incident may be reimbursed to a maximum of $2,000. Travel and accommodation expenses to attend counselling may also be reimbursed.

Witnesses are individuals who were in close proximity to the crime and personally viewed the incident. They are entitled to reimbursement for expenses incurred as a result of the incident as well as compensation for counselling services (VBR, art. 48.1(1)).

Limitations The victim must apply within one year of the crime. If a person eligible for compensation is under 18 years of age, the deadline for applying for compensation is extended until one year after the person reaches the age of (VBR, art. 51(3)).

If victims were involved in a crime when their injury or death happened, they or their dependents will be denied compensation (*Regulation* 6.2(1)). Witnesses, however, remain entitled to compensation regardless of the conduct of the victim (VBR, art. 48.1(2)).

If the victim or witness (VBR, art. 48.1(3)) has been convicted of certain serious offences prior to the victimization, this can result in their exclusion from the program (VBR, art 54.1(1)). Schedule B of the VBR includes a list of so-called *prescribed* offences, such as impaired driving causing death (s. 255(3) of the Criminal Code) and failure to stop at the scene of an accident involving bodily harm (s. 252(1.2)). Victims who have been convicted of any of these offences are automatically excluded from the program. Only if the offence was more than 10 years before the victimization and they have had no new convictions since then will they be eligible for compensation.

If the victim or witness has been convicted of two or more *nonprescribed* offences under the Criminal Code or the *Controlled Drugs and Substances Act* within the five years prior to the victimization, or if they were convicted at any time *after* the victimization, then the amount of his or her claim may be reduced or denied (VBR, art. 54.1(4)).

If the victim or witness does not help police or testify in court against the person who committed the crime (the alleged offender), they may be denied access to the program (VBR, art. 54).

If the recipient is an inmate in a correctional facility, no compensation is payable in respect of loss of wages or earnings while in prison. Any other compensation payable to the recipient will not be paid until he or she has been released from the correctional facility (*Regulation* 6.2(2)).

Recourse Victims have the right to request reconsideration of a decision made by the program director. They must make their request for reconsideration within 60 days after receiving the notice. If they are not satisfied with the decision made on reconsideration, they can file an appeal. They have 30 days after receiving the notice to file an appeal with the appeal board.

New Brunswick

In 1971, the province of New Brunswick first adopted compensation for victims of crime (Burns, 1992; Canadian Resource Centre for Victims, 2015). The existing program was introduced in 1996 following the adoption of Regulation 96–81 under the *Victims Services Act*. Since then, the program has undergone some modifications, most recently in 2010.

The program offers financial compensation to (1) direct victims of crime, (2) a parent or guardian acting *on behalf of* a child victim of crime, and (3) any person incurring eligible expenses in relation to a deceased victim of crime (art. 3.1).

Eligibility In order to be eligible, the offence must have taken place in New Brunswick (art. 2) and have resulted in the death or injury of the victim. Unlike other provinces, New Brunswick does not use a list of eligible offences, and all violent crimes recognized under Canada's Criminal Code that result in death or injury are eligible. In the case of sexual assault, it is important that the offence occurred after 15 November 1971, the date on which the original compensation program was introduced in the province.

The victim is required to report the crime to the police and to cooperate fully with the criminal investigation (art. 4.1).

Awards The program is intended as a safety net to offer some financial assistance to those who would otherwise receive nothing. Article 5 of the regulation provides a list of eligible expenses and the maximum amount that can be awarded for each item, which was last updated in 2010. Regardless of the victim's losses, the maximum amount of financial compensation for eligible expenses that may be awarded, including any amount for pain and suffering, is $10,000 (art. 6.1). The victims' pain and suffering may be compensated to a maximum of $1,000 (art. 6.2). Awards are made as lump sum payments (art. 8).

Because the program is meant to be a safety net, any amount received, whether by civil action or otherwise, from the offender or insurance will be deducted from any benefits (art. 7). However, acceptance of an award does not affect the person's right to institute proceedings in respect of the death or injury of the victim.

Limitations Applications must be made within one year of the victimization, or in the case of a sexual offence within one year of disclosure of the offence to the police (art. 3.2). The applicant may be denied compensation if the victim's behaviour directly contributed to his or her death or injury (art. 4.2). It will also be denied if the applicant knowingly gave false information in the application for compensation or to the police.

Recourse An applicant may appeal in writing to the minster regarding their eligibility for financial compensation or the amount of compensation awarded (art. 10.1). The minister shall review the file, including any new information relating to the grounds of appeal, and notify the applicant in writing of the results of the appeal and state the reasons for the decision (art. 10.2). The regulation does not specify how much time the applicant has to file an appeal.

Nova Scotia

In 1975, Nova Scotia adopted its *Compensation for Victims of Crime Act*, but the legislation was not proclaimed into force until 1982 (Burns, 1992). Ten years later, in 1992, when federal transfer payments were terminated, the province immediately changed its program (Canadian Resource Centre for Victims, 2015). The *Compensation for Victims of Crime Act* was repealed, and the *Victims' Rights and Services Act*, which had been introduced in 1989, was amended to include criminal injuries compensation (Nova Scotia Department of Justice Victims' Services Division, 1999). The program continued to undergo various changes until 2009, when it was replaced by the Criminal Injuries Counselling Program (NS Reg. 270/2009).

The counselling program is available to (1) the direct victims of violent crimes, (2) the immediate family members of victims who are deceased, and (3) good Samaritans who were injured while trying to stop a crime.

Eligibility Victims of a violent crime committed in Nova Scotia may be eligible for counselling. Victims are required to have reported the crime to the police and to have cooperated with authorities.

Awards When the Criminal Injuries Compensation Program was terminated, it put an end to financial benefits for lost wages as well as medical or dental expenses. As a result, only victims of crimes that took place between 1989 and 1992 are eligible for such benefits.

The counselling program allows compensation for counselling only. Counselling awards can be provided to a maximum of $2,000 for a two-year period from the date of the award. However, immediate family members of homicide victims can be provided with counselling awards to a maximum of $4,000 for a period from the date of the award until one year after the prosecution is completed. Counselling is provided by private counselling practitioners within the community who are approved counsellors with the program. Counsellors must apply to become approved counsellors and must meet certain criteria.

Limitations Victims have up to one year after the crime to apply for assistance. This applies to all crimes except sexual assaults by a person in a position of power or authority, for which there is no time limit. The one-year time period does not commence for children until they reach the age of majority (19). Furthermore, the one-year filing requirement may be extended if there were circumstances that prevented the victim from applying within the one-year time limit.

Recourse Applicants may appeal a decision of the director, but only questions of law or jurisdiction can be appealed. Appeals must be made to the Nova Scotia Utility and Review Board within 30 days of receipt of an award or decision.

Ontario

Ontario's victim compensation program was first introduced in 1971. It replaced the *Law Enforcement Compensation Act*, which began in 1967 and provided awards in relation to injuries or deaths that resulted while assisting a peace officer in making an arrest or preserving the peace—the so-called good Samaritan. This was expanded in 1969 to include victims of violence, and was finally replaced in 1971 by the *Compensation for Victims of Crime Act* (Canadian Resource Centre for Victims, 2015). Since then there have been attempts to transform the program, and while some changes have been made the program has essentially retained its original form. It offers financial compensation to victims and the family members of deceased victims of violent crime in the province of Ontario.

Eligibility The act defines victims as individuals injured or killed by an act or omission in Ontario resulting from the commission of a violent crime constituting an offence against the Criminal Code. In addition, so-called good Samaritans who are injured or killed while lawfully arresting or attempting to arrest an offender or suspected offender or while preventing or attempting to prevent the commission of an offence are recognized as victims (art. 5). The Criminal Injuries Compensation Board may also provide compensation to a person who is responsible for the support of the victim.

In case of death, any family members that were dependent on the deceased person or who paid expenses as a result of the death (including expenses to care for one or more children of the deceased person or expenses for bereavement counselling) can apply for compensation (art. 5).

A person can also apply for compensation if he or she witnessed or came upon the scene of a crime that resulted in death and meets the criteria for a finding of "mental or nervous shock."

Awards Compensation may be awarded for expenses actually and reasonably incurred or to be incurred as a result of the victim's injury or death. This includes medical and dental treatment, prescription drugs, as well as counsel-ling. Victims and, in the case of death, their dependents may be compensated for loss of income. If the victim is temporarily or permanently unable to work because of injury, he or she may receive up to $1,000 a month. Applicants may also request compensation for pain and suffering as a result of the crime.

Victims of sexual assault who give birth to a child as a result of their victim-ization may receive financial support for the child (art. 7).

The maximum amount awarded regarding the injury or death of a victim is $25,000 in the case of lump sum payments or $1,000 per month in the case of periodic payments (art. 19(1)). For any one victimization, the total of payments to be paid to *all* applicants in respect of any one occurrence (e.g., dependents) shall not exceed a total of $150,000 in the case of lump sum payments or, in the case of periodic payments, a total of $365,000 (art. 19(2)). Thus, a mass victimization leading to the deaths of 10 people would mean that the families of each victim would receive no more than $15,000 in benefits.

The administrative process may be long, so the board offers interim awards to victims if it is likely that their application will be judged favourably.

Limitations An application for compensation must be made within two years after the date of the injury or death. The board may, however, extend the time if it considers an extension warranted (art. 6).

Any crime of violence constituting an offence against the Criminal Code is eligible (art. 5). Unlike other provinces, Ontario does not use a list of recognized offences. Any offence involving the use or operation of a motor vehicle other than assault by means of a motor vehicle is, however, excluded from the program.

Recourse A decision by the board is final. However, for questions of law the applicant may launch an appeal with the Divisional Court.

Prince Edward Island

In 1988, Prince Edward Island adopted its *Victims of Crime Act* (Canadian Resource Centre for Victims, 2015). The act includes criminal injuries com-pensation for injured victims and the dependents of victims who are killed as a result of crime. Dependents are individuals who were, in whole or in part, dependent on the income of a victim at the time of the victim's injury or death (art. 13.c). Injuries include emotional trauma, mental or nervous shock, actual bodily harm, as well as pregnancy resulting from sexual assault.

Eligibility In order to be eligible, the victim must have suffered an injury or death resulting from a crime that occurred in the province on or after 30 September 1989, the day on which this part of the act came into force. Not all violent crimes are eligible, however, and Schedule 1 of the *Victims of Crime Act Regulations* is a list of eligible Criminal Code offences. It includes crimes such as assault, sexual assault, murder, robbery, criminal negligence, and arson, but it excludes homicide (art. 222). Since 1999, the act also applies to victims of impaired driving offences (s. 249–255 of the Criminal Code).

The crime must be reported to the police, and the victim must cooperate with law enforcement during the criminal investigation. While compensation is not dependent on a conviction (art. 22.4), it is possible that compensation will be withheld until after the trial if there is any doubt that the applicant was actually a victim of crime. The conviction by a criminal court is considered conclusive evidence that an offence has been committed (art. 22.5).

If the victim is culpable in relation to the offence or was engaged in unlawful behaviour at the time of the victimization he or she is ineligible for compensation (art. 16.2.b). In addition, if the victim's or his or her dependent's past character and lifestyle is thought to have contributed in any way to the death or injury of the victim, he or she will be ineligible for compensation (art. 23). This does not mean that a victim with a criminal record will automatically be disqualified—there must be a connection with the victimization for which compensation has been requested. Furthermore, when assessing claims, previous criminal injuries compensation awards to the victim will be taken into consideration (art. 23).

Application for compensation must be made within one year after the date of the victimization. However, the minister may extend the time limit "as the Minister considers warranted" (art. 17).

Awards The compensation program is used as a last resort, which means that any money the victim receives from other sources (e.g., private insurance) will be deducted from the benefits (art. 24).

Victims or, in the case of death, their dependents can claim losses such as lost wages or salary, funeral expenses, pain and suffering, medical and dental expenses, and other reasonable expenses. Victims of sexual assault who gave birth to a child as a result of the offence can request support for the child's maintenance. Any property loss or damage cannot be claimed since the program does not cover it.

It can take up to two years for an application to be decided. In the meantime, if the applicant is in immediate financial need and the minister is likely to grant an award, interim compensation is possible. This will allow the victim to have some financial relief while the final decision in their case is pending.

Limitations The maximum amount of compensation that can be awarded to an applicant in respect of the injury or death of a victim is $15,000. When more than one victim is involved, the maximum that all applicants can receive is $30,000 (*Regulations*, art 5).

Recourse A decision of the minister is final. However, appeal is possible on questions of law. In that case, an appeal must be launched within 30 days of the minister's decision to a judge of the province's Supreme Court (art. 29).

Quebec

In Quebec, legislation was adopted in 1971 creating its compensation program. The *Loi sur l'indemnisation des victimes d'actes criminels* (IVAC) entered into force on 1 March 1972. The province tried to change its program in 1993 after the federal government cut transfer payments. However, while the changes were adopted by the province's legislative body, the National Assembly, they were never implemented. More recently, the law was revised in 2006 and again in 2013, expanding the benefits to include family members of victims. With the exception of these add-ons, the legislation has essentially remained unchanged since the early 1970s.

The program targets (1) the direct victims of violent crimes, (2) good Samaritans who tried to prevent a crime or help arrest a suspect, and (3) the dependents of deceased victims of violence. In addition, limited services are offered to family members of victims of violence.

Eligibility The law defines victims as individuals who are killed or injured as the result of a violent crime that was committed in Quebec on or after 1 March 1972. This includes good Samaritans, regardless of whether or not they were injured or killed. On November 14, 2016, Quebec's Ministry of Justice announced that it would also recognize as victims, parents of murdered children who were killed by the parent's ex-spouse.

Not all violent crimes are eligible; eligible offences are listed in an appendix to the law. These include murder (s. 229 of the Criminal Code), robbery (s. 343), and sexual assault (s. 271). However, it does not include trafficking in persons (s. 279.01) or hijacking a ship (s. 78.1). Crimes involving a motor vehicle and victimizations at the workplace are excluded from the program since they fall under other provincial social insurance programs.

The victim is not required to report the crime to the police to be eligible. However, it is necessary that a crime took place, and typically the police report provides proof of criminal victimization (Lippel & Doyen, 2000).

If the victim dies, his or her dependents (i.e., children under 18 years of age and spouse) can receive compensation. Also, a woman who becomes pregnant following a sexual assault can receive benefits for her child. Should she die, or if for any reason the child is raised by someone else, then that person may receive benefits for the child's maintenance.

Since 2006, limited services are available for the family members of victims of violence. Specifically, the following family members may be eligible for assistance: spouse, father, mother, stepfather, stepmother, child, stepchild, brother, sister, grandparent, stepbrother, and stepsister.

Awards The program offers financial assistance to direct victims, good Samaritans, and the dependents of victims who died as a result of the crime.

An injured victim who is unable to work may be awarded benefits for loss of income. In the case of a temporary inability to work, a victim who was employed at the time of the crime will receive 90 per cent of his or her net income. If the victim was unemployed at the time of the crime, he or she will receive 90 per cent of minimum wage. In the case of a child victim (under 18 years of age), an award of $35 a week is provided. If victims suffer a permanent injury they may receive up to 90 per cent of their net income until they reach retirement age.

Benefits are determined based on the level of incapacity suffered by the victim. For example, victims suffering a partial incapacity following the victimization and who will only be able to work at 50 per cent of their former capacity according to specialists will receive 50 per cent of 90 per cent of their income (in other words, 45 per cent of their income) and will be expected to work for the other 50 per cent. The program does offer a social stabilization program to allow victims suffering a permanent partial incapacity the same level of income they had prior to the crime. Returning to the above example of a victim whose inability to work is rated at 50 per cent, if the victim is unable to find work for 50 per cent and provided our victim was employed prior to the crime, the province's social stabilization program can top up the applicant's income, bringing it back up to what it was prior to the crime. Benefits for loss of income are governed by the province's work disability program (*Loi sur les accidents du travail*). Victims may choose to receive one lump sum payment instead of monthly payments, but in this case they will receive less money in all than what they would have received over their lifetime.

The program covers medical and dental expenses as well as prescriptions. The program also provides access to services that aim to help the victim during the rehabilitation process, such as psychotherapy or reimbursement of expenses related to the victim's safety and protection (e.g., moving expenses, alarm systems, or self-defence courses). If victims are no longer able to do the work they did prior to the crime, they may also receive vocational training so that they can find work in another field.

The administrative process may be long, so the program allows interim awards to be granted when it seems likely that the applicant will receive benefits from the program.

If the victim dies, the program will reimburse up to $5,000 for funeral expenses. This can be claimed by whoever paid for the funeral, which in practice will often be the family members of the victim. Similarly, anyone who pays for the cleaning of a crime scene following a homicide may receive up to $3,200 reimbursement.

If death results from a violent victimization, the program provides financial benefits to the victim's dependents. A spouse who was financially dependent on the victim and who is under 35 years of age and has no children may receive an income supplement for up to five years. At 35 years or older, the spouse with no children may receive an income supplement that will last until the time when the deceased would have turned 65 years of age. Children under 19 years of age will receive an income supplement until the age of 19, unless they enrol in postsecondary education, in which case they can receive an income supplement until the age of 25. While it is generous, the program still relies heavily on the traditional concept of the family and encounters problems when faced with issues such as divorce and reconstituted families.

Since 2006, the law allows the family members of victims to receive up to 20 sessions of counselling. If the victim was killed, the program offers counselling to family members, and there is no limit on the number of family members who may receive counselling. If the victim is alive, the program may provide support to one family member if it is deemed in the interest of the victim. In this case, only one person is eligible for counselling, and the victim must choose which family member should receive this support. However, in the case of young victims of sexual assault (i.e., under 18 years of age), both the victim's two parents are eligible for counselling.

Limitations If the victim is believed to have contributed to the victimization, he or she will be considered ineligible for benefits (art. 20b). While the law does not specifically identify those with a criminal record as ineligible, applicants who had a history of criminal activity (e.g., former gang members) have been excluded, even though they were not actually involved in a crime at the time of their victimization (Desjardine, 2010).

Application must be made within two years following the victimization. Specifically, it is two years from when the person realized he or she was the victim of a crime (art. 11). This provision allows flexibility for victims of serious crimes, such as sexual assault during childhood, who may not immediately fully realize what happened or may not be able to take action for quite some time.

Recourse All decisions can be contested. Generally, applicants have 30 days to file an appeal, although this extends to 90 days for anyone suffering a permanent disability. To begin with, applicants file a request with the board to reconsider a decision. If they are still unhappy with the decision, they may launch an appeal before an administrative tribunal. The tribunal's decisions are final.

Saskatchewan

In 1967, Saskatchewan was the first province in Canada to introduce compensation for victims. Over the years, the original program has undergone several changes. Following the termination of cost sharing with the federal government, the program was replaced with the Victims Compensation Program. In 1994, the government adopted the *Victims of Crime Act* (VCA), which integrated its victims' rights legislation and victim compensation program. In 1997, the province adopted the *Victims of Crime Regulations*, which addresses the surcharges imposed on offenders to pay for victims' services (discussed in Chapter 7) as well as the victim compensation program. The program subsequently underwent further modifications, the most recent in 2014 (Reg. 79/2014).

The program aims to assist victims of violence and serves (1) the direct victims of crime, (2) certain family members if the victim is deceased, and (3) certain witnesses.

Eligibility In order to be eligible for compensation, the person must have suffered harm as a result of a criminal offence or been injured while trying to help a peace officer. Harm includes physical or mental injury, emotional suffering, as well as economic loss. The crime has to have taken place in the province of Saskatchewan, and the offence must be listed in the appendix of the regulations.

In addition to direct victims, certain other groups are eligible for certain services under the act and regulations. In the case of death, anyone who was financially dependent on the victim, as well as so-called secondary victims, are also eligible for the fund. According to the VCA, "secondary victims" include the spouse or child of an adult victim and the parent or sibling of a child victim (art. 13.1). In other words, the parents of an adult homicide victim (18 years and older) are not eligible to apply for compensation.

On 1 October 2014, the regulations were modified to include certain witnesses of violent crime. Specifically, children who witnessed domestic violence as well as homicide witnesses are now eligible for the program (art 8.1–2). Anyone who witnessed a homicide, regardless of their relationship with the victim, may apply for compensation (art 8.2).

Awards The maximum award possible under the program for offences that occurred on or after 1 October 2014 is $100,000. For offences that occurred prior to that date, the maximum is $25,000. Compensation is intended to cover financial losses and expenses, including health care expenses (medical, dental, optometric, chiropractic, etc.) and loss of earnings (where it is not covered by employment insurance, workers' compensation, or an insurance plan). Compensation is not available for pain and suffering, personal property damage, or legal fees. These benefits are available to the direct victims of crime and, in the case of homicide, to the victim's dependents as well as so-called secondary victims.

If the victim or dependent is a child, then a person can claim expenses that result from accompanying the child to attend health care services (*Regulations*, art. 8 (4)). Eligible expenses include loss of earnings.

If the victim dies, the program offers compensation for funeral expenses (maximum $5,000). The parents of a child victim may receive up to $2,000 for counselling.

Children who witness domestic violence as well as anyone who witnesses a homicide may also receive compensation for counselling to a maximum of $2,000 per application. If the witness is a child, the parent or family member who loses earnings to accompany the child to attend counselling can be reimbursed for his or her time to a maximum of $2,000 (art. 8.1(1–2)).

Limitations If the victim's injury or death occurred while participating in a criminal offence, he or she is ineligible for compensation. In addition, the application must be made within two years of the date the offence was reported to the police (art. 14(4)).

Recourse If applicants are unhappy with a decision, they can make a written request to the minister to reconsider the decision. Together with their request they may provide additional information to the minister. If, after reconsideration by the minister, the applicant is still not satisfied, he or she can always appeal the minister's decision. The VCA provides for an appeal committee consisting of three members appointed by the lieutenant governor in council. The decision of the appeal committee is final.

Territories

Northwest Territories

In 1973, the Northwest Territories adopted legislation to create a Criminal Injuries Compensation Program (Burns, 1992). In 1996, after the federal government terminated its cost-sharing program for victim compensation, the territory repealed its victims' compensation plan (Canadian Resource Centre for Victims, 2015). Twelve years later, in 2008, the territory's victim services division introduced a Victims of Crime Emergency Fund. Thus, the Northwest Territories no longer offers compensation, but instead Victim Services has a short-term emergency fund for victims of serious violent crime who have suffered intentional emotional or physical harm or serious damage to property. The fund has limited resources. For example, in 2015 a grand total of $70,000 was available to provide emergency assistance to victims of serious violent crimes (McKeown, 2016).

The emergency fund is available to (1) the direct victims of serious violent crimes and (2) the victim's parent or guardian if the victim is a minor.

Eligibility In order to be eligible, it is not only important that the crime take place in the Northwest Territories, in addition, the victim must be a resident of the territory. Tourists or anyone victimized while visiting the territory are not eligible. It is also important that the crime occurred on or after 1 September 2008, when the fund was introduced.

Only victims of serious violent crimes may be eligible. These include sexual assault; (attempted) homicide; forcible confinement; assault with serious personal violence, including spousal assault; assault with a weapon; and assault causing bodily harm. Other violent victimizations may be considered at the discretion of the manager of NWT Victim Services.

Any funds received must be spent in the Northwest Territories. The applicant must have an immediate need for emergency assistance.

Victims are not required to report the crime to the police to be eligible for assistance.

Awards The program offers financial assistance to pay for short-term immediate counselling, crime scene cleanup, emergency home repairs for immediate safety, emergency accommodation, emergency childcare and dependent care, certain transportation costs, medical expenses (including eyeglasses, dental treatment, prescription replacement), or other emergency items. The program does not cover lost wages or business income caused by time off work, pain and suffering, or stolen items.

Limitations Application for funding must be made within two months of the date of the offence. The program is intended as a safety net, and injuries covered by other programs, such as workers' compensation, are excluded. If victims are hurt because of their own behaviour, they will be denied assistance. For example, if a victim was injured while committing a crime, he or she will be excluded from the program. If the victim already received funding from the emergency fund for an offence, he or she will be ineligible to receive funding for this type of offence again. Certain crimes, such as domestic violence or incest, are typically not limited to a single incident and are instead repetitive. The program categorically excludes anyone who falls prey to repeat victimization.

Recourse Applicants can ask that a decision by the fund be reviewed.

Yukon

There is no compensation fund for victims of crime in Yukon. However, the Victims of Crime Emergency Fund can provide immediate emergency assistance to victims of crime. It is a fund of last resort, designed for victims who haven't been able to get support from other sources, such as social assistance, First Nations associations, insurance, a shelter, or a community group.

Eligibility Eligible victims are direct victims, or if the victim is incapacitated (from injuries) or a minor, a family member or legal guardian can act on his or her behalf. In order to be eligible the crime must have been committed in Yukon, and the funds will be spent in Yukon. This is emergency relief immediately following the crime and it must be requested within 60 days. The victim may not receive funding more than once for the same offence. The victim is ineligible if he or she was committing a crime at the time of the victimization. Victims are not required to report the crime to the police to be eligible.

Awards Eligible victims may be able to get funding for short-term counselling, crime scene cleanup, emergency home repair for immediate safety, emergency accommodation, emergency childcare and dependent support, certain transportation costs, medical expenses, and other items considered as emergency at the discretion of Victim Services. It does not cover lost wages or income caused by time off work or pain and suffering.

APPENDIX 4

VICTIM IMPACT STATEMENT

Form 34.2

(Subsection 722(4))

This form may be used to provide a description of the physical or emotional harm, property damage or economic loss suffered by you as the result of the commission of an offence, as well as a description of the impact of the offence on you. You may attach additional pages if you need more space.

Your statement must not include

- any statement about the offence or the offender that is not relevant to the harm or loss you suffered;
- any unproven allegations;
- any comments about any offence for which the offender was not convicted;
- any complaint about any individual, other than the offender, who was involved in the investigation or prosecution of the offence; or
- except with the court's approval, an opinion or recommendation about the sentence.

You may present a detailed account of the impact the offence has had on your life. The following sections are examples of information you may wish to include in your statement. You are not required to include all of this information.

Emotional impact

Describe how the offence has affected you emotionally. For example, think of

- your lifestyle and activities;
- your relationships with others such as your spouse, family and friends;
- your ability to work, attend school or study; and
- your feelings, emotions and reactions as they relate to the offence.

_____

_____

_____

_____

_____

_____

_____

Physical impact

Describe how the offence has affected you physically. For example, think of

- ongoing physical pain, discomfort, illness, scarring, disfigurement or physical limitation;
- hospitalization or surgery you have had because of the offence;
- treatment, physiotherapy or medication you have been prescribed;
- the need for any further treatment or the expectation that you will receive further treatment; and
- any permanent or long-term disability.

_____

_____

_____

_____

_____

_____

_____

Economic impact

Describe how the offence has affected you economically. For example, think of

- The value of any property that was lost or damaged and the cost of repairs or replacement;
- Any financial loss due to missed time from work;
- The cost of any medical expenses, therapy or counselling;
- Any costs or losses that are not covered by insurance.

Please note that this is not an application for compensation or restitution.

_____

_____

_____

_____

_____

_____

_____

Fears for security

Describe any fears you have for your security or that of your family and friends. For example, think of

- Concerns with respect to contact with the offender; and
- Concerns with respect to contact between the offender and members of your family or close friends

_____

_____

_____

_____

_____

_____

_____

Drawing, poem or letter

You may use this space to draw a picture or write a poem or letter if it will help you express the impact that the offence has had on you.

[ ] I would like to present my statement in court.

To the best of my knowledge, the information contained in this statement is true.

Dated this _____ day of _____ 20___, at

_____.

Signature of declarant

If you completed this statement on behalf of the victim, please indicate the reasons why you did so and the nature of your relationship with the victim.

_____

_____

_____

_____

Dated this _____ day of _____ 20____, at _____.

Signature of declarant

GLOSSARY

abolitionism: A school of thought within criminology advocating the abolition of the criminal justice system.

community impact statement (CIS): A statement that allows individual members of a community that has been affected by a crime to submit a statement on behalf of the community in which the individual expresses the harm or loss suffered by the community as a result of the crime.

crime rate: Measures the volume of crime registered by police relative to the population size. In Canada, information about the crime rate is published annually by Statistics Canada.

dark number: The term used by criminologists to refer to the amount of undiscovered or unreported crime.

direct victim: The person who was the object of the victimization and directly experienced the crime.

exposure theories: Refers to a group of theories that explain victimization by examining the environments victims are exposed to while also understanding what makes a target more vulnerable or attractive within such contexts.

indirect victim: A person who is linked to the direct victim of a crime in such a way that they too suffer as a result of that relationship.

International Criminal Court (ICC): A criminal court established by the international community. The court is seated in The Hague, Netherlands, and has the jurisdiction to prosecute individuals for crimes against humanity, war crimes, and genocide.

multiple victimization: Refers to having experienced more than one victimization incident during a specified period.

polyvictimization: Refers to having experienced multiple types or forms of victimization during a specified period.

post-traumatic stress disorder (PTSD): A psychiatric disorder that can occur following direct or indirect exposure to traumatic events.

prevalence rate: The number of individuals in a specific population who experienced at least one victimization during a specific time divided by the total number of people in the population.

restitution order: An order imposed by a judge in a criminal court upon conviction or discharge of the offender involving the financial reimbursement of the victim by the offender for any damage to or loss of property.

risk heterogeneity: Also referred to as *flag theory*, a theory that suggests victims have some enduring characteristics or behaviours that repeatedly place them at risk for victimization.

secondary victim: A person who suffered harm while intervening to assist victims in distress or who witnessed the victimization. This includes bystanders who witnessed a crime as well as professionals who may not have directly witnessed the crime but who are repeatedly exposed indirectly to trauma because of their work helping victims.

secondary victimization: A victimologial notion that reflects the idea that victims are injured once by the crime and a second time by the insensitive reactions of others, in particular criminal justice authorities and their failure to respond to the victim's needs.

state dependence: Also referred to as *event dependence* or *boost theory*, a theory that assumes there is nothing that distinguishes victims from nonvictims before the initial victimization, but the initial victimization may boost or increase the probability of the victim continuing to be victimized.

strain theory: From a victimological perspective, the accumulation of strain (including prior victimization), which is thought to render the individual vulnerable to and at risk of victimization.

tertiary victims Refers to members in a victimized community.

victim impact statement (VIS): A description by the victim of how a crime has affected his or her life. This is usually a written statement, although in certain circumstances the victim may read the statement aloud.

victimization rate: The number of victimizations experienced by a specific population divided by the total number of people in the population.

victimization survey: Originally designed as a way to measure crime, the victimization survey canvasses members of a population to assess their victimization experiences during a given period.

witness: A person who is thought to have seen something (such as a crime) happen. In criminal law the witness may include the person who directly experienced the crime (i.e., the victim).

REFERENCES

Abramson, L.Y., Seligman, M.E.P., & Teasdale, J.D. (1978). Learned helplessness in humans: Critique and reformulation. *Journal of Abnormal Psychology, 87*(1), 49–74. http://dx.doi.org/10.1037/0021-843X.87.1.49

Adorjan, M., Christensen, T., Kelly, B., & Pawluch, D. (2012). Stockholm syndrome as vernacular resource. *Sociological Quarterly, 53*(3), 454–474. http://dx.doi.org/10.1111/j.1533-8525.2012.01241.x

Agnew, R. (1992). Foundation for a general strain theory of crime and delinquency. *Criminology, 30*(1), 47–88. http://dx.doi.org/10.1111/j.1745-9125.1992.tb01093.x

Agnew, R. (2001). Building on the foundation of general strain theory: Specifying the types of strain most likely to lead to crime and delinquency. *Journal of Research in Crime and Delinquency, 38*(4), 319–361. http://dx.doi.org/10.1177/0022427801038004001

Alam, S. (2015). *Statistiques sur les tribunaux de la jeunesse au Canada, 2013–2014.* Ottawa, ON: Statistique Canada, Centre canadien de la statistique juridique.

Alden, L.E., Regambal, M.J., & Laposa, J.M. (2008). The effects of direct versus witness threat on emergency department healthcare workers: Implications for PTSD Criterion A. *Journal of Anxiety Disorders, 22*(8), 1337–1346. http://dx.doi.org/10.1016/j.janxdis.2008.01.013

Allegrezza, S. (2015). Victim's statute within Directive 2012/29/EU. In L. Luparia (Ed.), *Victims and criminal justice: European standards and national good practices* (pp. 3–19). Milan, IT: Wolters-Kluwer.

Allen, M. (2014). *Victim services in Canada, 2011/2012.* Canadian Centre for Justice Statistics, Statistics Canada.

Allen, M. (2016). *Police-reported crime statistics in Canada, 2015.* Canadian Centre for Justice Statistics, Statistics Canada.

Allinne, J.P. (2001). Les victims: des oubliées de l'histoire du droit? In R. Cario & D. Salas (Eds.), *Oeuvre de justice et victims* (Vol. 1, pp. 25–58). Paris: L'Harmattan.

American Bar Association. (2006). *The victim in the criminal justice system.* Washington, DC: Author.

American Psychiatric Association. (1994). *Diagnostic and statistical manual of mental disorders* (4th ed.). Washington, DC: Author.

American Psychiatric Association. (2013). *Diagnostic and statistical manual of mental disorders* (5th ed.). Washington, DC: Author.

Amick-McMullan, A., Kilpatrick, D., Veronen, L.J., & Smith, S. (1989). Family survivors of homicide victims: Theoretical perspectives and an exploratory study. *Journal of Traumatic Stress, 2*(1), 21–35. http://dx.doi.org/10.1002/jts.2490020104

Amick-McMullan, A., Kilpatrick, D.G., & Resnick, H.S. (1991). Homicide as a risk factor for PTSD among surviving family members. *Behavior Modification, 15*(4), 545–559. http://dx.doi.org/10.1177/01454455910154005

Amnesty International. (2004). Canada: Stolen sisters: A human rights response to discrimination and violence against Indigenous women in Canada. Retrieved from http://www.amnesty.ca/sites/default/files/amr200032004enstolensisters.pdf

Anderson, K.M., Renner, L.M., & Danis, F.S. (2012). Recovery: Resilience and growth in the aftermath of domestic violence. *Violence against Women, 18*(11), 1279–1299. http://dx.doi.org/10.1177/1077801212470543

Angel, C. (2005). *Crime victims meet their offenders: Testing the impact of restorative justice conferences on victims' post-traumatic stress symptoms.* Unpublished doctoral dissertation, University of Pennsylvania.

Angel, C.M., Sherman, L.W., Strang, H., Bennett, S., Inkpen, N., Keane, A., & Richmond, T. (2009). Effects of restorative justice conferences on post-traumatic stress symptoms among robbery and burglary victims: A randomized controlled trial. Paper presented at the International Symposium of the International Society of Criminology, Barcelona, Spain.

APA. (2016). *Traumatology.* Retrieved from http://www.apa.org/pubs/journals/trm/

Armour, M.P. (2002). Experiences of co-victims of homicide: Implications for research and practice. *Trauma, Violence & Abuse, 3*(2), 109–124. http://dx.doi.org/10.1177/15248380020032002

Aromaa, K. (2012). Victimisation surveys: What are they good for? *Temida, 15*(2), 85–93.

Aronowitz, A.A. (2009). *Human trafficking, human misery: The global trade in human beings.* Westport, CT: Praeger.

Ashworth, A. (1986). Punishment and compensation: Victims, offenders and the state. *Oxford Journal of Legal Studies, 6*(1), 86–122.

Ashworth, A. (1993). Victim impact statements and sentencing. *Criminal Law Review*, 498–509.

AuCoin, K., & Beauchamp, D. (2007). Impacts and consequences of victimization. *Juristat, 27*(1).

Bacik, I., Maunsell, C., & Grogan, S. (1998). The legal process and victims of rape. Dublin, IR: Dublin Rape Crisis Centre. Retrieved from http://www.drcc.ie/wp-content/uploads/2011/03/rapevic.pdf

Baranowsky, A., Young, M., Johnson-Douglas, S., Williams-Keeler, L., & McCarrey, M. (1998). PTSD transmission: A review of secondary traumatization in Holocaust survivor families. *Canadian Psychology, 39*(4), 247–256. http://dx.doi.org/10.1037/h0086816

Bard, M., & Sangry, D. (1979). *The crime victim's book*. New York, NY: Basic Books.

Baril, M. (1984). L'envers du crime. *Les Cahiers de recherches criminologiques, 2*. https://depot.erudit.org/id/000977dd

Baril, M. (1985). Vers une distribution équitable des droits et des libertés: Le cas des criminels et de leurs victimes. *Mémoires de la Société Royale du Canada, quatrième série, 23*, 105–113.

Baril, M. (2002). *L'envers du crime*. Paris: L'Harmattan.

Baril, M., Durand, S., Cousineau, M.M, & Gravel, S. (1983). *Mais nous, les témoins …* Montreal, QC: École de criminologie, Université de Montréal.

Baril, M., Laflamme-Cusson, S., Boisvert, R., Boudreau, N., & Gravel, E. (1990). *La déclaration de la victime au palais de justice de Montréal. Rapport final*. Montreal, QC: Association québécoise Plaidoyer-Victimes.

Barnes, A., & Ephross, P. (1994). The impact of hate violence on victims: Emotional and behavioral responses to attacks. *Social Work, 39*(3), 247–251.

Bassiouni, M. (1982). Quesas crimes. In M. Bassiouni (Ed.), *The Islamic criminal justice system* (pp. 203–209). Dobbs Ferry, Oceana Publishing Inc.

Bazemore, G. (1999). Crime victims, restorative justice and the juvenile court: Exploring victim needs and involvement in the response to youth crime. *International Review of Victimology, 6*(4), 295–320. http://dx.doi.org/10.1177/026975809900600404

Beattie, S., & Hutchins, H. (2015). Shelters for abused women in Canada, 2014, *Juristat*. Catalogue no. 85–002-X.

Bedau, H.A. (1978). Retribution and the theory of punishment. *Journal of Philosophy, 75*(11), 601–620. http://dx.doi.org/10.5840/jphil197875114

Beloof, D.E. (1999). The third model of criminal process: The victim participation model. *Utah Law Review, 2*, 289–331.

Beloof, D.E. (2005). The third wave of crime victims' rights: Standing, remedy and review. *Brigham Young University Law Review, 255*, 261–267.

Ben-David, S. (2009). Victim blaming in the context of rape. In O. Hagemann, P. Schäfer, & S. Schmidt (Eds.), *Victimology, victim assistance and criminal justice: Perspectives shared by international experts at the Inter-University Centre of Dubrovnik* (pp. 153–162). Mönchengladbach: Hochschule Niederrhein.

Bennett, T. (1995). Identifying, explaining and targeting burglary hot spots. *European Journal on Criminal Policy and Research, 3*(3), 113–123. http://dx.doi.org/10.1007/BF02242932

Berg, M.T., Stewart, E.A., Schreck, C.J., & Simons, R.L. (2012). The victim–offender overlap in context: Examining the role of neighbourhood street culture. *Criminology, 50*(2), 359–390. http://dx.doi.org/10.1111/j.1745-9125.2011.00265.x

Besserer, S. (2007). Attitudes toward sentencing in nine industrialized countries. In P. Nieuwbeerta (Ed.), *Crime victimization in comparative perspective: Results from the International Crime Victims Survey, 1989–2000* (pp. 391–412). The Hague, NL: Boom Juridische Uitgevers.

Besserer, S., Brzozowski, J.A., Hendrick, D., Ogg, S., & Trainor, C. (2001). *Un profil de la victimization criminelle: Résultats de l'enquête sociale générale 1999*. Ottawa, ON: Statistique Canada.

Biderman, A.D. (1967). *Report on a pilot study in the District of Columbia on victimization and attitudes toward law enforcement. President's Commission on Law Enforcement and Administration of Justice.* Washington, DC: US Government Printing Office.

Bienkowska, E. (1992). What is victimology? Some reflections on the concept of victimology. In S. Ben-David & G.F. Kirchhoff (Eds.), *International faces of victimology* (pp. 81–88). Mönchengladbach: World Society of Victimology Publishing.

Bies, R.J. (2008). Are procedural justice and interactional justice conceptually distinct? In J. Greenberg & J. Colquit (Eds.), *Handbook of organizational justice* (pp. 85–112). New York, NY: Psychology Press.

Bitti, G. (2011). Les droits procéduraux des victimes devant la Cour pénale internationale. *Criminologie, 44*(2), 63–98. http://dx.doi.org/10.7202/1005792ar

Black's Law Dictionary. (2015). Retrieved from http://thelawdictionary.org/

Blader, S.L., & Tyler, T.R. (2003). A four-component model of procedural justice: Defining the meaning of a "fair" process. *Personality and Social Psychology Bulletin, 29*(6), 747–758. http://dx.doi.org/10.1177/0146167203029006007

Blondel, E. (2008). Victims' rights in an adversary system. *Duke Law Journal, 58*(2), 237–274.

Bolton, P., Neugebauer, R., & Ndogoni, L. (2002). Prevalence of depression in rural Rwanda based on symptom and functional criteria. *Journal of Nervous and Mental Disease*, *190*(9), 631–637. http://dx.doi.org/10.1097/00005053-200209000-00009

Bombay, A., Matheson, K., & Anisman, H. (2014). The intergenerational effects of Indian residential schools: Implications for the concept of historical trauma. *Transcultural Psychiatry*, *51*(3), 320–338. http://dx.doi.org/10.1177/1363461513503380

Booth, T. (2016). *Accommodating justice: Victim impact statements in the sentencing process*. Annandale, NSW: The Federation Press.

Bouten, E., Goudriaan, H., & Nieuwbeerta, P. (2002). Criminal victimization in seventeen industrialized countries. In P. Nieuwbeerta (Ed.), *Crime victimization in comparative perspective: Results from the International Crime Victims Survey 1989–2000* (pp. 13–28). The Hague, NL: Boom Juridische Uitgevers.

Bowling, B. (1994). Racial harassment in East London. In M. Hamm (Ed.), *Hate crime: International perspectives on causes and control* (pp. 2–36). Cincinnati, OH: Anderson Publishing.

Boyce, J. (2015). *Police-reported crime statistics in Canada, 2014*. Catalogue no. 85–002-X. Ottawa, ON: Statistics Canada, Canadian Centre for Justice Statistics.

Boyce, J., & Cotter, A. (2013). Homicide in Canada, 2011. *Juristat*. Catalogue no. 85–002-X.

Bradford, B. (2011). Voice, neutrality and respect: Use of victim support services, procedural fairness and confidence in the criminal justice system. *Criminology & Criminal Justice*, *11*(4), 345–366. http://dx.doi.org/10.1177/1748895811408832

Brassard, R. & Cousineau, M.M. (2002). L'enfermement des femmes autochtones: une reconstruction d'objet. *Criminologie*, *32*(2), 73–90.

Brennan, I.R. (2016). When is violence not a crime? Factors associated with victims' labelling of violence as a crime. *International Review of Victimology*, *22*(1), 3–23. http://dx.doi.org/10.1177/0269758015610849

Brennan, S. (2011). Canadians' percepetions of personal safety and crime. *Juristat*, Catalogue No. 85–002-X.

Breslau, N., Davis, G.C., Andreski, P., & Petersen, E. (1991). Traumatic events and posttraumatic stress disorder in an urban population of young adults. *Archives of General Psychiatry*, *48*(3), 216–222. http://dx.doi.org/10.1001/archpsyc.1991.01810270028003

Brienen, M., & Hoegen, E. (2000). *Victims of crime in 22 European criminal justice systems*. Nijmegen: Wolf Legal Productions.

Brodeur, J.P. (2003). *Les visages de la police: pratiques et perceptions*. Montreal, QC: Les Presses de l'Université de Montréal.

Brookes, G., Pooley, J.A., & Earnest, J. (2015). *Terrorism, trauma, and psychology: A multilevel victim perspective on the Bali bombings*. Abingdon, UK: Routledge.

Brown, J.D., & Siegel, J.M. (1988). Attributions for negative life events and depression: The role of perceived control. *Journal of Personality and Social Psychology, 54*(2), 316–322. http://dx.doi.org/10.1037/0022-3514.54.2.316

Bryant-Davis, T., & Ocampo, C. (2005). The trauma of racism: Implications for counseling, research and education. *Counseling Psychologist, 33*(4), 479–500.

Bunch, J., Clay-Warner, J., & McMahon-Howard, J. (2014). The effects of victimization on routine activities. *Criminal Justice and Behavior, 41*(5), 574–592. http://dx.doi.org/10.1177/0093854813508286

Bureau of Justice Statistics. (1991). *Sourcebook of criminal justice statistics*. Washington, DC: US Department of Justice, Bureau of Justice Statistics.

Bureau of Justice Statistics. (2016). *Data collection: National Crime Victimization Survey (NCVS)*. Retrieved from http://www.bjs.gov/index.cfm?ty=dcdetail&iid=245

Burns, P. (1992). *Criminal injuries compensation* (2nd ed.). Toronto, ON: Butterworths.

Byrne, C.A., Kilpatrick, D.G., Howley, S.S., & Beatty, D. (1999). Female victims of partner versus nonpartner violence: Experiences with the criminal justice system. *Criminal Justice and Behavior, 26*(3), 275–292. http://dx.doi.org/10.1177/0093854899026003001

Calhoun, K.S., Atkeson, B.M., & Resick, P.A. (1982). A longitudinal examination of fear reactions in victims of rape. *Journal of Counseling Psychology, 29*(6), 655–661. http://dx.doi.org/10.1037/0022-0167.29.6.655

Campbell, K.M. (2015). Judicial attitudes regarding victim impact statements: Perspectives from Quebec. *Canadian Criminal Law Review, 19*(3), 341–372.

Campbell, R. (2005). What really happened? A validation study of rape survivors help-seeking experiences with legal and medical systems. *Violence and Victims, 20*(1), 55–68.

Campbell, R. (2008). The psychological impact of rape victims. *American Psychologist, 63*(8), 702–717. http://dx.doi.org/10.1037/0003-066X.63.8.702

Campbell, R., & Raja, S. (1999). Secondary victimization of rape victims: Insights from mental health professionals who treat survivors. *Violence and Victims, 14*(3), 261–275.

Campbell, R., & Raja, S. (2005). The sexual assault and secondary victimization of female veterans: Help-seeking experiences with military and civilian social systems. *Psychology of Women Quarterly, 29*(1), 97–106. http://dx.doi.org/10.1111/j.1471-6402.2005.00171.x

Campbell, R., Sefl, T., Barnes, H.E., Ahrens, C.E., Wasco, S.M., & Zaragoza-Diesfeld, Y. (1999). Community services for rape survivors: Enhancing psychological well-being or increasing trauma? *Journal of Consulting and Clinical Psychology, 67*(6), 847–858.

Campbell, R., Wasco, S.M., Ahrens, C.E., Sefl, T., & Barnes, H.E. (2001). Preventing the second rape: Rape survivors experiences with community service providers. *Journal of Interpersonal Violence, 16*(12), 1239–1259. http://dx.doi.org/10.1177/088626001016012002

Canadian Mental Health Association. (2015). *Mental health: Getting help.* Retrieved from http://www.cmha.ca/mental_health/getting-help/#.VYq_ooe8JnI

Canadian Resource Centre for Victims of Crime. (2015). *Victims' rights in Canada.* Retrieved from https://crcvc.ca/wp-content/uploads/2011/10/victims-rights_paper_DISCLAIMER_Feb2015.pdf

Caplan, J.M. (2007). What factors affect parole? A review of empirical research. *Federal Probation, 17*(1), 16–19.

Carlson, E.B., & Dalenberg, C. (2000). A conceptual framework for the impact of traumatic experiences. *Trauma, Violence & Abuse, 1*(1), 4–28. http://dx.doi.org/10.1177/1524838000001001002

Carr, P.J., Logio, K.A., & Maier, S. (2003). Keep me informed: What matters for victims as they navigate the juvenile criminal justice system in Philadelphia. *International Review of Victimology, 10*(2), 117–136. http://dx.doi.org/10.1177/026975800301000202

Casarez-Levison, R. (1992). An empirical investigation of coping strategies used by victims of crime: Victimization redefined. In E. Viano (Ed.), *Critical issues in victimology: International perspectives* (pp. 46–57). New York, NY: Springer Publishing.

Cassell, P., Mitchell, N.J., & Edwards, B.J. (2014). Crime victims' rights during criminal investigations? Applying the Crime Victims' Rights Act before criminal charges are filed. *Journal of Criminal Law & Criminology, 104*(1), 59–104.

Cavadino, M., & Dignan, J. (1997). Reparation, retribution and rights. *International Review of Victimology, 4*(4), 233–253. http://dx.doi.org/10.1177/026975809700400401

Cédilot, A. (2001, June 29). Une victime d'agression sexuelle refuse de témoigner à nouveau: le deuxième process de Gilles Dégarie s'en trouve menace. *La Presse.*

Chan, K.L. (2014). Polyvictimisation et comportements à risque chez des élèves chinois du high school. *Criminologie, 47*(1), 85–103. http://dx.doi.org/10.7202/1024008ar

Cheon, A., & Regehr, C. (2006). Restorative justice models in cases of intimate partner violence: Reviewing the evidence. *Victims & Offenders, 1*(4), 369–394. http://dx.doi.org/10.1080/15564880600934138

Child Advocacy Centres Canada. (2014). Building blocks: Update on CAC. Retrieved from http://cac-cae.ca/

Christie, N. (1977). Conflicts as property. *British Journal of Criminology, 17*(1), 1–15.

Christie, N. (1985). The ideal victim. In E.A. Fattah (Ed.), *From crime policy to victim policy* (pp. 17–30). Basingstoke, UK: MacMillan.

Chu, J.A. (1992). The re-victimization of adult women with histories of childhood abuse. *Journal of Psychotherapy Practice and Research, 1,* 259–269.

Clarke, R. (2012). Opportunity makes the thief. Really? And so what? *Crime Science, 1*(3), 1–9. http://dx.doi.org/10.1186/2193-7680-1-3

Clarke, R., Perkins, E., & Smith, D. (2001). Explaining repeat residential burglaries: An analysis of property stolen. In G. Farrell & K. Pease (Eds.), *Repeat Victimization* (pp. 119–132). Monsey, NY: Criminal Justice Press.

Cluss, P.A., Boughton, J., Frank, E., Stewart, B.D., & West, D. (1983). The rape victim: Psychological correlates of participation in the legal process. *Criminal Justice and Behavior, 10*(3), 342–357. http://dx.doi.org/10.1177/0093854883010003009

Cohen, L., & Felson, M. (1979). Social change and crime rate trends: A routine activity approach. *American Sociological Review, 44*(4), 588–608. http://dx.doi.org/10.2307/2094589

Colquitt, J.A. (2001). On the dimensionality of organization justice: A construct validation of a measure. *Journal of Applied Psychology, 86*(3), 386–400. http://dx.doi.org/10.1037/0021-9010.86.3.386

Cornaglia, F., & Leigh, A. (2011). *Crime and mental wellbeing,* Centre for Economic Performance Discussion Paper No. 1049, London School of Economics and Political Science.

Cornish, D., & Clarke, R. (Eds.). (1986). *The reasoning criminal.* New York, NY: Springer-Verlag.

Correctional Service Canada. (2012). Restorative opportunities program. Retrieved from http://www.csc-scc.gc.ca/restorative-justice/003005-1000-eng.shtml

Cougle, J.R., Resnick, H., & Kilpatrick, D.G. (2009). A prospective examination of PTSD symptoms as risk factors for subsequent exposure to potentially traumatic events among women. *Journal of Abnormal Psychology, 118*(2), 405–411. http://dx.doi.org/10.1037/a0015370

Couture, R., & Hétu, M. (1996). L'IVAC au service de la personne. In J. Coiteux, P. Campeau, M. Clarkson and M.M. Cousineau (Eds.), *Question d'équité: l'aide aux victimes d'actes criminels* (pp. 135–156). Montreal, QC: Association québécoise Plaidoyer-Victimes.

CQLC. (2014). *Rapport annuel de gestion 2013–2014.* Quebec, QC: Author.

CQLC. (2015). *Rapport annuel de gestion 2014–2015.* Quebec, QC: Author.

Craig-Henderson, K., & Sloan, R. (2003). After the hate: Helping psychologists help victims of racist hate crime. *Clinical Psychology: Science and Practice, 10*(4), 481–490. http://dx.doi.org/10.1093/clipsy.bpg048

Crenlinsten, R.D. (1977). *Dimensions of victimization in the context of terrorist acts.* Montreal, QC: International Centre for Comparative Criminology, Université de Montréal.

Cuevas, C.A., Finkelhor, D., Turner, H.A., & Ormrod, R.K. (2007). Juvenile delinquency and victimization: A theoretical typology. *Journal of Interpersonal Violence, 22*(12), 1581–1602. http://dx.doi.org/10.1177/0886260507306498

Cusson, M. (1993). In memoriam: Micheline Baril. *Criminologie, 26*(2), 3–5. http://dx.doi.org/10.7202/011178ar

Cyr, K. (2008). *Empowerment et système de justice pénale: l'expérience des victimes d'actes criminels.* Doctoral dissertation, Université de Montréal.

Cyr, K., Chamberland, C., Clément. M.E., & Lessard, G. (2014). Victimisation: réalité préoccupante pour les jeunes pris en charge par la DPJ. *La polyvictimisation des jeunes, 47*(1), 187–211. http://dx.doi.org/10.7202/1024013ar

Cyr, K., Clément, M.E., & Chamberland, C. (2014). Lifetime prevalence of multiple victimizations and its impact on children's mental health. *Journal of Interpersonal Violence, 29*(4), 616–634. http://dx.doi.org/10.1177/0886260513505220

Cyr, K., & Wemmers, J. (2011). Empowerment des victimes d'actes criminels. *Criminologie, 44*(2), 125–155. http://dx.doi.org/10.7202/1005794ar

Daly, K. (2011). Conventional and innovative justice responses to sexual violence. *ACSSA Issues, 12.* Retrieved from https://aifs.gov.au/sites/default/files/publication-documents/i12.pdf

Danieli, Y. (Ed.). (1998). *International handbook of multigenerational legacies of trauma.* New York, NY: Plenum Press. http://dx.doi.org/10.1007/978-1-4757-5567-1

Danieli, Y. (2014). Healing aspects of reparations and reparative justice victims of crimes against humanity. In J. Wemmers (Ed.), *Reparation for victims of crimes against humanity: The healing role of reparation* (pp. 7–21). London, UK: Routledge.

Danieli, Y., Engdahl, B., & Schlenger, W.E. (2004). The psychosocial aftermath of terrorism. In F.M. Moghaddam & A.J. Marsella (Eds.),

Understanding terrorism: Psychosocial roots, consequences, and interventions (pp. 223–246). Washington, DC: American Psychological Association. http://dx.doi.org/10.1037/10621-011

Davis, R., Lurigio, A., & Skogan, W. (1997). *Victims of crime*. Thousand Oaks, CA: Sage.

Davis, R., & Mulford, C. (2008). Victim rights and new remedies: Finally getting victims their due. *Journal of Contemporary Criminal Justice, 24*(2), 198–208. http://dx.doi.org/10.1177/1043986208315474

Davis, R., O'Sullivan, C., Farole, D., Jr., & Rempel, M. (2008). A comparison of two prosecution policies in cases of intimate partner violence: Mandatory case filing versus following the victims' lead. *Criminology & Public Policy, 7*(4), 633–662. http://dx.doi.org/10.1111/j.1745-9133.2008.00532.x

Davis, R., Taylor, B., & Titus, R. (1997). Victims as agents: Implications for victim services and crime prevention. In R. Davis, A. Lurigio, & W. Skogan (Eds.), *Victims of crime* (2nd ed., pp. 167–179). Thousand Oaks, CA: Sage.

Davis, R.C., & Smith, B. (1994). The effect of victim impact statements on sentencing decisions: A test in an urban setting. *Justice Quarterly, 11*(3), 453–469. http://dx.doi.org/10.1080/07418829400092351

De Léséleuc, S., & Brzozowski, J.-A. (2006). *Victimization and offending in Canada's territories*. Catalogue No. 85F0033MIE. Ottawa, ON: Canadian Centre for Justice Statistics, Statistics Canada.

De Mesmaecker, V. (2014). *Perceptions of criminal justice*. Oxon, UK: Routledge.

Dekel, R., & Goldblatt, H. (2008). Is there intergenerational transmission of trauma? The case of combat veterans' children. *American Journal of Orthopsychiatry, 78*(3), 281–289. http://dx.doi.org/10.1037/a0013955

Dempsey, M.M. (2009). *Prosecuting domestic violence: A philosophical analysis*. New York, NY: Oxford University Press. http://dx.doi.org/10.1093/acprof:oso/9780199562169.001.1

Denkers, A. (1996). *Psychological reactions of victims of crime: The influence of pre-crime, crime and post-crime factors*. Doctoral dissertation, Vrije Universiteit, Amsterdam.

Denkers, A., & Winkel, F.W. (1998). Crime victims' well-being and fear in a prospective and longitudinal study. *International Review of Victimology, 5*(2), 141–162. http://dx.doi.org/10.1177/026975809800500202

Department of Justice Canada (2004). *Values and Principles of Restorative Justice in Criminal Matters*. Retrieved from http://www.iirp.edu/pdf/RJValues-DOJCan.pdf

Department of Justice Canada. (2012). Harper government announces Federal Income Support for Parents of Murdered and Missing Children grant to be available on January 1st, 2013. Retrieved from http://news. gc.ca/web/article-en.do?nid=713599

Department of Justice Canada. (2015a). *Canadian Victims Bill of Rights.* Retrieved from http://laws-lois.justice.gc.ca/eng/acts/C-23.7/ page-1.html

Department of Justice Canada. (2015b). Financial assistance for Canadians victimized abroad. Retrieved from http://www.justice.gc.ca/eng/ fund-fina/cj-jp/fund-fond/abroad-etranger.html

Department of Justice Canada. (2015c). PMMC eligibility criteria. Retrieved from http://www.servicecanada.gc.ca/eng/sc/pmmc/ eligibility.shtml

Department of Justice Canada. (2016). Community impact statements. Retrieved from http://www.justice.gc.ca/eng/cj-jp/victims-victimes/ sentencing-peine/cis-drc.html

Desjardine, C. (2010, September 15). L'artisan de son malheur, tranché la Cour d'appel: homme devenu paraplégique en frayant avec les gangs de rue. *La Presse,* A12.

Deutsch, M. (1975). Equity, equality and need: What determines which value will be used as the basis of distributive justice? *Journal of Social Issues, 31*(3), 137–149. http://dx.doi.org/10.1111/j.1540-4560.1975. tb01000.x

Deutsch, M. (1985). *Distributive justice: A social-psychological perspective.* New Haven, CT: Yale University Press.

Dichter, M., Cerulli, C., Kothari, C., Barg, F., & Rhodes, K. (2011). Engaging with criminal prosecution: The victim's perspective. *Women & Criminal Justice, 21*(1), 21–37. http://dx.doi.org/10.1080/08974454.2011.5 36053

Doak, J. (2005). Victims' rights in criminal trials: Prospects for participation. *Journal of Law and Society, 32*(2), 294–316. http://dx.doi. org/10.1111/j.1467-6478.2005.00325.x

Doak, J. (2008). *Victims' rights, human rights and criminal justice: Reconceiving the role of third parties.* Oxford, UK: Hart Publishing.

Doak, J. (2015a). Enriching trial justice for crime victims in common law systems: Lessons from transitional environments. *International Review of Victimology, 21*(2), 139–160. http://dx.doi.org/10.1177/0269758015571469

Doak, J. (2015b). *Victims of crime in the criminal trial process.* Submission to the Victorian Law Reform Commission, Australia, 15 October.

Doerner, W., & Lab, S. (2005). *Victimology.* Newark, NJ: Anderson Publishing.

Donnelly, J. (2003). *Universal human rights in theory and practice.* Ithaca, NY: Cornell University Press.

Drapkin, I., & Viano, E. (1974). *Victimology*. Lexington, MA: Lexington Books.

Dugan, L. (1999). The effect of criminal victimization on a household's moving decision. *Criminology, 37*(4), 903–930.

Dunn, J.L. (2012). *Judging victims: Why we stigmatize survivors, and how they reclaim respect*. Boulder, CO: Lynne Riener Publishers.

Dussich, J., Underwood, T., & Petersen, D. (2003). New definitions for victimology and victim services: A theoretical note. *Victimologist, 7*(2), 1–3.

ECOSOC (United Nations Economic and Social Council). (2002). Basic principles on the use of restorative justice programmes in criminal matters. Resolution 2002/12.

Edwards, I. (2004). An ambiguous participant: The crime victim and criminal justice decision-making. *British Journal of Criminology, 44*(6), 967–982.

Elias, R. (1983). The symbolic politics of victim compensation. *Victimology, 8*(1–2), 213–224.

Elias, R. (1985). Transcending our social reality of victimization: Toward a victimology of human rights. *Victimology, 10*, 213–224.

Elias, R. (1993). *Victims still: The political manipulation of crime victims*. Newbury Park, CA: Sage Publications. http://dx.doi.org/10.4135/9781483326412

Ellenberger, H. (1954). Relations psychologiques entre le criminel et la victime, *Revue de droit pénal et de criminologie, 8*(2), 103–121.

Elliott, E. (2016, January 19). Compensation for victims of crime, Manitoba. Personal communication.

Epstein, J.N., Saunders, B.E., & Kilpatrick, D.G. (1997). Predicting PTSD in women with a history of childhood rape. *Journal of Traumatic Stress, 10*(4), 573–588. http://dx.doi.org/10.1002/jts.2490100405

Erez, E. (1991). Victim impact statements. *Trends and Issues in Crime and Criminal Justice, 33*.

Erez, E. (1994). Victim participation in sentencing: And the debate goes on . . . *International Review of Victimology, 3*(1–2), 17–32.

Erez, E. (1999). Who's afraid of the big bad victim? Victim impact statements as victim empowerment and enhancement of justice. *Criminal Law Review (London, England), 545*, 550–551.

Erez, E., Ibarra, P.R., & Downs, D.M. (2011). Victim welfare and participation reforms in the United States: A therapeutic jurisprudence perspective. In E. Erez, M. Kilchling, & J. Wemmers (Eds.), *Therapeutic jurisprudence and victim participation in justice: International perspectives* (pp. 15–40). Durham, NC: Caroline Academic Publishing.

Erez, E., & Roberts, J. (2007). Victim participation in the criminal justice system. In R. Davis, A. Lurigio, & S. Herman (Eds.), *Victims of crime* (pp. 277–297). Los Angeles, CA: Sage.

Erez, E., & Roeger, L. (1995). The effect of victim impact statements on sentencing patterns and outcomes: The Australian experience. *Journal of Criminal Justice, 23*(4), 363–375. http://dx.doi.org/10.1016/0047-2352(95)00026-M

Erez, E., Roeger, L., & Morgan, F. (1994). *Victim impact statements in South Australia: An evaluation (Series C, No. 6).* Adelaide, South Australia: Office of Crime Statistics, Attorney General's Department.

Erez, E., Roeger, L., & Morgan, F. (1997). Victim harm, impact statements and victim satisfaction with justice: An Australian experience. *International Review of Victimology, 5*(1), 37–60. http://dx.doi.org/10.1177/026975809700500103

Erez, E., & Tontodonato, P. (1992). Victim participation in sentencing and satisfaction with justice. *Justice Quarterly, 9*(3), 393–417. http://dx.doi.org/10.1080/07418829200091451

European Union Agency for Fundamental Rights. (2014). *Violence against women: EU wide survey main results.* Luxembourg: Publications Office of the European Union.

Evans-Campbell, T. (2008). Historical trauma in American Indian/Native Alaska communities: A multilevel framework for exploring impacts on individuals, families and communities. *Journal of Interpersonal Violence, 23*(3), 316–338. http://dx.doi.org/10.1177/0886260507312290

Farrell, G. (1995). Preventing repeat victimization. In M. Tonry & D.P. Farrington (Eds.), *Crime and justice: Vol. 19. Building a safer society: Strategic approaches to crime prevention.* Chicago, IL: University of Chicago Press.

Farrell, G., & Pease, K. (1993). *Once bitten, twice bitten: Repeat victimization and its implications for crime prevention. Crime Prevention Unit Series,* Paper 46. London, UK: Home Office.

Farrell, G., & Pease, K. (2001). *Repeat victimization.* Monsey, NY: Criminal Justice Press.

Farrell, G., Phillips, C., & Pease, K. (1995). Like taking candy. *British Journal of Criminology, 35*(3), 384–399.

Farrell, G., & Sousa, W. (2001). Repeat victimization and hot spots: The overlap and its implications for problem-oriented policing. In G. Farrell & K. Pease (Eds.), *Repeat Victimization* (pp. 221–240). Monsey, NY: Criminal Justice Press.

Fattah, E.A. (1966). Quelques problèmes posés à la justice pénale par la victimologie. *Annales internationales de la criminologie, 5*(2), 335–361.

Fattah, E.A. (1967). Toward a criminological classification of victims, *International Criminal Police Review, 22,* 163–169.

Fattah, E.A. (1971). *La victime est-elle coupable? Le role de la victim dans le meurtre en vue de vol.* Montréal, QC: Les Presses de l'Université de Montréal.

Fattah, E.A. (1991). *Understanding criminal victimization: An introduction to theoretical victimology.* Scarborough, ON: Prentice-Hall Canada.

Fattah, E.A. (1993). The rational choice/opportunity perspective as a vehicle for integrating criminological and victimological theories. In R.V. Clarke & M. Felson (Eds.), *Routine activity and rational choice* (pp. 225–258). New Brunswick, NJ: Transaction.

Fattah, E.A. (1998). A critical assessment of two justice paradigms: Contrasting the restorative and retributive justice models. In E. Fattah & T. Peters (Eds.), *Support for crime victims in a comparative perspective* (pp. 99–110). Leuven: Leuven University Press.

Fattah, E.A. (1999). From a handful of dollars to tea and sympathy: The sad history of victim assistance. In J.J.M. Van Dijk, R. Van Kaam, & J. Wemmers (Eds.), *Caring for crime victims: Selected proceedings of the 9th International Symposium on Victimology* (pp. 187–206). Monsey, NY: Criminal Justice Press.

Fattah, E.A. (2001). Victims' rights: Past, present and future: A global view. In R. Cario & D. Salas (Eds.) *Œuvre de justice et victims: Vol. 1.* (pp. 81–108). Paris: L'Harmattan Sciences Criminelles.

Fattah, E.A. (2008). *The future of criminology as a social science and academic discipline: Reflections on criminology's unholy alliance with criminal policy and on current misguided attempts to divorce victimology from criminology.* Keynote address at the 15th World Congress of the International Society of Criminology, Barcelona, 20–25 July.

Fattah, E.A. (2010). The evolution of a young, promising discipline: Sixty years of victimology, a retrospective and prospective look. In W.G. Shoham, P. Knepper, & M. Kett (Eds.), *International handbook of victimology* (pp. 43–94). Boca Raton, FL: CRC Press. http://dx.doi.org/10.1201/EBK1420085471-c3

Feldthusen, B., Hankivsky, O., & Greaves, L. (2000). Therapeutic consequences of civil actions for damages and compensation claims by victims of sexual abuse. *Canadian Journal of Women and the Law, 12,* 66–116.

Ferstman, C. (2012). *A review of practice and consideration of options for the future.* London, UK: Redress Trust.

FIDH. (2007). *Victims rights before the ICC.* Paris: Féderation internationale des ligues des droits de l'Homme.

Field, N.P., & Filanosky, C. (2009). Continuing bonds, risk factors for complicated grief, and adjustment to bereavement. *Death Studies, 34*(1), 1–29. http://dx.doi.org/10.1080/07481180903372269

Fijneault, C., Nuijten-Edelbroek, E., & Spickenheuer, J. (1985). *Politiële misdaadbestrijding: De ontwikkeling van het Amerikaanse, Engelse en Nederlandse onderzoek aangaande politiële misdaadbestrijding sedert de jaren 60. Onderzoek en beleid, 56.* The Hague: Staatsuitgeverij.

Finkelhor, D. (1997). The victimization of children and youth: Developmental victimology. In R. Davis, A. Lurigio, & W. Skogan (Eds.), *Victims of crime* (2nd ed.). Thousand Oaks, CA: Sage.

Finkelhor, D. (2007). Developmental victimology: The comprehensive study of childhood victimizations. In R. Davis, A. Lurigio, & S. Herman (Eds.), *Victims of crime* (3rd ed., pp. 9–34). Thousand Oaks, CA: Sage.

Finkelhor, D., Ormrod, R.K., Turner, H., & Holt, M. (2009). Pathways to poly-victimization. *Child Maltreatment, 14*(4), 316–329. http://dx.doi.org/10.1177/1077559509347012

Finkelhor, D., Ormrod, R.K., & Turner, H.A. (2007). Poly-victimization: A neglected component in child victimization. *Child Abuse & Neglect, 31*(1), 7–26. http://dx.doi.org/10.1016/j.chiabu.2006.06.008

Finkelhor, D., Ormrod, R.K., Turner, H.A., & Hamby, S. (2005). The victimization of children and youth: A comprehensive national survey. *Child Maltreatment, 10*(1), 5–25. http://dx.doi.org/10.1177/1077559504271287

Finkelhor, D., Turner, H., Hamby, S., & Ormrod, R. (2011). *Polyvictimization: Children's exposure to multiple types of victimization.* Washington, DC: US Department of Justice, Office of Justice Programs.

Finkelhor, D., Turner, H.A., Ormrod, R.K., Hamby, S., & Kracke, K. (2009). Children's exposure to violence: A comprehensive national survey. *Juvenile Justice Bulletin.*

Finn, M.A. (2013). Evidence-based and victim-centred prosecutorial policies. *Criminology & Public Policy, 12*(3), 443–472. http://dx.doi.org/10.1111/1745-9133.12049

Fiselier, J. (1978). *Slachtoffers van delicten: een onderzoek naar verborgen criminaliteit.* Utrecht: Ars Aequi Libri.

Fisher, B., & Jerin, B. (2014). The evolution of victimology: Pedagogy, research, services and advocacy. *Journal of Criminal Justice Education, 25*(4), 403–404. http://dx.doi.org/10.1080/10511253.2014.969477

Fitzgerald, R. (2008). Fear of crime and neighbourhood context in Canadian cities. *Crime and Justice Research Paper Series.* Catalogue no. 85–561-M-013.

Flatley, J. (2016). *Crime in England and Wales, year ending September 2015.* Statistical Bulletin, Office for National Statistics. Retrieved from http://

www.ons.gov.uk/peoplepopulationandcommunity/crimeandjustice/
bulletins/crimeinenglandandwales/yearendingseptember2015

Fleming, J., Mullen, P.E., Sibthorpe, B., & Bammer, G. (1999). The
long-term impact of childhood sexual abuse in Australian women.
Child Abuse & Neglect, *23*(2), 145–159. http://dx.doi.org/10.1016/
S0145-2134(98)00118-5

Folger, R. (1977). Distributive and procedural justice: Combined
impact of "voice" and improvement of experienced inequity. *Journal
of Personality and Social Psychology*, *35*(2), 108–119. http://dx.doi.
org/10.1037/0022-3514.35.2.108

Ford, D.A. (1991). Prosecution as a victim power resource: A note on
empowering women in violent conjugal relationships. *Law & Society
Review*, *25*(2), 313–334. http://dx.doi.org/10.2307/3053801

France, K. (2014). *Crisis intervention: A handbook of immediate person-to-person
help* (6th ed.). Springfield, IL: Charles C. Thomas Publisher.

Freeman, K., & Smith, N. (2014). Understanding the relationship between
crime victimisation and mental health: A longitudinal analysis of
population data. *Contemporary Issues in Crime and Justice: Crime and Justice
Bulletin*, *177*.

Freeman, L. (2013). *Support for victims: Findings from the crime survey for
England and Wales*. London, UK: Ministry of Justice Analytical Series.

Friedman, K., Bischoff, H., Davis, R.C., & Person, A. (1982). *Victims and helpers:
Reactions to crime*. Washington, DC: US Government Printing Office.

Fry, M. (1959). Justice for victims. *Journal of Public Law*, *8*, 191–194.

Gagné, H. (2008). *Vivre*. Montreal, QC: Libre Expression.

Gannon, M., & Mihorean, K. (2005). Criminal victimization in Canada,
2004. *Juristat*, *25*(7).

Garkawe, S. (2004). Revisiting the scope of victimology—How broad a
discipline should it be? *International Review of Victimology*, *11*(2–3), 275–
294. http://dx.doi.org/10.1177/026975800401100205

Garkawe, S. (2005). The need for a victims' convention. *The Victimologist*, *9*,
4–6.

Garland, D. (2001). *The culture of control: Crime and social order in contemporary
society*. Chicago, IL: University of Chicago Press.

Garvin, M., & Beloof, D. (2015). Crime victim agency: Independent lawyers
for sexual assault victims. *Ohio State Journal of Criminal Law*, *13*(1), 67–88.

Gibbons, D.C. (1979). *The criminological enterprise: Theories and perspectives*.
Upper Saddle River, NJ: Prentice-Hall.

Gilberti, C. (1991). *Victim impact statements in Canada, Vol. 7*. Ottawa, ON:
Research and Development Directorate, Department of Justice Canada.

Goetz, M. (2014). Reparative justice at the International Criminal Court: Best practice or tokenism? In J. Wemmers (Ed.), *Reparation for victims of crimes against humanity: The healing role of reparation* (pp. 53–70). Oxon, UK: Routledge.

Goldscheid, J. (2004). Crime victims compensation in a post-9/11 world. *Tulane Law Review, 79,* 167–233.

Goodey, J. (2005). *Victims and victimology: Research, policy and practice.* Essex, UK: Pearson Longman.

Goodrum, S. (2007). Victims' rights, victims' expectation, and law enforcement workers' constraints in cases of murder. *Law & Social Inquiry, 32*(3), 725–757. http://dx.doi.org/10.1111/j.1747-4469.2007.00075.x

Gravel, E. (2008, February 10). Guest lecture on victims and the criminal justice system at the École de criminologie, Université de Montréal.

Gray, S. (2005). *Crime victim's psychological trauma and satisfaction with the criminal justice system: Mediated by coping style.* Master's thesis, Université de Montréal.

Green, S. (2006). The victims' movement and restorative justice. In G. Johnstone (Ed.), *Handbook of restorative justice* (pp. 171–191). Cullompton, UK: Willan Publishing.

Greenberg, J. (1993). The social side of justice: Interpersonal and informational classes of organizational justice. In R. Cropanzano (Ed.), *Justice in the workplace: Approaching fairness in human resource management* (pp. 79–103). Hillsdale, NJ: Lawrence Erlbaum Associates.

Greenberg, M.S., & Ruback, R.B. (1992). *After the crime: Victim decision making.* New York, NY: Plenum Press. http://dx.doi.org/10.1007/978-1-4615-3334-4

Greeson, M.R., & Campbell, R. (2011). Rape survivors agency within the legal and medical systems. *Psychology of Women Quarterly, 35*(4), 582–595. http://dx.doi.org/10.1177/0361684311418078

Groenhuijsen, M. (1999). Victims' rights in the criminal justice system: A call for more comprehensive implementation theory. In J.J.M. Van Dijk, R. Van Kaam, & J. Wemmers (Eds.), *Caring for victims of crime* (pp. 85–114). Monsey, NY: Criminal Justice Press.

Groenhuijsen, M. (2014). The development of international policy in relation to victims of crime. *International Review of Victimology, 20*(1), 31–48. http://dx.doi.org/10.1177/0269758013511740

Groenhuijsen, M., & Pemberton, A. (2009). The EU framework decision for victims of crime: Does hard law make a difference? *European Journal of Crime Criminal Law and Criminal Justice, 17*(1), 43–59. http://dx.doi.org/10.1163/157181709X400386

Guidi, S., Homel, R., & Townsley, M. (1997). *Hot spots and repeat break and enter crimes: An analysis of police calls for service data.* Brisbane, AU: Queensland Criminal Justice Commission.

Hagan, J., Rymond-Richmond, W., & Parker, P. (2005). The criminology of genocide: Death and rape of Darfour. *Criminology, 43*(3), 525–562. http://dx.doi.org/10.1111/j.0011-1348.2005.00016.x

Hassija, C.M., & Gray, M.J. (2012). Negative social reactions to assault disclosure as a mediator between self-blame and posttraumatic stress symptoms among survivors of interpersonal assault. *Journal of Interpersonal Violence, 27*(17), 3425–3441. http://dx.doi.org/10.1177/0886260512445379

Hay, D., Varga-Toth, J., & Hines, E. (2006). *Delivering services to vulnerable populations.* Research Report F63. Ottawa, ON: Canadian Policy Research Networks. Retrieved from http://www.cprn.org/documents/45652_en.pdf

Haynes, S.H., Cares, A.C., & Ruback, R.B. (2015). Reducing the harm of criminal victimization: The role of restitution. *Violence and Victims, 30*(3), 450–469. http://dx.doi.org/10.1891/0886-6708.VV-D-13-00049

Health Canada. (2013). *Canada Health Act: Annual report 2012–2013.* Ottawa, ON: Health Canada. Retrieved from http://www.hc-sc.gc.ca/hcs-sss/pubs/cha-lcs/2013-cha-lcs-ar-ra/index-eng.php

Hébert-Dolbec, M.-L. (2014). *De l'émergence d'un espace participatif pour les victimes devant la cour pénale internationale: Quelle émancipation de la victime?* Montreal, QC: UQAM.

Herbert, C., Rioux, C., & Wemmers, J. (2014). Reparation and recovery in the aftermath of widespread violence. In J. Wemmers (Ed.), *Reparation for victims of crimes against humanity: The healing role of reparation* (pp. 22–37). Oxon, UK: Routledge.

Herman, J.L. (2003). The mental health of crime victims: Impact of legal intervention. *Journal of Traumatic Stress, 16*(2), 159–166. http://dx.doi.org/10.1023/A:1022847223135

Herman, J.L. (2005). Justice from the victim's perspective. *Violence against Women, 11*(5), 571–602. http://dx.doi.org/10.1177/1077801205274450

Herman, S., & Wasserman, C. (2001). A role for victims in offender re-entry. *Crime and Delinquency, 47*(3), 428–445. http://dx.doi.org/10.1177/0011128701047003008

Hill, J. (2009). *Working with victims of crime: A manual applying research to clinical practice* (2nd ed.). Ottawa, ON: Department of Justice Canada.

Hindelang, M., Gottfredson, M., & Garofalo, J. (1978). *Victims of personal crime: An empirical foundation for a theory of personal victimization.* Cambridge, MA: Ballinger.

Hochstetler, A., DeLisi, M., Jones-Johnson, G., & Johnson, W.R. (2014). The criminal victimization–depression sequela: Examining the effects of violent victimization on depression with a longitudinal propensity score design. *Crime and Delinquency, 60*(5), 785–806. http://dx.doi.org/10.1177/0011128710382261

Hodges, E.V.E., & Perry, D.G. (1999). Personal and interpersonal antecedents and consequences of victimization by peers. *Journal of Personality and Social Psychology, 76*(4), 677–685. http://dx.doi.org/10.1037/0022-3514.76.4.677

Holmstrom, L.L., & Burgess, A.W. (1978). *The victim of rape: Institutional reactions*. New York, NY: Wiley.

Holstein, J., & Miller, G. (1990). Rethinking victimization: An interactional approach to victimology. *Symbolic Interaction, 13*(1), 103–122. http://dx.doi.org/10.1525/si.1990.13.1.103

Hope, T., Bryan, J., Trickett, A., & Osborn, D. (2001). The phenomena of multiple victimization: The relationship between personal and property crime risk. *British Journal of Criminology, 41*(4), 595–617. http://dx.doi.org/10.1093/bjc/41.4.595

Hough, M. (2012). Researching trust in the police and trust in justice: A UK perspective. *Policing and Society, 22*(3), 332–345. http://dx.doi.org/10.1080/10439463.2012.671826

Hoyle, C., Cape, E., Morgan, R., & Sanders, A. (1998). *Evaluation of the "one stop shop" and victim statement pilot projects*. London, UK: Home Office, Research Development and Statistics Directorate.

Hulsman, L.H.C. (1977). Slachtoffers van delicten. *Delikt en delinkwent, 7*, 577–585.

Human Rights Centre. (2015). *The victims' court? A study of 622 participants at the International Criminal Court*. Berkley, CA: UC Berkley School of Law. Retrieved from https://www.law.berkeley.edu/wp-content/uploads/2015/04/VP_report_2015_final_full2.pdf

Huo, J.Y., Smith, H.J., Tyler, T.R., & Lind, E.A. (1996). Superordinate identification, subgroup identification and justice concerns: Is separatism the problem; is assimilation the answer? *Psychological Science, 7*(1), 40–45. http://dx.doi.org/10.1111/j.1467-9280.1996.tb00664.x

Huyse, L. (2003). Victims. In D. Bloomfield, T. Barnes, & L. Huyse (Eds.), *Reconciliation after violent conflict: A handbook* (pp. 54–66). Stockholm: International IDEA.

Hydon, S., Wong, M., Langley, A.K., Stein, B.D., & Kataoka, S.H. (2015). Preventing secondary traumatic stress in educators. *Child and Adolescent Psychiatric Clinics of North America, 24*(2), 319–333. http://dx.doi.org/10.1016/j.chc.2014.11.003

Ignatieff, M. (2001). The attack on human rights. *Foreign Affairs, 80*(6), 102–116.

Illingworth, H. (2016, February 1). Canadian Resource Centre for Victims of Crime. Personal communication.

Jacob, B.R. (1974). Reparation or restitution by the criminal offender to his victim: Applicability of an ancient concept in the modern correctional process. In I. Drapkin & E. Viano (Eds.), *Victimology* (pp. 215–220). Lexington, MA: Lexington Books.

Jacobs, S.C. (1993). *Pathologic grief: Maladaptation to loss.* Washington, DC: American Psychiatric Press.

Janoff-Bulman, R. (2006). Schema-change perspectives on posttraumatic growth. In L.G. Calhoun & R.G. Tedeschi (Eds.), *Handbook of posttraumatic growth: Research and practice* (pp. 81–99). Mahwah, NJ: Lawrence Erlbaum Associates.

Jensen, G.F., & Brownfield, D. (1986). Gender, lifestyles and victimization: Beyond routine activity. *Violence and Victims, 1*(2), 85–99.

Jimenez, E. (2013). La criminalisation du trafic de migrants au Canada: un outil de lutte contre les menaces à la sécurité. *Revue Criminologie 46*(1), 131–156.

Johnson, H., & Dawson, M. (2011). *Violence against women in Canada: Research and policy perspectives.* Toronto, ON: Oxford University Press.

Johnstone, G. (2011). *Restorative justice: Ideas, values, debates.* Oxon, UK: Routledge.

Jones, N., Parmentier, S., & Weitekamp, E. (2014). Transitional justice in Bosnia-Herzegovina: Understanding accountability, reparation and justice for victims. In J. Wemmers (Ed.), *Reparation for victims of crimes against humanity: The healing role of reparation* (pp. 143–154). Oxon, UK: Routledge.

Jorg-Birol, A. (2010). *Victims' rehabilitation versus criminal justice and victim assistance agencies: Are they going the same direction?* Doctoral dissertation, Université Lausanne.

Jost, J.T., & Banaji, M. (1994). The role of stereotyping in system-justification and the production of false consciousness. *British Journal of Social Psychology, 33*(1), 1–27. http://dx.doi.org/10.1111/j.2044-8309.1994.tb01008.x

Joyce, S., Modini, M., Christensen, H., Mykletun, A., Bryant, R., Mitchell, P.B., & Harvey, S.B. (2016). Workplace interventions for common mental disorders: A systematic meta-review. *Psychological Medicine, 46*(04), 683–697. http://dx.doi.org/10.1017/S0033291715002408

Julich, S., McGregor, K., Annan, J., Landon, F., McCarrison, D., & McPhillips, K. (2011). *Yes, there is another way!* Victoria University, New Zealand, Retrieved from http://www.nzlii.org/nz/journals/CanterLawRw/2011/14.pdf

Junger-Tas, J., & Haen-Marshall, I. (1999). The self-report methodology in crime research. *Crime and Justice, 25*, 291–367. http://dx.doi.org/10.1086/449291

Junger-Tas, J. & Zeefkens, A.A. (1978). *Publiek et politie: Ervaringen, houdingen en wensen. Een onderzoek onder de Nederlandse bevolking.* The Hague: Ministerie van Justitie, WODC.

Karmen, A. (2010). *Crime victims: An introduction to victimology* (7th ed.). Belmont, CA: Wadsworth.

Karstedt, S. (2010). From absence to presence, from silence to voice: Victims in international and transitional justice since the Nuremberg trials. *International Review of Victimology, 17*(1), 9–30. http://dx.doi.org/10.1177/026975801001700102

Kelling, G., Pate, T., Dieckman, D., & Brown, C. (1991). L'expérience de Kansas-City sur la patrouille préventive. *Les cahiers de la sécurité intérieure, 5*, 277–315.

Kelly, D.P. (1984). Victims' perceptions of criminal justice. *Pepperdine Law Review, 11*, 15–22.

Kenney, J. (2010). *Canadian victims of crime: Critical insights.* Toronto, ON: Canadian Scholars Press.

Kessler, R.C., Sonnega, A., Bromet, E., Hughes, M., & Nelson, C.B. (1995). Posttraumatic stress disorder in the national Comorbidity Survey. *Archives of General Psychiatry, 52*(12), 1048–1060. http://dx.doi.org/10.1001/archpsyc.1995.03950240066012

Kessler, R.C., Chiu, W.T., Demler, O., & Walters, E.E. (2005). Prevalence, Severity, and Comorbidity of Twelve-month DSM-IV Disorders in the National Comorbidity Survey Replication (VCS-R), Archives of General Psychiatry, 62(6) 617-27.

Kilchling, M. (1995). *Opferinteressen und Strafverfolgung.* Freiburg im Breisgau: Max-Planck-Institut für ausländisches und internationles Strafrecht.

Kilpatrick, D.G., Acierno, R., Resnick, H.S., Saunders, B.E., & Best, C.L. (1997). A two-year longitudinal analysis of the relationship between violent assault and substance use in women. *Journal of Consulting and Clinical Psychology, 65*(5), 834–847. http://dx.doi.org/10.1037/0022-006X.65.5.834

Kilpatrick, D.G., Beatty, D., & Smith-Howley, S. (1998). The rights of crime victims—Does legal protection make a difference? *National Institute of Justice Research in Brief.* https://www.ncjrs.gov/pdffiles/173839.pdf

Kilpatrick, D.G., Best, C.L., Veronen, J., Amick, A.E., Villeponteaux, L.A., & Ruff, G.A. (1985). Mental health correlates of criminal victimization: A random community survey. *Journal of Consulting and Clinical Psychology, 53*(6), 866–873. http://dx.doi.org/10.1037/0022-006X.53.6.866

Kilpatrick, D.G., Edmunds, C.N., & Seymour, A.K. (1992). *Rape in America: A report to the National.* Arlington, VA: National Victim Center & Medical University of South Carolina.

Kilpatrick, D.G., Saunders, B., Veronen, L.J., Best, C.L., & Von, J.M. (1987). Criminal victimization: Lifetime prevalence, reporting to police and psychological impact. *Crime and Delinquency, 33*(4), 479–489. http://dx.doi.org/10.1177/0011128787033004005

Kilpatrick, D.G., Saunders, B.E., Amick-McMullan, A., Best, C.L., Veronen, L.J., & Resnick, H.S. (1989). Victim and crime factors associated with the development of crime-related post-traumatic stress disorder. *Behavior Therapy, 20*(2), 199–214. http://dx.doi.org/10.1016/S0005-7894(89)80069-3

Kirchengast, T. (2006). *The victim in criminal law and justice.* Houndmills, UK: Palgrave Macmillan. http://dx.doi.org/10.1057/9780230625778

Kirchengast, T. (2011). Les victimes comme parties prenantes d'un process penal de type accusatoire. *Criminologie, 44*(2), 99–124. http://dx.doi.org/10.7202/1005793ar

Kirchengast, T. (2013). Victim lawyers, victim advocates and the adversarial criminal trial. *New Criminal Law Review, 16*(4), 568–594. http://dx.doi.org/10.1525/nclr.2013.16.4.568

Kirchhoff, G.F. (1994). Victimology—History and basic concepts. In G.F. Kirchhoff, E. Kosovski, & H.J. Schneider (Eds.), *International debates of victimology* (pp. 1–81). Mönchengladbach: WSVN.

Kirchhoff, G.F. (1999). Why do they stay? Why don't they run away? In J.J.M. Van Dijk, R. Van Kaam, & J. Wemmers (Eds.), *Caring for victims of crime* (pp. 221–238). Monsey, NY: Criminal Justice Press.

Kirchhoff, G.F. (2010). History and theoretical structure of victimology. In W.G. Shoham, P. Knepper, & M. Kett (Eds.), *International Handbook of Victimology* (pp. 95–124). Boca Raton, FL: CRC Press. http://dx.doi.org/10.1201/EBK1420085471-c4

Klaus, P.A. (1994). *The costs of crime to victims: Crime data brief.* Washington, DC: Bureau of Justice Statistics.

Kleemans, E. (1996). Herhaald slachtofferschap van het delict woninginbraak. *Tijdschrift voor Criminologie, 38,* 232–244.

Koss, M.P. (2014). The RESTORE Program of restorative justice for sex crimes: Vision, process and outcomes. *Journal of Interpersonal Violence, 29*(9), 1623–1660. http://dx.doi.org/10.1177/0886260513511537

Kunst, M.J.J. (2010). *The burden of interpersonal violence: Examining the psychosocial aftermath of victimisation.* Doctoral dissertation, Intervict Tilburg University.

Kunst, M.J.J., Rutten, S., & Knijf, E. (2013). Satisfaction with the initial police response and development of post-traumatic stress disorder symptoms in victims of domestic burglary. *Journal of Traumatic Stress, 26*(1), 111–118. http://dx.doi.org/10.1002/jts.21774

Kury, H., & Kilchling, M. (2011). Accessory prosecution in Germany: Legislation and implementation. In E. Erez, M. Kilchling, & J. Wemmers (Eds.), *Therapeutic jurisprudence and victim participation in justice: International perspectives* (pp. 41–66). Durham, NC: Carolina Academic Press.

Kyl, J., Twist, S.J., & Higgins, S. (2005). On the wings of their angels: The *Scott Campbell, Stephanie Roper, Wendy Preston, Louarna Gillis, and Nila Lynn Crime Victims' Rights Act. Lewis & Clark Law Review, 9*(3), 581–628.

La Prairie Associates. (2004). *Multi-site survey of victims of crime and criminal justice professionals across Canada.* Ottawa, ON: Department of Justice Canada.

Lagelée, G., & Manceron, G. (1998). *La conquête mondiale des droits de l'homme.* France: UNESCO.

Lamboley, M. (2016). Le mariage forcé de femmes immigrantes au Québec. Doctoral dissertation, Université de Montréal.

Landau, T.C. (2000). Women's experience with mandatory charging for wife assault in Ontario, Canada: A case against the prosecution. *International Review of Victimology, 7*(1–3), 141–157. http://dx.doi.org/10.1177/026975800000700308

Langton, L., & Truman, J.L. (2014). *Socio-emotional impact of violence crime: Special report, Bureau of Justice Statistics.* Washington, DC: US Department of Justice Office.

Laroche, N. (2002). Réseau des CAVAC et la justice réparatrice: Position du Réseau des CAVAC. In J. Wemmers & K. Cyr (Eds.), *La justice réparatrice et les victimes d'actes criminels.* Montreal, QC: Centre international de la criminologie comparée.

Laurin, C., & Viens, C. (1996). La place de la victime dans le système de justice pénale. In J. Coiteux, P. Campeau, M. Clarkson, & M.M. Cousineau (Eds.), *Question d'équité: L'aide aux victimes d'actes criminels* (pp. 109–134). Montreal: Association québécoise plaidoyer-victimes.

Lauritsen, J.L. (2003). *How families and communities influence youth victimization.* Washington, DC: Office of Juvenile Justice and Delinquency Prevention.

Lauritsen, J.L., & Davis-Quinet, K. (1995). Repeat victimization among adolescents and young adults. *Journal of Quantitative Criminology, 11*(2), 143–166. http://dx.doi.org/10.1007/BF02221121

Lauritsen, J.L., & Rezey, M. (2013). *Measuring the prevalence of crime with the National Crime Victimization Survey,* Washington, DC: Bureau of Justice

Statistics, U.S. Department of Justice. Retrieved from http://www.bjs. gov/content/pub/pdf/mpcncvs.pdf

Laxminarayan, M., Henrichs, J., & Pemberton, A. (2012). Procedural and interactional justice: A comparative study of victims in the Netherlands and New South Wales. *European Journal of Criminology*, *9*(3), 260–275. http://dx.doi.org/10.1177/1477370812439641

Leahey, T.H. (1980). *A history of psychology*. Englewood Cliffs, NJ: Prentice-Hall.

Lebeau, A., Wemmers, J., Cyr, K., & Chamberland, C. (2014). Comparison de deux enquêtes de victimisation. *Criminologie*, *47*(1), 105–126.

Lemieux, D., & Riendeau, L. (1996). Éliminer la violence faite aux femmes, une longue route. In J. Coiteux, P. Campeau, M. Clarkson, & M.M. Cousineau (Eds.), *Question d'équité: L'aide aux victimes d'actes criminels* (pp. 249–274). Montreal, QC: Association québécoise Plaidoyer-Victimes.

Lens, K., Pemberton, A., & Bogaerts, S. (2013). Heterogeneity in victim participation: A new perspective on delivering a victim impact statement. *European Journal of Criminology*, *10*(4), 479–495. http://dx.doi.org/10.1177/1477370812469859

Lerner, M. (1980). *Belief in a just world: A fundamental delusion*. New York, NY: Plenum Press. http://dx.doi.org/10.1007/978-1-4899-0448-5

Lerner, M., & Simmons, C. (1971). Observers' reactions to the "innocent victim": Compassion or rejection? *Journal of Personality and Social Psychology*, *20*, 127–135.

Letschert, R., & Van Boven, T. (2011). Providing reparation in situations of mass victimization. In R. Letschert, R. Haveman, A.-M. De Brouwer, & A. Pemberton (Eds.), *Victimological approaches to international crimes: Africa* (pp. 153–184). Anwerpen: Intersentia.

Leung, A. (2004). *The cost of pain and suffering from crime in Canada*. Ottawa, ON: Justice Canada.

Levasseur, J. (2015, April 15). Manitoba Justice refuses to help with funeral for slain aboriginal woman, *CBC News*. Retrieved from http://www.cbc.ca/beta/news/canada/manitoba/iteam/manitoba-justice-refuses-to-help-with-funeral-for-slain-aboriginal-woman-1.3033253

Leventhal, G., Karuza, J., & Fry, W.R. (1980). Beyond fairness: A theory of allocation preferences. In G. Mikula (Ed.), *Justice and social interaction* (pp. 167–218). New York, NY: Springer-Verlag.

Lind, E.A., MacCoun, R.J., Ebener, P.A., Felstiner, W.L.F., Hensler, D.R., Resnik, J., & Tyler, T.R. (1989). *The perception of justice: Tort litigants' views of trial, court-annexed arbitration, and judicial settlement conferences*. Santa Monica, CA: RAND: The Institute for Civil Justice.

Lind, E.A., & Tyler, T. (1988). *The social psychology of procedural justice*. New York, NY: Plenum Press. http://dx.doi.org/10.1007/978-1-4899-2115-4

Lippel, K., & Doyen, I. (2000). *L'indemnisation des victimes d'actes criminels: une analyse jurisprudentielle.* Cowansville: Editions Y. Blais.

Llewellyn, J., Demsey, A., & Smith, J. (2015). An unfamiliar justice story: Restorative justice and education: Reflections on Dalhousie's Facebook incident 2015. *Our Schools/Our Selves, 25*(1), 43–56.

Lloyd, S., Farrell, G., & Pease, K. (1994). *Preventing repeated domestic violence: A demonstration project on Merseyside.* London, UK: Home Office.

Logan, R. (2001). Statistiques de la criminalité au Canada, 2000. *Juristat, 21.*

Logan, T.K., Walker, R., Cole, J., & Leukefeld, C. (2002). Victimization and substance abuse among women: Contributing factors, interventions and implications. *Review of General Psychology, 6*(4), 325–397. http://dx.doi.org/10.1037/1089-2680.6.4.325

MacDonald, S., Scrim, K., & Rooney, L. (2013). Building our capacity: Children's advocacy centres in Canada. *Victims of Crime Research Digest, 6*, 2–11.

Maguire, M. (1980). The impact of burglary upon victims. *British Journal of Criminology, 20*(3), 261–275.

Maguire, M. (1985). Victims' needs and victim services: Indications from research. *Victimology, 10*(1–4), 539–559.

Maguire, M. (1991). The needs and rights of victims of crime. In M. Tonry (Ed.), *Crime and justice: A review of the research* (Vol. 14, pp. 363–433). Chicago, IL: University of Chicago Press. http://dx.doi.org/10.1086/449190

Maguire, M., & Shapland, J. (1997). Provisions for victims in an international context. In R. Davis, A. Lurigio, & W. Skogan (Eds.), *Victims of crime* (2nd ed., pp. 211–230). Thousand Oaks, CA: Sage Publications.

Manikis, M. (2012). Recognizing victims' role and rights during plea bargaining: A fair deal for victims of crime. *Criminal Law Quarterly, 58*(3–4), 422.

Manikis, M. (2015). Imagining the future of victims rights in Canada: A comparative perspective. *Ohio State Journal of Criminal Law, 13*(1), 163–186.

Manirabona, A., & Wemmers, J. (2014). It doesn't go away with time: Victims' need for reparation following crimes against humanity. In J. Wemmers (Ed.), *Reparation for victims of crimes against humanity: The healing role of reparation* (pp. 71–91). Oxon, UK: Routledge.

Manrique-Rueda, G. (2014). Lands, wars and restoring justice for victims. In J. Wemmers (Ed.), *Reparation for victims of crimes against humanity: The healing role of reparation* (pp. 190–199). Oxon, UK: Routledge.

Marchand, A., Guay, S., Boyer, R., Iucci, S., Martin, A., & St-Hilaire, M.-H. (2006). A randomized controlled trial of an adapted form of individual critical incident stress debriefing for victims of an armed robbery. *Brief Treatment and Crisis Intervention, 6*(2), 122–129. http://dx.doi.org/10.1093/brief-treatment/mhj007

Marshall, B.K., Picou, J.S., & Gill, D.A. (2003). Terrorism as disaster: Selected commonalities and long-term recovery for 9/11 survivors. *Research in Social Problems and Public Policy, 11*, 73–96. http://dx.doi.org/10.1016/S0196-1152(03)11006-X

Marshall, T. (1999). *Restorative justice: An overview.* London, UK: Home Office, Research Development and Statistics Directorate.

Martin, C.G., Cromer, L.D., De Prince, A.P., & Freyd, J.J. (2013). The role of cumulative trauma, betrayal, and appraisals in understanding trauma symptomology. *Psychological Trauma: Theory, Research, Practice, and Policy, 5*(2), 110–118. http://dx.doi.org/10.1037/a0025686

Maslow, A.H. (1968). *Toward a psychology of being* (2nd ed.). New York, NY: Van Nostrand Reinhold.

Mattinson, J., & Mirrlees-Black, C. (2000). *Attitudes to crime and criminal justice: Findings from the 1998 British Crime Survey.* London, UK: Home Office.

Maxwell, A. (2015). *Statistiques sur les tribunaux de juridiction criminelle pour adultes au Canada, 2013–2014.* Ottawa, ON: Statistiques Canada, Centre canadien de la statistique juridique.

Mayhew, P., Clarke, R., Sturman, A., & Hough, J.M. (1976). Crime as opportunity. *Home Office Research Study, 34.* London, UK: Her Majesty's Stationary Office.

McCann, I.L., & Pearlman, L.A. (1990). Vicarious traumatization: A framework for understanding the psychological effects of working with victims. *Journal of Traumatic Stress, 3*(1), 131–149. http://dx.doi.org/10.1007/BF00975140

McCold, P. (2004). What is the role of community in restorative justice theory and practice? In H. Zehr & B. Toews (Eds.), *Critical issues in restorative justice* (pp. 155–171). Monsey, NY: Criminal Justice Press.

McFarlane, J., Maddoux, J., Nava, A., & Gilroy, H. (2015). Abused women with children who are first-time users of a shelter or applicants for a protection order: Entry data of a 7-year prospective analysis. *Violence against Women, 21*(2), 249–268. http://dx.doi.org/10.1177/1077801214564680

McGlynn, C., Westmarland, N., & Godden, N. (2012). 'I just wanted him to hear me': Sexual violence and the possibilities of restorative justice. *Journal of Law and Society, 39*(2), 213–240. http://dx.doi.org/10.1111/j.1467-6478.2012.00579.x

McGonigle-Leyh, B. (2011). *Procedural justice? Victim participation in international criminal proceedings*. Cambridge, UK: Intersentia.

McKeown, R. (2016, January 20). NWT victim services. Personal communication.

Mégret, F. (2009). The International Criminal Court statute and the failure to mention symbolic reparation. *International Review of Victimology, 16*(2), 127–147. http://dx.doi.org/10.1177/026975800901600202

Mégret, F. (2014). The case for collective reparations before the International Criminal Court. In J. Wemmers (Ed.), *Reparation for victims of crimes against humanity: The healing role of reparation* (pp. 171–189). Oxon, UK: Routledge.

Mendelsohn, B. (1956). Une nouvelle branche de la science bio-psycho-sociale: La victimologie. *Revue de droit pénal et de criminologie, 10*(2), 95–109.

Mendelsohn, B. (1963). The origin of the doctrine of victimology. *Excerpta Criminologica, 3*, 239–245.

Menzies, P. (2006). Intergenerational trauma and homeless Aboriginal men. *Canadian Review of Social Policy, 58*, 1–24.

Mercer, V., & Sten-Madsen, K. (2011). *Doing restorative justice in cases of sexual violence: A practice guide*. Daphne III—JUST/2011/DAP/AG/3350.

Meredith, C., & Paquette, C. (2001). *Victims of crime research series: Summary report on victim impact statement focus groups*. Ottawa, ON: Policy Centre for Victims Issues, Department of Justice Canada.

Middleton, W., Burnett, P., Raphael, B., & Martinek, N. (1996). The bereavement response: A cluster analysis. *British Journal of Psychiatry, 169*(2), 167–171. http://dx.doi.org/10.1192/bjp.169.2.167

Miers, D. (2014). Offender and state compensation for victims of crime: Two decades of development and change. *International Review of Victimology, 20*(1), 145–168. http://dx.doi.org/10.1177/0269758013508683

Mihorean, K., Besserer, S., Hendrick, D., Brzozowski, J.-A., Trainor, C., & Ogg, S. (2001). *A profile of criminal victimization. Results of the 1999 General Social Survey*. Catalogue No. 85–553-XIE. Ottawa, ON: Statistics Canada.

Miller, J. (1998). Up it up: Gender and the accomplishment of street robbery. *Criminology, 36*(1), 37–66. http://dx.doi.org/10.1111/j.1745-9125.1998.tb01239.x

Miller, K.-L. (2014). Relational caring: The use of the victim impact statement by sexually assaulted women. *Violence and Victims, 29*(5), 797–813. http://dx.doi.org/10.1891/0886-6708.VV-D-13-00056

Miller, T., Cohen, M.A., & Wiersema, B. (1996). *Victim costs and consequences: A new look*. Washington, DC: National Institute of Justice.

Milliken, R. (1950). The sex offender's victim. *Federal Probation, 14*, 22–26.

Mills, K.L., Teesson, M., Ross, J., & Peters, L. (2006). Trauma, PTSD, substance use disorders: Findings from the Australian National Survey of Mental Health and Well-Being. *American Journal of Psychiatry*, *164*, 651–658.

Mitchell, A.M., Sakraida, T.J., & Kameg, K. (2003). Critical incident stress debriefing: Implications for best practice. *Disaster Management & Response*, *1*(2), 46–51. http://dx.doi.org/10.1016/S1540-2487(03)00008-7

Moffett, L. (2014). *Justice for victims before the International Criminal Court.* Oxon, UK: Routledge.

Mohr, A. (2006). Family variables associated with peer victimization: Does family violence enhance the probability of being victimized by peers? *Swiss Journal of Psychology*, *65*(2), 107–116. http://dx.doi.org/10.1024/1421-0185.65.2.107

Morgan, K., & Smith, B.L. (2005). Victims, punishment and parole: The effect of victim participation on parole hearings. *Criminology & Public Policy*, *4*(2), 333–360. http://dx.doi.org/10.1111/j.1745-9133.2005.00025.x

Morissette, M., & Wemmers, J. (2016). L'influence thérapeutic de la perception de justice informationnelle et interpersonnelle sur les symptômes de stress post-traumatique des victimes de crimes. *Revue canadienne de criminologie et justice pénale*, *58*(1), 31–55. http://dx.doi.org/10.3138/cjccj.2014.F03

Morris, A., & Maxwell, G. (1998). Restorative justice in New Zealand: Family group conferences as a case study. *Western Criminology Review*, *1*(1), 1998.

Moulden, H.M., & Firestone, P. (2007). Vicarious traumatization: The impact on therapists who work with sexual offenders. *Trauma, Violence, and Abuse,* *8*(1), 67–83.

Munch, C. (2012). Les services aux victimes au Canada, 2009–2010. *Juristat*, Catalogue No. 85-002-X.

Muscat, B.T. (2010). Victim services in the United States. In S.G. Shoham, P. Knepper, & M. Kett (Eds.), *International handbook of victimology* (pp. 397–428). Boca Raton, FL: CRC Press. http://dx.doi.org/10.1201/EBK1420085471-c15

Mustaine, E.E., & Tewksbury, R. (1998). Specifying the role of alcohol in predatory victimization. *Deviant Behavior*, *19*(2), 173–199. http://dx.doi.org/10.1080/01639625.1998.9968082

Nagel, W. (1949). *De criminaliteit van Oss.* Doctoral dissertation, The Hague, NL: Daamen.

Nagel, W. (1959). Victimologie. *Tijdschrift voor Strafrecht*, *68*, 1–26.

Nagel, W. (1963). The notion of victimology in criminology. *Ecerpta Criminologica*, *3*(3), 245–247.

Native Women's Association of Canada. (2014). Sexual exploitation and trafficking of Aboriginal women and girls: Literature review and key informant interviews. Retrieved from http://canadianwomen.org/sites/canadianwomen.org/files/NWAC%20Sex%20Trafficking%20Literature%20Review_2.pdf

Neimeyer, R. (2000). *Meaning reconstruction and the experience of chronic loss.* Washington, DC: American Psychological Association.

Nofziger, S., & Kurtz, D. (2005). Violent lives: A lifestyle model linking exposure to violence to juvenile violent offending. *Journal of Research in Crime and Delinquency, 42*(1), 3–26. http://dx.doi.org/10.1177/0022427803262061

Noll, D.E., & Harvey, L. (2008). Restorative mediation: The application of restorative justice practice and philosophy to clergy sexual abuse cases. *Journal of Child Sexual Abuse, 17*(3–4), 377–396. http://dx.doi.org/10.1080/10538710802330021

Normandeau, A. (2000). Politiques et pratiques en matière de droits et de services aux victimes d'actes criminels au Canada. Colloque sur les victimes d'actes criminels, Université de Pau, France, 5 May.

Norris, F. (2007). Impact of mass shootings on survivors, families and communities. *PTSD Research Quarterly, 18*(3), 1–8.

Norris, F.H., & Kaniasty, K. (1994). Psychological distress following criminal victimization in the general population: Cross-sectional, longitudinal and prospective analyses. *Journal of Consulting and Clinical Psychology, 62*(1), 111–123. http://dx.doi.org/10.1037/0022-006X.62.1.111

Norris, F.H., Kaniasty, K., & Thompson, M.P. (1997). The psychological consequences of crime: Findings from a longitudinal population-based study. In R. Davis, A.J. Lurigio, & W.G. Skogan (Eds.), *Victims of crime* (2nd ed., pp. 146–166). Thousand Oaks, CA: Sage Publications.

NOVA. (1988). *Victim rights and services: A legislative directory.* Washington, DC: National Organization of Victim Assistance.

Nova Scotia Department of Justice Victims' Services Division. (1999). Activity report, April 1, 1998–March 31, 1999. Retrieved from http://www.novascotia.ca/just/publications/docs/victim99.pdf

Ochberg, F. (1978). The victim of terrorism: Psychiatric considerations. *Terrorism, 1*(2), 147–168. http://dx.doi.org/10.1080/10576107808435404

Office for National Statistics. (2016). *Crime survey for England and Wales (CSEW).* Retrieved from http://www.crimesurvey.co.uk/HomeReadMore.html

Ontario Parole Board. (n.d.). Victims and the Ontario Parole Board. Retrieved from http://www.slasto.gov.on.ca/en/OPB/Pages/Victims-and-the-Ontario-Parole-Board.aspx

Organisation for Economic Co-operation and Development (OECD) (2014). *New rural policy: Linking up for growth*. Retrieved from https://www.oecd.org/rural/rural-development-conference/documents/New-Rural-Policy.pdf

Orth, U. (2002). Secondary victimization of crime victims by criminal proceedings. *Social Justice Research, 15*(4), 313–325. http://dx.doi.org/10.1023/A:1021210323461

Orth, U., & Maercker, A. (2004). Do trials of perpetrators retraumatize crime victims? *Journal of Interpersonal Violence, 19*(2), 212–227. http://dx.doi.org/10.1177/0886260503260326

Outlaw, M., Ruback, B., & Britt, C. (2002). Repeat and multiple victimizations: The role of individual and contextual factors. *Violence and Victims, 17*(2), 187–204. http://dx.doi.org/10.1891/vivi.17.2.187.33648

Oxford Dictionary. (1989). Oxford, UK: Oxford University Press.

Ozer, E.J., Best, S.R., Lipsey, T.L., & Weiss, D.S. (2003). Predictors of posttraumatic stress disorder and symptoms in adults: A meta-analysis. *Psychological Bulletin, 129*(1), 52–73. http://dx.doi.org/10.1037/0033-2909.129.1.52

Packer, H.L. (1964). Two models of the criminal process. *University of Pennsylvania Law Review, 113*(1), 1–68. http://dx.doi.org/10.2307/3310562

Padfield, N., & Roberts, J.V. (2010). Victim input at parole: Probative or prejudicial? In A. Bottoms & J.V. Roberts (Eds.), *Hearing the victim: Adversarial justice, crime victims and the state* (pp. 255–280). Cullompton, UK: Willan Publishing.

Parmentier, S., & Weitekamp, E. (2007). *Sociology of crime, law and deviance: Vol. 9. Crime and human rights*. Amsterdam, NL: Elsevier.

Parsons, J., & Bergin, T. (2010). The impact of criminal justice involvement on victims' mental health. *Journal of Traumatic Stress, 23*(2), 182–188.

Patterson, D., & Campbell, R. (2010). Why rape survivors participate in the criminal justice system. *Journal of Community Psychology, 38*(2), 191–205. http://dx.doi.org/10.1002/jcop.20359

Pease, K. (1998). Repeat victimization: Taking stock. *Crime Detection and Prevention Series*, Paper 90. London, UK: Home Office.

Pemberton, A. (2015). Victims and mediation in the Netherlands. In I. Vanfraechem, D. Bolivar, & I. Aertsen (Eds.), *Victims and restorative justice* (pp. 126–152). Oxon, UK: Routledge.

Pena, M., & Carayon, G. (2013). Is the ICC making the most of victim participation? *International Journal of Transitional Justice, 7*(3), 518–535. http://dx.doi.org/10.1093/ijtj/ijt021

Perreault, S. (2004). *Visible minorities and victimization. Canadian Centre for Justice Statistics Profile Series.* Ottawa, ON: Canadian Centre for Justice Statistics.

Perreault, S. (2015). Criminal victimization in Canada, 2014. *Juristat,* Catalogue No. 85–002-X.

Perreault, S., & Brennan, S. (2010). Criminal victimization in Canada, 2009. *Juristat,* Catalogue No. 85–002-X.

Perreault, S., & Hotton-Mahony, T. (2012). Criminal victimization in the territories, 2009. *Juristat,* Catalogue no. 85–002-X.

Perreault, S., Sauvé, J., & Burns, M. (2010). Multiple victimization in Canada. *Canadian Centre for Justice Statistics Profile Series.* Ottawa, ON: Statistics Canada.

Perreault, S., & Simpson, L. (2016). Criminal victimization in the territories, 2014. *Juristat,* Catalogue no. 85–002-X.

Perry, D., Hodges, E., & Egan, S. (2001). Determinants of chronic victimization by peers: A review and new model of family influence. In J. Juvonen & S. Graham (Eds.), *Peer harassment in school: The plight of the vulnerable and victimized* (pp. 73–104). New York, NY: Guilford Press.

Petersilia, J. (2000). *Sentencing and corrections: Issues for the 21st century: Vol. 9. When prisoners return to the community: Political, economic, and social consequence.* Washington, DC: U.S. Department of Justice, National Institute of Justice. Accessed on February 8th, 2016 at: https://www.ncjrs.gov/pdffiles1/nij/184253.pdf

Peterson, C., Schwartz, S., & Seligman, M. (1981). Self-blame and depressive symptoms. *Journal of Personality and Social Psychology, 41*(2), 253–259. http://dx.doi.org/10.1037/0022-3514.41.2.253

Pham, P.N., Weinstein, H.M., & Longman, T. (2004). Trauma and ASD/PTSD in Rwanda: Implications for attitudes toward justice and reconciliation. *Journal of the American Medical Association, 292*(5), 602–612. http://dx.doi.org/10.1001/jama.292.5.602

Polvi, N., Looman, T., Humphries, C., & Pease, K. (1990). Repeat break-and-enter victimization: Time course and crime prevention opportunity. *Journal of Police Science and Administration, 17*(1), 8–11.

Postmus, J., Severson, M., Berry, M., & Yoo, J.A. (2009). Women's experiences of violence and seeking help. *Violence against Women, 15*(7), 852–868. http://dx.doi.org/10.1177/1077801209334445

Poulson, B. (2003). A third voice: A review of empirical research on the psychological outcomes of restorative justice. *Utah Law Review, 15*(1), 167–203.

Pruitt, D.G., Peirce, R.S., McGillicuddy, N.B., Welton, G.L., & Castrianno, L.M. (1993). Long-term success in mediation. *Law and Human Behavior, 17*(3), 313–330. http://dx.doi.org/10.1007/BF01044511

Public Safety Canada. (2013). *Information guide to assist victims: Federal corrections and conditional release* (8th ed.). Ottawa, ON: National Office for Victims.

Public Safety Canada. (2015). Correctional Service of Canada 2015–2016: Report on Plans and Priorities. Retrieved from http://www.csc-scc.gc.ca/publications/005007-2603-eng.shtml

Quinney, R. (1972). Who is the victim? *Criminology, 10*(3), 314–323. http://dx.doi.org/10.1111/j.1745-9125.1972.tb00564.x

Radford, L., Corral, S., Bradley, C., & Fisher, H.L. (2014). La victimisation, la polyvictimisation et la délinquance chez les enfants et les jeunes adultes au Royaume-Uni. *Criminologie, 47*(1), 59–83. http://dx.doi.org/10.7202/1024007ar

Randall, M. & Haskell, L. (2013). Trauma-informed approaches to law: Why restorative justice must understand trauma and psychological coping. *Dalhousie Law Journal, 36*(2), 501–534.

Raphael, B., & Wooding, S. (2004). Debriefing: Its evolution and current status. *Psychiatric Clinics of North America, 27*(3), 407–423. http://dx.doi.org/10.1016/j.psc.2004.03.003

Redress. (2015). Victim participation in criminal law proceedings: Survey of domestic practice for application to international crimes prosecutions. London, UK. Retrieved from http://www.redress.org/downloads/1508victim-rights-report.pdf

Reeves, H., & Mulley, K. (2000). The new status of victims in the UK: Opportunities and threats. In A. Crawford & J. Goodey (Eds.), *Integrating a victim perspective within criminal justice* (pp. 125–145). Aldershot, UK: Dartmouth Publishing.

Regan, P. (2011). *Unsettling the settler within.* Vancouver, BC: UBC Press.

Regel, S., & Dyregrov, A. (2012). Commonalities and new directions in post-trauma support interventions: From pathology to the promotion of post-traumatic growth. In R. Hughes, A. Kinder, & C.L. Cooper (Eds.), *International handbook of workplace trauma support* (pp. 48–67). Chichester, UK: Wiley-Blackwell. http://dx.doi.org/10.1002/9781119943242.ch4

Reichel, P.L. (1994). *Comparative criminal justice systems: A topical approach.* Upper Saddle River, NJ: Prentice-Hall.

Reiss, A.J. (1967). *Studies in crime and law enforcement in major metropolitan areas.* Washington, DC: Office of Law Enforcement Assistance.

Roach, K. (1999). *Due process and victims' rights: The new law and politics of criminal justice.* Toronto, ON: University of Toronto Press. http://dx.doi.org/10.3138/9781442674127

Roberts, J.V. (2009). Listening to the crime victim: Evaluating victim input at sentencing and parole. In M. Tonry (Ed.), *Crime and justice: A review of research* (pp. 347–412). Chicago, IL: University of Chicago Press. http://dx.doi.org/10.1086/599203

Roberts, J.V., & Edgar, A. (2006). *Judicial attitudes to victim impact statements: Findings from a survey in three jurisdictions.* Ottawa, ON: Policy Centre for Victim Issues, Department of Justice Canada.

Roberts, J.V., & Erez, E. (2004). Expression in sentencing: Exploring the expressive function of victim impact statements. *International Review of Victimology, 10*(3), 223–244. http://dx.doi.org/10.1177/026975800401000302

Roberts, J.V., & Erez, E. (2010). Communication at sentencing: The expressive function of victim impact statements. In A. Bottoms & J.V. Roberts (Eds.), *Hearing the victim: Adversarial justice, crime victims and the state* (pp. 232–254). Cullompton, UK: Willan Publishing.

Roberts, J.V., & Manikis, M. (2010). Victim impact statements at sentencing: The relevance of ancillary harm. *Canadian Criminal Law Review, 15*(1), 27–29.

Rock, P. (1986). *A view from the shadows: The ministry of the solicitor general of Canada and the justice for victims of crime initiative.* Oxford, UK: Clarendon Press.

Rock, P. (2010). Hearing victims of crime: The delivery of impact statements as ritual behaviour in four London trials of murder and manslaughter. In A. Bottoms & J.V. Roberts (Eds.), *Hearing the victim: Adversarial justice, crime victims and the state* (pp. 200–231). Cullompton, UK: Willan Publishing.

Ruback, R.B., Clark, V.A., & Warner, C. (2014). Why are crime victims at risk of being victimized again? Substance use, depression and offending as mediators of the victimization-revictimization link. *Journal of Interpersonal Violence, 29*(1), 157–185. http://dx.doi.org/10.1177/0886260513504626

Ruback, R.B., & Thompson, M.P. (2001). *Social and psychological consequences of violent victimization.* Thousand Oaks, CA: Sage. http://dx.doi.org/10.4135/9781483345413

Ruby, C.C. (2012). *Sentencing* (8th ed.). Markham, ON: LexisNexis Canada.

Rugge, T.A., & Scott, T.-L. (2009). *Restorative justice's impact on participants' psychological and physical health.* Ottawa, ON: Public Safety Canada.

Sacco, V.F., & Johnson, H. (1990). *Profil de la victimisation au Canada: Enquête social générale Série analytique.* Ottawa, ON: Statistique Canada.

Sampson, A., & Phillips, C. (1992). *Multiple victimisation: Racial attack on an East London estate.* London, UK: Home Office.

Sandberg, D.A., Lynn, S.J., & Matorin, A.I. (2001). Information processing of an acquaintance rape scenario among high- and low-dissociating college women. *Journal of Traumatic Stress, 14*(3), 585–603. http://dx.doi.org/10.1023/A:1011168808683

Sanders, A., Hoyle, C., Morgan, R., & Cape, E. (2001). Victim impact statements: Don't work, can't work. *Criminal Law Review,* 447–458.

Sauvé, J. (2009). Victim services in Canada 2007/2008. *Juristat, 29*(4).

Sauvé, J., & Burns, M. (2009). Residents of Canada's shelters for abused women, 2008. *Juristat, 29*(2).

Sauvé, J., & Hung, K. (2008). An international perspective on criminal victimization. *Juristat,* 28(10).

Schafer, S. (1968). *The victim and his criminal: A study in functional responsibility.* New York, NY: Random House.

Schafer, S. (1977). *The victim and his criminal.* Reston, VA: Reston Publishing.

Schauben, L.J., & Frazier, P.A. (1995). Vicarious trauma: The effects on female counsellors working with sexual violence survivors. *Psychology of Women Quarterly, 19*(1), 49–64. http://dx.doi.org/10.1111/j.1471-6402.1995.tb00278.x

Schmid, A.P., & Jongman, A. (1988). *Political terrorism: A new guide to actors, authors, concepts, data bases, theories, and literature.* London, UK: Transaction Publishers.

Schneider, H.J. (2001). Victimological developments in the world during the last three decades: A study of comparative victimology. In A. Gaudreault & I. Waller (Eds.), *Tenth International Symposium on Victimology* (pp. 19–68), Montreal: AQPV.

Screvens, R. (1959). Journées crimonologiques Hollando-Belges. *Revue de droit pénal et de criminologie, 39*(7), 669–673.

Seligman, M., Abramson, L., Semmel, A., & Von Baeyer, C. (1979). Depressive attributional style. *Journal of Abnormal Psychology, 88*(3), 242–247. http://dx.doi.org/10.1037/0021-843X.88.3.242

Sellin, J.T., & Wolfgang, M. (1964). *The measurement of delinquency.* New York, NY: John Wiley and Sons.

Shapland, J. (1985). The criminal justice system and the victim. *Victimology: An International Journal, 10*(1–4), 585–599.

Shapland, J. (2014). Implications of growth: Challenges for restorative justice. *International Review of Victimology, 20*(1), 111–127. http://dx.doi.org/10.1177/0269758013510808

Shapland, J., Atkinson, A., Atkinson, H., Colledge, E., Dignan, J., Howes, M., . . ., & Sorsby, A. (2006). Situating restorative justice within criminal justice. *Theoretical Criminology*, *10*(4), 505–532. http://dx.doi.org/10.1177/1362480606068876

Shapland, J., & Hall, M. (2007). What do we know about the effect of crime on victims? *International Review of Victimology*, *14*, 175–217.

Shapland, J., Robinson, G., & Sorsby, A. (2011). *Restorative justice in practice*. Oxon, UK: Routledge.

Shapland, J., Wilmore, J., & Duff, P. (1985). *Victims in the criminal justice system*. Aldershot, UK: Gower Publishing.

Shaw, M. (2001). Time heals all wounds. In G. Farrell & K. Pease (Eds.), *Repeat Victimization*. Monsey, NY: Criminal Justice Press.

Shear, M.K., Simon, N., Wall, M., Zisook, S., Neimeyer, R., Duan, N., . . ., & Keshaviah, A. (2011). Complicated grief and related bereavement issues for DSM-5. *Depression and Anxiety*, *28*(2), 103–117. http://dx.doi.org/10.1002/da.20780

Sherman, L.W. (1995). Hot spots of crime and criminal careers of places. *Crime Place*, *4*, 35–52.

Sherman, L.W., & Strang, H. (2003). Repairing the harm: Victims and restorative justice. *Utah Law Review*, *15*, 15–42.

Sherman, L.W., & Strang, H. (2007). *Restorative justice: The evidence*. London, UK: Smith Institute.

Sherman, L.W., Strang, H., Angel, C., Woods, D., Barnes, G.C., Bennett, S., & Inkpen, N. (2005). Effect of face-to-face restorative justice on victims of crime in four randomized, controlled trials. *Journal of Experimental Criminology*, *1*(3), 367–395. http://dx.doi.org/10.1007/s11292-005-8126-y

Silver, W., Mihorean, K., & Taylor-Butts, A. (2004). Hate crime in Canada. *Juristat*, *24*(4).

Silverman, R.A. (1975). Victim precipitation: An examination of the concept. In I. Drapkin & E. Viano (Eds.), *Victimology: A new focus: Vol. 1. Theoretical issues in victimology* (pp. 99–110). Lexington, MA: Lexington Books.

Singer, S. (1986). Victims of serious violence and their criminal behaviour: Sub-cultural theory and beyond. *Violence and Victims*, *1*, 61–70.

Sinha, M. (2013). Measuring violence against women: Statistical trends. *Juristat*. Catalogue no. 85–002-X.

Skogan, W. (1999). Victim surveys at the century's end. In J.J.M. Van Dijk, R. Van Kaam, & J. Wemmers (Eds.), *Caring for victims of crime* (pp. 41–53). Monsey, NY: Criminal Justice Press.

Slachtofferhulp Nederland. (2016). *Onze werkwijze*. Retrieved from https://www.slachtofferhulp.nl/Over-Ons/Werkwijze/

Smith, A. (2011). Victim impact statements: Redefining "victim." *Criminal Law Quarterly (Toronto)*, *57*, 346–369.

Smith, B., Watkins, E., & Morgan, K. (1997). The effect of victim participation on parole decision: Results from a southeastern state. *Criminal Justice Policy Review*, *8*(1), 57–74. http://dx.doi.org/10.1177/088740349700800103

Smith, E.C. (2015). *The world would start turning again: Identifying and measuring victims' restorative justice needs at the International Criminal Court.* Doctoral dissertation, Bournemouth University.

Solicitor General of Canada. (1983). *Victims of crime, Canadian Urban Victimization Survey. Bulletin 1.* Ottawa, ON: Research and Statistics Group.

Solicitor General of Canada. (1985). *Cost of crime to victims, Canadian Urban Victimization Survey. Bulletin 5.* Ottawa, ON: Research and Statistics Group.

Solicitor General of Canada. (1988). *Multiple victimization, Canadian Urban Victimization Survey. Bulletin 10.* Ottawa, ON: Research and Statistics Group.

Spreitzer, G.M. (1995). An empirical test of a comprehensive model of intrapersonal empowerment in the workplace. *American Journal of Community Psychology*, *23*(5), 601–629. http://dx.doi.org/10.1007/BF02506984

Spungen, D. (1998). *Homicide: The hidden victims.* Thousand Oaks, CA: Sage. http://dx.doi.org/10.4135/9781483327389

Starzyck, K., Gaucher, D., Boese, G., & Neufeld, K. (2014). Framing reparation claims for crimes against humanity: A social psychological perspective. In J. Wemmers (Ed.), *Reparation for victims of crimes against humanity: The healing role of reparation* (pp. 113–125). Oxon, UK: Routledge.

Statistics Canada. (1994). *Tableaux sur la victimization: L'enquête sociale générale de 1993, décembre.* Ottawa, ON: Author.

Staub, E. (2003). Notes on cultures of violence, cultures of caring and peace, and the fulfilment of basic human needs. *Political Psychology*, *24*(1), 1–21. http://dx.doi.org/10.1111/0162-895X.00314

Staub, E. (2004). Basic human needs, altruism and aggression. In A.G. Miller (Ed.), *The social psychology of good and evil* (pp. 51–84). New York, NY: Guilford Press.

Staub, E. (2007). Preventing violence and terrorism and promoting positive relations between Dutch and Muslim communities in Amsterdam. *Peace and Conflict*, *13*(3), 333–360. http://dx.doi.org/10.1080/10781910701471397

Steinmetz, C. (1990). *Hulp aan slachtoffers van ernstige misdrijven: Effecten van slachtofferhulp en primaire opvang.* Onderzoek en Beleid, 98. Arhnhem: Gouda Quint bv.

Stover, E. (2005). *The witnesses: War crimes and the promise of justice in The Hague.* Philadelphia: University of Pennsylvania Press. http://dx.doi.org/10.9783/9780812203783

Stover, E., Balthazard, M., & Koenig, K.A. (2011). Confronting *Duch*: Civil party participation in Case 001 at the Extraordinary Chambers in the courts of Cambodia. *International Review of the Red Cross, 93*(882), 503–546. http://dx.doi.org/10.1017/S1816383111000439

Strang, H. (2002). *Repair or revenge: Victims and restorative justice.* Oxford, UK: Oxford University Press.

Strang, H., Barnes, G.C., Braithwaite, J., & Sherman, L. (1999). *Experiments in restorative policing: A progress report on the Canberra reintegrative shaming experiments (RISE).* Canberra: Australian National University. Retrieved from http://www.aic.gov.au/media_library/aic/rjustice/rise/progress/1999.pdf

Strang, H., Sherman, L.W., Angel, C.M., Woods, D.J., Bennett, S., Newbury-Birch, D., & Inkpen, N. (2006). Victim evaluations of face-to-face restorative justice conferences: A quasi-experimental analysis. *Journal of Social Issues, 62*(2), 281–306. http://dx.doi.org/10.1111/j.1540-4560.2006.00451.x

Strentz, T. (1980). The Stockholm syndrome: Law enforcement policy and ego defenses of the hostage. *Annals of the New York Academy of Sciences, 347*(1), 137–150. http://dx.doi.org/10.1111/j.1749-6632.1980.tb21263.x

Strobl, R. (2004). Constructing the victim: Theoretical reflections and empirical examples. *International Review of Victimology, 11*(2–3), 295–311. http://dx.doi.org/10.1177/026975800401100206

Strobl, R. (2010). Becoming a victim. In P. Knepper & S. Shoham (Eds.), *International handbook of victimology* (pp. 3–26). Boca Raton, FL: Taylor Francis Group. http://dx.doi.org/10.1201/EBK1420085471-c1

Stuart, B. (1996). Circle sentencing: Turning swords into ploughshares. In B. Galaway & J. Hudson (Eds.), *Restorative justice: International perspectives* (pp. 193–206). Monsey, NY: Criminal Justice Press.

Stubbs, J. (1995). 'Communitarian' conferencing and violence against women: A cautionary note. In M. Valverde, L. MacLeod, and K. Johnson (Eds.), *Wife assault and the criminal justice system* (pp. 260–289). Toronto, ON: Centre of Criminology, University of Toronto.

Stubbs, J. (2010). Restorative justice, gendered violence and Indigenous women. In J. Ptacek (Ed.), *Restorative justice and violence against women* (pp. 103–122). New York, NY: Oxford University Press.

Sullivan, S. (1998). *Équilibrer la balance: L'état des droits des victimes au Canada*. Ottawa, ON: Centre canadien de resources pour les victims de crimes.

Symonds, M. (1980). The second injury. *Evaluation and Change, Special Issue*, 36–38.

Szabo, D. (1979). *Victimologie et criminologie: Tendances et applications*. Troisième Symposium International de Victimologie, Münster, Germany, 2–8 September.

Tabor, P.D. (2011). Vicarious traumatization: Concept analysis. *Journal of Forensic Nursing, 7*(4), 203–208. http://dx.doi.org/10.1111/j.1939-3938.2011.01115.x

Tahone, R. (1952). Le consentement de la victim. *Revue de droit pénal et de criminologie, 35*, 323–342.

Taylor, A.J.W. (2003). Justice as a basic human need. *New Ideas in Psychology, 21*(3), 209–219. http://dx.doi.org/10.1016/j.newideapsych.2003.09.004

Tedeschi, R.G., & Calhoun, L.G. (2004). Posttraumatic growth: Conceptual foundations and empirical evidence. *Psychological Inquiry, 15*(1), 1–18. http://dx.doi.org/10.1207/s15327965pli1501_01

Ten Boom, A., & Kuijpers, K. (2012). Victims' needs as basic human needs. *International Review of Victimology, 18*(2), 155–179. http://dx.doi.org/10.1177/0269758011432060

Thibaut, J., & Walker, L. (1975). *Procedural justice: A psychological analysis*. Hillsdale, NJ: Wiley.

Tillyer, M.S. (2013). Violent victimization across the life course: Moving a "victim careers" agenda forward. *Criminal Justice and Behavior, 41*(5), 593–612. http://dx.doi.org/10.1177/0093854813509370

Tobolowsky, P. (2001). *Crime victim rights and remedies*. Durham, NC: Carolina Academic Press.

Tobolowsky, P. (2015). Mandamus muddle: The mandamus review standard for the federal *Crime Victims' Rights Act*. *University of Denver Criminal Law Review, 5*, 109–172.

Tochilovsky, V. (1999). Victims' procedural rights at trial: Approach of continental Europe and the International Tribunal for the Former Yugoslavia. In J.J.M. Van Dijk, R. Van Kaam, & J. Wemmers (Eds.), *Caring for victims of crime* (pp. 287–292). Monsey, NY: Criminal Justice Press.

Truman, J.L., & Langton, L. (2015). *Criminal victimization, 2014*. Washington, DC: Bureau of Justice Statistics, U.S. Department of Justice.

Trust Fund for Victims. (2016). About us. Retrieved from http://www.trustfundforvictims.org/about-us

Tseloni, A., & Pease, K. (2003). Repeat personal victimization: Boosts or flags? *British Journal of Criminology, 43*(1), 196–212. http://dx.doi.org/10.1093/bjc/43.1.196

Tucker, C.J., Finkelhor, D., Turner, H., & Shattuck, A.M. (2014a). Family dynamics and young children's sibling victimization. *Journal of Family Psychology, 28*(5), 625–633. http://dx.doi.org/10.1037/fam0000016

Tucker, C.J., Finkelhor, D., Turner, H., & Shattuck, A.M. (2014b). Sibling and peer victimization in childhood and adolescence. *Child Abuse & Neglect, 38*(10), 1599–1606. http://dx.doi.org/10.1016/j.chiabu.2014.05.007

Tufts, J. (2000). Public attitudes toward the criminal justice system. *Juristat, 20*(12).

Turner, H.A., Finkelhor, D., Hamby, S.L., & Shattuck, A. (2013). Family structure, victimization and child mental health in a nationally representative sample. *Social Science & Medicine, 87*, 39–51. http://dx.doi.org/10.1016/j.socscimed.2013.02.034

Turner, H.A., Finkelhor, D., & Ormrod, R.K. (2007). Family structure variations in patterns and predictors of child victimization. *American Journal of Orthopsychiatry, 77*(2), 282–295. http://dx.doi.org/10.1037/0002-9432.77.2.282

Turner, H.A., Vanderminden, J., Finkelhor, D., Hamby, S.L., & Shattuck, A. (2011). Disability and victimization in a national sample of children and youth. *Child Maltreatment, 16*(4), 275–286. http://dx.doi.org/10.1177/1077559511427178

Tyler, T.R. (1990). *Why people obey the law.* New Haven, CT: Yale University Press.

Tyler, T.R. (2000). Social justice: Outcome and procedure. *International Journal of Psychology, 35*(2), 117–125. http://dx.doi.org/10.1080/002075900399411

Tyler, T.R. (2003). Procedural justice, legitimacy and the effective rule of law. *Crime and Justice: A Review of Research, 30*, 257–283. http://dx.doi.org/10.1086/652233

Tyler, T.R. (2005). *Procedural justice.* Aldershot, UK: Ashgate. http://dx.doi.org/10.4135/9781412952552.n228

Tyler, T.R., & Huo, Y.J. (2002). *Trust in the law: Encouraging public cooperation with the police and courts.* New York, NY: Russel Sage Foundation.

Tyler, T.R., & Lind, E.A. (1992). A relational model of authority in groups. *Advances in Experimental Social Psychology, 25*, 115–191. http://dx.doi.org/10.1016/S0065-2601(08)60283-X

Umbreit, M., Bradshaw, W., & Coates, R. (1999). Victims of severe violence meet the offender: Restorative justice through dialogue. *International Review of Victimology, 6*(4), 321–343. http://dx.doi.org/10.1177/026975809900600405

United Nations General Assembly. (1985). *Declaration of basic principles of justice for victims of crime and abuse of power.* Geneva: United Nations. Retrieved from http://www.un.org/documents/ga/res/40/ a40r034.htm

United Nations Office on Drugs and Crime. (2010). *Manual on victimization surveys.* Geneva: United Nations. Retrieved from https://www.unodc. org/documents/data-and-analysis/Crime-statistics/Manual_on_ Victimization_surveys_2009_web.pdf

Van Ameringen, M., Mancini, C., Patterson, B., & Boyle, M.H. (2008). Post-traumatic stress disorder in Canada. *CNS Neuroscience and Therapeutics, 14*(3), 171–181.

Van Camp, T. (2014). *Victims of violence and restorative practices: Finding a voice.* Oxon, UK: Routledge.

Van Camp, T., & De Mesmaecker, V. (2014). Procedural justice for victims of crime: Are victim impact statements and victim–offender mediation rising to the challenge? In I. Vanfraechem, A. Pemberton, & F.M. Ndahinda (Eds.), *Justice for Victims: Perspectives on rights, transition and reconciliation* (pp. 277–299). London, UK: Routledge.

Van Camp, T., & Wemmers, J. (2013). Victim satisfaction with restorative justice: More than simply procedural justice. *International Review of Victimology, 19*(2), 117–143. http://dx.doi.org/10.1177/0269758012472764

Van Camp, T., & Wemmers, J. (2016). Victims' reflections on the proactive and protective approach to the offer of restorative justice: The importance of information. *Canadian Journal of Criminology and Criminal Justice, 58*(3), 415–442. http://dx.doi.org/10.3138/cjccj.2015.E03

Van den Bogaard, J.W. (1992). *Slachtoffers van woninginbraken benaderd.* Enschede: Univesiteit Twente.

Van den Bos, K. (1996). *Procedural justice and conflict.* Doctoral thesis, Rijksuniversiteit Leiden.

Van den Bos, K. (2008). What is responsible for the fair process effect? In J. Greenberg & J. Colquitt (Eds.), *Handbook of organizational justice* (pp. 273–300). New York, NY: Psychology Press.

Van den Bos, K., & Lind, E.A. (2002). Uncertainty management by means of fairness judgements. *Advances in Experimental Social Psychology, 34,* 1–60. http://dx.doi.org/10.1016/S0065-2601(02)80003-X

Van Denderen, M., De Keijser, J., Kleen, M.N., & Boelen, P.A. (2015). Psychopathology among homicidally bereaved individuals: A systematic review. *Trauma, Violence & Abuse, 16*(1), 70–80. http://dx.doi. org/10.1177/1524838013515757

Van der Merwe, H. (2008). What survivors say about justice: An analysis of the TRC victim hearings. In A. Chapman & H. Van der Merwe (Eds.),

Truth and reconciliation in South Africa (pp. 23–44). Philadelphia, PA: University of Pennsylvania Press.

Van Dijk, J.J.M. (1983). Victimologie in theorie en praktijk. *Justitiële Verkenningen, 6,* 5–35.

Van Dijk, J.J.M. (1988). Ideological trends within the victims' movement: An international perspective. In M. Maguire & J. Pointing (Eds.), *Victims of crime: A new deal?* (pp. 117–126). Milton Keynes, UK: Open University Press.

Van Dijk, J.J.M. (1997). Het victimologische perspectif in het verleden, heden en toekomst. *Tijdschrift voor Criminologie, 39*(4), 292–309.

Van Dijk, J.J.M. (1999). Criminal victimization and victim empowerment in an international perspective. In J.J.M. Van Dijk, R. Van Kaam, & J. Wemmers (Eds.), *Caring for victims of crime* (pp. 15–39). Monsey, NY: Criminal Justice Press.

Van Dijk, J.J.M. (2009). Free the victim: A critique of the Western conception of victimhood. *International Review of Victimology, 16*(1), 1–34. http://dx.doi.org/10.1177/026975800901600101

Van Dijk, J.J.M. (2011). Dutch sociologist discovers unpublished victimological data dating from 1937. *Journal international de victimologie, 9*(2), 302–304.

Van Dijk, J.J.M., & Steinmetz, C. (1983). Victimization surveys: Beyond measuring the volume of crime. *Victimology, 8,* 291–309.

Van Dijk, J.J.M., Van Kesteren, J., & Smit, P. (2007). *Criminal victimisation in international perspective: Key findings from the 2004–2005 ICVS and EU ICS.* The Hague, NL: Boom Juridische Uitgevers.

Van Emmerik, A.A.P., Kamphuis, J.H., Hulsbosch, A.M., & Emmelkamp, P.M.G. (2002). Single session debriefing after psychological trauma: A meta-analysis. *Lancet, 360*(9335), 766–771. http://dx.doi.org/10.1016/S0140-6736(02)09897-5

Van Genugten, W., Van Gestel, R., Groenhuijsen, M., & Letschert, R. (2006). Loopholes, risks and ambivalences in international lawmaking: The case of a framework convention on victims' rights. *Netherlands Yearbook of International Law, 37,* 109–154.

Van Hecke, T. & Wemmers, J. (1992). *Schadebemiddelingsproject Middelburg.* Onderzoek en Beleid, 116. Arnhem, NL: Gouda Quint bv.

Van Ness, D. (2003). The shape of things to come: A framework for thinking about a restorative justice system. In E. Weitekamp & H.J. Kerner (Eds.), *Restorative justice: Theoretical foundations* (pp. 1–20). Cullompton, UK: Willan Publishing.

Van Swaaningen, R. (1999). Reclaiming critical criminology: Social justice and the European tradition. *Theoretical Criminology, 3*(1), 5–28. http://dx.doi.org/10.1177/1362480699003001001

Vanfraechem, I., & Bolivar, D. (2015). Restorative justice and victims of crime. In I. Vanfraechem, D. Bolivar, & I. Aertsen (Eds.), *Victims and restorative justice* (pp. 48–76). Oxon, UK: Routledge.

Verhoeven, M., Van Gestel, B., De Jong, D., & Kleemans, E. (2015). Relationships between suspects and victims of sex trafficking: Exploitation of prostitutes and domestic violence parallels in Dutch trafficking cases. *European Journal on Criminal Policy and Research, 21*(1), 49–64. http://dx.doi.org/10.1007/s10610-013-9226-2

Vermunt, R., & Steensma, H. (2008). How can justice be used to manage stress in organizations? In J. Greenberg & J. Colquit (Eds.), *Handbook of organizational justice* (pp. 383–410). New York, NY: Psychology Press.

Veronen, L.J., & Kilpatrick, D.G. (1980). Self-reported fears of rape victims: A preliminary investigation. *Behavior Modification, 4*(3), 383–396. http://dx.doi.org/10.1177/014544558043007

Viau, L. (1996). Victimes des ambitions royales. *La Revue Juridique Thémis, 30*, 117–141.

Victorian Law Reform Commission. (2016, August). *The role of victims of crime in the criminal trial process: Report.*

Viscusi, W.K. (1993). The value of risks to life and health. *Journal of Economic Literature, 31*(4), 1912–1946.

Volhardt, J.R. (2012). Collective victimization. In L.R. Tropp (Ed.), *The Oxford handbook of intergroup conflict* (pp. 136–158). Oxford, UK: Oxford University Press. http://dx.doi.org/10.1093/oxfordhb/9780199747672.013.0009

Von Hentig, H. (1948). *The criminal and his victim.* New Haven, CT: Yale University Press.

Waldman, E.A. (1998). The evaluative-facilitative debate in mediation: Applying the lens of therapeutic jurisprudence. *Marquette Law Review, 82*, 155–170.

Walgrave, L. (2006). Integrating criminal justice and restorative justice. In G. Johnstone (Ed.), *Handbook of restorative justice* (pp. 171–191). Cullompton, UK: Willan Publishing.

Waller, I. (2011). *Rights for victims of crime: Rebalancing justice.* Toronto, ON: Rowman & Littlefield Publishing.

Waller, I., & Okihiro, N. (1978). *Burglary: The victim and the public.* Toronto, ON: University of Toronto Press.

Walther, S. (2000). Reparation in the German criminal justice system: What is and what remains to be done. *International Review of Victimology, 7*(4), 265–280. http://dx.doi.org/10.1177/026975800000700404

Walther, S. (2011). Victims' rights: Procedural and constitutional principles for victim participation in Germany. In E. Erez, M. Kilchling, & J. Wemmers (Eds.), *Therapeutic jurisprudence and victim participation in justice: International perspectives* (pp. 97–112). Durham, NC: Carolina Academic Press.

War Crimes Research Office. (2007). *Victim participation before the International Criminal Court.* Washington, DC: International Criminal Court Legal Analysis and Education Project, Washington College of Law.

Weiss, J.C. (2005). Working with victims of hate crimes. In G. Greif & P. Ephross (Eds.), *Group work with populations at risk* (2nd ed., pp. 197–211). New York, NY: Oxford University Press.

Weitekamp, E. (1999). The paradigm of restorative justice: Potentials, possibilities, and pitfalls. In J.J.M. Van Dijk, R. Van Kaam, & J. Wemmers (Eds.), *Caring for victims of crime* (pp. 115–126). Monsey, NY: Criminal Justice Press.

Wells, J. (2014, June 11). *20 years later, winning the OJ civil case was never a "pot of gold."* CNBC. Retrieved from http://www.cnbc.com/2014/06/10/oj-simpson-murder-money-trial.html

Wemmers, J. (1996). *Victims in the criminal justice system.* Amsterdam, NL: Kugler.

Wemmers, J. (1999). Victim notification and public support for the criminal justice system. *International Review of Victimology, 6*(3), 167–178. http://dx.doi.org/10.1177/026975809900600301

Wemmers, J. (2002). Restorative justice for victims of crime: A victim-oriented approach to restorative justice. *International Review of Victimology, 9*(1), 43–59. http://dx.doi.org/10.1177/026975800200900104

Wemmers, J. (2003). *Introduction à la victimologie.* Montreal, QC: Les Presses de l'Université de Montréal.

Wemmers, J. (2005). Victim policy transfer: Learning from each other. *European Journal on Criminal Policy and Research, 11*(1), 121–133. http://dx.doi.org/10.1007/s10610-005-3624-z

Wemmers, J. (2006). *Reparation and the International Criminal Court: Meeting the needs of victims.* International Centre for Comparative Criminology, Université de Montréal. Retrieved from http://www.cicc.umontreal.ca/files/prod/publication_files/reparation_icc.pdf

Wemmers, J. (2008a). Victim participation and therapeutic jurisprudence. *Victims & Offenders, 3*(2-3), 165–191. http://dx.doi.org/10.1080/15564880801938318

Wemmers J. (2008b). Victims and the International Criminal Court: Transforming justice. *Access: Newsletter for the Victims Rights Working Group, 6.*

Wemmers, J. (2009a). A short history of victimology. In O. Hagemann, P. Schäfer, & S. Schmidt (Eds.), *Victimology, victim assistance and criminal justice: Perspectives shared by international experts at the Inter-University Centre of Dubrovnik* (pp. 33–42). Mönchengladbach: Niederrhein University of Applied Sciences.

Wemmers, J. (2009b). Victims and the International Criminal Court (ICC): Evaluating the success of the ICC with respect to victims. *International Review of Victimology, 16*(2), 211–227. http://dx.doi.org/10.1177/026975800901600205

Wemmers, J. (2009c). Where do they belong? Giving victims a place in the criminal justice process. *Criminal Law Forum, 20*(4), 395–416. http://dx.doi.org/10.1007/s10609-009-9107-z

Wemmers, J. (2010a). The meaning of justice for victims. In P. Knepper & S. Shoham (Eds.), *International handbook of victimology* (pp. 27–42). Boca Raton, FL: Taylor Francis Group. http://dx.doi.org/10.1201/EBK1420085471-c2

Wemmers, J. (2010b). Victims' rights and the International Criminal Court: Perceptions within the court regarding victims' right to participate. *Leiden Journal of International Law, 23*(3), 629–643. http://dx.doi.org/10.1017/S0922156510000257

Wemmers, J. (2011a). Aider la victime ou prévenir la criminalité? *Revue internationale de criminologie et de police technique et scientifique, 64*, juillet-septembre, 259–266.

Wemmers, J. (2011b). Victims in the criminal justice system and therapeutic jurisprudence: A Canadian perspective. In E. Erez, M. Kilchling, & J. Wemmers (Eds.), *Therapeutic jurisprudence and victim participation in justice* (pp. 67–82). Durham, NC: Carolina Academic Press.

Wemmers, J. (2012). Victims' rights are human rights: The importance of recognizing victims as persons. *Temida, 15*(2), 71–83. http://dx.doi.org/10.2298/TEM1202071W

Wemmers, J. (2013). Victims' experiences in the criminal justice system and their recovery from crime. *International Review of Victimology, 19*(3), 221–233. http://dx.doi.org/10.1177/0269758013492755

Wemmers, J. (2014). *Reparation for victims of crimes against humanity: The healing role of reparation.* Oxon, UK: Routledge.

Wemmers, J., & April-Ménard, S. (2013). *Brief written for Justice Canada in the framework of public consultations on a bill of rights for victims.* Montreal, QC: International Centre for Comparative Criminology, Université de Montréal.

Wemmers, J., & Canuto, M. (2002). *Victims' experiences, expectations and perceptions of restorative justice: A critical review of the literature.* Ottawa, ON: Department of Justice Canada.

Wemmers, J., & Cousineau, M.M. (2005). Victim needs and conjugal violence: Do victims want decision-making power? *Conflict Resolution Quarterly, 22*(4), 493–508. http://dx.doi.org/10.1002/crq.117

Wemmers, J., & Cyr, K. (2004). Victims' perspectives on restorative justice: How much involvement are victims looking for? *International Review of Victimology, 11*(2–3), 259–274. http://dx.doi.org/10.1177/026975800401100204

Wemmers, J., & Cyr, K. (2005). Can mediation be therapeutic for crime victims? An evaluation of victims' experiences in mediation with young offenders. *Canadian Journal of Criminology and Criminal Justice, 47*(3), 527–544. http://dx.doi.org/10.3138/cjccj.47.3.527

Wemmers, J., & Cyr, K. (2006a). *Victims' needs within the context of the criminal justice system.* Montreal, QC: International Centre for Comparative Criminology, Université de Montréal.

Wemmers, J., & Cyr, K. (2006b). What fairness means to crime victims: A social psychological perspective. *Applied Psychology in Criminal Justice, 2*(2), 102–128.

Wemmers, J., & Cyr, K. (2015). *Étudier et comprendre les liens entre la vicitmisation et la délinquance.* Rapport Final, Centre international de criminologie compare, Université de Montréal.

Wemmers, J., & Cyr, K. (2016). Gender and victims' expectations regarding their role in the criminal justice system: Towards victim-centred prosecutorial policies. In H. Kury, S. Redo, & E. Shea (Eds.), *Women and children as victims and offenders: Background, prevention, reintegration* (pp. 233–248). Geneva: Springer International Publishing. http://dx.doi.org/10.1007/978-3-319-28424-8_9

Wemmers, J., & De Brouwer, A.M. (2011). Globalization and victims of crime. In R. Letschert & J. Van Dijk (Eds.), *The new faces of victimhood: Globalisation, transnational crimes and victim rights* (pp. 279–300). Dordrecht, NL: Springer. http://dx.doi.org/10.1007/978-90-481-9020-1_12

Wemmers, J., Lafontaine, L., & Viau, L. (2008). Racial victimization in Canada. In J. Winterdijk & G. Antonopoulos (Eds.), *Racist victimization* (pp. 43–66). Aldershot, UK: Ashgate.

Wemmers, J., & Manirabona, A. (2014). Regaining trust: The importance of justice for victims of crimes against humanity. *International Review of Victimology, 20*(1), 101–109. http://dx.doi.org/10.1177/0269758013511163

Wemmers, J., & Raymond, E. (2011). La justice et les victimes: l'importance de l'information pour les victimes. *Criminologie, 44*(2), 157–169. http://dx.doi.org/10.7202/1005795ar

Wemmers, J., & Van Camp, T. (2011). *The offer of restorative justice to victims of violent crime: Should it be protective or proactive?* Montreal, QC: International Centre for Comparative Criminology, Université de Montréal.

Wemmers, J., Van der Leeden, R., & Steensma, H. (1995). What is procedural justice? Criteria used by Dutch victims to assess the fairness of criminal justice procedures. *Social Justice Research*, *8*(4), 329–350. http://dx.doi.org/10.1007/BF02334711

Wertham, F. (1949). *The show of violence*. Garden City, NY: Doubleday.

Westermeyer, J.M., & Williams, M. (1998). Three categories of victimization among refugees in a psychiatric clinic. In J.M. Jaranason & M. Popkin (Eds.), *Caring for victims of torture* (pp. 61–87). Washington, DC: American Psychiatric Association.

Wexler, B., & Winick, D. (1991). *Essays in therapeutic jurisprudence*. Durham, NC: Carolina Academic Press.

Wexler, D. (1993). Therapeutic jurisprudence and the criminal courts. *William and Mary Law Review*, *35*(1), 279–299.

Wexler, D., & Winick, B. (1996). *Law in a therapeutic key: Developments in therapeutic jurisprudence*. Durham, NC: Carolina Academic Press.

Widom, C.S. (1998). Child victims: Searching for opportunities to break the cycle of violence. *Applied & Preventive Psychology*, *7*(4), 225–234.

Widom, C.S., Schuck, A.M., & White, H.R. (2006). An examination of pathways from childhood victimization to violence: The role of early aggression and problematic alcohol use. *Violence and Victims*, *21*(6), 675–690. http://dx.doi.org/10.1891/0886-6708.21.6.675

Widom, C.S., & Wilson, H.W. (2015). Intergenerational transmission of violence. In J. Lindert & I. Levav (Eds.), *Violence and mental health* (pp. 27–45). Netherlands: Springer.

Williams, J.E. (1984). Secondary victimization: Confronting public attitudes about rape. *Victimology*, *9*, 66–81.

Williams, L.M., & Herrera, V.M. (2007). Child maltreatment and adolescent violence: Understanding complex connections. *Child Maltreatment*, *12*(3), 203–207. http://dx.doi.org/10.1177/1077559507304427

Winick, B. (1997). The jurisprudence of therapeutic jurisprudence. *Psychology, Public Policy, and Law*, *3*(1), 184–206.

Winick, B. (2000). Redefining the role of the criminal defense lawyer at plea bargaining and sentencing: A therapeutic jurisprudence/preventive law model. In D. Stolle, D. Wexler, & B. Winick (Eds.), *Practicing therapeutic jurisprudence: Law as a helping profession* (pp. 245–308). Durham, NC: Carolina Academic Press.

Winick, B. (2011). Therapeutic jurisprudence and victims of crime. In E. Erez, M. Kilchling, & J. Wemmers (Eds.), *Therapeutic jurisprudence and victim participation in justice: International perspectives* (pp. 3–14). Durham, NC: Carolina Academic Press.

Winkel, F.W. (1987). *Politie en voorkoming misdrijven: Effecten en neveneffecten van voorlichting*. Amsterdam, NL: Mens en Recht.

Winkel, F.W., Spapens, A.C., & Letschert, R.M. (2006). *Tevredenheid van slachtoffers met "rechtspleging" en slachtofferhulp: Een victimologische en reschtspychologische secundaire analyse.* Tilburg, NL: Intervict, Universiteit van Tilburg.

Wittebrood, K., & Nieuwbeerta, P. (2000). Criminal victimization during one's life-course: The effects of previous victimization and patterns of routine activity. *Journal of Research in Crime and Delinquency, 37*(1), 91–122. http://dx.doi.org/10.1177/0022427800037001004

Wolfgang, M. (1958). *Patterns in criminal homicide.* Philadelphia, PA: University of Pennsylvania Press.

Wolitzky-Taylor, K.B., Resnick, H.S., McCauley, J., Amstadter, A.B., Kilpatrick, D.G., & Ruggiero, K. (2011). Is reporting of rape on the rise? A comparison of women with reported versus unreported rape experiences in the national women's study—replication. *Journal of Interpersonal Violence, 26*(4), 807–832. http://dx.doi.org/10.1177/0886260510365869

World Society of Victimology. (2010). Draft convention on justice and support for victims of crime, abuse of power and terrorism. http://www.worldsocietyofvictimology.org/wp-content/uploads/2014/12/Draft-Convention.pdf

Xie, M., & McDowall, D. (2008). Escaping crime: The effects of direct and indirect victimization on moving. *Criminology, 46*(4), 809–840. http://dx.doi.org/10.1111/j.1745-9125.2008.00133.x

Yantzi, M. (2005). *Victim–offender reconciliation program: In the beginning.* Ottawa, ON: Correctional Service Canada.

Yeager, K.R., & Roberts, A.R. (2015). *Crisis intervention handbook: Assessment, treatment and research* (4th ed.). Oxford, UK: Oxford University Press.

Young, A. (2001). *Le rôle de la victime au sein du processus judiciaire: une analyse bibliographique 1989 à 1999.* Ottawa: Ministère de la Justice, Centre de la politique concernant les victimes.

Young, A. (2005). Crime victims and constitutional rights. *Criminal Law Quarterly, 1,* 432–471.

Young, I.T., Iglewicz, A., Glorioso, D., Lanouette, N., Seay, K., Ilapakurti, M., & Zisook, S. (2012). Suicide bereavement and complicated grief. *Dialogues in Clinical Neuroscience, 14*(2), 177–186.

Young, M. (2001). Victims of crime: A confluence of forces. Address at the First National Symposium on Victims of Federal Crime, Washington, DC, 10 February 1997. https://www.trynova.org/wp-content/uploads/file/victimsmovement.pdf

Zambrowsky, J., & Davies, D.T. (1987). *Victims' rights and the judicial process. Proceedings of the First National Seminar.* Ottawa, ON: Canadian Criminal Justice Association.

Zaykowski, H., & Campagna, L. (2014). Teaching theories of victimology. *Journal of Criminal Justice Education, 25*(4), 452–467. http://dx.doi.org/10.1080/10511253.2014.965410

Zehr, H. (2015). *The little book of restorative justice: Revised and updated.* New York, NY: Good Books.

LAWS CITED IN THE TEXT

Canadian Laws and Regulations

Alberta, *Victims of Crime Act*, Revised Statutes of Alberta 2000, chapter V-3. http://www.qp.alberta.ca/documents/Acts/v03.pdf

Alberta, *Victims of Crime Act, Victims of Crime Regulation*, Alberta Regulation 63/2004, with amendments up to and including Alberta Regulation 224/2012. http://www.qp.alberta.ca/documents/Regs/2004_063.pdf

British Columbia, *Crime Victims Assistance Act*, SBC 2001, Chapter 38. http://www.bclaws.ca/civix/document/id/complete/statreg/01038_01

British Columbia, *Crime Victims Assistance (General) Regulation*, BC Regulation 161/2002. http://www.bclaws.ca/civix/document/id/loo97/loo97/161_2002

British Columbia, *Crime Victim Assistance (Income Support and Vocational Services or Expenses Benefits) Regulation*, BC Regulation 162/2002. http://www.bclaws.ca/civix/document/id/loo88/loo88/162_2002

Canada, Bill C-479, *Act to Amend the Corrections and Conditional Release Act (Fairness for victims)*; Short title: *An Act to Bring Fairness for the Victims of Violent Offenders*. http://www.parl.gc.ca/HousePublications/Publication.aspx?DocId=7935229&Language=E&Mode=1

Canada, *Canadian Statement of Basic Principles of Justice for Victims of Crime, 2003*. http://www.justice.gc.ca/eng/rp-pr/cj-jp/victim/03/princ.html

Canada, *Canadian Victims Bill of Rights*, SC 2015, c. 13, s.2. http://laws-lois.justice.gc.ca/eng/acts/C-23.7/page-1.html

Canada, *Charter of Rights and Freedoms, Constitution Act, 1982*, Part 1. http://laws-lois.justice.gc.ca/eng/const/page-15.html

Canada, *Constitution Act, 1867*, 30 and 31 Victoria, c.3 (UK), s. 91(27) and 92(14). http://laws-lois.justice.gc.ca/eng/Const/page-1.html

Canada, *Corrections and Conditional Release Act*, SC 1992, c. 20. http://laws-lois.justice.gc.ca/eng/acts/C-44.6/

Canada, *Crimes Against Humanity and War Crimes Act*, SC 2000, c. 24. http://
laws-lois.justice.gc.ca/eng/acts/C-45.9/

Canada, *Youth Criminal Justice Act*, SC 2002, c. 1. Part 1, Extra Judicial
Measures. http://laws-lois.justice.gc.ca/PDF/Y-1.5.pdf

Manitoba, *The Victims' Bill of Rights*, CCSM c.V55. https://web2.gov.mb.ca/
laws/statutes/ccsm/_pdf.php?cap=v55

Manitoba, *Victims' Rights Regulations* (214/98). http://web2.gov.mb.ca/
laws/regs/current/_pdf-regs.php?reg=214/98

New Brunswick, *Regulation 96–81*, under the *Victims Services Act*, OC
96–378. http://laws.gnb.ca/en/showpdf/cr/96-81.pdf

Northwest Territories, *Consolidation of Victims of Crime Act*, RSNWT 1988, c.
9 (Supp.). http://www.canlii.org/en/nu/laws/stat/rsnwt-nu-1988-c-9-
supp/latest/part-1/rsnwt-nu-1988-c-9-supp-part-1.pdf

Northwest Territories, *Victims of Crime Act*, RSNWT 1988, c. 9. https://
www.justice.gov.nt.ca/en/files/legislation/victims-of-crime/
victims-of-crime.a.pdf

Nova Scotia, *Compensation for Victims of Crime Act*, RS c. 83, s. 1, 1989,
amended 1992, c. 36, s. 7(1). http://nslegislature.ca/legc/statutes/
compnvic.htm

Nova Scotia, *Criminal Injuries Compensation Regulations* made under Section
14 of the *Victims' Rights and Services Act*, SNS 1989, c. 14, and Clause
4(1)(b) of the *Utility and Review Board Act*, SNS 1992, c. 11. https://www.
novascotia.ca/just/regulations/regs/vrscomp.htm

Ontario, *Compensation for Victims of Crime Act*, RSO 1990, c. C.24. https://
www.ontario.ca/laws/statute/90c24

Prince Edward Island, *Victims of Crime Act*, c.V-3.1. https://www.
princeedwardisland.ca/sites/default/files/legislation/v-03_1.pdf

Prince Edward Island, *Victims of Crime Act Regulations*, c.V-3.1. https://www.
princeedwardisland.ca/sites/default/files/legislation/v03-1g.pdf

Quebec, *Loi sur les accidents du travail*, c. A-3. http://www2.
publicationsduquebec.gouv.qc.ca/dynamicSearch/telecharge.
php?type=2&file=/A_3/A3.html

Quebec, *Loi sur le système correctionnel du Québec*, RLRQ, c. S-40.1. http://
www2.publicationsduquebec.gouv.qc.ca/dynamicSearch/telecharge.
php?type=2&file=/S_40_1/S40_1.htm

Quebec, *Loi sur l'indemnisation des victimes d'actes criminels*, c. 1–6. http://
www2.publicationsduquebec.gouv.qc.ca/dynamicSearch/telecharge.
php?type=2&file=/I_6/I6.html

Saskatchewan, *The Victims of Crime Act, 1995*, c.V-6.011. http://www.qp.gov.
sk.ca/documents/English/Statutes/Statutes/V6-011.pdf

Saskatchewan, *The Victims of Crime Regulations, 1997*, C.V-6.011 Reg. 1. http://
www.qp.gov.sk.ca/documents/English/Regulations/Regulations/
V6-011R1.pdf

Canadian Jurisprudence

R. v. Bremner (2000), 146 CCC (3d) 59 (BCCA)
R. v. Lonechild, 2007 SKQB 224 (CanLII)
Vanscoy v. Ontario (1999) OJ No. 1661 (Ont. Sup. Ct. J.)

European Laws and Regulations

Council of Europe, *European Convention on the Compensation of Victims of
Violent Crimes*, ETS No. 116.
European Union, *Council Directive 2004/80/EC of 29 April 2004 Relating to
Compensation of Crime Victims*.
European Union, *Council Framework Decision on the Standing of Victims in
Criminal Proceedings*, 2001/220/JHA.
European Union, *Directive 2012/29/EU of the European Parliament and the
Council of Europe, of 25 October 2012, Establishing Minimum Standards on
Rights, Support and Protection of Victims of Crime and Replacing Council
Framework Decision 2001/220/JHA*.

US Laws and Jurisprudence

*Scott Campbell, Stephanie Roper, Wendy Preston, Louarna Gillis, and Nila Lynn
Crime Victims' Rights Act*, 108th Congress (2003–2004).
Kenna v. US District Court (2006: 435 f, 3d, 1011), para. 11.
Payne v. Tennessee (111 S.Ct. 2597 (1991)).

International Law

International Criminal Court, *Rome Statute of the International
Criminal Court*, A/Conf.183/9. https://www.icc-cpi.int/nr/
rdonlyres/ea9aeff7-5752-4f84-be94-0a655eb30e16/0/rome_statute_
english.pdf
International Criminal Court, *Rules of Procedure and Evidence*, Rule 85,
ICC-ASP/1/3. https://www.icc-cpi.int/iccdocs/PIDS/legal-texts/
RulesProcedureEvidenceEng.pdf
United Nations, *Basic Principles and Guidelines on the Right to a Remedy
and Reparation for Victims of Gross Violations of International Human
Rights Law and Serious Violations of International Humanitarian Law*, A/
RES/60/147. http://www.ohchr.org/EN/ProfessionalInterest/Pages/
RemedyAndReparation.aspx

United Nations, *Declaration of Basic Principles of Justice for Victims of Crime and Abuse of Power*, A/RES/40/34. http://www.un.org/documents/ga/res/40/a40r034.htm

United Nations, *Universal Declaration of Human Rights*, A/RES/217A. http://www.un.org/en/universal-declaration-human-rights

United Nations Economic and Social Council (ECOSOC), *Basic Principles on the Use of Restorative Justice Programmes in Criminal Matters*, Resolution 2002/12.

INDEX

Figures and tables indicated by page numbers in italics